Screenwriters' Masterclass

Screenwriters Talk About
Their Greatest Movies

Edited by

Kevin Conroy Scott

Newmarket Press • New York

To my Mother
For giving me an open mind

This book is published in the United States of America.

First Edition

ISBN-13: 978-1-55704-692-5
ISBN-10: 1-55704-692-1

10 9 8 7 6 5 4 3 2 1

Library of Congress Cataloging-in-Publication Data

Screenwriters' masterclass : screenwriters talk about their greatest movies / edited by Kevin Conroy Scott.— 1st U.S. ed.
p. cm.
ISBN 1-55704-692-1 (pbk. : alk. paper)
1. Motion picture authorship. 2. Screenwriters—Interviews. I. Scott, Kevin Conroy.
PN1996.S373 2006
808.2'3—dc22
2005028510

QUANTITY PURCHASES

Companies, professional groups, clubs, and other organizations may qualify for special terms when ordering quantities of this title. For information, write Special Sales Department, Newmarket Press, 18 East 48th Street, New York, NY 10017; call (212) 832-3575; fax (212) 832-3629; or e-mail info@newmarketpress.com.

www.newmarketpress.com

Contents

List of Illustrations

"When I am writing I talk about what I feel and what I want to see. The screenplay is words, sentences, which make the picture. It's a beautiful craft because I have to create the pictures in my mind."

Krzysztof Piesiewicz

Introduction

After working for a Hollywood film studio in my early twenties and reading a lot of screenplays on the weekends, I tried my hand at writing a script. Why not? Everyone else in LA was doing it. What followed was a bit of a mess, a 140-page detective comedy about a forty-two-year-old bachelor who lives in his parents' garage and thinks he's Magnum P.I. Sensing a foul odor, I only asked one friend to read it. He hated it. I put it in a drawer and it hasn't been seen since.

Six years, a different country, and hundreds of "coverage reports" later, I was still interested in screenwriting. I was curious to know how things were done, and I'd been searching for the elusive answers for some time. I started with Syd Field's ubiquitous book *Screenplay*, I read Christopher Vogler's clever review of Joseph Campbell's ideas, I flipped through Robert McKee's bible, I watched nine hundred films in three years, and I even earned a Masters Degree in Film History. But when it came down to writing a screenplay, I still didn't know how it was done.

Then I envisioned a book wherein aspiring screenwriters could learn about the craft from professionals as they revisit their work. Imagine the possibilities: instead of poring over story charts or pondering mythical archetypes, the student could have a private audience with the professional screenwriter as they are guided through the creation process of the film. The screenwriter could have the space to comment on what worked and what didn't in the finished film; why that happened; and how they handled the painstaking process of creating a three-dimensional world out of images previously seen only within the privacy of their own mind. The more I thought about the idea, the more it appealed to me. *Screenwriters' Masterclass* could offer an innovative approach to the subjective task of learning the trade of screenwriting. In the process, it could create a valuable case history of the films explored, offering film historians and enthusiasts a rare glimpse behind the scenes to learn about how these movies came into existence.

Of course, the quality of this book would depend on the writers interviewed. That's why I then considered widening the spectrum, interviewing not only the top Hollywood pros, but also leading European screenwriters, whose relationship to the audience is inevitably different. Falling in love with the sound of my own logic, I also realized, selfishly, that if I could find a publisher then I could also get them to pay for my travels to call upon my favorite screenwriters in person. Imagine it! New York City, London, Hollywood (not so exciting, but still . . .), Paris, Mexico City, even Malmö, Sweden.

I did indeed travel to some amazing places and, more importantly, met some amazing people. I sat in the window of a hotel bar on the southern tip of Sweden and watched passersby gawk at Lukas Moodysson, the director of *Together*, which was more popular in Sweden than *Titanic*. I played basketball in Mexico City with Guillermo Arriaga, the screenwriter of *Amores Perros*. He was like the mayor of his neighborhood, challenging his young son and his friends to take him on (he won every game). In New York, I sat in Wes Anderson's office, under the family portrait of the Blumes that you see in the opening of his film, *Rushmore*. Bill Murray in an oil painting. Where else can you see that but in Wes Anderson's office? In Paris I spent a cold spring morning with Michael Haneke in his flat off rue Jacob. When I greeted him I was hungover and cotton-mouthed, and he offered me pretzels instead of water. The interview fared much better. I returned to Paris and spent a hot summer afternoon with François Ozon. He was both elegant and funny and made jokes about Eric Rohmer being a cheapskate. I liked him very much. In fact, I liked them all very much. I hope this book doesn't suffer as a result. There's nothing worse than an interviewer who kisses ass.

What was very important from the outset was that we focus on one film in each writer's body of work. This way, we could go deep into that film's creation process and discover each writer's individual working methods. The original concept behind this book was to watch one movie with each screenwriter. I did this in my first interview. The guinea pig was the Academy Award winner Ted Tally, the film *The Silence of the Lambs*. It was an amazing experience, sitting there in his hotel room as he told me what it was like to be on set with Jonathan Demme, Jodie Foster and Hannibal the Cannibal. His lucid comments brought this book to life. Other screenwriters elected not to watch their films for different reasons. I found that their interviews were just as fascinating as Ted Tally's as they travelled back in time and revisited a time of intensive writing and revisions (and writing and revisions, and writing and revisions . . . and hand-wringing and, as a final kick in the teeth, crippling moments of self-doubt).

These interviews are here to both entertain and inform. They are meant to give film students hope, aspiring screenwriters knowledge, film enthusiasts the inside dirt and professional screenwriters a stick by which to measure themselves. More importantly, this book endeavors to treat screenwriters as artists, something that is often forgotten amid the translation of words into images and the never-ending battle for screen credits.

Kevin Conroy Scott

Ted Tally

TED TALLY

The Silence of the Lambs

"Refrigerator Questions"

After studying theater as an undergraduate at Yale, Ted Tally wrote plays in New York for ten years. He transitioned into writing for TV and film; his first feature credit was the Susan Sarandon drama *White Palace* (1991). Shortly thereafter he won an Oscar for Best Adapted Screenplay for *The Silence of the Lambs* (1992). Tally has a reputation in Hollywood for making beautiful screenplays out of difficult adaptations, as witnessed in his work on Cormac McCarthy's novel *All the Pretty Horses* (2000).

Synopsis

The United States, the present. Young FBI agent Clarice Starling is assigned to help find a missing woman and save her from a serial killer named "Buffalo Bill," who skins his victims. Clarice attempts to gain a better insight into the twisted mind of the killer by talking to an incarcerated psychopath, Dr. Hannibal "The Cannibal" Lecter, who prior to his capture was a respected psychiatrist. Starling's mentor, FBI agent Jack Crawford, believes that Lecter might have the answers to questions that will help them locate the killer. Starling's twisted relationship with Lecter not only forces her to confront her psychological demons, but also leads her face-to-face with Buffalo Bill himself.

* * *

KEVIN CONROY SCOTT: *Ted, who were your artistic heroes growing up? I'm thinking mainly in terms of playwrights, novelists and filmmakers.*

TED TALLY: Well, I didn't read or see much theater growing up, not until I was about eighteen. There weren't that many opportunities to see live theater around where I grew up. But I did read voraciously, I loved adventure books and science fiction—anything that was a thumping good read; and that could be Charles Dickens, too. Movies were just another world to me, though: I liked to go see them, but I didn't figure these things were actually made by *people*—certainly not people like me.

You didn't think of filmmaking as a tangible ambition?

Not at all. But theater, as I began to act in plays and stuff, I thought was a viable kind of thing to pursue, because you could get a bunch of people together and put on a play. I didn't know how to get a bunch of people together to make a movie . . .

So what was your first acting role on stage?

God, it was probably in the ninth grade, in a play called *I Remember Mama.* It's sentimental, based on a book of memoirs about a Norwegian family in New York, it had been on Broadway. I just remember a bunch of North Carolina kids with terrible accents, trying to be Norwegian and play roles much older than themselves. But I was very bitten by theater. I just loved the whole camaraderie of it. And I started doing tons of plays—summer theater and community theater, and every so often some pretty good university theater, where occasionally they would let local kids be spear carriers. I was always in a couple of things at a time.

Can you pinpoint a certain time where you thought you could create plays yourself?

Well, I was in a summer program in North Carolina, it still exists, called the Governor School. It's a six-to-eight-week summer program for high school students, with teachers from all over the state. You have to apply and audition. So I went into the theater program and it was mostly acting and acting exercises, and we put on two productions during the course of that summer. And after the first production they said, "OK, for the last one we're going to give you a chance to write your own play. And if you ever wanted to write a play, now's your chance, because if they're any good we're going to put them on." It had never occurred to me to write a play before, but I couldn't pass up that opportunity, so I wrote a strange kind of pantomime play with music and dance, and no dialogue. It was very arty—kind of like performance art. But it was very well-performed and some local person got wind of this and decided to tape it as a local television special. So I thought, "That was easy enough. Maybe next time I'll try dialogue . . ." Then I wrote a more conventional one-act play, a historical drama, and sent it off to a play competition, which it got picked for. And so that play was also staged.

Were you solely interested in writing at that time?

No, I was directing, I was designing sets, you had to do what you had to do, and in college I still mostly acted—I didn't write a full-length play until I was a senior at Yale. I majored in drama, and I went to Yale because they had such a strong tradition of undergraduate productions with virtually no limitation on them; they had sixty or seventy a year. Each individual college there would put on a play; then there was the Yale Rep which was a professional theater, and the Yale Drama School which had its own theater activities. That was the attraction for me.

Was there anyone working in theater at that time whom you especially admired?

This was the late sixties, so it was a time of great turbulence and a lot of very strange things were going on in the theater, which I didn't care very much for, because I'm innately conservative. But there were playwrights who I admired very much: Pinter, Arthur Kopit who I met and had a seminar with at Yale, Jack Gelber. There were a series of youngish off-Broadway playwrights of that generation that we all admired. We got such heavy doses of the classics academically that it was a turn-off— Ibsen, Strindberg, they just weren't very 1969 for us . . . But we were constantly being told we should concentrate on Chekhov, that he was more modern than we realized, so we did read a lot of Chekhov.

Really, I was like a sponge at that point. I was also seeing lots of movies, because the college had cheap film societies. Every night they would show real prints on projectors in a huge law school auditorium, and for twenty-five cents you could go in and see great films that I'd never seen on television. I saw movies there that made up ninety per cent of my film education. I can remember seeing Truffaut films, which were an eye-opener to me. I'd even never seen a foreign film before. But they would also show *Citizen Kane* and *Casablanca*, and they would have "Hitchcock Week."

Was there a particular Hitchcock film that stuck with you?

My favorite is *Rear Window*. I love a lot of them, he's extraordinary, but I think *Rear Window* is the most wonderful combination of romance and claustrophobia. He would set himself such challenges, like "Can I do an entire film in a rowboat? Can I do a whole film in a courtyard . . . ?"

Are you still involved in the theater at all?

No, my theater career, if you can call it a career, lasted for about ten years. I reached a point in my early thirties where I just thought I wasn't really pushing to the next level in the theater because it wasn't going to happen. And I was also getting more interested in the movies.

It took you eight years to get your first film made. Living in New York City, what did you do to make ends meet financially?

Well, my plays were all getting staged, they just didn't play for very long. But then they were getting subsequent production in regional theaters, and occasionally abroad. So I had a fairly good income from theater royalties and publications. I kept getting writing grants too, so that helped. I graduated in drama in 1977 and right away had a professional production, and an agent, and a teaching grant, so I never had to work at any other job. And then pretty quickly I started getting asked if I would do TV scripts, within two or three years I think. Then I rewrote a TV movie called *The Father Clements Story* with Louis Gossett, Malcolm-Jamal Warner, and Carroll O'Connor, directed by Edwin Sherin, a good director. I had nothing to do with the actual making of it but they did a very good job of it and finally after all those years it gave me a little bit more credibility. I had a credit, and that helped me to get the job writing *White Palace*, which was the first feature film that I made. I'd been like somebody hanging by his fingertips from a wall for years, and now finally I felt like I'd got my foot up on it.

Funnily enough, it seems like you had a very easy entry into professional writing, but then getting through the glass ceiling was another story.

I have a strange career in that way; it took me forever to get going and then I had a lot of early success, and then I went into a trough and nothing got made. It always seems like feast or famine. I don't have any kind of game plan. I can go for three or four years without any movie being made, and then two or three will be made at once. I don't think there's a lot of rhyme or reason in this business.

You've said that one of the big breaks in your career came at the hands of Lindsay Anderson?

Yes, this must have been about 1979, 1980. He sort of took me under his wing and he was a tough guy, very fierce and very proud, a very angry man. I think he had a real chip on his shoulder about a lot of things. But he *really* loved movies, and not just as a filmmaker but as a *cinephile*. He even wrote a book on John Ford.

When he first called me up, I was so green I'd never even seen a screenplay, didn't even know what they looked like, but he said he'd show me one. I didn't understand all the camera angles and those kinds of things, and he said, "Just leave them out; nobody reads them or takes any notice of them anyway." He told me to just write it like a play, where you have a lot more freedom to change the scene, and that was good advice. It was based on the Indian Mutiny and specifically the siege of Delhi in 1857. Lindsay grew up in India, it was very much in his blood, and he always wanted to make a movie set there: a Ford-style Western epic set in India. That was his obsession. And he would say things like, "This *must* be an epic. What do *you* think is an epic?" And I would say, "*Lawrence of Arabia* is an epic," and he'd say, "Don't be ridiculous!" Then all I could think of was Lean's *The Bridge on the River Kwai* and he'd say, "That's not an epic, that's a war adventure." I kept trying to get him to define what an epic was, and I could never really get a clear answer, except that he would snort at anything I suggested. But I think he thought that an epic was something that really expressed a great national movement of people. It couldn't just be a love story set against an epic background—it had to be *War and Peace*. It had to really suggest a change in ethics.

But Lindsay was his own worst enemy when it came to Hollywood and the making of films, because not only would he not suffer fools gladly, he wouldn't suffer them at all. And you would cringe when you went to a studio meeting with him because you knew he just wasn't going to censor himself if he thought he was speaking to an idiot. So, not surprisingly, most of his Hollywood movies never got made, including mine . . . But he was a patient and sometimes sarcastic teacher. I went back and forth from New York, where I was living then, to London or LA, working over a screenplay with him and he would say, "Yes, OK, well, that's nice enough, and let's have a scene where so-and-so happens." And I would go off and come back with reams of more pages. He never had any interest in editing this stuff, the final script was about 150 pages long and completely unfilmable in its length. But it had great scenes, great passion, great characters. He was a great teacher; it was like getting paid to learn how to write a screenplay. Anyway, we worked for a year, and then we just sort of abandoned it, he just never called again.

You've said elsewhere that when you're adapting a book into a screen-play, you turn the book into a treatment before you do the first draft. Can you describe what this treatment consists of?

It's about twenty-five or thirty single-spaced pages normally, in paragraph outline, and it has a very conventional three-act structure and it's my attempt to describe the movie scene-by-scene. If it's an important movie, I'll go into some detail about what happens and why. There's virtually no dialogue in it unless it's really important to the scene—it's suggested but I don't want anybody to pin me down on that. And if it's a small scene or a sequence of them I might just say "And now there's a montage" without going into too much detail. But it's pretty specific; act one, scene one, two, three . . .

You actually number the scenes?

Oh yeah, there tend to be eight-to-ten scenes per act, and I reference the book. If I give this kind of thing to a producer or a director, I don't know if they'll sit there with the treatment in one hand and the book in the other, but if they care to look, I cross-reference, say, "Scene four of the movie uses pages thirty-five to forty-seven of the book, but with the following changes," and I will suggest how it will change. It's already beginning to change from the book by the time it's a treatment. And then, usually by the time I've finished the treatment and maybe done some revision, I've absorbed almost everything from the book I'm ever going to. Very often the book is hardly referred to from that point, and the treatment becomes the blueprint for the screenplay. Only if I'm confused about some point or if I really want some bolstering of specific details am I going to go back to the book—or if I want to crib some dialogue. But basically I work off the treatment as I work. The treatment is really intended as a tool for myself, it's to reduce the book to a manageable level and to give me the illusion that I have a road map for the screenplay. It never quite works out that way: when you're writing you're continually finding out what you thought you needed and didn't need after all, so you tear out three pages of the treatment, throw them away and do something else, wing it. I wish there was a way of knowing those things in advance; you'd save a lot of time and a lot of heartache. But I can't, I just have to write my way into it—which you wouldn't think would be true with an adaptation but it happens anyway. I said to Jonathan Demme one time, we were talking about cutting a scene and I said, "I worked for weeks on this, we got it polished and you were happy with it, Kristi made the set, we got the costumes, the actors there, we shot it.

Wouldn't it be better if we had known in advance that we didn't need it?" And he said, "If we'd *known*, it would have been boring . . ."

You've said that the first act is always a struggle for you. Is this because you're trying to get the audience involved as well as getting exposition out of the way?

Partly. It's also just that you're coming to grips with a story and characters that are not your own and that you've got to try to *make* your own, and that's just an almost physical struggle until you feel some mastery over it. It may be a world you've never lived in or imagined before, it may be science fiction or a western, or something that you don't really have the dramatic vocabulary for—you've faked your way into getting the job and now you've got to actually sit down and do it. So that first half of the first act is a tremendous struggle, and those pages get constantly rewritten. But by the time you get to the last part of the act, it goes by in a blur and you hand it in.

Other writers have said the same thing, about how hard it is to get momentum.

Well, you put a lot of pressure on yourself because you're so conscious of the importance of those first ten or twelve pages. Somebody said, and it's not much of an exaggeration, "The only thing that matters in a screenplay is the first ten pages, and the only thing that matters in a movie is the last ten minutes." From a Hollywood point of view there's some truth in that. If the first ten pages don't grab the agent then they're not going to tell the client to read it, or the studio person, or whatever. If the audience doesn't walk out happy after the last ten minutes then they're not going to recommend the movie to their friends. I don't agonize so much over the last ten pages of the script, because by then I've got the rhythm going and I feel like I know what I'm doing. The first draft in particular, I feel like it's mine—it's the one time during the process of making the movie where I have total control over what I'm doing, I don't really have to answer to anybody.

Do you then feel a lot of pressure when you turn in the first draft to the producer?

I didn't use to. And in truth, now, from the point of view of worrying if they are going to like it, or hate me, or am I going to get fired or whatever, I don't feel that way. After I stick that first draft into a FedEx envelope and send it off, I sleep like a baby! Because I feel like

I've done the best I could and if they don't like it there's not much else I could have done. But I'm very conscious that there's pressure on a first draft now that didn't used to be—that they're hiring me to do it and paying me a lot of money, and the first draft has got to be as polished as I can possibly make it.

I've had movies where I've still never written anything but the first draft, I have movies where the first draft hung around for eight years and then got green-lit. I've had movies where the first draft was on the internet within a week of me posting it into the studio. It's a first draft, but there's no privacy anymore, it gets leaked somewhere, and suddenly people are reviewing my first draft. That happened with *Red Dragon*. And it's a weird feeling. "Guys, it's not done yet! Can I get the director's notes before I get yours?" So there is that feeling that once a script leaves your hands, you don't know where it's going or who's going to see it, and it's very important to make it good. From the moment you turn in a first draft, it's either on its way to being a movie or it's on its way to development hell—one or the other is going to happen. It's not like anybody's going to say, "This is an interesting idea, let's gently nurture and develop this and maybe in a year after a lot of work we'll have something . . ."

How did you come across Thomas Harris's novel, The Silence of the Lambs?

It was actually sent to me by Tom Harris, who was a client at an art gallery where my wife worked and was great friends with the gallery owner, and still is. I met Tom a couple of times, once at an art exhibit in New Haven, and I had dinner with him a couple of times. So I knew him socially and I admired his books and he knew I was a playwright, but I don't think he'd seen anything that I'd written. So I said, "What are you working on?" And he just mailed a soft-cover press copy, and I read it, and because I knew the Lecter character from *Red Dragon*, I was just beside myself, I couldn't believe how powerful this story was. But I assumed that someone was already doing the screenplay since the publication date was only three or four weeks away. Throughout my career I'd never been able to catch up to a good book before it's too late: by the time I would see it in a bookstore, the screenplay was already written. That's one of the main reasons I switched agencies and went to ICM because they have a literary department in New York and they have people who hunt down books, and I thought I needed to get in that pipeline before it's too late.

So I was weeping and wailing and saying, "This is too good to be available still," and my wife said, "Call your agent and find out." She's never let me forget that she was the one who nagged me into getting that job . . . So I called my then-agent and she called Orion Pictures. And they said they didn't have a screenwriter yet, and they remembered me because I wrote that Lindsay Anderson script for them and they liked it. They thought I was an interesting idea for this, but they were buying the book for Gene Hackman to direct and act in, and he wanted to write the screenplay too. But basically Orion said, "Hang in there, because we don't think he can do this." Sure enough, three or four weeks later they called up again and said, "He was up to page thirty of the screenplay and only on page thirty of the book, so that's not going to work out." I had to have a writing sample to show to him, and I had *White Palace*, which had just been green-lit. So again, after a year of bad timing it was suddenly good timing, because I could say there was this movie with Susan Sarandon that Universal were going to make, so now I have some credibility. Hackman read it and said, "OK, let's talk." And I had to convince him to give me the job.

Did you find that daunting?

Yeah, a little scary. He's a giant figure, and I had to go to his home in Santa Fe to meet him. I guess he still had some questions after our first meeting, because he then made me fly to Chicago and talk to him for four hours. His back was bothering him too, so he lay on the floor with a pillow under his head while I was talking and talking and talking. Every once in a while he would toss out some little bomb, he had some weird ideas for things he wanted to try visually, to which I just had to say, "Yes, that's a good idea."

Which role was he considering playing?

He couldn't decide whether he was going to play Lecter or Crawford; he thought he might be taking on too much to play Lecter. And then when I was halfway through the first draft he got cold feet about the whole thing and dropped out. He didn't call, which really offended me, since I'd done the whole song and dance for him and was beavering away on this job. For him to quit and not even call, I think, is appalling manners.

Going back, can you describe the excitement that you felt when reading the story?

First of all, I just thought it was so smart, so literary and knowing, and not just in a technological, police-procedural, serial-killer way—which Tom is extremely knowledgeable about. It's so knowing about people and human nature and character, and the dialogue is so good. It was "the thriller" raised to literature. And the story is just so unpredictable; to have the twinned killers, two bad guys instead of one, and the whole intricacy of the criminal plot. But, above all, it was the relationship between this young woman and this mad psychiatrist which was not like anything I'd ever seen. Jonathan and I were talking about it and he said, "This is new, dramatically; there has never been a relationship of two main characters like this."

And then, for reasons I'm not even sure of, I felt very moved, and still do, by Clarice Starling. By her courage and vulnerability—and I probably respond more to courage in a main character than any other quality. She's in a male world, and she's a student, and she's orphaned . . . I was just deeply moved by her. And Thomas Harris had so artfully worked in mythic underpinnings—it just had this feeling that there's the orphaned young woman making her way in the world, and there's the good stepfather in Crawford and the evil stepfather who's Lecter who are taking on her education. That's a huge part of the story, in fact it's the emotional heart of the whole story; her search for a missing father and her attempt to replace that void which is never going to go away. The whole thing of saving the lamb and being able to save Catherine Martin is all tied up with her inability to save her own father when she was a child.

And this is what you saw clearly in your first read?

Oh yeah. And I also thought these are just incredible parts to attract actors. I guess from my theater background I always think of that. I don't see a specific actor when I'm writing a part but I always think of trying to give actors great stuff to do, because that's what gets movies made and that's what makes them memorable for audiences.

You said that when you're adapting a novel you try to write the scenes that stick out in your mind. In the case of The Silence of the Lambs, *I assume that the meeting of Clarice and Lecter was the first one.*

Right. You've got to start with her tutorial from Crawford where he, as it turns out, is being quite manipulative and not entirely nice in sending her into this rat's nest. Then you've got to have a journey into the labyrinth of Dr Chiltern . . . most of those building blocks as you adapt a book are pretty evident. But there are nine or ten key scenes that will tell the story. Then the question is what do you do with the really interesting ones that don't fit into that scenario? And what do you do when you've got these grisly gaps between them: what is the new connective material and what is the new rhythm? Because you're not going to have the rhythm of the book.

Jodie Foster commented that if we'd had a less sympathetic studio they would have made us cut down those long scenes between Clarice and Lecter, eight-page scenes where they're just static, two people talking to each other. They wouldn't have accepted it or understood that it's the heart of the movie, it's not just filler waiting for the next action sequence.

Each one of those scenes really crackles.

Well, it's just great dialogue, and a lot of it is just verbatim from Thomas Harris. It's like a fencing match, but with sexual overtures. Those things play like they're theater. I was a little worried that I was giving a director a very difficult job to keep that visually interesting. I was aware that I was dumping a very big slab on him and normally I try to be more sensitive towards a director. But there was no other way to do this. I kept them as short as I could but there was a limit to how much they could be cut.

There are numerous points of view in the novel. When did you figure out that you had to tell the screenplay from Clarice's?

Well, that was part of the interest of the book. Then I was confronting this mountain of pages knowing I'd probably be ending up with only one-fifth or one-sixth of the text. So the first thing you'd better do in a case like that is to find an organizing principle, or an editing principle; and in that one it seemed pretty clear to me that Clarice is the character that we care most about, our surrogate going into this world. So it would also be more moving for the audience if we were made to see the story through her eyes.

At times I thought Clarice was in danger of being a do-gooder, a go-getter, or an annoyingly keen character. How did you overcome that?

Well, she's smart and she is ambitious but not in a way that I think the audience would be offended by. But the biggest help there, is to have Jodie Foster play the part, because she's such a great actress and so smart that it's impossible for the audience not to respond to her and like her. As a screenwriter you always assume that an audience is much like yourself and so I assumed that if I cared this much about this character then so would the audience. As it went on and we had more perspective on it making the movie, we gradually began to realize that we were breaking all kinds of thriller rules, not only did we have a woman in the central role but we also had no action until the last half of the third act, we had no car chases. Not only that, but we didn't even have our heroine in physical jeopardy until almost the very end of the movie. She's in emotional jeopardy but she's not in physical danger. It just broke rule after rule after rule in that way.

I didn't know until later that a bunch of people in Hollywood had turned down the book and some very famous screenwriters had said it was unfilmable. Apparently some thought it was either too dark, or too complicated, or too ugly. I'm glad I was naïve enough not to think of it that way, because to me I felt like it was a home run; it was easy, except that it's an embarrassment of riches. You've got a great hero, you've got a great villain, you've got great dialogue, great twists and turns, a fabulous finale.

What did you think of Jonathan Demme as the director? He was known for quirky character-driven films like Something Wild *and* Melvin and Howard.

Well, I wasn't suspicious of him. I liked him personally, his sense of humor and his talent. I didn't quite know what was going to happen when he bashed heads with this material. I know that Jodie was the same, she told me she was terrified that he was going to bring some kind of irony to it. Jonathan is so liberal and so sweet that she was afraid he was going to do some goof on the FBI and make them look like fools. When she realized that wasn't going to happen, she felt much better. And the moment I first started seeing the dailies, I knew he was going to nail it.

After which draft did Demme get hired?

He read the book after Gene Hackman dropped out, but before I finished the first draft, probably a month or two before. Initially he'd had no interest in reading the book because he thought it was just some slasher story, but once he read it he began to see possibilities. He read my first draft not long after it was finished, and we met, then I was just startled by the speed of things. We met in May 1989 and we were shooting in November. I don't remember any big revisions.

And he invited you to be on the set . . .

Well, he wanted me to be there as much as I could be. It was hard, as I had a new child and I couldn't spend the whole time in Pittsburgh. He was very nice, he said, "I don't want you to come for two or three weeks at the start, because I need to establish my authority over this set and these actors and I don't want them looking out of the side of their eye at you if I say something, because the actors will come to the screenwriter looking for emotional shortcuts and they need to have their own process to find a way into it." But he then told me that, any time after that, he hoped I'd come as often as I could, and if I couldn't he'd send me dailies. He kept me very involved.

Considering you'd had some negative experience before that, how did that help you as a writer, being invited on set?

Oh, it was great, it made it real to me in a way that it had never been for my screenplays. Either they weren't made, or they were made and I wasn't involved in production. So it was an enormous payoff, both emotionally and artistically, after all the years in the wilderness—to see what was happening with all that time I'd spent alone in that room. It's satisfying to write a play or a novel, but there "coming to life" means it appears in print. The realization of the life you've created as a screenwriter is an astonishing thing to witness, especially for the first time. William Goldman says the most exciting day of a screenwriter's life is the first day he is on the set of a movie that he wrote, and the most boring day of his life is the second day. Which is kind of true! [*laughs*] I'd been in theaters and seen sets and performances, but you can't compare. I remember going into this giant abandoned turbine factory in Pittsburgh where they were building Lecter's asylum and Gumb's basement. I walk into an enormous three-story set, and outside there are these girders and ladders, and it felt like there were hundreds of workers swarming over this thing, painters, people applying dust to the stones, people distressing the bars of the cell, costume people, lighting people, electricians, cables everywhere. I'm standing there staring at this, and Ed Saxon, the producer, says to me, "What hath Ted wrought!?" And that was the feeling, an astonishing feeling, to see your ideas turning into a three-dimensional construction.

Now I've written a screenplay for *Alexander the Great* . . . well, it's one thing for me to sit there and write, "The trumpet sounds and five thousand horsemen launch themselves across the plain." But to make that actually *happen* is a very difficult thing, and I'm sure I'll have that same feeling if I'm standing there in Morocco watching that cavalry charge. It begins years before with a screenwriter, then it becomes somebody else's problem! Thank god I'm not there having to feed those horses and clean up after them. I spent years writing plays hoping that, if I got lucky, one hundred and fifty people a night would come to see them. Then you write a movie and it opens and fifteen million people see it all over the world. That's an astonishing thing for a writer.

Did you ever get notes from Orion on Silence of the Lambs?

No. At least, *I* never did. I've had two or three experiences where I never saw a single note from a studio. Either the director would absorb them and pick and choose the ones that they had some interest in, or just toss them out the window and say, "It's too late, this ship will sail!" When a movie is being made, in my experience, the studio tends to be very supportive; they just want to give you the best tools they can to make the best movie you can. Where they torment you, like a cat with a mouse, is when a script is in development hell and probably will never be made but they will never admit that—that's where it can be agonizing. It's all about diplomacy and studio politics, in ways that you'll never be able to understand if you don't live out here and know what's going on behind the scenes: who's in, who's out, who has power and who doesn't. It becomes about a lot of things besides about what's going to make a script better . . . That part of it is no fun. And I always like the idea that it's either quickly going to get green-lit or going into development hell. I lose interest quickly if it's not going to become a movie. I just want to move on to something else. I've been in situations where there's a lot of money still on the table but I've just made an amicable parting, if they're not serious about making the movie, so they can keep the money and let me have my time back. There's nothing deader than an unproduced screenplay.

Did you find it easier to adapt a thriller than a more literary screenplay?

I guess, in general, thrillers are easier to adapt. They give you a strong motor to drive the narrative, which other movies don't necessarily do. *All the Pretty Horses*, from a structural point of view, wasn't a difficult adaptation because it's a simple plot—too simple, many critics may say. But it's very dense so that's a problem. Sometimes you can read a book and immediately there's a hundred pages that just go right out, you know you don't need them. But that book was very beautifully and densely written, with no wasted scenes. So it was kind of like *Silence of the Lambs*, an embarrassment of riches. And so much so, I would have liked to have done a TV mini-series of it. That's how I feel when I hit a really good book, I feel it's sad to reduce it to two hours, but that's what they want and that's what I do.

When you wrote the first draft of Silence, *who did you think of playing Lecter?*

I didn't visualize an actor. I did think of Jodie Foster as Clarice, and that was hardly a leap of genius. In fact she called me as I was writing it, because she loved the book and was aware that I was doing the script. Tony Hopkins's name came up when Jonathan and I started talking about casting. He'd played a lot of loonies, he'd done thrillers, and he had been very good on the stage, and we thought that to play that character we needed an actor with that kind of theatrical grounding. His language is so baroque and epigrammatic that it was not going to sound like credible speech unless there was a classically trained actor doing it. Also Tony is a handsome guy, we thought that was important too—that evil of that kind should have an attractiveness, it shouldn't just be repugnant.

Were you worried about Lecter upstaging Clarice?

A little bit, but I knew that we wouldn't care about him like we did her. He would impress people and be exciting but he wouldn't move people as she did. And in the end she's got a lot more to do, so she will be the star. Jodie said one time that it wasn't the kind of part that gets awards, you do a lot of quiet listening and he's got all the flashy stuff. I said I thought she was wrong: I didn't think there would be a bigger woman's role that year . . .

Lecter serves many different purposes in the story. Did you find it difficult making each facet of his character work? Mentor, sexual tormentor, friend, murderer, cannibal . . .

No, he just leaps right off the page. In *Red Dragon* I had to invent a lot more stuff that just didn't exist in the book but with *Silence* I played very close. He is very much Thomas Harris's invention and I was just hanging on to his coattails. Every once in a while I had to make up some new dialogue for him, or find some movie equivalent—something that could be spoken and acted—for the cryptic games he plays. But when a character is that well-written you just try to mimic what the novel is already doing.

Much of Crawford's story is cut out. What was the logic behind that?

Well, that was very sad to me. I regretted that we couldn't keep more of that in the movie because it's very moving that his wife is dying. While he's trying to find this killer his own life is a shambles and he's trying to hold back the pain of that. Also, in some weird way it does inform his sort of muted sexual attraction to Clarice too. I struggled to keep that stuff in the screenplay. I think in the first draft there were a few scenes relating to Crawford's wife. Bits of it might have stayed into the second draft but finally Jonathan said we had to face it, it wasn't important enough, and we couldn't afford it, and he was right.

There was other stuff: we had a whole sequence involving Senator Martin, where Clarice goes to Catherine's apartment and Senator Martin finds her there finding the nude Polaroids and gets in trouble. That was one of the first things Jonathan shot, in Washington, and they're not in the movie: scenes where Senator Martin is pissed off and Lecter has escaped and Clarice and Crawford get blamed for that and dismissed from the case. Jonathan always said it was his fault—he'd just started the movie, he didn't know the actors well enough, and he didn't direct the scenes very well. But the truth is, they were what he thought was "fake suspense." In every cop film there's always a point where the cop gets suspended from the case, but we always know that they're going to come back on the case and solve it. We had truckloads of *real* suspense in this movie and we had trouble enough fitting all that in—we didn't have room for fake suspense. But he didn't know that until he shot it and it went into the edit. And I think they were one of the last things to come out.

Apart from Crawford's story, what was the biggest change from the book to the film?

Gumb is a much richer character in the book. In the movie he's really reduced to a cipher, we don't know what makes him tick, he's just kind of a bugaboo. And I regretted that, but I couldn't see any way around it. I was trapped in my own logic; if it was from Clarice's point of view, she doesn't know anything about Gumb. I had to go to Catherine Martin for the suspense, for the famous Hollywood ticking clock, but I really didn't want to know too much about Gumb if Clarice didn't know it. I didn't want to put the audience in a superior position to her as it would have broken the bond with her. I think the strategy worked but it shortchanged the Gumb character in a sad way. Jonathan said he made up for that with some extravagant improvisation, they managed to find something for him to do, some kind of weirdness, and it's very creepy and effective but it shortchanges the book a bit.

The music in that scene where he tries on his "wig" was particularly . . .

That's them, there's not much in the script there. That was a desperate actor and director thinking, "What the hell do we do now? What is this guy doing?" When I first saw it I thought, "A nipple ring?" I was horrified, but then I thought, "What would I have done in their shoes?" You can't have him just sitting there reading a *TV Guide*.

I just wanted to stay with Clarice at every possible moment and only cut from her in a case of dire necessity. I had to cut away from her for Lecter's escape, which did affect the rest of the plot, but even that made us nervous. Jonathan said we were breaking another rule; we were cutting away from our main character for twelve minutes in the third act. He said, "Does that make you nervous?" But I said it was just the greatest set piece of action: and if you didn't have that, why make the movie?

In terms of not empowering the audience, another thing you change from the book is when Clarice comes to Lecter with the offer. In the book the reader knows it's a bogus offer. In the film, the audience doesn't know until later that Clarice is trying to dupe him . . .

It's definitely a better strategy to try to sell them while you're selling Lecter. We used the book as our bible, and where we saw an opportunity to take it further, we did. The piece at the end where Clarice thinks she's missed the real action, just doing grunt work, and she comes to Gumb's house just to ask a few questions—that slight overlap is suggested in the book, it happens for a beat, and you have to be reading it closely or you'll miss it. Jonathan thought we could run with it, overlap, slice and dice, and have some fun. So we did.

I'd just like to take you through the film and ask you some questions about some specific scenes. For example, in the opening sequence where Clarice is running through the woods, alone, were the atmospherics and the sense of isolation important?

Well, it's very much in character to see her alone in the woods in this strange setting. It's quite a brilliant sequence by Jonathan. Is she chasing someone or is she running from someone? It's ambiguous and it doesn't particularly register that she's in a training regiment. It has a wonderful physical intensity, Jodie had to actually do all of those things, which are not easy; she had to climb over a tall netting wall and flip over to the other side. So spunky little Jodie actually does all of these tasks, which was good for her getting into the part. We had talked about different kinds of credit sequences; at one point it was going to be very arty, closeups on moths' wings that were so abstracted that you didn't know what you were looking at.

Did you write a credit sequence of your own?

In my experience it's hard to get the director to film what you want the credit sequence to be, it almost never happens. They consider it their own perk to devise that sequence, so I hardly ever even write them in the screenplay. I did for *Red Dragon*, which actually got made the way I wrote it, but that's very rare. For *Silence* I just thought, "I'm not even going to bother. I'll start with her approaching Crawford's office." But Jonathan did something that I love, which is that he carries us into the movie, into this world and into this character, before we've had any dialogue. He doesn't waste the credit sequence.

There are a lot of smooth transitions between scenes in Silence; *words echoed, overlapping dialogue. Are they something that you pay close attention to?*

I'm a sucker for that kind of transition, I like to do leap-forward transitions and dialogue where the next scene segues with this scene. Transitions are just as important as anything else that happens; they can be very important. And I'm always looking for what makes the strongest transition—it maybe something visual, it may be something in the music, it may be something verbal, I'm just trying to stitch the scenes together tightly.

Can you tell me something about when Clarice first meets Lecter at the hospital/prison. There is something of a buildup to get to his cell.

That kind of sequence, where Dr Chiltern is walking with Clarice and giving her the rules of how to talk to Lecter in his cell, is fun to write because, even though it's all exposition, if you break it up enough and have it in an interesting visual space it doesn't feel heavy. And this is such a creepy world we're entering that I knew that a dry exposition would pay off against the setting.

So it's like the audience takes in the exposition without knowing it?

Right, and there's also something wonderfully creepy about layer upon layer upon layer of security here. It's one of the longest build-ups to meeting a character you'll ever see. The point is you want the audience so thoroughly rattled at the point they meet Lecter that anything will scare them.

There is a moment in that scene where we don't see what she's looking at, only her reaction. That's the kind of thing we tried to do throughout the movie with violence. We wanted the audience's imagination to be supplying images rather than having them on screen, if we could help it.

When Miggs says "I can smell your cunt"—when that line comes out you know exactly where you are in the screenplay. Did you think it was really important?

We talked about that a lot, of course, and the throwing of the semen on her later—"Is it something we can really bear to have in here?" And I thought, as disgusting as it is, it's a way of absolutely pulling the rug out from the audience. If you do those things, they are going to now know for the rest of the movie that there are no rules—that anything might happen. So the unsettling effect of those moments carries over the next hour.

It was Tony Hopkins' idea to discover Lecter standing upright in the middle of the cell, like he's just been beamed down from a spaceship. But he also understood really well, after the enormous build-up to meeting this character, the value of now underplaying. I didn't know what he was going to do with the part yet, I said, "I guess you have to pick and choose your moments where the madness is." He said, "If you're mad, you're mad all the time." So I was worried that we might get some hammyness or something if he played it mad all the time. He knew better, of course . . .

What about the moment when they first meet and he starts sniffing her through his Plexiglas, that wasn't something written in the screenplay, was it?

No. The screenplay reflected the book, which had bars and netting in the cell. Jonathan made the discovery in the eleventh hour that they couldn't shoot that effectively—you couldn't get an unobstructed look at their faces, therefore the emotion was blunted. So the Plexiglas was a desperate improvisation on the set. And then they found the Plexiglas would help Jonathan visually but the actors couldn't hear each other, so then the holes were an improvisation on the improvisation. It's an interesting illustration of what happens when the screenplay turns into a movie, how you have to adapt to the physical reality. Also of course it feels much more dangerous if it seems like there's no visual separation between them. It feels like they could touch each other and it's much scarier.

And his famous line, "A census taker once tried to test me. I ate his liver with some fava beans and a nice Chianti." Was that from the book as well?

In the book it's a nice Amarone, and I didn't know what that was, but it turns out that it's a very well-known Italian wine, big and heavy like a Cabernet. But I thought that if I don't know that, and I like wine, then the audience is going to stop dead at that word. So I had to change it to something more conventional.

What sort of techniques did you use to write sexually? You always notice the sexual energy in the film because there are always people looking at Clarice in a sexual way even though there is no "love story" in the film.

Well, Jodie Foster's very beautiful . . . You know, another way in which this isn't a conventional story is that there is no love story, no romance. It doesn't interest Clarice to talk about pornographic scenes with Lecter or to imagine pornographic scenes with Crawford. I was very conscious that all of the events of this movie basically take place over a week, so there's no way to cram a boyfriend in here, realistically. She's got too much going on. Still, I like the sense that when she's in a scene, the men are always checking her out.

There's a nice moment when Clarice visits Lecter and she is wet . . . It's wonderful, he sees her wet hair and sends the towel through his drawer . . . the whole way that their relationship evolves from the first scene up until the last, the way that they become a bit more intimate.

In a way that's the love story.

Yes, it's a kind of love story, controversially. And it's the absolute heart and soul of the book. It's almost like the whole Buffalo Bill investigation only exists to justify having these scenes.

Were you worried about Catherine Martin being the daughter of a senator—that it might put the audience off because it's too convenient?

It seemed a bit coincidental, but I accepted that it would escalate the stakes for the plot in a way that nothing else could. You've got to have a ticking clock and now you have a ticking clock getting national attention, so it puts a lot more pressure on this rookie, that if she screws up now it could be her career going down the drain.

You said Thomas Harris really knows his police procedurals. Does he do a lot of research on serial killers too?

Buffalo Bill's method of abducting a potential victim came straight out of the book, but Tom Harris got it from the Ted Bundy case, the idea of a fake injury to illicit sympathy was something Ted Bundy used to do sometimes. I think, even though this is fictional, Tom Harris uses a lot of things from real life cases. Also, there was a famous serial killer who had a basement where he kept women in Philadelphia. I think he's put different pieces of different killers together to create someone like this.

Going back to violence offscreen, can you give me an example of that?

Yeah, people think that it's a very violent movie but actually there's only about a minute of on-screen violence in two hours. It's usually offscreen completely or by implication. You just have to be extremely careful on a movie like this. Scaring an audience is a pleasure up to a point and then they just turn on you, they are repelled. And in fact the first time we saw the movie we were actually nervous, that it was too scary, that we'd miscalculated and made too scary a movie because there was such dead silence after the movie. Then we just realized that it was stunned silence, not unhappy silence . . .

How do you handle writing in reaction shots for actors? The off-screen violence is now transmitted through their faces.

You're always trying to help actors with this. What's important is not the emotion they're playing but the emotion they're trying to conceal, that's what makes for a great scene.

How was your relationship with Thomas Harris as you were working on the screenplay?

Well, we didn't know each other well and he was very polite and respectful about what I had to do. He stayed at arm's length throughout the movie and said, "Do what you have to do and don't worry about me." He was an unusual writer in that way, good at letting go and letting us do our thing without trying to manage the process. He offered to help me in any way I needed, he offered to read the script but not if I didn't want to. He said, "I understand that movies have a different agenda from the book and if you want to do things differently, that's OK."

Can you tell me something about shooting the flashbacks and why you didn't shoot more of them?

I could see that if we were going to have flashbacks, they should culminate, there should be some climactic thing, and we should see the child Clarice encountering the slaughter of the lambs and trying to save one of them. Jonathan was willing to shoot them, it was going to be the last thing we shot as we had to wait for the lambing season in spring, and it was going to cost a million dollars to set up the whole thing. Then Jonathan shot the scene where Clarice tells Lecter about the killing of the lambs. He sent the dailies to me and said to watch them and give him a call. So I watched these performances, and they were extraordinarily powerful, and Jonathan said, "How can I cut away from these performances to a flashback? It's all there: she's telling us the entire story in her face, in her words, we don't need to see it as well." He said it's just a primary rule of filmmaking that if you can show it instead of telling it, you show it, but don't show it *and* tell it. He was right, but it was scary to me.

When did you realize it was right?

When I saw the dailies and saw it cut together. It was extraordinary. He actually said to me, "Watch Jodie's performance, she could win an Academy Award because of this scene with Lecter." This was a year and a half before the movie opened. But it scared me because I hadn't conceived it that way and I wasn't actually sure that it could hold up without this flashback.

And then they did this very brilliant thing here where you're aware of the bars of his temporary cell but as the scene gets more intense and more emotional they push the camera in so that the bars disappear and there's just no space between them at all, which is just very good.

We also had a lot of discussions about this because Jonathan said, "We've had this enormous build-up to this revelation about her trying to save this little lamb. It's not a person, it's a lamb. And you like rack of lamb and so do I, so why should I care about this lamb?" And I said, "I don't care about the lamb, I care about her, and if she cares that deeply, I care too." He said, "I accept the logic of that," and that sort of removed his last doubt about this scene.

The one thing we would have seen, which is very screenwriterly, is that at the end of the sequence of flashbacks when she got all the way to the barn and she sees somebody in an apron with a dead lamb in front of him, when the cowboy or rancher turns around to look at her, it's Lecter. Which is the kind of thing screenwriters get excited about but directors don't like because you're trying too hard. It's gilding the lily.

Yes, but in another way, when you're writing a scene, you're thinking about trying to get the story across so the reader understands it, not how the actors are going to deliver it.

Right, but you're also trying to play all the parts in your own head. And I think some of the best preparation for being a writer is to have been an actor.

You found that useful?

It sort of informs you as you write because you think, "If I was playing this part, I would feel like I wanted a big scene, I haven't had a big scene yet." Even if you were playing a small part, you'd think, "If I were playing this part I'd want something interesting to do even if it was in one scene, one page of the movie, I wouldn't want to just be a spear-carrier." It forces more creativity. It makes you not take any character for granted if you try to play the parts in your own mind. Or you say, "If I were trying to read this line, I would have trouble trying to make this line clear."

And do you find yourself speaking out loud?

Not out loud, because then they lock you up . . . but in my mind I'm saying, "I would stumble on this word, I should change this word."

All screenwriting and all of movie writing seems to be coming back to the same thing, which is learning what you can do without. Screenplays are always longer than the finished movie, more footage is shot than can actually be used. Movies are actually quite wasteful, because nobody knows until it's too late. It's always striking in your own movies that it seems like eight hours' work and it turns into thirty seconds in the movie.

You were saying sometimes you'll write three pages a day and sometimes one day is spent erasing two-and-a-half pages?

Yeah, you're right, two pages one day and then the next day your whole day of work is spent erasing one of those pages.

Were you ever worried that the audience would guess that Lecter was playing dead in the ambulance, under the mask of skin?

No, I don't see how you could possibly guess. I've seen this trick imitated since in other movies, but this is just a stunningly imaginative leap on the part of Thomas Harris. There are two great leaps, two great twists, this is the first and the second is when Clarice turns up alone at Gumb's house just as you think the SWAT team is at Gumb's house. Those two great sleights of hand that he pulls off are something that I could never have done.

In our discussions working on this movie, Jonathan was always the one taking the big leap and I was always the logic maker. So I was saying, "OK, you need to kill the medic at the back of the van, but there's the driver of the van and he's got to take care of him too, can we at least see the van swerve violently?" We shot it but we had to shut down the entire tunnel to do it, which wasn't easy. And it was all cut.

Were you ever worried about the logic of Lecter's escape scene not working?

No, I never worry about that kind of thing, what Jonathan called "refrigerator questions." The first time I heard that, I asked Jonathan what he meant, and he said, "You've seen the movie, you've enjoyed it, you get home and open the refrigerator and say, "Wait a minute! How could that guy have done that?" He said, "If it doesn't occur to you until you get to the refrigerator, it's not important enough for us to worry about."

Can you give me another example of a refrigerator question?

When I saw the house Gumb lives in, I thought the exterior location didn't look big enough to have that gigantic basement, it would be confusing for the audience, and Jonathan said, "Refrigerator question!"

But you do need to make certain leaps of logic in filmmaking.

Sooner or later you do cheat in every movie; you just hope it's not too glaring.

Talking about pacing, when you have a frenetic scene like Lecter's violent escape, are you self-consciously letting the audience adjust and slow down now with a slower scene next?

Well, in the case of Lecter's escape, which is the big action sequence in the movie, I thought that we'd really got to get off that. We're well into the third act and you've got to move on. Enough noodling around with the clues, the characters and the audience need a breakthrough. So we were trying to jump forward to the breakthrough.

I'm very anxious because I know as a screenwriter here I'm adrift in the ocean! I've just had this great thing with Lecter and I know if I can just get Clarice to Gumb's house, then that's going to save me. But in between it's hard. I know it's going to work, even though it's kind of very familiar: madman in the basement chasing somebody in the dark, I know it's going to work.

When I wrote this first draft I was borrowing an office from Robert Benton, the film director and writer, and he knew the book and once in a while I would try to talk to him, thinking that he'd have better ideas than me. He never wanted to talk about it that way. But I did one time sit there moaning about how hard it was, and I said, "You know what? All this work, this whole thing, it just adds up to a madman in a basement chasing a girl, and you've seen that a million times—is that going to be enough?" And he said, "That's what you've promised the audience, that's what it sets up for two hours so you've got to deliver that whether it's been in a million movies or not, that's what you've promised." The two characters have been coming to this collision for the entire movie. And yeah, it's a madman in a basement but the night-vision goggles will help.

It's not where you go, it's how you get there.

Right, it's how you get there and how much you care about the character.

This is the other thing I love; Catherine Martin is not just a victim, Catherine Martin is working as hard as she can to save her own life, she's not waiting for someone to come and save her. It's typical Thomas Harris that he cares about every character and he cares about every character's self-interest, and in this situation you would try to think of something, you wouldn't just sit there and wait to be killed. It just gives you one more plot line going on here.

Gumb's basement lair feels like something out of a horror film, it's almost a grotesque funhouse.

Jonathan was told once by Roger Corman, "The scariest shot in all of movies is the camera approaching a closed door, that you know somebody's got to open it. The anticipation is much scarier than anything, it's the most terrifying shot in the movie, it's not expensive, it's not special effects." So that scene uses this theory with a vengeance. I like how chaotic it is, it's just like neither Clarice nor Catherine is in control, they're just upset and they're angry, neither one of them has a clue, they don't know what they're doing. It's a long way from an Arnold Schwarzenegger action sequence.

So, after the denouement, how do you bring Hannibal back in at the end so the audience can, in a way, say good-bye and thanks?

This was another question. At one point I was even toying with the idea that he was in the back of the audience of the graduation, then I thought, "I can't get away with that, it's pushing too far." Or that he makes some comment on the phone that indicates that he was physically there, "You look lovely today" or something. I think it's enough that he calls her. I thought, "How would he possibly get this number, at this moment?" And then I thought, "Refrigerator question."

But Hannibal ringing her at her graduation was written differently in the book . . .

Initially when he calls, it turns out that he's at Chiltern's house and as he talks he's strolling across a lawn, you see the sea, he steps over a body into the house, walks down the hall, and at the end of the scene he's in Chiltern's study where Chiltern is all bound and gagged and just very terrified. And it ended up with Lecter hanging up from her and saying, "Well, Dr. Chiltern, shall we begin?" And Jonathan said, "It's great but it's too horrific; even though Chiltern's a slime-bag we have to give him at least some vague fighting chance of getting away." Then we came up with the idea that he would try to escape to a tropical island and maybe Lecter is already there ahead of him. And we don't know how but maybe that would be more fun. Jonathan loved that idea, especially because it meant he could get a trip to a tropical island at the end of shooting this movie; after a winter in Pittsburgh, he could take a cruise in this case to Bimini or somewhere. Of course then he went through all that and the weather didn't cooperate, it stayed overcast for days and they couldn't get that pretty tropical thing that the script called for. But Ed Saxon said, "It's OK, it's atmospheric, the wind blew a lot, it's kind of strange and gloomy for the tropics but it's still got atmosphere."

And this was a joke throughout the entire shoot. I said, "Jonathan, can I have my crane shot at the end? Nobody ever lets me end a movie with a crane shot." He said, "I will give you your crane shot." And in fact they had to get a barge to haul the crane to Bimini, you can't just go to Bimini and find a movie crane, you had to haul it there. But he had promised me a crane shot.

It's a good thing you saved a million bucks on the last flashback sequence.

Exactly. The other frustrating thing was that I didn't get to go to Bimini. It would have been a fun thing but it just didn't fit into my schedule.

Could you have predicted that Silence of the Lambs *would do as well as it did?*

Well, I couldn't have predicted. This movie now appears in books of the greatest films ever made, and the top hundred this and that. We couldn't predict that but we knew it was a really good movie. We knew early on. I went to the set and they'd just shot that stuff in the storage unit where she finds the head. And I ran into Jonathan's producer Kenneth Utt and asked, "How's it going?" He said, "We're making a great movie." And this was only after three weeks; Anthony Hopkins hadn't shot a single scene yet. Kenneth said, "I haven't had this feeling on a movie since *Midnight Cowboy*; it's going to be a classic." So there was kind of that feeling throughout that something really cool was happening.

And Jonathan Demme, the way that he treated people—you were having fun?

You have to keep it light; you're in Pittsburgh, it's freezing, it's February and you're making a really dark movie. So there were a lot of practical jokes on set, a lot of goofing around, sometimes he would even make somebody deliberately do something wrong just to see if they could crack up Jodie Foster on camera, which is hard to do but he managed it once or twice. And dailies would be a thing where you'd bring popcorn and soda like going to a movie, even though it might only be fifteen minutes. People would see themselves on the screen and throw popcorn at the screen if it was bad. It was a great atmosphere and we knew, especially by the time Jodie and Anthony shot their scenes together, we knew it was amazingly powerful. The question was whether it was *too* powerful.

The first time I saw it other than in a screening room was at a private screening in New York with just people who were working on it. And then I came to Hollywood with Jonathan and wanted to show it to some friends here, just in a little screening room. I remember there were a few movie-star people there, who were just friends. Jonathan introduced me to Jessica Lange, and I said to her, "I just hope the critics allow Jonathan this movie, because it's so different from his other work. They like to feel as if they determine what he does, and they like him doing comedies. I'm afraid they won't allow him this movie." And Jessica Lange said, "I don't think they have a choice . . ."

Beverly Hills, California

Lisa Cholodenko

2

LISA CHOLODENKO

High Art

"It's about ordinary lives at ordinary moments."

Lisa Cholodenko is a native of Los Angeles who studied film in New York and made her debut feature as a writer-director in 1998 with *High Art*, starring Ally Sheedy. The original screenplay won the Waldo Salt Screenwriting Award at the Sundance Film Festival. Her second feature, *Laurel Canyon* (2002), starred Frances McDormand as a hedonistic record producer who seduces the young stars she works with, much to the chagrin of her conservative son.

Synopsis

New York, the present. Syd, an ambitious but inexperienced magazine editor, discovers that the woman living above her flat is none other than the famous photographer Lucy Berliner. Syd becomes acquainted with Lucy's work and her junkie friends. Locating a step up the career ladder, Syd encourages Lucy to shoot new pictures for her magazine. At the same time, a strong attraction starts to develop between them. As the photo assignment continues, Syd and Lucy fall in love but with drastic consequences.

* * *

KEVIN CONROY SCOTT: *Lisa, you're from Los Angeles. Did you have a lot of exposure to the film business when you were growing up?*

LISA CHOLODENKO: Well, I guess growing up here you get more exposure to it than the average American citizen . . . and I did have relatives who were in the business; I had an uncle who was married to my blood aunt who was a producer, and a first cousin who was an entertainment lawyer. So I was seeing it peripherally, I was conscious of what they did. But they weren't involved in my getting interested or involved in film. And I wasn't one of those kids who'd put on plays or run around with a Super-8 in the back yard. I wasn't sitting through double features at the weekends . . . I was aware of growing up in a cinema-obsessed city but it really wasn't until I got to film school that I actually was exposed to a lot of the classic films. I went to college in San Francisco, did my undergraduate degree and became friends with people who were in the film school at San Francisco State, and that's when I first got exposed to films by Fassbinder, Fellini, those people.

Did your parents encourage you at all to express yourself artistically?

My mom is an elementary school principal and my father is a graphic designer. He went to art school when he was younger, he painted and he's an artist. So there were art books around and a general appreciation of aesthetics, they were very aesthetic people. I think because my father was aesthetically driven, he liked things to be pleasing and beautiful. My mom was like that too, but I think what was interesting about my upbringing was that on the one hand my father is a person who was trained and interested in aesthetics and himself a working artist in a commercial way, and then he is married to this person who was a school principal. I think both of those qualities combined are very similar to the things that comprise the personality of a film director.

Your mother being in charge and then your father having an eye for the frame?

Yeah, exactly.

What did you study at San Francisco State?

Oh, I just went there to go to college. I only got into college by the skin of my teeth. It wasn't that I was a bad student, I just wasn't present. I was just way more interested in late seventies' sex, drugs and rock 'n' roll.

Even when you were in high school?

Yeah. I mean I grew up in LA and it was fast, and I was kind of fast! I was just distracted. I was just more interested in the music and social things, and I went to an open public high school and I just wasn't that focused. So by the time I got to San Francisco State I had to learn how to be academic.

What kind of music were you into then?

I just tapped into what was going on in LA in the late seventies, early eighties—Patti Smith, the Go-Gos. There was a late punk scene that was going on here that largely had its life around the Sunset Strip; it was where punk was giving way to New Wave. X was the largest of the bands and everything that came after them, Split Enz, all of that. So I saw a lot of gigs and was very interested in experimental bands.

How did your education take shape?

I found a major at San Francisco State that really appealed to me; it was an interdisciplinary major in Social Sciences, and basically it had these core classes that taught you how to synthesize a lot of different disciplines and pick a subject that you could study and write a thesis on. So I took classes in Critical Theory, Ethnic Studies, Women's Studies and Anthropology, and I invented something, some place where they all intersected. It was an abstract degree . . .

Was writing something that came to you naturally or was it something that you had to really learn?

Because I was so half-in, half-out at high school I felt that I didn't really learn how to write until I went to college. I had an experience that was kind of central to me. I took classes with Angela Davis and later became her teaching assistant. Before that I was a freshman in one of her classes and I got a C on a paper and I was really bereft about it, ashamed that Angela Davis gave me a C. I went to see her in her office and she said, "You know, you can rewrite this and I'll re-grade you. Let's talk about how to organize your ideas." And she went over it with me, patiently telling me about how to think through my writing.

Did you learn something about structure then?

Yeah, from that point on I realized that I really cared. I wanted to learn how to express myself. These were academic ideas, but it really was important to me to learn how to express myself clearly and succinctly and I think that was a moving moment, a galvanizing moment. It was like, "Now I have something to say, there's something in there, and if I muddle it, it's not going to come out so I have to discipline myself."

Were you a light reader or a voracious reader at this time?

I was a casual reader. I really didn't become a big reader until my mid-to-late twenties. But I do remember my sister had a boyfriend who was studying literature at UCLA and I really admired him. He would give me books and one that was so hugely impressive to me was Thomas Mann's *Death in Venice*. In college I was more interested in reading theory, like Roland Barthes, rather than literature. But I did get turned on to Virginia Woolf. *To the Lighthouse* had a huge effect on me. I remember reading an interview with the author of *The Hours* and he was talking about what impressed him about Virginia Woolf; he said her subject matter is ordinary lives at ordinary moments. The detail of the interior neurotic experience was fascinating to me. I was new to literature, so I thought that maybe everybody wrote about that, I don't know, but for me I was just really taken by that modernist stream of consciousness writing. It had a neurotic pace, the way thoughts beget thoughts, and it was something that felt familiar to me; a world could be invented that I can enter and totally identify with. So that was the first time I felt intimacy with a character through literature—it had a visceral, psychic identification for me.

Can you tell me about the development of your awareness of cinema?

I'd met these eccentric people at San Francisco State who were doing experimental film; a big person at that time was Trinh Minh-ha, a Vietnamese experimental filmmaker. There was also a pretty interesting faculty for a while, all these people were making personal and experimental films and I was struck by them. But I never thought there was anything viable in it, it seemed like something you indulge yourself in but it's not a vocation. So I never really thought about it myself in a sustained way, but it lodged itself in my imagination somewhere. I finished my undergraduate studies and went overseas for a couple of years, and when I came back I needed a job so I moved back to LA and got a job at the American Film Institute.

That's a good place to get a job . . .

Yeah, well, it was like, "I've got to do something and it seems kind of cool to be at the American Film Institute." Two friends of mine were working there, had been there for years, and they got me in. So I worked in the conservatory at their film school.

Did you see a lot of films there?

I saw a lot of the *students'* films.

And were you starting to think that you might be able to do something similar?

It was the first time I could say, "This is a profession, there's a place for this." I was in this institute that was like the smorgasbord of everything. There's the film festival, there was an archive, there was a foundation for training women film directors, there was a film school, all of these things going on like a culture, a society and system and a training place. I thought, "Finally, this makes sense." And it flicked a switch in me and I was sparked by this. Filmmaking was the first profession I'd come across in my mid-twenties that I thought I could devote myself to honestly. It took me a long time to figure out what I was going to focus on. But it didn't feel right to not have a focus, I'm not the sort of person who can just hang. So it was exciting, and I was like "Ready, set, go." I got myself into a summer film program at Stanford, we did a couple of theory classes and made a film, so I made my first little film up there and learned some rudimentary things about editing and shooting and whatever else I could learn in two months. And then I came back down to LA, left the AFI, and got a job as an assistant editor.

How did that come about?

Well, that's the great thing about having grown up in LA, you don't know who's coming out of the woodwork. I knew somebody who was an executive at Columbia Pictures, her sister-in-law is one of my best friends, and she was the person responsible for *Boyz N the Hood*. They were gearing up to start filming it and I got a job as an apprentice editor in the cutting room.

I read somewhere that a lot of editors could make good screenwriters. Why do you think that is? Were there any lessons or techniques that you picked up?

I think the most important thing I learned in there is that you start with this huge bear of a film which really has no pacing or no point in a way, because you're just pasting all the footage together. And that, I discovered later, is almost identical to screenwriting in that you have to keep whittling it down until it has its perfect amount of information to communicate what you need and retain tension. So I think the editing of the film is really the same as the editing of the script.

Basically—and this is what you are prone to do in film school—it's really important not to get caught up in one piece of the film. If you put everything into getting that one piece into some kind of fine cut, it will be out of balance with the rest of the film. What editors do—or what I've done on my films, at least, and I think it's a standard convention—is that you do capsules of the film. You go through it and make some cuts and get it in some kind of shape and then *everything* gets narrowed down, it's like sculpting. So you never just go to the first ten minutes of the film and cut it till it's perfect and then go to the next ten minutes. You keep slicing through the whole film.

That's a really interesting analogy.

It's really the same in a script, because I think if you just keep on the first three scenes you end up with a script that's tight and good in the beginning and then just falls apart, and doesn't even know what it wants to say. So it's really important to know not to panic, it's all going to come together; you've just got to keep pushing forward. You can't just get hung up in one place.

High Art *is primarily about photography and photographers in general. Was photography something that you were always interested in?*

There was a group of photographers whose work I admired and were part of the inspiration for the film. They knew each other from living in Boston and studying at the Museum School in the 70's. They're referred to as the "Boston School" in art literature. Jack Pierson and David Armstong were among them, and Nan Goldin is probably the best known of the crew. There's a sensibility that they all share—a kind of personal documentary style that I was very attracted to. Larry Clark is also in this tradition. He did a famous book called *Tulsa* and basically used people who were leading underground lives, involved in sex, drugs and rock 'n' roll in a kind of depraved way, and he made art of it. And then it was appropriated in fashion photography in the early nineties and it became what was known as "heroin chic," you know— skinny, strung out. That was all ripped off from these photographers who were shooting their friends shooting up and fucking and passed out in cars. I was trying to make a meditation on that for *High Art* because I was struck by this chain of exploitation that was kind of overlooking the tragedy at its core.

So then when you went to Columbia University film school the story goes that you came under the tutelage of Milos Forman. How did that happen?

I was writing and directing, and in our third year the chair of the department, Annette Insdorf, decided to organize this class called "Mentors" where she paired up ten or twelve of us with working directors. I was supposed to be paired with Alan Pakula and we had one meeting but he was really busy and couldn't take me on. So I was

the only one of ten students who was matched up, and Milos Forman
had been the chair of the department and did Annette a favor and said,
"I'll take one of those students on if you need a back-up." So he made
himself available and I had a semester of being mentored by him,
which really consisted of him reading a draft of *High Art* that I had
been writing while I was a student. He met with me to talk about the
script and, ultimately, about how to make the film.

How many drafts did you write before Milos Forman saw it?

I had spent less than a year on it, so probably four major drafts or something. I was nervous; I'd given him this script and then I went to meet
him in his house on Central Park South. I sat down in this big fat chair
and he sat in the other one and lit up a big cigar, and I was smoking
cigarettes at the time so I lit up. And in his thick Slavic accent, he said,
"This is a great script, this is great writing." I was really flattered. At the
time he was making *The People vs. Larry Flynt* and he felt like we were
dealing with quite similar themes—the magazine world, heroin; there
were things that crossed over. He also said there were one or two places
where he didn't buy it. Then we proceeded to have a conversation about
casting and how to make the film in a certain way.

At Columbia, did you know that you wanted to be a writer-director?
Was writing very important to you?

Yeah, I felt like there was a lot of attention being given to independent
cinema and "New Queer Cinema," a lot of things were going on in New
York in the late eighties, early nineties. Jim Jarmusch had become an
acclaimed director. And I was really keen to get out of LA and figure
things out. It seemed like there was a road map, there was a way that you
could take it into your own hands, and I thought that I had stories to tell.

Was High Art *your first attempt at a feature length screenplay?*

No, I'd written another one before that. It was inspired by some girl I
was involved with who was bourgeois and had a gay brother who was
whoring around New York. I thought it would be interesting to do a
story about these two gay siblings who had these radically different
lives. So the script was about this brother and sister, both gay, and the
sister has a wife and they live in San Francisco. And the brother is
decadent, a real sleep-around guy. The story starts when his lover
informs him that he's HIV, and then it's about how the brother and
sister come back together and help each other out. It was kind of

great, but it felt too gay. And it's still in my drawer. But one of the guys who was in my screenwriting class became a successful producer, and he recently asked me about it so maybe one day I'll take it out and revisit it. I think I just reached a point where I moved on.

The student short films you made, Souvenir *and* Dinner Party: *were they also inspired by things going on around you?*

Pretty much, but they're both fiction, from my imagination. I was very precious about *Souvenir* and really painstakingly put it together. I mean, it was expensive; it cost ten or twelve grand to make. It was an ordeal. But I made it, and it was fine for a first film, but I was frustrated and I felt it just didn't have energy. So with my next short I wanted to do something Cassavetes-ish. One day I said, "I want to make this little film, it'll only take one day or two. We'll do it in a loft and it's loosely scripted; here's the script, you can improvise, I just want to do a Cassavetes thing, it'll be black and white, not a big deal, I just feel I've got to blow off some of this preciousness." And the long and the short of it is that it took way longer than two days to make. We shot for a couple of days and I needed to shoot more and we couldn't get back together for four months and then it was like a sloppy job because I just got my friends from film school to do jobs that they didn't know how to do. So it took me two years to do this film, but I persevered and I just thought, "I could throw this away because it's kind of a mess and it's kind of ridiculous but I think there's something cool here."

And in fact it ended up I made more money on that film than I did on *High Art*. It struck some chord and was bought by Canal+. They have affiliates all over Europe and they bought it to screen on TV so it screened in Scandinavia, France, Bulgaria, Poland. And then some Internet company owns it now and shows it on the Internet.

Wow, a profitable short film . . . I'm interested in hearing about what was the thread for the narrative. Was there an outline or some kind of signposts?

I really wanted to do a voice-over, I really felt like I wanted that kind of immediacy, I always like voice-over when it works, with the dramatic irony that it's meant to be done with. And so I constructed this little narrative about a girl who's been spurned by her girlfriend, they lived together in this loft. The real impulse for me to do it was so that I could get into this character's head, and what we're hearing her say to herself in her head is completely counter to what she's doing when she's at this dinner table with her ex-girlfriend and some girl that she's attracted to. So she's an unreliable narrator.

Was it important to you to have lesbian themes in those short films? You talk about the New Queer Cinema; is that something that you're preoccupied with or is it just a matter of you showing what's around you?

I just felt like instead of presupposing what I'm supposed to be doing, I'm just going to try to do the world in which I live and the people who I know. And not be bothered by where to depart from my own experience to be broader, more mainstream or whatever.

Were you ever concerned that people would label you as a strictly "gay filmmaker?"

I felt really proud of *High Art* in that it did transcend its world in a way; it's not like some gay cult thing. I think people see beyond its sexuality. But I really felt with *Laurel Canyon* that I wanted to stretch personally, in my imagination, and I also wanted to see if I could create a world that had some kind of weight and truth to it but wasn't a world that was exactly my own.

Thinking about where High Art *came from, I was curious about the kind of friends you had in New York because you said you hung out with interesting artists . . .*

I lived uptown for a long time, then I moved downtown and one of my oldest friends from California, who I travelled with a lot after college, had recently moved to New York and she was a photographer—she ended up doing all the photographs for *High Art*. So I was spending time with her and thinking about her world and what her concerns were. And then there was the Nan Goldin thing which was around, and I became intrigued by that kind of photography, and it felt exciting and interesting to me. New York's townie in a way, so you meet one person and then suddenly you have a network of friends, and it turned out that a lot of my friends were either filmmakers or visual artists: photographers, painters. And for some reason the people that I knew, many of them had recently been through a period in their lives where they were pretty heavy heroin dabblers.

I knew going in that High Art *was a movie about heroin but I didn't realize people would just sit around sniffing it in such a casual way. Is that really how it was?*

Yeah, well, I think people do it in all kinds of ways, depending on how heavy you are into it. But it had had a sort of resurgence, there had been a lot of really clean heroin around at one point, and it all corresponded to this weird Nan Goldin kind of imagery. Everything was coalescing into that weird heroin-chic moment. And unsuspecting people, young girls from Columbia University, were going downtown and checking out heroin: hanging out, sniffing it, chasing the dragon.

It's often said that the mood or state of mind you're in when you're high on drugs is very subjective and difficult to convey in a screenplay. Did that concern you at all?

I'm not a heroin user but I've done enough drugs and been around all that to know what it looks like. And when you're making a film like that in lower Manhattan, people who know that world are working on the film. So we had consultants.

How did writing High Art *differ to your writing experience on* Laurel Canyon?

With *Laurel Canyon* I really wanted to get another film out, fast, and I was broke so I decided I would try to generate an idea quickly and take it to October Films who, at the time, were still in existence and had taken *High Art*. I had a germ of an idea already in my head. I'd begun thinking it up when I was cutting *High Art*; I had been listening to a Joni Mitchell record. I started talking about a character loosely based on that. I had a sketch of the thing but it really wasn't fleshed out at all. I felt like I really needed to get paid to write but nobody was going to do a blind writing deal, "Here's some cash, everything's going to be great!" So I came up with a treatment, went in and pitched it, and got a very small amount of money to write a draft. But it became a lot more arduous than I really wanted. I think I'm just not a believer in writing a treatment—to have a loose sketch of where you might go is cool, but I really think truly inspired work comes from going into the dark hole and trying to write your way to the other end and see what you have. I've done two films, and done them in radically different ways, and I just feel like my experience on the first one was so much freer.

Didn't you find it hard to write on your own in that way, finding a way in the dark?

You know, it goes all ways and I think it's really hard to say. For me there's been a lot of pressure to push forward; you have your early career and then you're on the wave; it's a very self-conscious and anxious position to be in and unfortunately I think it's not made writing any easier.

How did you handle moments of self-doubt, where you felt like the idea wasn't working, or the scene wasn't working?

I slept a lot . . . I sometimes wonder if all writers have the same dysfunctional patterns. But I was like a narcoleptic, I slept so much, it was hard to sit at my desk. I had a couple of friends I would call, who were filmmakers who I would melt down with. You really want to know a typical day? It's like the office never closes, right? So the minute you get up you're like, "Fuck, I've got to go back to that fucking script," like there's this monkey on your back. So you get up at the crack of dawn and you make coffee, go back into your bedroom and read the *New York Times*—and that's the most beautiful period of the day. You're entitled to have that coffee, you're entitled to read your copy of the *Times*.

And check your e-mails as well.

And check your e-mails, right. And then it's like, "Now's the time!" So you get up and you hobble into your kitchen and you're like, "I may have something to eat," and then you finally get to your desk, and sit there, and then you rewrite the opening scene for like the seven *hundredth* time. And basically it's not rewriting, it's just taking four words of dialogue and looking in your thesaurus for maybe a better word, or saying it in your mind and seeing if the cadence is right. Really, really, minute, pedantic, unnecessary shit. And then at that point you're spent—you've been there for twenty minutes and you lie down on the couch. Then you get up and have more coffee.

Basically I felt like I was a little rat in my apartment. I would just go from the bed to the kitchen, to the desk, to the couch, to the kitchen, to the bed, to the desk, to the couch. And maybe I'd go out or go running, that and reading the *Times* was the high point of my day.

Did running clear your mind a little bit?

Yeah, I discovered that if I sweat really hard, I could handle the stress better.

Can you talk about how you construct characters? Do they just evolve through drafts or do you have certain constructs, like writing biographies?

With *Laurel Canyon* I really tried to objectify the characters, write biographies of them, psychoanalyze them, give them details on paper.

Maybe it helped—but in retrospect it feels like it was a really awkward thing to synthesize this information that I'd objectively made up about these characters while I was writing this story.

It doesn't feel like they're three-dimensional people at that point?

Yeah, and it's like a feat to try and make them come alive. Jane, played by Fran McDormand, was really considered the most vivacious and magnetic of the characters in the piece, and she was the first person to come into my imagination—she had a voice before I sat down with any objective details about her; she just told me what she was about. And I feel like that's the way the characters in *High Art* came about too.

You said that some of the people you were hanging out with in New York made it into High Art. *Where did Lucy come from and how did she get to where she is in the film?*

She was really less of a developed character. The piece really centered on Syd. In the first draft she works at a shitty job, and it was all about how she's abused by her boss. Then she figures out her neighbor is this famed photographer, and they get to be friends. Actually, in the first draft, Syd sneakily gets hold of some of Lucy's photographs and takes them to somebody that she knows who's a receptionist at *Interview* and they get published. So it was really all about this chick's desire for notoriety, to be recognized, and how that corrupts her. It was super-cynical. And Lucy was really just a prop at that stage, until the story developed. Then I felt I really wanted to do parallel character studies, and have characters intersect at the right and wrong times. I had a sketch of Lucy; she was a photographer, and then it descended into this alienated, heroin-addled world, inspired by Nan Goldin's photographs and so on. I think there were a lot of little pieces that I knew about Nan Goldin that I took— people at the time were critical of the fact that this character resembled Nan Goldin. But one of the things that was interesting to me was, I'm Jewish and I knew Nan Goldin was Jewish, so I pumped up the fiction a few notches and made the character—this so-called Nan Goldin-like character, Lucy—a trust-fund, heroin-addled daughter of a holocaust survivor with a German mother.

And then one of the three producers on the movie, Dolly Hall, one of her major notes to me which was invaluable was that we had to make it more sympathetic; we have to really think about Syd's over-tures to Lucy and maybe pull a love story out of this rather than make it this cynical dance of seduction. And I took heed. I think it's more interesting and accessible if I make it that this girl is caught off-guard by things that conflict with her ambitions, and that she has sex with Lucy because of her affection and desire for her and her impulse to save her. And that was a better way to go than some mad-dog descent into trying to get to the top by fucking somebody over. I think it was a more special film by getting into something that was a paradox.

By challenging the audience to care for someone who might also be duplicitous?

Yeah, exactly.

I thought the moment Syd crosses the heterosexual line and starts kissing Lucy was underplayed. Wouldn't somebody of Syd's ambitious nature, living in a corporate environment, do a lot of hand wringing about going for another woman?

I think what was really important to me was to be true to the time, and I think what I realized about women under thirty, this last generation and the one before it, is that they've been much more liberal about checking out heroin or crystal meth, and things that are fucking *hard core* like stripping or sleeping with other girls. At least in New York City, if you compare and contrast college girls of different generations and of a certain sophistication, maybe not the heroin, but there is this vogue around bisexuality, and I think it was important to me to portray this character as an emblem of part of a culture.

You wrote the screenplay with the intention of directing it. How did this affect your writing?

In a couple of ways. Again, Dolly Hall, who helped me a lot in the early stages of writing and thinking about making a film, encouraged me to keep writing and to think about the budget and not make it unwieldy, that it was something that I could actually do for half a million dollars. And then I was also thinking, "There's got to be something in here that I can connect to, or I won't be able to direct it." And I learned from those short films that I made; where I connected it worked, and where I didn't connect it didn't work. So I spent a long time working with the dialogue and the scenes and figuring out the emotional subtext of this story, scene to scene. In a way it was preparation or homework, so that when I got on the set I wouldn't be standing there with my mouth open, not knowing how to perform it or what it means. I'd already been through the subtext so I could give the direction as to what spin to put on the performance, so you elicit that from the actor and the audience can see and understand what's being said and what it means.

You were worried that the humor and irony necessary to tell this story would turn absurdist. Why are humor and irony necessary in depicting this part of the New York art world?

I think it's just a sensibility that I relate to, this comic-tragic tone, because I think there's a little of both in each thing. And it felt like— this has to do with both films but particularly in *High Art*—it's so heavy and interior and dark at times that I felt there had to be some levity and it had to be offset by these strains of absurdism, just like a gallows sensibility where somebody in a grave situation cracks a joke. Also I felt it had to be in there for the audience, to make it feel dynamic, so there was a point of entry.

You enjoy a few laughs related to the people at Frame *magazine because they are so unrelentingly pretentious. Did you have prior experience working with people like that?*

I had a job in film distribution when I first got to New York and I really didn't get on with my boss. I just felt really oppressed and denigrated. And I think the original idea for *High Art* came out of this incredible humiliation I felt at being around this person, how much repulsion I felt at the time and how unconscious and indifferent she was as to how she made people around and under her feel. I was raging, in a way, and this was my outlet.

Were you worried about these characters at Frame *magazine being a little bit too transparent, which is what they are?*

It's something that came up a lot when people would be critical of the film and I think, in retrospect, now that I know more than I did then and am probably a more sophisticated writer, I would flesh those characters out better. At the time I just thought it was funny, and that was what I needed to do to bring the point home.

I was very struck by the moment when we know that Greta, played by Patricia Clarkson, acted for Fassbinder. First, it makes her world of heroin sniffing in the afternoons completely plausible, secondly it recalls the Fassbinder film The Bitter Tears of Petra von Kant, *an adaptation of a stage play where a famous fashion designer falls in love with her model, making her live-in lover very jealous. Was that resonance intentional?*

Greta was always German, but I think there was a Fassbinder retrospective going on at the Museum of Modern Art at the time. And while I was aware of Fassbinder and had seen his films or pieces of films, I'd never really taken the time, so I decided to really check this out. I would look at these women in his films and I thought that was something I could add to this character to make her really interesting. And I knew that Fassbinder himself was this great neo-melodramatist and that he was hugely cynical; he fucked with his friends, they'd screw each other over, and he had a drug-addled history, so I thought, "This is perfect." Greta was a little bit young to make it perfectly plausible, but I think it's a great spin.

There is a scene when Lucy admits to Syd that she is attracted to her. Lucy's also taking a risk by admitting that she'd had a breakdown before. What were you thinking when you wrote that?

I was thinking that it's where the conflict and the tension are becoming heightened between Syd's involvement with Lucy personally, or her responsibility to her personally, to her condition, which involves exploiting her. And it was really important to me to have a scene where we understand what happened to Lucy, so there was exposition needed for that scene; there was a need to have Syd make the overture, "I want you to come to the magazine, it's a good thing" — it's a plot point, but also having that information puts Syd in a conundrum because here's this woman saying, "I've basically had a kind of breakdown, and I'm sharing that with you." But it was also important to me to have it not being like an older, art-star, lesbian photographer who's preying on this young woman; that there's something between them, the younger woman is awed by her allure, she's drawn to her and turned on. She's excited by it, it's all really heady.

And it's something that Syd's boyfriend is very quick to pick up on.

Yeah, because he thinks that it's a ridiculous, pretentious world, and it is. And now on top of it she's up there snorting heroin with these people? What's up with that?

It's pretentious, the things she's saying, almost like someone who's got a newly minted Masters degree sounding off on everything they've just learned.

That was deliberate. I wanted Syd to be pulling every art-theory idea she ever read. And when you read those art-speak books you're like, "For fuck's sake!" I wanted her to be kind of an emblem for that. Lucy just rolls her eyes and says, "I haven't been deconstructed in a long time."

That was one of the most oft-quoted lines from the film. Moving on to the relationship between Greta and Lucy, they have an interesting way of interacting . . .

It was important to me that there was a contrast in these questions of fidelity, that Syd's in a more conventional relationship and they're going through a complication regarding an infidelity, and the hipsters upstairs are so far beyond keeping a rein on each other, they're so out of the box, their relationship is so unconventional, so codependent and dysfunctional that shit like this happens. It's not like "You've cheated on me," it's like "I hate that fucking teenager. Fine, go fuck whoever you want." I thought that it was important to the reality of how these women were living out of the box, not to have conventional tropes of monogamy.

Ally Sheedy is a brave casting choice as Lucy. When she became interested in the role, did you find it ironic that Lucy's career had certain parallels with Ally Sheedy's own Hollywood trajectory: once famous, now in a kind of casual retirement and a laid back recluse?

Yeah, it piqued my curiosity; I had mixed feelings, because I think that Ally's had a mixed reception in the industry. But she pursued the role doggedly; it wasn't like I went after her. Somebody gave her the script, I got a phone call from her saying that she wanted to read for me, so I said, "OK, if you fly out here." I was living in New York at the time and she was in LA. And she did. She did that darkroom scene and it was intense, really moving.

I was wondering why you decided to have Lucy's death happen off-screen? It was foreshadowed with Greta's overdose; you know it's a possibility but it's still unexpected.

Well, it went on longer, it was scripted a lot of different ways. One is where she does more heroin and lies down on the bed and their friend Arnie comes into the room and he lies down and he discovers she's cold and not breathing, and there's all this mayhem upstairs and Syd comes out. And it felt like I didn't need to show all that to communicate what needed to be communicated. I did shoot more than what got left in the film, which is when Arnie wakes up and he goes into the bedroom and he lies down next to them and we see Greta stir like she wakes up when he comes in and Lucy doesn't and then they go back to sleep, the three of them are sleeping in the bed and that's the close of that. And then the next morning happens. That didn't feel like it added anything to the scene and it didn't feel like the most powerful way to end. I think it was just confusing. I didn't take it to the point where he discovers she's gone, so to go from three of them lying in that bed to cut to the next morning and Arnie in the car felt like it muddled the point more than just ending on Ally and then the next day.

And what happens to Syd? Hypothetically, where did she go after that? Do you think she dated strictly women after that or was it a one-time experience?

I thought of it as a one-time experience. I always saw her going back, in a way, to where she was, but as a more informed, expansive person. I saw her as somebody who probably tucked it away, like one of those things you have in your early life where it kicks your ass but you have to compartmentalize it because you don't really know exactly how to assimilate it or what it means. It's just like one of those anomalous, "Oh my fucking God, that was a trip that I just went through."

It felt with Syd that she's had sex before this, but her relationship with Lucy is the first time she's really been intimate and intense.

For me it was really important that it wasn't like, "Oh my god, this girl's coming out of the closet, she's having a revelation and it's blowing her mind." I really wanted to try to do a portrait of all the things that go into passion, and from her perspective it was intrigue and mystery and romanticizing this woman's decadence and debauchery and her tragic past and her notoriety. There was something that she wanted from Lucy. Here was this woman who was going to enable her to climb up. It felt like it was important to me to take it out of gay/straight and all these illogical components that go into attraction.

It reminds me of your comment on Virginia Woolf and these very small moments made large.

I think for me it's really important not just to drop into a moment, but to lead the viewer to the moment, so they experience it, no matter how slight, for themselves. That's the real challenge of writing on any scale; if you can give the audience the right moments, if you can choose one of the right moments to show and take somebody there in an organic, step-by-step way, then it's really gratifying. You're in it with the characters.

Hollywood, California

Carlos Cuarón

3

CARLOS CUARÓN

Y *Tu Mamá También*

"I wanted to be García Márquez, man!"

At the 2003 Academy Awards Carlos Cuarón and his older brother, the writer-director Alfonso Cuarón, were nominated for a Best Original Screenplay for their film *Y Tu Mamá También* (*And Your Mother Too*), an amazing feat considering that the film was written in Spanish. *Y Tu Mamá* went on to become a huge international success and won many awards, including the Best Screenplay Award at the 2001 Venice Film Festival. Their first collaboration, *Love in the Time of Hysteria* (*Sólo con tu Pareja*), broke records at the Mexican box office in 1991. Carlos has written and directed prize-winning short films, including his most recent, *You Owe Me One* (*Me la Debes*), which was made with the shortends from *Y Tu Mamá*.

Synopsis

Mexico City, the present. Abandoned by their girlfriends for the summer, teenagers Tenoch and Julio meet the older Luisa at a wedding. Trying to impress her, the friends tell her they are headed on a road trip to a beautiful, secret beach called Boca del Cielo. Intrigued with their story and desperate to escape her cheating husband—as well as coping with the news of her terminal illness—Luisa asks if she can join them. Soon the three are headed out of Mexico City, making their way towards the fictional destination. Along the way Luisa seduces the two young men, and they begin to argue over her.

* * *

KEVIN CONROY SCOTT: *You and your brother Alfonso grew up in Mexico City. Can you help me understand how two men from the same household became so proficient in the arts? Were you both encouraged from an early age?*

CARLOS CUARÓN: No. First of all, I guess that we became artistically inclined precisely because we didn't come from an artsy family. My father was a nuclear physicist; he died last year. And my mother is very eclectic: I think she did chemistry in college, then she became an editor at a publishing house; now she has a banana plantation and she's a full-time mystic. My parents separated when I was five, and divorced when I was seven. Alfonso is five years older than I am, and when he was eleven or twelve our father gave him a Super-8 camera and a Retina camera. Alfonso started taking photographs and shooting Super-8 films. My sister and I became his props, his actors, his assistants and whatever else. So I guess he was probably twelve, at the most thirteen, when he decided what he wanted to be when he grew up. And he was very specific: he wanted to be a film director. Back then, I was like a victim—I was being victimized by this guy harassing me, basically.

Then when I turned fourteen, I decided that I wanted to be a writer. Now, my notion of a writer was a completely different thing. Back then, I thought that movies were not written, they were just shot. I thought of myself more like García Márquez or Carlos Fuentes, you know—being a novelist and having dinners with diplomats and politicians and things like that. It didn't happen that way . . .

Your mother was a book editor by then, so I assume you had a lot of books in the house.

Yes, always, both my parents loved reading.

Do you remember what sort of books you were into?

I became a reading freak when I was twelve. Before that, I hated reading because my mother would inflict it like a punishment, ten pages a day or something, from classics that I didn't give a shit about. There's an Italian book called *Cuore: The Heart of a Boy* and it was one of her favorites when she was a kid, so I had to read it, but it was just overwhelmingly boring, I hated it. What happened when I turned twelve was that I discovered another literature, and I discovered that these books could tell me stories, that I could be entertained, that I could laugh, even cry, at moments. That to me was a new thing—and not boring at all. So by the time I was fourteen, I was already reading *The Catcher in the Rye*, Boris Vian, Carlos Fuentes, the Mexican modern classics, García Márquez—he's not Mexican but he lives there—Octavio Paz, Juan Rulfo and other very important writers from Mexico like Jorge Ibargüengoitia and José Augustín. At the same time I was reading Sartre and all the existentialists, because I think I was at the right age to sort of . . . self-whip myself.

"Self-flagellate"?

That's the word!

As a teenager, what did you and your friends get up to? What part of Mexico City were you hanging out in?

We were originally from Colonia Roma, which is like a *barrio* or neighborhood, central, close to downtown. When I was eight we moved to the southern part of the city and remained there. My school was in that part of the city, and most of my friends were from the south. I still live there. The south part of the city was more like the suburban life, but culture-wise it's very strong—there are these *barrios* in Mexico City like Coyoacán that used to be pre-Hispanic towns, where the culture is so vivid: not only the Spanish culture but also the pre-Hispanic culture and the current culture. So most intellectuals either live or work in Coyoacán, and that's the south part of the city. And that's probably why we got so artistically inclined—because we would go to La Cineteca, which is like the Cinemathèque in Paris, where you would go to see films you couldn't see in any other part of Mexico: films by Kurosawa, or Bergman, or the French *nouvelle vague*, very good international cinema.

What about Mexican films of that time? Were you at all influenced by them?

Not really. There were a few Mexican films that I really liked, mostly from the seventies: films like *Canoa* or *El Apando*, both by Felipe Cazals, and then also Arturo Ripstein's films. But there was a terrible gap in Mexican filmmaking from the seventies through until the late eighties: twenty years of very artsy—and therefore very difficult—films, most of them boring. So Mexican audiences wouldn't go to see a Mexican movie because they don't like to be bored. And then in the eighties what happened was that the private producers started to make movies with a lot of sex and whoring. As a kid growing in the seventies in Mexico, I remember watching a lot of "luchadores" films (masked wrestlers films) with "El Santo" and "Blue Demon," all the classic melodramas from the forties and fifties, comedies starring Cantinflas, Tin Tán and Mauricio Garcés. I remember two films by Alfonso Arau that I specially loved: *El Águila Descalza* and *Calzonzin Inspector*, two very Mexican delightful comedies.

As a kid, did you go to the movies with your friends or with your family?

In my family we all loved movies. We are four siblings—my big brother, then Alfonso, then I had a sister, then me; and my mother would take us to any kind of movie—I could go see *Star Wars* on Saturday and then the next day I would be seeing Bergman's *The Magic Flute*. Because not only did we have La Cineteca, there was another artsy place which would screen these kinds of films on weekends. Then when I was still a teenager the National University opened two new cinemas in the south part of the city. So I would go with my friends to see whatever Hollywood movie was showing one day, and then the day after we were watching a Kurosawa movie.

Back in the early eighties, what would you say was the general attitude of you and your friends towards the United States?

Well, for the common Mexican, the U.S. is like the natural enemy. And it's not the American people—it is because we have been so oppressed by American governments. And it is because we have had so many corrupt governments of our own that have not helped our own people. There are many things we have to clear up: one, when a Mexican says *gringo* it is not a derogatory term, *gringo* is just *gringo*—it's an American, not a Canadian, not British, not Danish—it's just a word we use, and we don't use it derogatorily. As you have a word for "ship," which is "ship," you have a word for "heaven," which is "heaven"—we have a word for *gringo,* it's *gringo.* And that's very important, because usually Americans freak out with this *gringo,* and it's not derogatory at all, it's almost friendly. We even say *gringita,* so you know . . .

So our attitude has always been like that. It started to change in the seventies. When I was a kid, the U.S. was, like, *the* enemy. In the eighties that had changed, because we started to have more contact with the American people. Mexican migration towards the U.S. increased and became illegal at the same time that the Mexican government shifted from nationalist populism to the here-I-come-so-just-lubricate-your-ass-neoliberalism so loved by Ronald Reagan and the like. In the seventies we would have voted against the U.S. in every way, in the eighties that was not so, it was almost the other way around. I guess we also started to differentiate between the American government and the American people. But it's always been a very complex love/hate, poor/rich, needy/need-you relationship.

From seeing Y Tu Mamá También, *and from meeting a lot of Mexicans in London, I see that I've lived so close to that country my whole life and yet I know so little about it.*

Well I think that's precisely one of the things that made the Y Tu Mamá so successful, for someone from abroad who doesn't know Mexico, it's a new thing, suddenly they can see the many "Mexicos" that we have—and we have many more, but you cannot put them all in one movie. And for people who do really know Mexico, like my American friends, it's like "Wow man, I know that, you really captured that place, that character . . ."

Your brother Alfonso said that before you two collaborated as screen-writers that you were married to a beautiful, amazing woman called Literature. Then, as his story goes, he introduced you to a hooker called Screenwriting. Can you tell me something about your aspirations to be a novelist, and when that stopped, and when your screenwriting began?

The truth is my aspiration to be a novelist has never stopped. Earlier this year I started a novel, a story that has been sort of clogged within me for the last fifteen years—I needed to, you know, just puke it out. But until it's finished it's all mental masturbation, so I remain a novelist in the closet—I'll let you know when I get out. Alfonso and I still laugh about his theory, and what he says is that I preferred the great blow jobs that a hooker gives instead of the sweaty hand of my first love . . . But I also have to be very pragmatic about it. I knew you can't really make a living writing novels, not in Mexico, you have to teach or do something. Only if you become García Márquez will you be able to do it full-time. So I thought that writing scripts would pay my living, and I wrote a bunch of scripts for TV before *Sólo con tu Pareja* (*Love in the Time of Hysteria*), our first feature. Then right after *Sólo con tu Pareja* I moved to LA and started writing for the American industry. The movie wasn't released in the States but after we screened it at the Toronto Film Festival Alfonso stayed here in LA on the way back, and I moved to LA three months later and started writing for various people, in English.

Did you find that difficult?

At the beginning, yes, but not for long. I had been reading English since I was twelve and then I did English Literature at university, so I was used to writing essays in English. The difficult thing was to write dialogue with a good ear. I do have a good ear, and as I had been doing that for such a long time, what I do is just listen, listen, listen for what kind of thing I want. And if I am adapting a novel then it's even easier, because if the novel has good dialogue it sort of gets into my system.

Where did you attend university?

I went to the National University in Mexico which is, I guess, the biggest university in the world, at least the most populated. I did finish—I did everything except my thesis. [*laughs*] So I can't say I have a B.A. The reason was that my thesis was probably too ambitious. When I was in my second semester in the university I started writing scripts, so by the time I finished school I was fed up with academia. It was like, "Oh I don't want to hear about Derrida or Barthes anymore. I hate them all! I need something more practical." And that was screenwriting.

Do you remember any of your first efforts to write feature-length stuff?

Well, the first long feature I wrote was *Sólo con tu Pareja* but before that I wrote I-don't-know-how-many scripts for TV. There were at least six that I remember: scripts for a TV show in Mexico in the late eighties that was a sort of Mexican *Twilight Zone*. The good thing was that it had a filmmaking structure, because you weren't shooting two cameras, only one. And you had to shoot a twenty-two page script in two to three days.

How did that job come about?

There was a producer in Televisa—the most important Mexican TV network—who is the daughter of a famous Mexican actor, and she created this concept, and she was looking for filmmakers. Back then, filmmakers were completely depressed because we weren't producing movies, so this show became like the school for mine and Alfonso's generation. We sort of learned our craftsmanship there. For example, I learned the three-act structure, because the show would go out in four blocks, separated by three commercial breaks. So we would have Act One, block one, and then Act Two would be block two and three, and then the fourth block would be Act Three. That taught me structure—I learned it there and didn't go back.

Where did you get the idea for Sólo con tu Pareja?

The idea came from Alfonso, but his idea was somehow different from what we ended up doing. He read a book called *Journal of the Plague Years*. And he started writing this idea about a main character, an intellectual, writing an essay on Daniel Defoe's book about the plague. At the same time, I was studying the myth of Don Juan at the university. We discussed his approach and decided that it was too intellectual. So we both agreed it had to be someone more pragmatic but creative, and we ended up with a publicist/copywriter, and the plague became AIDS. What Alfonso wanted to make originally was a parallel between the plague in the seventeenth century and AIDS nowadays. And that was not working at all. What we decided to go with was basically a screwball comedy about a Don Juan who thinks he is HIV-positive. And it did tremendously well in Mexico.

That brings me to my next question, which is how does life differ for a screenwriter working in Mexico City as opposed to Los Angeles?

Well, in the actual writing process there is no difference because when I'm working for the studios I'm doing it in Mexico, not LA, because I don't have a work permit. The big difference is, if I'm writing a Mexican project, I'm not being paid, I'm taking the risk, as in *Y Tu Mamá También*, so I become a partner and I get a share of whatever, and that was the same thing with *Sólo con tu Pareja*, and with the other two projects that I have written in Mexico. So the main difference is that, the economic difference. The second difference is that the American studios and producers tend to put a lot of pressure on the writers. My commitment is always the same, but if I'm writing a Mexican project, the salaries are so dismal, so if a Mexican director calls me, mad and hysterical and says, "When is my script going to be ready?" I may just answer, "Fuck you, sir!" if I'm caught in the middle of a bad day. But if a studio executive calls me and very efficiently says, "When is my script ready?" first I say, "What script?" [*laughs*] And then I remember I'm getting paid, so I promise I'll do my best to finish before Christmas or something. That is the difference there . . .

When did you stop living in LA?

In 1992. I came back to Mexico with an assignment. But I stopped writing for Hollywood in 1995–6, and the reason was because I wanted to start directing, and I had to do that in Mexico because otherwise it was just too difficult.

I was just about to ask you about the short films that you have directed. Why did you want to take it up another level and start directing?

I started doing shorts out of frustration. It was just after Alfonso did *A Little Princess*, he was in Mexico, and we were having dinner with the director Guillermo del Toro who has done *Hellboy, Mimic* and *Blade II*. And I guess I looked sad because he said, "What's wrong with you? You look depressed." And I said, "Well, I've been doing so many scripts, and they don't get produced, and when you're a writer and your script doesn't get produced it's like a dead thing. And you don't like to create death. Your self-esteem starts to wane." And they looked at me with strange faces, and said, "Well, why the fuck don't you direct them?" And I was like, "Oh, I never thought of that . . ."

You'd really never thought about that?

No, because I was a writer. I wanted to be García Márquez, man! So I considered it for like a nanosecond, and then I said, "You know, there are so many bad directors that I am sure I can do a better job than them." But I had to learn, you know? And then it was December 1997 that I got my first chance to direct. The producer originally wanted to make one feature with three short films like *New York Stories*, but he ended up with only one good script, which was mine, so the two other scripts he never produced. Then the Mexican Film Institute took away more than half the money from him to produce all the movies, because the others weren't ready. So he said, "OK, we have chosen you to be the director of our project, but it can't be the script that you gave me, it has to be this other script—because the National Lottery is paying for it." There was a National Lottery theme in a short script written by three friends of mine, and I knew it, so I told the producer and I told the Mexican Film Institute, "OK, but I cannot shoot that script, it's really bad." Even my friends knew it was bad. Well, two of them knew it was bad, the other one thought it was a piece of genius . . .

It's always the way.

Yeah, but that guy is not a filmmaker . . . so I convinced them I would keep elements that they liked from that script. They proposed three things, the National Lottery theme, the Mexican Bingo theme, and a twenty-two minute length, and the reason was that they wanted to show it on national TV. I said, "OK, but I'll do my own script," and they agreed to it. So I kept the title, and shot it in December 1997, finished it the next year. And when I'd finished they said, "But the title had nothing to do with the film!" So I actually did whatever I wanted . . . And I cast interesting people, I had Salma Hayek playing an ugly nun. We did such good work in characterizing her that the guy who did the music, Santiago Ojeda, when I showed him the film—and he knew beforehand that Salma was starring in it— laughed at the nun and said, "Who's that?" When I told him, he said, "No way, man!" That short won some awards in Mexico and around the world, and it's the longest thing I've shot as a director. I love it because it's my first thing, and I hate it because it's so flawed.

When did you make Me la Debes (You Owe Me One)?

That I made right after we shot *Y Tu Mamá También*. I used the short ends. We made thirty-five copies of it and ran it before *Y Tu Mamá* in Mexico . . .

It's very similar in tone: it depicts sexual relations between three different couples in one short film which is quite busy, but it's not glamorized, only shown in a matter-of-fact, honest way.

I wrote *Me la Debes* a long time before, probably 1997, and I wanted it to be my first short film, but it didn't happen that way. And I'm glad, because in the end I had a lot more experience; I learned a lot in the *Y Tu Mamá* process. But I didn't want it to be like *Y Tu Mamá*. The most important thing to me was the social criticism.

The upstairs-downstairs aspect?

That double morality that pervades everyone and everything in the world. That's something that really happens in Mexico, something like the father going and having sex with the maid or the cook; it's so common. So Mexicans related to that. My uncle, who is very conservative and probably did that when he was young, he hated the film! [*laughs*]

I thought it was hilarious. Where did the idea for that come from?

I wanted to direct, I was writing films and long features and things to see what I could do, so I was trying to adapt a story by Anton Chekhov. I'm a big Chekhov fan, and there is a great short story about a doctor crying because his son just died. So I wrote that the son died from a scorpion sting, which is very Mexican. But what happened for the next three nights was that when I was writing, I would go and give my child a good night kiss and there would be a huge scorpion there on the wall. So after the third night—I don't kill animals—so I took the scorpion out and I took the decision that I couldn't do that story because somehow I was bringing that energy to my son.

Then I remembered, "Hey, what was that other short story by Chekhov, "In the Dark"? That's a good one!" It's about an aristocratic couple who are going mad; the woman hears noises so she says, "Why don't you check on the maid, she's probably with her boyfriend, that fireman?" And the guy says, "Oh, you're so paranoid, why can't you trust the servants? I'm going to look ridiculous." So he goes down, sees that everything is all right, and seizing his moment he says to the maid, "Oh, by the way, you were brushing my robe, do you have it?" And he takes his robe in the dark, goes upstairs and says to his wife, "Hey, I told you, there is nothing to worry about, you're totally paranoid." And the wife just says, "How come you're wearing the fireman's overcoat?" So with that in mind, what I did was Mexicanize the story all the way.

Are your other short films so rambunctious and playful?

Yes.

Do you think you're seen in Hollywood as a playful, mischievous writer?

I don't know in Hollywood—in Mexico I am. Yes, I pass for that, everybody thinks I only write comedy, which is a big lie. It's a problem with definitions. I mean, people in Mexico and also in LA say that *Y Tu Mamá También* is a comedy and it's not, it's a drama with a sense of humor. People tend to confuse "comedy" and "sense of humor." Sense of humor is related to the English idea of wit. It's a deeper knowledge of character and humanity, which obviously gives a lot of dimension. It has nothing to do with laughter, more to do with cracking a smile. The thing about sense of humor is that it always makes you think. Comedy doesn't do that—at least, not always. The classic premise of comedy is to correct your customs and manners by laughing—it always involves social criticism, especially classic comedy. For me, one of the masters of sense of humor is García Márquez. You are not laughing when you are reading but you have this smile on your face. The same happens with Sam Shepard. It's so terrible what is happening, but you still find yourself smiling.

Where are you standing now in terms of your directorial ambitions?

Before we starting making *Y Tu Mamá* I was trying to put my first feature together, *Orders from Above*. But the financing collapsed—it was a very acute criticism on vertical power and corruption in Mexico during the last regime. So what happened was that the guys who wanted to pay for it discovered that they were a part of that old regime. The reason why Alfonso and I did *Y Tu Mamá* was because both of our projects collapsed at the same time. Right now I'm writing what I hope will be my first long feature film.

Seven years before you started writing Y Tu Mamá *you and Alfonso had written an outline for a comedy—a road movie about two kids who go to the beach. Would you say it was a teen comedy at that point?*

Yes, *Y Tu Mamá* is a very old idea, from around 1987, and it came from *Y Tu Mamá*'s DP, El Chivo Lubezki, who said, "Why don't we make a road movie about two guys who go to the beach?" We took that and in the next ten years we came up with a new idea for the characters and the plot. In the end we were very grateful that we didn't make this movie ten years ago because it would have been like *Porky's*, basically. What we needed was those ten years of personal growth. That's what made it a different movie.

You've talked in interviews about your writing "rhythm." Can you explain what that means?

It's always hard to start writing, *whatever* you're writing. I've written short stories, plays and scripts. Page one is always terrible. Beginnings are always difficult and I don't know why that is, because I always know how I want to start the story. Once I get over that I start to get a rhythm with my work. It's an internal writing rhythm. It's an intuition. When I don't feel entertained I go backwards and either cut something or make it longer. Sometimes, not always, good writing rhythm may translate into good narrative rhythm. When that happens it's just like a wet dream come true.

How do you approach your writing day?

I wish I was more disciplined . . . I read that F. Scott Fitzgerald, when he was trying to write screenplays in Hollywood, would get to his office and write dialogue for an hour and then he would just take those pages and throw them out and then start in earnest. So I sort of do the same. For example, I'll get to my office and I'll start writing prose, just whatever: texts I've been writing through the years, scattered ideas or anecdotes or a diary that is not a diary. The creative juices are flowing so I'll leave a good paragraph in the middle so the day after I come back to it and have something to finish. Then I start to work on whatever screenplay. The thing about writing is that you don't spend most of the time writing, you spend most of the time thinking. So the difficult part of the writing is not the writing but the thinking you do before the writing.

When you are feeling discouraged and having serious doubts about the quality of your writing, how do you handle those feelings of self-doubt that occur?

[*A long sigh . . .*] I am my toughest critic . . . and that's terrible. It's good because it means that I care about my work but at the same time it creates a lot of insecurities. Then I find myself rewriting a stupid scene for the thousandth time and I take twenty days to do it. I hate that. But then some days I write twenty pages and that's it, I don't question it.

I don't like people who are very receptive towards my work, because it doesn't help me. When I finish something I usually give it to my wife and to Alfonso and in the last years I also give it to Alejandro González Iñárritu and Guillermo Arriaga. That's because they are all so critical. We have a deal between us: if we see or read the other person's work, we have to be 100 per cent honest and tell the truth about what we think. It's not always nice, but it's very cool, and it always helps.

Does Alfonso usually find things that you instinctively knew about but weren't willing to address or does he surprise you with his criticism?

Both. Good criticism always surprises. And then there are also things that I have thought of before but didn't put in or things that I was afraid of writing and repressed myself. I think we know each other so well that he knows when I am repressing myself.

Is music an integral part of your writing process? There is that well-known story about how you and Alfonso were listening to a Frank Zappa song when you revisited Y Tu Mamá *and started writing it again . . .*

Music has always been important to me and also to Alfonso. For example, with *Sólo con tu Pareja* Alfonso always knew he wanted to use a very specific Mozart piece, the "Gran Partita." He gave me a copy when I started writing and I listened to it until exhaustion. It helped me a lot to get the tone right. With *Y Tu Mamá* it was Frank Zappa and also Brian Eno and Pink Floyd. Something happens to me where I understand the tone of the movie through music. As soon as we agreed that *Sólo con tu Pareja* was going to have Mozart in it I just understood so much better. The same happened when Alfonso played "Watermelons in Easter Hay" by Frank Zappa—I knew what it was. There was a wistful melancholy. I understand that was the tone. Why? Because I knew I would have two teenagers saying teenager things.

Am I overreaching by saying that you were being a bit mournful about that period in your life as well?

Yeah, that has a lot to do with it. Zappa, Pink Floyd and Brian Eno, this kind of stuff we would listen to when we were teenagers.

Does being brothers help the writing process because you know each other so well or is it a hindrance because you know each other so well? I mean, I know I can get away with talking to my older brother in a way that his business partner can't.

We have our own codes and vocabulary that only we understand. That is very convenient because it serves as a useful shorthand for us. For example, in *Y Tu Mamá* when we reach the pool scene in the country, he said, "My image of it is a rundown hotel with a pool covered by leaves on the surface." And I said, "Yeah, that hotel that we stayed at when we were kids." And he says, "Yeah, man, that's it!" So our common experience can be very useful.

What about the other part of that relationship?

The other part is sometimes tough. I mean, we are brothers.

But he gets to take phone calls when you're writing together, even though you're not allowed to?

Exactly. And he is allowed to distract himself with *whatever* but if I distract myself just one millimeter out of what we are talking about he gets mad. All brothers tend to fight, so when we don't agree on something it can be very tiresome. Because he's the director. I can get my point of view across but I know he's got the last word. I push until I know I am going to lose the battle because it is a waste of energy.

Does he then sometimes come back to that point and admit that you were right?

Yes, but not that way. He'll say, "I was thinking that this . . ." and I'll say, "That's what I was fucking saying yesterday!" And he'll say, "Well, it works perfectly, man. Let's do it." That happens a lot. And it happens a lot because it is very normal. I'm sure it also happens to me. I know him so well and I know when he is being stubborn for no good reason. I know that he is playing with his ego or whatever he's boiling in his mind and that the next day he will come around to my idea or to any idea that is worth the while for the project.

So even if you have a disagreement it will only go so far because you are brothers?

I usually back out because otherwise you cannot work. There is something that we are clear about: the most important thing is the project.

So whatever I am confronting him about, it's about having a better project. And the same goes for him.

On paper, Y Tu Mamá *has a very erotic premise. It almost sounds like a fantasy letter a teenage boy might write to* Penthouse *magazine. But, like your short film, the sex is hardly erotic; it's doggedly realistic in its depiction. Can you tell me something about how you decided to approach the sexual situations?*

When I flew to New York to sit down with Alfonso at his place to conceptualize and plot the outline, we were very clear about the plot, but we weren't clear about character. We knew we were missing something but we didn't know what that something was. What happened was that Alfonso decided that he wanted this to be like a "New Wave" film. I know what the *nouvelle vague* is but I didn't know what he meant by that. He thought that a narrator could be very helpful, and I was totally against it because I didn't want the movie to be like that television show *The Wonder Years,* where it is nostalgic and sentimental. I hate those kinds of movies. But Alfonso said that a narrator that would work was a narrator like in Godard's *Masculin Féminin.* I said, "Well, that one I haven't seen." So we stopped what we were doing and we crossed the street to the video store and rented it. I was blown away by the very first scene, and I got his visual and narrative concept. And Alfonso got all excited about this narrator.

And what's interesting about the narrator is that he is telling us everything that we would never find out, a lot of expository information. It doesn't get in the way of the narrative. What were the rules you had behind this narrator?

The rules were very simple. One is that it had to be deadpan and very objective. Another was that he couldn't tell the story—he could give a lot of information but we couldn't use him as you usually do in movies, you know, to fill in a gap in the story and bring the audience up to speed on what's happening. So what we discovered, was through the narrator we could discover a complete character, which is Mexico, the narrator together with the visuals. Once I understood why the narrator was there and what his purpose was and what he was going to say, everything was clear. So instead of having a scene between Tenoch and Julio saying, "Oh, your father is a politician." "Oh yes, and your father left you when you were five and you have a mother who is a secretary!" "Oh, yes! And your mother is mystical!" . . .

You make expository dialogue sound clumsier than it normally is.

You need expository scenes in every script, and they're difficult because you want them to sound natural but they don't.

What we wanted was to make the point that these two guys were travelling with a girl, caught up in their own universe, but around them, the whole universe was moving. So that's why the narrator tells these stories that don't belong to the main characters but do belong to the movie and belong to Mexico as a character. For example, when they are on the highway and the narrator says, "If they had driven to this place ten years before they would have seen a truck full of chickens turned over, two people dead and one woman crying"—those are images that we have seen. Those are images that help to create Mexico as a character.

So having a narrator helped make it more mature; less Porky's, *more* Jules et Jim?

Yes. I had to cut out a lot of the third person narration because I found that it was too repetitive; or that I was giving information that we didn't need. You have to be very pragmatic. When Alfonso is in the cutting room he loves the cutting key, and when I am working on the screenplay I love the delete key, so we don't have attachment problems. I love killing scenes.

How did Godard's Masculin Féminin *relate to how you handled the sex scenes?*

Alfonso was very clear about what he wanted, that the camera would be very far away and we wouldn't have any closeups and that he didn't want to glamorize sex with a lot of cuts. He approached the sex scenes just like any other scene in the script. In most of my work I guess all of my short films feature sex, and to me it's natural. I was criticized in Mexico by a critic who said I only had sex on my mind. But to me there's nothing wrong with sex. Just let it flow. The important thing is not the sex but the relationship between the characters, their behavior, whatever they may show or tell about themselves in that intimate moment.

You poke fun at Julio and Tenoch when they say things like, "Left-wing chicks are hot, dude." But still, you can't help but like these two characters and empathize with them. How did you handle this, making fun of a character while embracing them at the same time?

It just came naturally. It was just Alfonso or myself giving the dialogue and just laughing. Actually the dialogue in Spanish is different. The literal translation from Spanish to English would be: "Women in demonstrations are actually fucking good." The guy who did the translation did it with Alfonso and I breathing over his shoulder. He's an American who lived in Mexico City with a Mexican wife. So when we translated that bit of dialogue he suggested "left-wing chicks" and it worked. We owe our friend Tim Sexton that line in the English subtitles.

Road movies are generally very episodic in their nature. How did you go about devising a structure that looks like it meanders but is actually very balanced and symmetrical?

We had a very clear idea of the plot. We knew that they were going to confess that they were keeping from each other about cheating with each other's girlfriends. You can have an episodic film that is still engaging. What you need to do is create a dramatic structure. Drama does not come from movement, it comes from inner conflict.

At what point in the writing process did you know that Luisa would be diagnosed with terminal cancer?

That happened years before. I remember that I came up with it. All the way we were questioning why she was doing this and leaving her husband. We didn't have a good motivation or solution for Luisa. It sounded like a vengeance movie. And we both hate vengeance movies. I don't know if I dreamt it or what, but I told Alfonso that she was dying of cancer and he thought that worked. The day after, he called me and said, "I don't think that's a solution." Then of course he called the next day and said, "I think that's the solution." [*laughs*]

Can you tell me something about where Julio and Tenoch came from? Are they close to anyone you and Alfonso know?

Julio and Tenoch and even Saba, the stoner, are all based on characters we used to know when we were teenagers—and yet they are very different. They are unique individuals, they weren't copied. We actually did character biographies for each of them. It may look schematic because Tenoch is a rich kid and Julio is poor. But if you are Mexican you know that it is not schematic because Tenoch is the son of a corrupt politician. Politicians in Mexico are very corrupt and they steal money and they become rich. Julio is not poor. He represents the real Mexican middle class. We have many different levels of wealth in Mexico.

There are some homoerotic elements in the movie, and the incident that drives Julio and Tenoch apart. It's foreshadowed brilliantly in the country club when they are in the showers. Is it an honest way of handling Mexican macho culture?

We just thought we were being honest and thought it was what the story needed. The first scene, where the characters get set up, is in the car where one farts and the other one has to smell the fart. The other farts to one-up him and the competition starts. That's the way I used to behave with my friends. About the homoerotic scenes—and I'm thinking of the diving board scene and the kissing scene—everyone has his or her own theory. When we thought of the diving board scene we just thought it would be fun to have a scene that ends with a cum shot in the pool. Some of my friends in high school, before I met them, they used to have penis-size contests or they would masturbate together to see who could shoot further. [*laughs*] So that was information that I had that we decided to use.

In the script the kissing scene is written like this: "They kiss, a kiss of love." If these guys are honest in any moment of the movie it is right then and right there. Because they love each other. They don't have to be gay, they just love each other. I can also tell you that a Mexican director who is a friend of ours, he is openly gay, he said, "You have finally captured Mexican machismo with that kiss." And I was blown away because coming from this guy, that is a huge compliment.

The radical gay community interpreted Tenoch's morning-after puke as discrimination, basically. They said, "Why is he puking? Just because he had a gay experience?" Our answer was, "Well, yeah, because he's not gay." If you are not gay that would be a common reaction. He's also totally hungover because he was very drunk the night before. In Mexico it was a big deal. What was very interesting was at the opening day of the film. We were in a huge theater, over a thousand people there, all the Mexican machos were shouting "No!" and whistling in a particular way, which in Mexico means that someone is a son of a bitch. And when my friends saw the movie in different theaters they said, "Man, there was a couple behind and when the two guys kissed the boyfriend demanded to leave but the girlfriend wanted to stay until the end of the film." Mexico is such a macho society that most men were offended by the kiss and most females didn't like looking at Gael García kissing Diego Luna. They didn't see the characters; they saw the famous heart-throb actors. They are fans of theirs and they want to fuck those guys. So girls didn't like to see their heroes kissing.

You could make the argument that the film is preoccupied with death. Luisa is diagnosed with her illness but Julio and Tenoch are completely and blissfully unaware of their own death. Was that intentional?

We wanted that to be a leitmotif. We didn't want it to be an obvious leitmotif because we wanted it to be a surprise at the end. So we just used a lot of innuendoes that you only see once and not twice.

Your approach to this leitmotif reminded me of Nick Adams's short story by Hemingway where the son is in a canoe after witnessing an Indian die while at his father's side. And on the way back the son thinks to himself, "I'm never going to die." And in my own mind, I feel quite sure that both Julio and Tenoch think they will never die.

They don't consider death because they are so young and only teenagers. The only moment they consider death is for a brief moment when Luisa is telling them about her teenage love and they make a joke about him and she says, "No, he died in a motorcycle accident at the age of seventeen." Which is their age—and you can see their faces thinking of death for the first time.

You were on the set during filming. What was your role?

Usually when I work with Alfonso he gives me a lot of freedom to say what I think on the set.

Doesn't that create problems with the actors getting mixed signals?

No it doesn't because I don't tell the actors my views, I tell Alfonso. We have a private conversation. If I see something I don't like or that can be improved I will go to Alfonso; if he agrees then usually what he does is he'll say, "OK, then go tell them." Alfonso always includes me in the creative process and I am glad he does because otherwise I wouldn't work with him.

How did you incorporate the actors' ideas into the screenplay?

Well, there is such a generational gap between Alfonso and I and Gael and Diego that sometimes it was very useful. For example, they were saying a word that their generation didn't use but my generation did, because we are the MTV generation. When we got MTV in Mexico we would call music videos a different phrase. And Gael and Diego would mock us for our anachronisms: "These guys, they are so old."

Overall the dialogue didn't change; the actors respected it as written. However, Luisa's dialogue changed because we flew to Madrid to see Maribel Verdú, and she sat me down and gave me some notes on how a woman would speak Spanish the way a Spanish person would speak it. I wrote the dialogue based on the way I thought a Spanish woman would speak, but I was wrong because I am Mexican and our language is different. So I asked her to give Luisa a voice because I didn't know the syntactical structures. I could hear it when she changed it, but I couldn't write it myself. I studied at a Spanish school and I have a lot of contact with Spanish culture so I can hear when it was right. If she did something too radical, I could feel that as well.

You also came up with a clever way of introducing her character and getting inside her head. Luisa is waiting in the doctor's office and she is taking a test in a magazine and we learn that she doesn't like to take risks and is not very happy.

Alfonso wanted a different way of talking about her character and I said, "How?" And we came up with the *Cosmo* test, basically. The whole idea is that she is so very well defined by what she answers in that test and it worked well. She is a certain type, maybe even slightly boring. But she disagrees with that—and it's a kind of foreshadowing for later in the story.

You introduce Luisa when she is actually getting the news about her terminal cancer. Even though you don't let the viewer in on what the result of that visit to the doctor was, were you and Alfonso at all worried about giving this away to the audience?

Yes and no. Yes, because you don't want the audience to know things before they should. And no, because I knew how he was going to do it. If you watch that scene with the doctor, it is just like a routine visit to the doctor. In the next scene you see her on her bed, with a tissue in her hands and red eyes. She knows she is going to die, but then it quickly becomes a scene about infidelity when her husband rings from Villahermosa to say that he's cheated on her.

Were you at all worried that it wouldn't be believable that Luisa would go on a journey to a beach with some teenage boys?

Not at all, because I think it is a universal human fantasy, probably part of the collective unconscious, and because at the end of the day it all depends on Luisa's motivation until the end. Right now, everybody thinks that she wants to have this trip because it's an act of vengeance.

Were you involved with the rehearsals at all?

Actually, I started casting the movie, because Alfonso was in New York, so the first part of the casting I did with the casting director. And that was good, because it gave me some more ideas. Like when Saba, who's always stoned, is showing Julio and Tenoch the way to the beach on the map and he says, "You take this road here and then you go down this road." And then one of them says, "That's not a road, that's a river!" That always gets a good laugh, and that came from being around from the casting, because someone actually said that. Then we would send Alfonso the videos and we'd talk about it. He says he'd rather have me direct the casting sessions than the casting director, because I understand better what he's looking for. I was also involved in the rehearsals during pre-production and whenever I was on the set. I basically took notes to improve the script and gave my opinion whenever I felt like it or whenever it was needed.

I thought the Charolastra Rules was a really good device because it helps define the boys and what is important to them. Among these rules are which football team not to support, and a rule about never cheating with a fellow Charolastra's girl. Can you tell me something about how this came about? Later in the film, Luisa commandeers the manifesto for her own devices, which is a nice touch.

When I was a teenager I didn't have a manifesto or a set of rules, but there were these unspoken rules between friends; like not fucking your friend's girl, which we all broke, obviously . . . We needed to create a code that these guys identified with so we knew what kind of guys they were. The whole thing was that they were very radical and yet they are like Victorian characters, in a way. They all say these things about virgins and so on, but if you scratch them just a little, they're not radical, they're puritanical, which you can see at the end.

Then there is also the rule "Pop beats poetry" which I have to argue against.

"Pop beats poetry" is the only rule that Gael came up with. Originally I had, "In case of a fight during a party, flee." And I liked that because it actually *was* one of those unspoken rules I had as a teenager. But Alfonso didn't like it, and the guys didn't like it either. So in one of those rehearsals we asked them to come up with a new rule, and they decided it. But I hated it, just because all of the other rules are on the level of promiscuity and teenage interest. And then you have this thing that sounds kind of intellectual . . .

Towards the end of the film there is a scene which lasts nine pages of the script. It's their last night at the beach before they have to head back. That's a climax without a car chase, a climax without anyone fighting . . .

Yeah, a climax with everyone agreeing! Once I figured out that scene, I wrote it in about an hour and a half to two hours. It just came to me. A writer usually writes between one to two pages an hour. But I didn't want to stop because I had the whole thing in my head, and if I stopped then the rhythm would stop. I even had my wife type the scene and she kept trying to slow me down so she could get everything as it was spilling out of my head. Before that, we knew what was supposed to happen at the end but we didn't know how to *make* it happen. Something similar happened to Alfonso during the shooting: he originally planned to make that scene in three consecutive nights with a lot of coverage, but he suddenly found himself making a very long shot and he ended up doing the entire thing in only six hours!

The morning after the threesome scene, Luisa is very matter-of-fact and businesslike. Why?

Because she has put everything in order. The balance is back. She broke the balance by fucking Tenoch, then Julio. But they had a threesome and now the balance is perfect. So yes, she is very happy, she has made up her mind and she is going to stay there because she is going to die soon.

One Mexican critic had a sour response to the film, calling it a "South of the Border Beavis and Butthead." Did that upset you?

No, we used his tagline to promote the film! He also said that it was a good film for the *Penthouse* readers, and we used that line too. Even for my short film *Me la Debes* I used his line, "Carlos Cuarón has only one thing in mind: sex and all its variations . . ." I put it on the poster for the short film, because it had a family portrait and they all looked very rigid and repressed—so that tagline was actually very funny and the film became a huge success. I believe Truman Capote when he said, "Don't humiliate yourself by answering a critic." So who gives a fuck, you know?

Beverly Hills, California

4

CHRIS WEITZ

About a Boy

"I was anthropologically suited to adapt *About a Boy*."

Chris Weitz and his older brother Paul made their feature film debut as directors on the hit teenage comedy *American Pie* (1999). They then directed the comedian Chris Rock in *Down to Earth* (2001), a re-make of Warren Beatty's 1978 film *Heaven Can Wait*. They achieved considerable success in their first writing–directing role, nominated for Best Adapted Screenplay, along with Peter Hedges, at the 2003 Oscars for co-writing *About a Boy* (2002).

Synopsis

London, the present. Will, a rich, child-free and irresponsible Londoner, searches for available women by inventing an imaginary son so he can attend single-parent meetings. As a result of one of his new relationships, he meets Marcus, an odd twelve-year-old boy with problems at school. Reluctantly, Will takes a liking to Marcus, helping him become more confident. In turn, Marcus helps Will accept that he is an adult.

* * *

KEVIN CONROY SCOTT: *Chris, your father was a fashion designer and a writer, and your mother was an actress. So was creativity something that was encouraged in your household?*

CHRIS WEITZ: My mom [Susan Kohner] won two Golden Globes and was nominated for an Oscar for *Imitation of Life*, the Douglas Sirk movie. But it was funny, because she never really talked about making movies when we were little—I think she was glad to put it aside. And I grew up in New York, so there wasn't much talk of the film industry. It was only when my grandfather and grandmother would roll into town—my grandfather was an agent, he was Ingmar Bergman's agent, and John Huston's, and Billy Wilder's, so he represented a lot of the European talent that came to Hollywood in the thirties, forties and fifties. He was born in what is now the Czech Republic, and he was extremely literate, like a man of letters from two centuries ago. So the idea that people who made films could also be literate and have ideas, and be inspired not only by a visual culture but by a literary one—that came from my grandparents. My grandmother too had been a silent film actress, and she starred in Mexico's first talking picture. So there's a weird lineage there . . .

My father also served in intelligence in the Second World War, and he was writing biographies of Nazi leaders as well as designing clothes. So he was also very well-read, and really he didn't like designing; it was basically just what he made his money from. So he encouraged me and my brother to seek careers in the arts, and I think there were points where he regretted it, because he thought we would just be deadbeats. And for a long time, that's definitely how it looked . . .

But my brother and I did grow up with very hierarchical ideas about writing, and to this day I'm still not sure that screenwriting is "writing" in that literal sense. I don't think it's literature, really—rarely and unintentionally does it achieve that status. It's not even as important as architectural drawings—and that's the thing it's similar to, in that a script is a map that's meant to be undertaken. But I always feel uncomfortable calling myself "a writer," because that's not what I think screenwriting really is. It's a much more pragmatic event.

So how did the pair of you get into screenwriting, given that it was so frowned upon?

I was working as a journalist and my brother as a playwright, and we just started writing something together for fun. I don't think we ever realized it would be our business at all. And so it's always been done— not on a wing and a prayer—but we've just improvised a lot of it as we've gone along. Whereas I think a lot of young Hollywood screenwriters really set out to be "screenwriters" and have a lot of set ideas about what that means.

How was you and your brother's relationship when you were growing up?

Paul is four years older than me, and he was very nice, which was, for me, the first reason we worked together. He didn't beat me up constantly . . . My parents had very strong ideas about child rearing and it was definitely on the European model rather than the American—meaning curfews, and strict ideas on etiquette and what we were supposed to wear. So we lived in a little enclave, it was very old-fashioned, in a way, and it left my brother and me under pressure to conform a lot—as well as to create fantasy worlds for ourselves. We used to constantly come up with strange characters who had weird shticks that they would do, and these became obsessions with us. They were odd, little running skits, and they drove our parents crazy but kept us sane. In that sense, it became easy for us to write comedies. Eventually it would be harder to change from that to write more *grown-up* comedies. But it happened eventually, I guess . . .

Have you and Paul always stayed good friends?

We always got along really well, we were very close and we still are. We get on each other's nerves probably more now than we ever have, especially because when you're directing a movie you're living on top of one another. So we do have arguments on the set, but we're very careful at keeping them away from the actors, because they get spooked easily. And when we disagree about writing—this holds especially when you're writing comedy, because the question of what's funny or not is very much open to judgment—things can get quite personal. For example, we go through so many drafts that there can be a running battle over one joke that can last the course of a year, and in the end one of us comes out on top. But then it still happens that we'll agree on a joke, agree that it's hilarious, and then nobody will laugh in a screening. And our attitude is, "Screw them!" If you have enough stuff that's actually funny, you can afford to have stuff that drops . . .

How does someone who grew up in New York end up studying English literature at Cambridge?

My dad was born in Berlin in 1923 and was sent away in '33 when Hitler came to power. He went to the Hall School in London, then to St. Paul's, and then to Oxford. So he always liked the idea of one of his sons going to St. Paul's—it was a very important place that restored his sense of worth after being made a second-class citizen in Germany. I originally went there for a year to look at things, I was fourteen, and I ended up deciding to stay and finish there because it was a great school, I had really good friends and I liked it there. Then it was kind of logical to apply to Oxbridge, and once I got into Cambridge I stayed on.

Your American accent hasn't changed.

Yeah, but I came back to the U.S. afterwards. At fifteen I sounded like an English public schoolboy, because I was a kid and tried not to stick out. But then I came home and was accused of being a fake, so I actually had to relearn the American accent to survive. But if I'm hanging around English people, it goes again . . .

What were your impressions of Cambridge? Did you row in the boat race against Oxford or any of that stuff?

I played rugby, but not at a high enough level of becoming a Blue. I had a shot at becoming a Blue at basketball but I didn't even make that. No matter what school you went to beforehand, it's a shock to the system. It's still quite anachronistic in many ways. For instance, it's very difficult to study other disciplines while you're there. There are a lot of things American universities would find barbaric: there's no creative writing program—it's discouraged, if anything. It's seen as too keen, too enthusiastic, amateurish. Whereas they figure that if you're a real writer, it'll happen anyway. There certainly wasn't a film program. I don't think there is a film camera within fifty miles of Cambridge. But there's a really good arts cinema there, which definitely helped.

Were you harboring any ambitions to be a novelist when you chose your major there?

English literature was the only thing I could imagine doing at that young age. But I don't think I ever thought I would be a novelist. I still think that writing a novel is on a completely different scale of magnitude in terms of the effort and thought involved compared to writing a screenplay, which is really pretty light when you compare it to the work of writing a novel. Also—and this is a slight digression—the question of style in a novel is also much more difficult than in a screenplay, where you're really dealing with images and dialogue. You have more strictures in a screenplay, and I find that much easier than imagining how you would go about the degree of detail you would express in a novel. You don't have to go into that in a screenplay, because you know that the details will be handled by a production designer or a director. In a novel, there are more perspectives—you can go inside a *chair*'s head if you want. You can do anything, and that variety of choice is crippling. I've had a few stabs at writing a short story or a novel and I can't get my head around it. Whereas films start with a relatively small number of opening moves. You can start it with an image, and it would be preposterous to describe it to the nth degree in the way you could justifiably do in a novel. And you usually don't have to convey someone's state of mind except in as much as they display it outwardly. But if you're writing a novel, it would be a shame if you didn't address some of the inner narrative of the characters expressed in the book. And that was certainly the case with *About a Boy*; not only was the dialogue in the novel excellent, the inner commentary was fantastic as well, and why we decided to do voice-overs in the film. That way, we're converting from—beware, something pretentious is coming up—what Flaubert called *"style indirect libre,"* which is the influence of a person's state of mind on the description of the events, or the characters that he's noticing. In other words, the narrative voice takes on the tones of the character's feelings. You can't do that in the same way if your characters are stating things outright in voice-over. There are passages in *About a Boy*, the novel, which are expressed as the third-person narrative voice but are clearly tinged by the perceptions of the child or Will, and we have to state them directly. So that means you have to be careful with the nuance of how you do it.

Which English literature really inspired you when you were doing your MA?

Lord Byron was my guy, because he was a lot of fun to begin with and much more intelligent than people gave him credit for. I mean *Don Juan* is kind of a philosophical poem on a really grand scale, as much, I think, as *Paradise Lost* is. It's not so coherent but in terms of the kind of scope of ideas it's concerned with, it's really amazing. Byron is consistently underestimated and just thought of as a guy who had sex with his half-sister—and everyone else he could get his hands on. I find that he's the figure of English literature that I'm most devoted to.

One English critic called you an Anglophile in his review of About a Boy. *Would you agree with that?*

Well, I love being one, but it's from having lived there and partially growing up there more than anything else. I'm not sure if that makes me an Anglophile. I feel sort of like that anthropologist who went to live with the Yanomami in the Amazon. I feel like *that* guy. I do know their language, their ways more than a lot of people. So I guess I was anthropologically suited to adapt *About a Boy*.

Was it your idea or the studio's to have an English to American-English dictionary on the DVD of About a Boy *to explain phrases like "shag" and "bugger off"?*

It was the studio's idea. They always come up with these ideas for bonus items to encourage people to buy the DVD instead of the VHS. It wasn't a terrible idea, and it wasn't horrifically executed. Although it was mistaken that the biggest audience for the film would be in

America, not England . . . A big question did come up during the writing process: should we say "sneakers" instead of "trainers"? And we decided against it. It didn't feel right; we didn't feel comfortable with it. We knew that the characters wouldn't say it, that people living in London wouldn't say it, and that it would bother British people who watched it; whereas it wouldn't necessarily be that hard to understand in context. I think people take too much effort to tailor films to an imagined audience and in doing so, lose grasp of what's particularly interesting about something.

Stephen Frears filmed Nick Hornby's High Fidelity *in Chicago, and you must have been under a lot of pressure to relocate* About a Boy. *Why didn't you capitulate?*

I think we wouldn't have shot in the U.S. with Hugh, and since he came with the package when we came on board—and we were very happy with that—that was one very strong reason. The strongest, really. But you could transpose those characters, and I think they did that really well in *High Fidelity* but for us, I think there was something particularly London in the setting. Also the fact that it's so dialogue-driven and the characters are so hyper-articulate—even Marcus—that seems more of a British trait. And the kind of misery the kid was in seemed particularly British to me.

What would you say was so "particularly London" in the setting?

If it was set in Los Angeles, it's very hard to fight against the visuals of bright skies and hills and palm trees, whereas depression has a particular resonance in London because of the rain, the grayness, and those gothic piles of schools. Actually, the bizarre thing was we had a choice of two specific locations and in each case the school was exactly the same. There were some buildings that were built exactly to the same plan.

What happened to those aborted short stories you mentioned? What were they about?

Of course, the first things I thought about writing were autobiographical self-justifications which were just awful. Whatever relationship I just had gotten out of at the time and I felt aggrieved about became the basis for a novel . . . The one thing I think I might even follow through on is that I have an idea for a novel about four kids who play Dungeons & Dragons. So that's taking place on one level, and on another level it's a fantasy novel about the characters who the kids play, who think they're not characters but actual people. So, on one level, it would be sort of about self-determination and free will but in the light of this ludicrous fantasy world; and on the other level, about these kids and how the personas that they're playing reflect what they're going through.

It sounds almost like something J. K. Rowling would write.

Weirder. One of the kids would be realizing he was gay; all the kinds of things that happen when you're fourteen or fifteen and that get transposed to the Dungeons & Dragons characters, the barbarians, or magicians or whatever.

So you played some Dungeons & Dragons with your brother?

We did, and it's embarrassing to say, but it had such an influence on my life. I'd like to write an article on this some day. There are a lot of people who played and are horribly embarrassed about it and won't admit it, because it's part of their lives they put behind, but it had an incredible influence as to how they've gone about things. I was never as fervent about doing anything as I was about Dungeons & Dragons. Making movies might be a close second. I think the brilliance of it is how you live out these stories with such fervent care and attention to detail. There really was something to it, a consensual story told by lots of different people at once. Things that happened within the game had no objective value whatsoever—the idea of finding treasure was totally imaginary but it still breeds some sense of real worth. In fact, I still wonder why the hell anyone would get into a movie knowing it's a two-dimensional, clearly artificial process. Even the act of cutting and editing around a scene is so artificial, it's so unlike any actual experience of real life. But people take it on board as if it was tapping into a dream.

After university, you wrote some articles for some London newspapers: The Sunday Times *and the* Independent. *How did these come about?*

My director of studies was a great guy and he hooked me up with someone who wrote for the arts pages of the *Evening Standard*. His name is Ian Irvine, and he's an extremely lovely guy. Having only seen stuff I had written for some really bad Cambridge magazines and newspapers, he gave me a chance to write an article and I just did a terrible job and it was never published because I was making literary references totally out of context to what the articles were supposed to be about. I wrote about books and about films too, but very much what they call "think pieces"—you just sort of bullshit for a while.

What was your relationship to cinema like at that point?

I didn't really have a sense of film history at all, which was stupid because my grandfather was in the thick of everything. I wasn't out in LA where he worked to get a sense of that. And, growing up, I never went to a school in which film was thought to have a history at all and it really wasn't considered a subject, which was a blind spot for me. And that's something about Cambridge, the canonical view about English literature and of subjects in general. If things don't fit into one of the established subjects, either you have to create a whole new department or manage to dovetail it in some way. So I had no idea about it. I mean, I loved watching films and I think I've got a decent grounding, but not a true film-nerd grounding in film. I know what I love and, in a way, I wish I had had the time to watch classic films and have an excuse—because now it's hard to find an excuse to sit and watch a three-hour Japanese film. But I've been able to follow my enthusiasms, which is cool.

And you're still reading a lot . . .

When I can. I actually want to re-gear my life and make reading more of a priority, to the extent that I really do think of re-ordering my time and other responsibilities because I can sort of do a little less work now and read more. Because I feel it's slipping out of my grasp. There's not enough time to read. I read slowly and I'm not comfortable when reading is not a big part of my life.

Is it true that you got interested in international relations after Cambridge?

Well, I didn't know what the hell I was going to do as a job, I was still living abroad, and I thought I could maybe keep living abroad if I worked for the State Department. So, ironically, the task was to figure out how to become an American again—to be interested enough in the world for them to send you out, but American enough so they don't think you'll go native. So I also had to teach myself macroeconomics at least to the level they wanted for the exams. The first level was largely informational, American history and economics and government. The second was weird role-playing exercises, like D & D International Relations—"Write a cable to the Embassy," or "Propose this aid package for this imaginary country." I went through that, too, and I was ready to sign up, but there was a backlog in hiring because of a recent lawsuit which was allowing in a lot of female applicants who had previously been rejected. And while I was waiting to get hired and assigned, my brother and I started writing. It was a *much* more appealing thing to do. And I'm really, really glad I didn't do work for the Department of State, because I'm pretty gloomy, and I know for a fact that if I had to go to another country and start over again, I would have hated it.

Your brother had written some plays which had been produced in New York. Why did you think it was a good idea to collaborate together?

We had both reached a bit of a dead end. I'd realized I wasn't a very good journalist and Paul realized he was a really good playwright, but no one was going to pay him very much to do it. I was twenty by now, and he was twenty-four. And halfway through writing *Legit,* our first screenplay, I moved back to New York. It was about a porn director who wanted to make an art film—a fairly broad comedy about people with no talent trying to do something very ambitious. We were definitely at that point dealing with pretty buffoonish types. Paul Thomas Anderson did a much more difficult thing with *Boogie Nights* because those characters have much more pathos and humanity, and at the same time they were laughable and were fun. I suppose we did *Legit* for fun and thought, "Wow, wouldn't it be great if someone wanted to buy it?" Nobody did, but it got us some meetings and we sold a pitch.

Did the thought occur that your family might be able to open a door?

Actually, the one contact that worked for us was through my brother's work as a playwright: David Seltzer, a screenwriter and director who had a production deal at MGM, and had seen my brother's plays, so he didn't think we were complete idiots. That's kind of how we got our first job.

How did you and Paul work together then as compared to how you work together now?

Well, it's changed, because we used to sit in the same room at the same computer for six to eight hours a day. That was horrible. Sometimes it was funny, because you would crack each other up, but we'd also get into fights and be kind of wrestling for the keyboard. And it was also really forcing blood from a stone, which isn't great if you're writing a comedy.

Now we're at the stage where we very carefully outline a script so that we know what should precisely happen in which scene. And then we'll divvy up sequences so that someone isn't just writing a single scene, but a sequence with a particular feel to it, so you can get a run-up to something. And then we'll just swap them over and edit each other's stuff. That still occasionally leads to fights but at least we resolve them.

And sometimes there are bizarre gaps in logic where for instance, I've written a sequence where a character ends up in Ohio whereas in the next sequence Paul has him in New York for no particular reason, and these things have to be straightened out. But that's usually pretty straightforward. Actually, the most important thing is that we agree on the tone of the particular script we're doing. And that's the problem I find in most of the scripts that I read. If it's a comedy, people will sacrifice the consistency of tone for something funny because obviously it's a comedy, it's supposed to be funny—but that can lead to a weird jarring of the audience where they suddenly realize they're watching a film that's trying to make them laugh, rather than being seduced into a particular frame of mind in which things happen to be funny. That's the worst thing about most comedy writing that goes wrong: nobody has respect for the tone of the piece they're trying to do.

How do you and Paul find that consistency of tone in a piece yourselves?

It really comes out of the outline. We don't start out saying, "OK, what's the tone of this movie going to be?" But I think there's a basic understanding of what it is. With *About a Boy*, the tone of the book was somewhat established, but in terms of movies, it was going to be Wilderesque in tone but also Lubitsch, everything that Lubitsch paid attention to, that particular brand of light comedy of Austro-Hungarian origin, really. And we do understand each other well enough that we come up with the same reaction to a situation in real life, a joke—it's bizarre but there must be some genetic encoding, a humor gene of that particular type as opposed to another.

Do you consider yourself a comedy screenwriter?

I guess I've got to admit to that, because that's mostly what I've done.

Do you think that's what you're hired to do when you're not writing your own stuff?

No, I don't. We are hired to do various things, and sometimes it is to write a comedy. But you tend to get pigeonholed into various arcane definitions of what you actually do. We wouldn't necessarily be considered comedy writers so much as people think we're "the guys with heart": the bizarre notion that we or anybody else can bring some kind of emotion to a piece which before that was completely lifeless. That's probably our reputation in the industry. "Heart" is shorthand for characters who behave like human beings might, and there's occasionally a problem for scripts that don't have that.

But, technically, we probably are comedy writers. The thing I like about comedy is that it doesn't ignore an aspect of human life, which is that human life is occasionally bizarre and ridiculous and laughable. And dramas can ignore that at their peril, because you haven't presented a rounded view of things if you haven't shown something funny or amusing. I think a lot of Oscar-grab movies go for what they imagine to be the emotion while ignoring humor. But, no—when I think about comedy writers in Los Angeles—I would like not to fall into that stereotype. At least I hope I'm not a bitter, cynical jokes–salesman type who's wearing tennis shoes and jeans, and slightly overweight from too much lobster tempura. And I don't think that the guys who write films that happen to be terribly funny in other countries really consider themselves "comedy writers" in that sense. Going back to Byron again, he wrote some comic verse at times, but his best work is incredibly funny as well as interesting and heartfelt and explorative of very important ideas. And I'd rather be more on that model.

So what is a normal writing day like for the two of you these days?

It's different for the two of us. Here's what Paul does: he wakes up at an early hour, sets himself down to work, concentrates very hard and earnestly and produces five pages. I wake up late, I go to Starbucks and dick around reading the paper. I go home, go online, check e-mail even though I don't need to and then I go to Book Soup and knock around the aisles there, and then at the end of the day I start really sweating, work really hard for half an hour and maybe produce five pages. Sometimes it's ten pages or sometimes none at all. I'm far more slipshod about it. There used to be one place where I would consistently get a lot of work done, which was this café in New York called Le Gamin on McDougal Street below Houston. I've written twenty pages there in a day, which is like a fifth of a script. But they closed it so I'm completely screwed. I need to find a backup.

Take me through your process a little bit more. Do you do character biographies or story charts or the like?

We don't do character biographies in the sense of really having an idea of what the character did at a given age, or even having a page of information about them. Occasionally we ask ourselves what we think

he was like, but it's done more on a case-by-case basis and the feel of
what a character has and what we think he might say—the intuition
we have about it, more than anything else.

The outlines are pretty detailed. It's embarrassing, because we do it
on index cards, one for each scene, which is how everyone does it. We
never say, "Let's just start with this scene and see where it goes,"
because we don't know how it will end. That would be sheer disaster
for us even though it isn't for other people. But, first of all, our plots
would never match up, we'd have to stay in the same room and end up
strangling each other.

Soon after that we would have no idea as to what was happening
which might lead to an interesting movie if someone else wrote it
but it would be a complete, horrible train wreck if we did. So we
need to be pretty detailed not only because we work separately a lot
but also because we really want a sense of the film as a whole. If you
plot out a film, it's clearly working like a machine in some fashion
going from point A to point B. And in that sense, it's non-intuitive and
can lead to characters who behave as though they're automata. So
it's a weird balance between that very mechanistic view of it and
trying to keep some life in your characters so that they can say and
possibly do things that you didn't necessarily specify at the beginning. So we start with a very, very detailed version of how things go,
and hope that we can roll with anything that sort of comes up
through inspiration.

That's the weakness of American screenwriting, I think—this
notion of the first, second, third act. The freedom that foreign films
have by contrast is sometimes really stunning. But having said that,
although some American films can be horrendous, the plots tend to
be less of a mishmash than films that are developed in a less formulaic
way.

*Do you think it's because American audiences expect things to be fig-
ured out for them while foreign audiences are allowed to figure things
out for themselves?*

It is that in part. Foreign audiences allow themselves to view screenwriting and film itself as more of an art form than a lot of
Hollywood filmmakers. My brother and I are on one edge of the
independent ghetto with *About a Boy*, with one foot in the studio
world, where there are happy endings. We didn't set out to do that.
To a horrible fault, Hollywood is very audience driven and ninety
per cent of the films that come out of these studios now are really
just engines for producing profit. I don't think that studio people

would even deny it. They call it "summer entertainment" but what else is it but fleecing people for nine dollars and making it loud enough so that they think that they've seen something?

I was a judge at the Tribeca Film Festival a little while ago and one of the features that I saw was a bizarre French film about a gay couple, where one of them leaves town. At first it seems to be a weird haunted-house story, with two strange bald men appearing in a basement in polka-dot summer dresses. But it doesn't end up being scary at all, it doesn't even have a plot per se that you can make out. When I saw the filmmakers at the interview afterwards, they said, "Yes, it came out of living with the idea of this picture we had seen." It wasn't really an explanation that demanded that you sympathize with them whatsoever. And I thought, "That must be really liberating."

On the other hand, I've probably fallen into the habit of entertaining mass audiences and wanting to. I don't think there's anything wrong with that, I really do like the idea of entertaining. Modern audiences don't have a lot of patience, but then they haven't been trained to have it. They certainly don't think, "I'll go to a movie and be patient." I guess it's a more European attitude to view film like any other art form and take time to understand it. Then again, I really like the fact that American films have very strong narratives. We tell a story better than anybody else—except maybe the Japanese, Kurosawa. But we tell a story better than the Europeans do.

Switching gears . . . how do you and your brother handle those moments in the writing process when things aren't working out and you are having periods of self-doubt?

Geez, wow. I'll try to throw caution to the wind and say I don't doubt myself as a screenwriter because, first of all, this goes hand in hand with not being a writer. Doubting yourself as a screenwriter would be like doubting yourself as a Rollerblader. Who cares, really? I'm certainly not going to beat myself up about it. I find that certain things can be going badly and not be coming out well but I just don't think it's going to be that difficult to sort it all out.

So I guess the way we get past it is like extreme arrogance in a way because we feel we understand as well as anybody else what has to be done to make something work well in a screenplay. I've had a lot of doubts about myself as a filmmaker because you're in a world of infinite possibilities and it's terrifying and gut-wrenching and then you have to take a deep breath and jump. Now, my brother would disagree, so I have to say this is me talking. But I don't feel like screenwriting is brain surgery: I feel like all you have to do is imagine the film

in your head, and that's what I've always done. I sort of fuck around
and procrastinate until I can get into a weirdly meditative state where
I can see the film playing out, and then it's more like transcribing it
than making it up.

*Having such a literary pedigree, how did you find yourself co-directing
the teen comedy* American Pie?

I enjoyed *Porky's* when it came out, but I was twelve years old then
and didn't know any better . . . Actually it's a horrible film with a lot
of horrible sentiments behind it. And I never really watched a lot of
John Hughes movies, so I never really knew those films or had a fond-
ness for them. *American Pie* wasn't the first directing job to occur to
me, but it *was* funny, and I liked the characters, so we decided to just
make the best possible teen sex comedy that we could. That having
been said, that vein of humor exists in literature and in the canon. In
Aristophanes there are giant phalluses all over the place, and Rabelais
is just disgusting when you get down to it. And I could say it was just
about the spirit of misrule and carnival, which is really sordid. But the
fact of the matter is, my father was German, he always enjoyed bawdy
toilet humor and I did too, and so we just knew it was going to be a
whole lot of fun. That said, the whole gross-out comedy movement, I
just can't wait for it to end. I think it is over, actually.

Has your mother being an actress helped your writing?

I know that it's terrifying to stand in an actor's shoes. So I'm more
inclined to trust actors when they say, "I can't say that line, it doesn't
sound right" — because when you write you don't have to speak the
lines, although you probably should because then you'll know whether
human beings can actually say certain lines of the dialogue. And that's
crucial, because an audience will be thrown by dialogue that seems to be
overly expository, or syntactically correct but not realistic, and not only
that, it will make life very difficult for the actor, and he'll have to adjust
his cadences to get it right. So I guess I'm more inclined to listen to
actors, because I know they're not a bunch of people prancing around —
it's really difficult to do, and especially difficult if the words that you're
saying don't fit the situation or the human voice either.

How did you first come across the novel About a Boy?

I read it, because I'd heard that it was a fun novel. And I thought that
it was incredibly absorbing but also in such an unpretentious and

powerful way, evoking certain feelings and emotions while dealing with human problems. At the crux of it, I could see the idea of a guy inventing a child in order to meet women as a Billy Wilder tactic. So we saw it as being similar to *The Apartment*.

How did you then become involved in the film?

New Line bought it for Tribeca, and Peter Hedges wrote the first draft. Iain Softley was going to direct it but he fell off to do *K-Pax*. It was still at New Line and by then Hugh Grant was attached but it was an American character in London. So that draft was obviously written before Hugh came on because they were thinking about an American star. The end of the film was in many ways similar to the end of the book, the element of Kurt Cobain's suicide being a focal point. But tying it to Cobain's death made it a period piece, 1994, which seemed strange and difficult for us to handle. Also I think it would have proved impossible to get the rights to play the music. At any rate, when we looked at the plot, the suicide wasn't central to the actual machinations, it was a red herring in fact. It represented all kinds of themes, about whether you're going to keep on living even if things seem to suck. But also, in the intervening time, Kurt Cobain's death became something different from what it was at that moment—the shock then had become part of a litany of tragedies since.

We obviously set about to re-Anglicize it. Peter had chosen to express the interior monologue by Hugh Grant's character communicating with various trendy friends of his, and you got the sense of his superficiality through theirs. But we wanted to actually strip it back a bit and make it much more about a depressed, alienated person who didn't realize how depressed he was. You could imagine he might have friends, but you were never going to see them in the movie if we could help it. We always wanted to keep him isolated in his apartment, or alone in big shops, so he doesn't have anyone to talk to. We didn't mind the audience imagining he was just some weird loner who spent time on the Internet and watching TV and didn't have any real contacts with human beings.

So how was your third act different?

In Peter Hedges's version, there was a finale in which it seemed as though Marcus was going to commit suicide, and it would take place in Piccadilly Circus. Visually it was a really big set-piece because obviously that's the most active, kinetic part of London. Well, first of all, we didn't see how we could actually film that, and second of all, we

felt that we just wanted to bring Marcus and Will together in a much
more familiar environment that we had already seen before. And we
felt it should be about Will being childish or at least dealing with what
we imagined to be his childish fears and the fear of not being cool
being a metaphor of never being accepted in the first place. So the
whole third act became about this performance Marcus was going to
make, and also about how to get the audience to give a shit about the
importance of a child performing a song and how that might be terrible
for him. There is an imagined suicide, which is the mother's suicide, but
it's not really about that. It's about the fact that the little boy thinks he'll
cheer up the mother if he sings for her, and that's a child's idea as to
how you can influence events. But how to convince an audience to
really care about this little kid being humiliated—frankly, there was no
way you could achieve that on the page. It was one of those cases
where I was blustery and overconfident about thinking it was going to
work, but people who read it weren't so sure. And really it was up in
the air until the actual kid did it on the day, and he was so winning
that we were able to pull it off, I think.

*This novel, more than any of Hornby's other novels, gives you more of
a challenge in balancing what's fantastical and what's realistic just by
its premise. And that's obviously what Billy Wilder did very well.*

He did. The S.P.A.T. (Single Parents, Alone Together) meeting posed a
difficulty and that's Nick Hornby's accomplishment in the novel. It is
actually fantastical when you think about it and only a slightly deranged
individual would actually think of it and that's where you really have to
depend on the actor. I don't think it would have been so easy for Billy
Wilder to do half of the stuff he did without Jack Lemmon who could,
when you look at *The Apartment*, be extraordinarily broad—he can be
like Jim Carrey—and yet he brings this sort of everyman feeling to it, a
terribly likeable quality. So Hugh Grant saves the S.P.A.T. scene literally, you can't do it without him. And the kid saves the rock concert. Yeah,
it's totally farfetched and just on the edge of "Hollywood" and I think
that it would have been a disaster if we had written that the crowd
erupts into applause—there had been suggestions that we do that. But I
think that the only thing that saves it is that there is this realistic aspect
of a few scattered claps, and that Hugh's character has managed to do it
to avoid the child being completely slaughtered. He's taken the damage
on to himself by the end of it.

*The novel is told from two different points of view, Marcus's and Will's.
However, you open with Will's point of view, and then we see a glimpse*

of Marcus during Will's date in Regent's Park. Did you ever consider introducing Marcus when Will meets his date in Regent's Park?

We did, and we thought that it was crucial that you care as much about Marcus as about Will, and we kind of bit off the challenge of justifying that degree of attention from the audience. We knew it would be surprising, first of all, to be introduced to this kid who no one had ever seen before except in the credits. But we thought it was easier to get them interested in that point of view by saying, "This guy is going to be playing equal to Hugh Grant, so get used to it," rather than introducing him later and seeing the kid as just a function of Hugh's story. That's only what the novel does; it alternates chapters in terms of whose point of view it is. But we did compromise by introducing Hugh's character first, whereas the novel introduces Marcus first. And although we argued with Hugh because he wanted to start with the boy, we wanted to come out with what they call the number one batsman—you put the strongest guy out there first.

I read somewhere that Casino *influenced the voice-over. Can you expand on that?*

Martin Scorsese is just great at voice-overs. He never uses them unnecessarily and he also uses them in imaginative ways, like in *Casino* when Joe Pesci's voice-over ends in mid-sentence when he's hit over the head with an aluminum baseball bat. Horrible scene, it's just gutwrenching. But Scorsese's just so good at doing that, and uses it as a real element instead of something that's clearly been added later to make up for deficiencies in the film. And also the idea is that there's such a thing as an unreliable voice-over in the way that there's an unreliable narrator: *Casino* does that as well and you get two different perspectives on an event, neither of which are completely correct. And that was really useful to us.

How did Hugh Grant get involved in the writing process?

He was the person we listened to most, because he's really smart and he knew the character really well. He's a good writer in his own right. He came up with a lot of the good dialogue, not only for himself but for other characters as well, and he was a really great sounding board as to what sounds like something a person might actually say. He's a much more technical actor than people give him credit for. Everything has been worked to death by the time he delivers his lines, so we're not just brown-nosing him when we say he was our collaborator when we were working on the script.

How did you handle his improvisation on set?

Sometimes we thought, "This is a really great piece of dialogue and we'll try to protect it as much as we can." But other times we knew it could always be better and so we were very happy. Not all actors can improvise. It's just like writing on the fly, really, when you're in the groove of the character—which is all you're doing when you're writing anyway and you're imagining yourself into these different voices. And it can be absolutely wonderful.

There are a lot of intricate camera movements in About a Boy. *Did you write them into the script?*

Mostly no, because it's really hard to do that. You can *suggest* camera moves. It would be lovely if sets are built entirely to instructions that are written down in the screenplay but that won't happen because all kinds of financial considerations will come into play. So you hope you'll have time to look at a location, and for shot-listing to be an additional writing period that you do with your cinematographer. We might start writing camera angles into things more, but there was a long period where every time I read somebody else's script where it said "Extreme Close-Up On" or "Angle Over," I thought, "Fuck yeah, when have you ever been on set making a movie?" I guess it helps the reader imagine things, but for any director reading it, it's just a red flag.

The scenario is very much a boy meets boy, boy loses boy setup.

Yeah, it's very much a romantic comedy between these two guys, absolutely not between any of the men and any of the women.

When the mother goes to see Will, there's a suggestion of pedophilia there. How did you manage to get the delicate balance on that issue?

We pretty much handled it the way that the book does, which is if we didn't address the question whether Hugh's character was interfering with the little boy, it would leave an open question. I find it very sad that it's become one of the tropes of American society, sexual abuse. I think we worried about it all along the way, how someone might say, "Why hasn't the mother done something to protect this child?" At the same time, the audience knows that Will isn't doing anything terrible with Marcus. So we just had to try to address it in a nuanced enough way so that the suggestion became laughable in the context of what the audience knew. The fact that Fiona overreacts at that point, first of all it's understandable, but it adds to the idea that she's very wrongheaded but very loving at the same time.

Were you worried about audience sympathy towards the shallow Will?

Hugh Grant helps a hell of a lot. We did worry. There's something Pauline Kael said about characters in screwball comedies that has been lost in modern or contemporary screenwriting: the best way to make a character likeable is to make them funny. She was talking about heroines in romantic comedies. If a character makes you laugh, he instantly becomes likeable no matter how much of a heel he is to begin with. And you have to walk a very fine line between undercutting moments in which Will is sympathetic and making sure they're not sentimental, and moments where he's really horrendous and seeing that actually the degree of his self-loathing isn't completely justified by the situation. And when he is actually being loathsome, he's also being amusing. It's there in the novel in the first place. When he's at S.P.A.T. lying, on one hand he's actually got a weird childish enthusiasm that develops, he's not being completely rational about it. There's a great line in the novel which we couldn't use because of an odd reason. He's kind of constructing his fake life story and talking about how he gets choked up and says, "I wasn't a creepy liar, I was Robert De Niro." Of course you can't use that line since De Niro was one of the actual film's producers . . . but it's in the book. He's finding his artistry. He's an artist at certain unpleasant things, like wasting his time and lying, and you sort of grow to love him in a certain way. The sins he commits are quite forgivable and identifiable. It's weaseling out of relationships, which everyone, male or female, has done at one point or other; and lying in order to gain something, which everyone does as well although not on such a grandiose scale.

Who came up with the idea of asking Badly Drawn Boy to score the film?

We usually have some set of music we listen to when we're writing something and it varies completely as to what we're into at the moment. When I was starting I used to write particular music cues into a screenplay, but what you learn the first time you make a movie is that you're not going to get the songs, because they're too expensive, or the guy who owns the rights is crazy, or someone else is using it in another movie. So you can only use music as tonal references; and it just became sad to ask for a particular song in a script so I think we tended to leave that out of consideration altogether.

Anyway, my friend Erik Feig said, "I've just heard a really good album by someone called Badly Drawn Boy, it's called *Hour of the Bewilderbeast*." It's so good, just one of the best single albums ever made in terms of the strength of every single song. I fell in love with it before I even read *About a Boy* and wrote a lot of the script while listening to it, both Paul and I did. We kind of realized that its air of melancholy and humor fitted perfectly to the film, so we had the crackpot idea of getting him to write all the songs, which isn't something that's usually done with a studio film. They usually think about it in terms of how a film can be made to market a kind of compilation album in the case of a comedy. But Nick Hornby had separately hit upon the idea of Badly Drawn Boy to do the music, so it was a really bizarre coincidence that we were both after the same guy. And the amazing thing was that we actually got him to do it largely because Badly Drawn Boy liked the book and was a big fan of movies and movie soundtracks and had been interested for a while in doing it. And we were able to do it because we weren't under the radar, we were in England and so Universal didn't really know what was going on until it was too late.

How did you work with Damon Gough?

Some of the songs were written by Damon just having read the screenplay and the book and he said, "This might work here, this might work there," and we fitted them in. And in some cases we had a cut of a given scene which was to a particular bit of music, like the Dylan piece for the suicide note. And we said, "We've been using Bob Dylan here, can you come up with something like it? Have you got the Nick Hornby *31 Songs?*" It's a CD and commentary by Nick Hornby and he includes that song which is called "A Minor Incident" and in fact the lyrics of the song are the content of the suicide note which is actually written out in Hornby's book. There's no way to do it in conventional terms. We're not going to have Toni Collette reading out this four-minute long letter, it would just be insanity. But the great thing is that Damon's lyrics were another part of the screenplay because he was able to convey what was contained in the letter but in an oblique, great way. And there are so many wonderful, gratuitous things that happened with the film just in terms of everybody coming up with great stuff at the right time.

How was your relationship with Nick Hornby throughout the whole process? How involved was he?

It was a little terrifying because, first of all, I loved the novel so much I didn't want to screw it up, so you feel a genuine responsibility to the guy who wrote the book. But he had a very permissive, Zen attitude to what we were doing. I think it was also fatalistic because what are you going to do eventually? As the writer you're always going to be overruled. If he'd wanted to, he could have seen every draft because he was one of the producers on the movie and he could have been copied into any distribution. But we never really got notes by draft. Occasionally we would hear from him about this thing or about that thing, and they were always pragmatic and useful. And he was actually working on a screenplay with Emma Thompson at the time, really busy, and I'm sure it was good for his sanity to not to have to face whatever we were doing to his work. But that was another really fortunate thing for us, that it was another relationship that worked really well. I think he understood that we cared a lot for his novel and that we weren't jobbing directors, guns for hire. Getting it right really mattered a lot to us. I think he was worried about *American Pie* at first. To adapt the novel demanded a lot of tact and a sense of nuance and a balance so it wouldn't turn into over-sentimental mush or Disney's *The Kid*. I think the fact that I had lived in England helped a hell of a lot, and also Paul is a very serious, earnest person—the moment you meet him you know he's not there to fuck around with your labor of love.

You've written for other people, directed other people's scripts, and produced and directed your own scripts. Which is your favorite? And which is your least favorite?

I guess my favorite would be directing something absolutely genius that we've come up with. On *About a Boy* there was such a resonant story with Nick's novel that you're halfway there—we only knew a good thing where we saw it, and were careful not to fuck it up. It's hard to come up with a great idea to begin with, so I'll take them in any form. I think a lot of the great films that I admire from the thirties, forties and fifties came from stage plays or from classic novels, history . . . So who cares, really, in terms of the inspiration? The only reason to direct something that you wrote is that you're less likely to think that the writer's an interfering asshole, and the writer's less likely to hate the director—although there's no guarantee of that either . . .

Hollywood, California

5

MICHAEL HANEKE

Code Unknown

"Explanations are limitations, and every limitation is an indirect lie."
Translated by Deborah Holmes

The Austrian-born writer-director Michael Haneke worked in German television for almost two decades before moving on to the European art-house stage to direct *The Seventh Continent* (*Der Siebente Kontinent*) (1989). He has received acclaim and consternation in equal measures from critics with intelligent but sometimes demanding films like *Funny Games* (1997) and *The Piano Teacher* (*La Pianiste*) (2001), starring Isabelle Huppert. *Code Unknown* (*Code Inconnu: Récit incomplet de divers voyages*) (2000), starring Juliette Binoche, was his first to be shot in French. Haneke divides his time between Vienna and Paris.

Synopsis

Paris, the present. Anne, an actress, meets Jean, the younger brother of her war-photographer boyfriend Georges. Jean has run away from his father's farm and asks her for the new entry code to her apartment; he discards a crumpled paper bag into the lap of Maria, an illegal immigrant who is begging on the street. Amadou, a teacher of deaf children, demands that Jean apologize to her. In the ensuing scuffle, policemen arrest Maria and Amadou. Maria is deported. Amadou's father leaves for Africa, Georges returns from the war, Maria makes ends meet in Romania, Anne stars in a thriller and Jean returns home to his father.

* * *

KEVIN CONROY SCOTT: *Michael, as far as I can see, you've been a poet, a pianist, an aspiring novelist, a TV development executive, a literary critic, a theater director . . .*

MICHAEL HANEKE: I deny it all . . . [*laughs*]

You were born into an artistic family—your mother was an actor and your father was a theater director. Was creativity something that was encouraged in your household?

Well, I didn't grow up with my parents. I grew up with my aunt, my mother's sister, on a farm about fifty kilometers south of Vienna. Of course, I was influenced by what my parents did, particularly in my adolescence, but I wasn't in a milieu of artists, surrounded by them on a day-to-day basis. I would go with my grandmother to go see my mother on stage, though.

And at a certain point you became interested in writing plays?

Like every teenager, I started writing poems and short stories. When I was fourteen I wanted to become a priest, when I was fifteen I wanted to become an actor, and when I was seventeen I snuck off to do the auditions for drama school. They didn't take me, thank god. Then I was forced to study philosophy, and I started writing literary reviews.

You are also a trained pianist?

Yes, I wanted to be a pianist as well. My stepfather was a composer and a conductor, and he gave me the advice at the right time not to pursue it, because he thought I wasn't talented enough. So many film directors you read interviews with, their dream job at one point is either being a conductor or a composer.

Robert Bresson once said, "Anyone who is interested in making films should study music first." Do you agree with that?

Everything Bresson says is a very good tip . . .

Since you've studied composing music and have also studied writing screenplays, I was wondering if you could see a correlation between the two?

The structure of feature films, at the very least, has a lot to do with musical structure. It can't do you any harm if you have an idea of how to compose music. If you are writing a novel, you can start off and not know what the end is going to be. But whether you start off composing a piece or writing a script, you have to know exactly what your material is going to be, and how it ends before you start working on it. It's the same as music; you have to have your material organized before you actually begin to develop it. If you're writing a fugue like Bach, you need a fixed theme before you start developing it, otherwise you'll be lost.

By your late teens what kind of films were you watching and what kind of literature were you interested in?

I always read things that were too difficult for my age. Thomas Mann once said, "You should always read things that are above your level so you are learning the whole time." That's what I was always trying to do. At the age of twelve or thirteen I was reading Chinese philosophers I didn't understand, but I still learned from it. Film was difficult, because I wasn't living in the capital at the time and there was no television, so what I was able to see was really a matter of chance. When I moved to Vienna to start studying it was completely different—then I started organizing my day around which films were playing where, seeing about two or three films a day, which is why my degree course wasn't very successful. [*laughs*] In fact, it's funny you mention Bresson because he had a seminal influence on me, and I actually wrote an essay on him while I was at university.

My very first memory of the cinema is going to see Laurence Olivier's *Hamlet* with my grandmother when I was five or six. My grandmother had to take me out after the first five minutes, because it started with the castle and the waves and I was terrified, screaming, and everyone complained about me.

A couple of years later, after the war, when a lot of Austrian children were being sent abroad to escape the country's poverty, I went to Denmark for three months to live with foster parents, to be fattened up. I didn't enjoy it, I was very unhappy because it was my first time away from home. To try and cheer me up, they took me to the cinema. I can distinctly remember this long auditorium where they were showing a nature film set in Africa with rhinos and long shots through the savannah. When the curtains fell at the end of the film and they opened the doors at the back of the cinema, it was still raining outside and it was still Copenhagen. I was deeply traumatized by the idea that I had been in Africa but here I was still in Denmark and it was still raining outside. It would be quite different for other people who grew up with television, because you never have that moment of realization that the pictures and reality are two different things. It's like those interesting experiments carried out with "primitive peoples"—as they are sometimes called—where cinema screens are put up and short scenes of dialogue shown where you just get a closeup of two people talking and they will run away screaming in terror. When they have calmed down and you ask them what they were screaming about they say, "They were severed heads. There were no bodies to them so they must have been spirits talking to each other!" We fill in the gaps and they just see what they see: two severed heads, talking to each other.

At the University of Vienna you studied philosophy and psychology. When did becoming a filmmaker become a tangible aspiration for you?

It had nothing to do with my degree course. While I was at university the idea of making films was great, but I didn't think it was very realistic. I was writing quite a lot back then, and my short stories were being well received by people "in the know," so I thought that was a more realistic thing to do. By the time I graduated I got a chance to do work experience with the ARD, Germany's public broadcasting company, who were taking people on three-month work placements straight out of university. That coincided with this particular channel looking for a "drama director"—the guy who was there at the time was just about to retire. They had been looking for someone for quite a while to fill his position, but they hadn't taken any of the previous people on work placements from university. By chance I turned up at the right time and they took me. So at a young age I was working in television.

You mentioned writing short stories. What kind of stories were you writing?

Once I started working in television, I stopped writing short stories and was writing drama scripts. But before that? I'd say my short stories were heavily influenced by D. H. Lawrence. That was all there was to them. [*laughs*]

So what were your responsibilities as a "drama director" for television?

Every day I had a large pile of scripts on my desk that were sent in by other people so I had to read through them and review them. That's the best way to learn, to read an awful lot of bad scripts. Not that there's a recipe: you can't automatically read a bad one and then write a good one yourself. In this case, they weren't that bad that you could call them rubbish, they were things that could have worked. It was my job to play around with them and see what could be changed so that they would work. So you would have to look at the mechanics of the thing and have to decide how to put it right. Reading through other people's scripts was the first two years. Later on I was working with professional writers to produce stuff ourselves.

The whole department had been created to make socially critical television drama. It doesn't really exist anymore. But we would take specific themes, like, "If you come from the working class, you don't get a good education and you stay underprivileged. What happens? How do you deal with that?" It was the golden age of German television, the end of the sixties and the beginning of the seventies.

I also read that you were a film critic as well at this point in your career.

Actually, it was mostly literary reviews I was doing, reading new books that were coming out for the newspapers. And when I was still studying in Vienna they had a radio station that dramatized the "great novels of world literature" over the course of ten weeks, so I worked on that to earn some extra pocket money.

And then you were also a theater director at some point here. How did that happen?

The ARD is based in Baden-Baden and there was a small theater there where my girlfriend at the time was working as an actress. She wasn't very happy with the way the theater was being run and the way that her director worked. I told her to show me what they were doing, and then I would try and make it better. In the end, she realized that some of the things I said actually helped, and the theater caught on to this. I helped out directing three productions and the actors were pleased to get the extra input. The first play I directed was Marguerite Duras's *Whole Days in the Trees* and I had just been working on it for television—we had this massively expensive set. So that's how I got them to let me direct it at the theater. I told them that if they let me, I would bring the set with me to the theater. I then did another couple of plays at the theater and went back to the television people and said, "It's working well at the theater. Let me do a little something that will air at midnight on the terrestrial channel."

You once said of film critics that you could approximate from their reviews whether or not they were raised before the advent of television. How so?

It hangs together with what I said earlier about people who have grown up around television since they were babies; they have a completely different experience. They see it as reality. They have a completely different method of accessing it. People who grew up before television are a lot more aware of the possible dangers of taking it as reality. But critics who didn't are a lot more susceptible to manipulation; they are so used to it that they are actually in favor of being manipulated.

Do you think that this current generation has lost the ability to have a better awareness? That there is no option but to lose it because we have been brought up in the world of media?

Yes, I think so. We live in a world that's been made completely unreal, yet we think it is reality. The pictures of the war in Iraq are a good example. We all know intellectually that the pictures have been manipulated and what we are seeing is not reality. It is dead knowledge, because we are not able to feel the same shock of experience that I had as a little boy in Copenhagen watching the African animals, then realizing I wasn't in Africa. The shock is not there. It's the difference between "knowing" something and actually experiencing or feeling something.

That's interesting because it is the core behind what you do and what your films are about—questioning reality. When did you become fascinated with this?

I started to explore it in television. But it was the thing that always concerned me most. For me, the first film that had this built-in shock experience was Tony Richardson's *Tom Jones*. There's a point when Tom Jones is being chased and he suddenly stops and looks into the camera and says something like, "I hope he's not going to catch me!" He breaks the illusion of fiction. It was a real shock for me as a spectator in the film, to realize that you can actually do that, and make people realize they can be manipulated rather than having them, when they buy their ticket at the box office, agree to accept the illusion and not question it.

You worked from 1973 to 1989 in television. In 1989 you made your first feature. What are some of the major differences between writing for television and writing a feature film?

When I first started writing for television I had written a script and handed it in to the German Film Foundation, who agreed to give me 300,000 marks. But that wasn't enough to make the film, and therefore the money expired and the script got put in a drawer somewhere. Then there were ten years where I did a lot of work for television and theater. The television work was commissioned, so it was a case of writing to order and getting paid for it. I was so busy with that that I was not prepared to think more about writing another script to make a feature film.

The turning point was when I started making films for Austrian television and they were very successful at a time in Austria when there weren't a lot of people making films of *any* kind. The people in Austria said, "Well, why don't you make a feature film?" At the same time I was working with people from the ARD in Bremen in northern Germany, and they were saying, "Why don't you write a television film for us?" So with that encouragement I took a story I read in *Stern* magazine of grim events that happened ten years before and wrote what became my first feature, *The Seventh Continent*. I was going to give it to the people in Bremen, but they said they didn't want to do it because people would not want to see it. I told them that, since they didn't want to make it into a television film, I would make it into a feature film in Austria.

There are two reasons why I went into making feature films. The first was that television was already developing the way it's gone today, not as interested in social criticism. After *The Seventh Continent* I carried on making television films but they were only literary adaptations because that was the only ghetto left in television to do critical stuff. The second reason was that I hadn't wanted to make a film beforehand. Before I wrote *The Seventh Continent* I never found a personal approach that was different from what everyone else was doing and that treated cinema as an art form rather than just a film that anyone else could have made. Then I found something that was mine and mine alone, not just in the content but also in the form. I had found a different way.

The article in *Stern* was about this family who commits suicide, but before they commit suicide they destroy everything they own. The journalist's way of writing about these things is to look for explanations; they didn't have enough money, it wasn't a happy marriage and all the rest of it. In finding explanations for everything and making it rational, they take away the horror and the shock of the act. That's what I wanted to get across. Television and genre films tend to explain everything and make it nice and neat and have the reasons, so you can go and watch it and then come out again and not be touched by it at all while thinking that the world is all OK. But the world is not all OK. Cinema is an art form and therefore cannot make us think that the world is OK.

This seems to be getting back to the question of reality. It's like you're trying to get your audience to look at cinema as if they were watching a film and looking at the world for the first time, to see it as it is and just look at it.

It would be good if I could manage this, to get people to feel as if they are seeing a film for the first time. The problem is, of course, if you want to tell the story without explaining it then you have to somehow work out a way to tell the story that doesn't have built-in explanations. I wrote *The Seventh Continent* on a Greek island, somewhere I often go when I am writing my films. I tried desperately to get it to work by showing the actual event of the suicides and then have flashbacks, but I realized I couldn't do that, because as soon as I have a flashback, it automatically works like a commentary, an explanation. It turns into journalism all over again. This is how I came to the method of chronicle, which is like taking Day One in the life of the family and then showing Day Two where not much happens. There may be some small indications of what is to come in Day Three when they commit suicide. So you have a chronological structure: one day in one year, the next year and then the next year. This way you can put the horror back into the story even though television doesn't want it anymore . . .

For almost all of the screenwriters I have talked to for this book, explanations are a very big part of their writing.

It's the American way of thinking. That's because it's a way of reassuring people. If cinema wants to earn money, then reassuring people and entertaining them is the way to do it.

Can you take me through the process of how you write an original screenplay? Do you outline, go through research, do numerous drafts . . . ?

It's different for every film, but if I'm starting from zero and it's completely new then I usually start with an idea or something interesting that occurs to me. Then I carry that around with me but it doesn't actually come to anything, because everyone has an idea for a film but one is not enough, so I wait until I have another idea that fits with the original idea. Then I collect other things that might fit and make notes and it starts to come together. When you have a few ideas that fit together, you put your feelers out and become obsessive about collecting material for your film. At some point I reach the stage where I feel I have enough material but up until then I'm constantly collecting notes.

The script that I had written that I was offered money for in Baden-Baden but I didn't take was actually *Funny Games*. But it was *Funny Games* without the self-reflexive bits, so it wasn't a film about a film about violence. It was just the plotline, and I wasn't interested in it because there are millions of films with similar plots. It was only fifteen years later when I had the idea to make it a film about a film about violence.

Once I get to the point where I have enough material I use the classic method of systematically writing every single idea down on a separate note card, putting them up on a board and playing around with them.

How do you start bringing characters and plot into it?

You can't separate the characters and the plot, they more or less happen at the same time. I already have a fairly good idea of who the main characters are going to be once I put the ideas on to the cards. I also write biographies of the characters, sometimes but not always. There are times when I don't want to define certain characters closely because I want them to remain a mystery to me as well as to the audience.

The main job is finding the construction of the piece. The writing is actually fun. The really hard work is putting these cards together. Once I have finished all the cards on the board, I put them into tables on the computer. It doesn't have to be finished to the absolute last detail or last scene, but the points where it branches and the points where it joins have to be decided and established. When I start writing I already know the number of scenes that the film will need. Sometimes I change these things while I'm writing, but that doesn't happen very often.

I am very systematic about the way I write. When I have a deadline or I set myself a deadline for a film, I know how long I have to write and I know how many pages I have to write. I'll divide them up and say, "Right, every day I have to write so many pages." And I will write that number of pages, however long it takes. The difficult thing is getting started, no matter what day it is . . . Of course I tidy my desk and do all those things to procrastinate. Everything I enjoy doing, like drinking, listening to music, I can do none of that while I'm writing.

The idea or the inspiration doesn't come when I'm writing. It generally comes at night when I am lying in bed trying to fall asleep. I have a dictaphone by my bed and in the last couple of weeks as I get closer to the writing process I find myself waking up in the middle of the night, dictating until my wife tells me to shut up.

How do you handle feelings of self-doubt, those moments when you are halfway through your mapped out story and it just doesn't feel right?

When the script is finished, you just hope no one else can see all the mistakes in it—there are always things you could have done better. Self-doubt is part of the profession. There are some bits that write themselves and it all seems to be going really well. There are other bits that are like getting blood out of a stone and you are fighting for every word because there are so many different ways of saying something and you can go through thousands of variants before you find what you are looking for. On the other hand, when it's writing itself and going really well, that isn't necessarily a guarantee of quality. Those are the bits you might read after and say, "That's not so good."

Have you ever directed someone else's screenplay?

The first two television films I did were other people's scripts. I also twice worked with co-authors on television projects, but they got completely frustrated with me because I'm not a very good collaborator. All the feature films are by me and just by me, apart from *The Piano Teacher* which is based on a novel but is still adapted by me.

As a writer-director could you ever direct a screenplay that wasn't written by you?

Never say never. I spent fifteen years in the theater directing other people's stuff so it's not impossible. However, I have to say it doesn't interest me much. To make a quality film, you have to be sure that the content and form are really identical; it's virtually impossible to do that with someone else's ideas when you use the kind of film language I do. It's so specific and pointed and has so much to do with my intellectual background, I really have to write the stories for it myself. There is one person I'd be really interested in working with, Michel Houellebecq, the novelist and author of *Platform*. The things he writes are very close to my writing. But for the moment, only him. [*laughs*]

You've worked a lot in theater and also done some acting yourself. Has that experience informed your writing at all?

Of course. Both as a director and a writer you must have a pretty good idea of acting to know what is a good role and what is a bad role, and how you can give the actor a chance to show themselves. It's like composers and opera singers, if you don't have an idea of how to sing then you can't write music for the singer.

Moving on to Code Unknown . . . *when I arrived in Paris this week I was talking to my translator and we were discussing the different meanings of what an "unknown code" might be. We parted ways and I went to a friend's flat, it was my first time staying with someone in Paris. I got to her place after getting lost due to my poor understanding of French and I went to the door only to realize that there was a code box there. I couldn't buzz up to her flat like you can in New York or London. I went around to a phone box, rang her, and discovered that no one was home. So I was alone, on the street with my luggage. Then I said to myself, "I think I understand what* Code Unknown *is about now."*

Yes. [*laughs*]

Did you ever have a similar experience to mine?

It was a fundamental experience for me in Paris, arriving from Vienna to find that if you don't have the code you can't get into the foyer to buzz up to the flat. It wasn't the first idea for the film, but it did give me the title.

Would it be fair to say that Code Unknown *originated in your interest in immigrant culture in France and the problems with communication barriers that exist there?*

My inner motivation was that for years I wanted to do a film about immigration in Austria because I think it is one of *the* themes of this century. People from poor countries will want to come and share our riches, and we won't be able to get away with not dealing with them. Then Juliette Binoche rang me and suggested that we make a film together; that was the external motivation. I started thinking about France, which I didn't know very well at the time. Then I came to Paris and researched for three months. Multicultural society already exists in Paris and London—it doesn't yet in Vienna.

The film features French and Romanian languages but not German. I know you speak French but still, how did you handle writing in a tongue not your own?

I wrote it all in German and had it translated; my French isn't good enough to do any different. I have a translator I always work with for my French films. But we go through the translation, sentence by sentence, because I have enough French to understand whether it is something I want or not. I just wouldn't know how to say it from scratch.

The plot of Code Unknown *might be called disjointed, focusing on several unrelated people and random acts of violence. Why not use more of a traditional method such as interlinking stories as seen in films like* Magnolia *or* Short Cuts *instead of using your Brechtian device of black spaces to separate the scenes?*

It's not the first film I've done like this. I did it on *The Seventh Continent* and *71 Fragments of a Chronology of Chance*; they're also done with the same structure. The point is that we don't perceive the world as a whole, we have separate impressions and we only put them together in our heads. Every scene, every take is one impression, they don't correspond, we create the correspondences. Although I find films like *Magnolia* and *Short Cuts* very elegant and very well done, they use aesthetic means to present an illusion of totality that does not exist; in reality our impressions are isolated. I present the fragments as they are which is why you see that black between the scenes. The only part of *Code Unknown* that is not broken by that black is the sequence where we show the film being filmed. That scene was supposed to be a hint to the viewer to help them understand, but in that scene you still fall for it. It's because there is a trap in every scene; the viewer gets caught up in the aesthetic. That's why the filmmakers can do what they want with the viewer.

Many of the scenes in the film are similar; you start off and you don't know where you are, like when Juliette Binoche is auditioning into the camera. You don't actually know if she's locked in the room with the gas on or not. You don't know where you are or what's happening; it's a way of showing the audience that we shouldn't be so quick to trust our perception of reality.

What is interesting about the structure of Code Unknown *is how we come back to where we started by seeing the code box outside Juliette Binoche's flat. This is the only moment where you use music to score the film, by using the drums as played by the deaf children.*

I thought a long time about whether I should have the music in there or not. It doesn't necessarily fit in with the rest of the film's strategy but I liked the ambivalence of the music. On the one hand it can sound quite threatening, serving as a marker for the fear that Westerners have about people coming into their country. On the other hand it also has positive energy, a sort of "We are coming, we are on our way." It was this ambivalence that made me decide to go with it, although it's against the strategy of not overlapping one scene to the next. I hope it is permissible. [*laughs*] It is something I do often in *The Piano Teacher*, where I let music drift in from one scene to the next.

I thought it worked perfectly. For me it served as a hopeful metaphor about the possibility of communicating.

Because it is the deaf mutes who are making the music.

Given that you use the music to create an effect and take a little bit away from the reality by having overlapping sounds, it seems like it's a moment where you are torn between wanting to transport the viewer in the way that art does and at the same time trying to get them to doubt their impressions. Were those two aims at odds for you?

I was torn in two directions and it was a question of, "Do I give up this effect on a matter of principle or do I close my eyes to my principles and keep the effect?" Besides, the rules are there to be broken. [*laughs*]

You said you wrote Juliette Binoche's role to be that of an actress in Code Unknown *because that is the only part she can play. Obviously, this is not due to her limitations as an actress.*

The problem is what do I do with Juliette Binoche in a film that is trying to be realistic? It's more realistic to have her playing an actress in the film than it would be to have her playing a servant girl, even though she doesn't play a *successful* actress. Also, it was a way to kill two birds with one stone because once you have that, you can show the breaks in reality by having her at work in the cinema and theater. You can have the film within the film, which is the most interesting formal feature of filmmaking as far as I'm concerned. What do you do with a star like Binoche when it is not a genre film? She is in my next film as well, but just as an ordinary woman, because it's a thriller.

What was the most difficult part of writing Code Unknown?

One of the most difficult things was with the girl at the beginning of the film—the deaf girl who's showing an emotion that her classmates are unsuccessfully trying to guess—trying to explain to her what she had to act out, while leaving it open to different interpretations.

Did you actually give her one emotion to work with?

Yes, I did but I am not going to tell you what it is. [*laughs*]

Some American critics found Code Unknown *to be hard to follow because the scenario is not constructed in a traditional cause and effect style. Do you ever worry about alienating an audience because you don't give them easy signposts to follow?*

No. It would be stupid to worry about it, especially in retrospect. My films are written for a very particular audience as compared with mass cinema. If you were writing a poem you are going to have a more limited audience than for a popular novel or whatever. You have to live with that. If you want to explore your ideas as precisely and in as much detail as possible, you have to decide: do I want to do that, or do I want to be successful?

You have said that the reason you don't give concrete explanations for your characters' behavior is because, "Every kind of explanation is just something that is there to make you feel better." Are you saying that explanations are lies?

It's not so much that explanations are lies in that you are willingly giving false information. An explanation gives the impression of explaining the world *in toto*. If it was possible to explain the world then it would probably look very different and we would look very different. Explanations are limitations, and every limitation is an indirect lie. They give the impression that in 90 minutes or in 200 pages of a book you can explain everything. Modern literature would never dare to claim that it explained the world, whereas genre cinema does just that but with the participation of the audience. They know they are paying for an illusion, but it still reassures them; not only is the illusion intentional, but the audience consents.

The notion of not explaining holds true for Code Unknown. *I am thinking of Maria when she is deported from Paris. She lives in a communicative, loving family in Romania. Then she goes back to Paris but we don't know why she doesn't stay. If an artist has an obligation to seek reality doesn't he also have an obligation to pursue emotional truth?*

I think it's very clear from the beginning why she has to go back. Ninety per cent of Romanians who work abroad are doing it so they can build a house at home. That's why you see all the empty shells of houses that they drive by. I think her emotional conflict is also expressed very clearly when she's walking down her road in Romania and is picked up by a friend of the family in his truck. They both lie to each other about how they are earning a living abroad. So now, at home, they are living a lie. The truth is that once they're abroad they live on the streets.

Anne is given a note through the door about the girl who screams upstairs from time to time. Anne initially thinks it is from her elderly neighbor, but she denies that it is from her. The next we see of this is the funeral of the girl and a very long tracking shot of Anne and her elderly neighbor walking away from the burial, not saying a word to each other. That little scenario is enough to make a whole film of. Did you ever worry that you were trying to do too much with all of these stories?

No, otherwise I wouldn't have done it. Thematically I think it all becomes clear, so it isn't too much. I think all of my films are about guilt and responsibility. The scene where they walk away from the burial is paradigmatic; each is isolated with her feeling of guilt, because they didn't take any action to save the girl. Perhaps they wouldn't have been able to do anything, but that is another matter. Things happen to us every day where we perhaps could have done something but mostly don't even realize that we could. I want to remind the viewers of their own sins of omission. That's the point of the stories. In the opening scene, the young black guy wants Jean to apologize to Maria, and it is actually his fault that she is deported back to Romania. He didn't mean to harm her at all but because of his trying to help, she is deported.

And the road to hell is paved with good intentions . . .

[*laughs*] Which doesn't mean that you should repress your good intentions! People who talk to me about this scene often ask what the point of it is, whether I'm actually trying to say that we shouldn't help each other. I say no, I'm trying to show how complex life is. That's the drama of human existence.

There are many different characters from many different cultures in the film and I thought that their experiences, which range from war photographer to taxi cab driver to immigrant beggar, were convincingly drawn. Can you tell me something about the research you did for each role?

In contrast to my other films practically nothing in *Code Unknown* was invented, at least as far as the themes of being an immigrant or foreigner are concerned. I just threw together stories of people I met. I put them together of course, but very little is made up. It's either things I saw, or things people told me. I met Romanian families and African families, the stories are real. For example, in the African family, the two women who quarrel all the time are both wives of the taxi cab driver.

That sums up your storytelling style for me, this man having two wives and you not pointing it out explicitly for the audience.

Yes, how the relationships work in these families is all real stuff that I went out there and discovered. Also, the war photographs in the film are taken by a friend of mine who is a war photographer. The story of George and Anne is actually based on a documentary that was going to be made in collaboration with *Libération* on the difficulties of being a war photographer. One of the people who was going to be profiled had written about his problems with his family. The documentary didn't get made so the material got passed on to me with the hope that I could do something with it.

How do you work on dialogue? Do you incorporate an actor's comments in rehearsals?

Once I get around to directing the script I want everything that is in the script to be realized on the screen, which applies to dialogue as well. Even when there are things that the production team says are too expensive I say, "I am just the director, I am here to make sure that the writer Haneke's work appears on screen as he wanted it to be. I can't have my writer frustrated." [*laughs*] Obviously, if I notice there are any things that the actors are having trouble getting out, then I will simplify it or modify it.

I was wondering if you could take me through how you approached writing the long opening scene that was shot in one take. I was thinking of how you went about establishing character, tone . . .

The main thing is introducing the characters and the relationships between them. You find out that Anne is an actress, that the boy is her boyfriend's brother. What I really wanted to do was to get the characters together at the beginning of the film rather than at the end of the film, which is more the convention. It's difficult to find something at the beginning which you can then repeat at the end which doesn't look unlikely. The difficult thing is to combine the aesthetic side and the plot side so that you have something that unites all the characters but is also realistic. Obviously you have the earthquake in *Short Cuts* and the television and the song in *Magnolia* that bring everyone together. And the raining frogs too! [*laughs*] There are very few possibilities in *Short Cuts* to get all the characters doing the same thing. You have them being sprayed with insecticide at the beginning, and the earthquake at the end, but in between it is very difficult to get everyone together.

How do you feel about expositional dialogue? It's necessary to set up your characters but it often feels dead on the screen.

Yes, it just depends on the setup of the scene. I have no recipe for it. I say to my students that when you are playing billiards you don't hit the ball straight on, you often try to bank it off a cushion.

The main problem in shooting this scene was that I had dialogue that needed careful timing, but since I had one take in one tracking shot it was difficult to get the written dialogue realized on screen with the right pauses in between. So we had to do things like plan when a certain pedestrian was going to walk past and mark a turning point in the dialogue. As a result, there are no passersby who aren't passing by for a specific reason. [*laughs*] So we ended up doing this long take thirty-eight times . . . the problem with such a long scene, of course, is that someone always forgets something or something goes wrong and even if it is three seconds before the scene ends you have to do the whole scene again.

In the original script the idea was that Jean would pass by a shop where there are lots of televisions running, where you see all the different pictures. The problem with that is that if you stop to look in a window, you have to pull back with the camera to see all the pictures he's looking at. Then we wouldn't have been able to catch him throwing his trash into the beggar's lap with any degree of accuracy. That's why he walked into the passageway, so he could walk by her and drop the trash in her lap instead of throwing it.

And what about when Juliette Binoche's character is shooting her film? We have already seen this scene before when she is auditioning in front of the camera. We see it again, through the lens of being an audience. Isn't this redundant?

It's a step back because you know you are watching the making of the film. During the filming of this scene the actual camera that films this scene is hidden in the woodwork of the flat she is viewing with the estate agent. There is a transition that you barely notice where you go from watching the film being made with the crew in the shot to actually being in the film. Then we come back to "reality" when she looks directly into the camera, then we know we are not in a film anymore.

Was this scenario a playful swipe at the French idea of a thriller? The film within Code Unknown *is about an estate agent who kills his clients, called* The Collector.

The whole plot of this film is told during the course of *Code Unknown*, so I was just trying to just show the self-reflection that is possible.

So your next film, the thriller starring Juliette Binoche, will it be called The Collector?

No, no . . . [*laughs*] "Thriller" is a bit of an exaggerated way to describe it. It uses the tools to tell another story of guilt and personal responsibility in a child who does something when he is young that is not particularly bad. But it has bad consequences.

Paris, France

Wes Anderson

6

WES ANDERSON

Rushmore

"There are always times when you don't know if it's a movie."

Wes Anderson's first feature, *Bottle Rocket* (1996), was co-written with his university friend and aspiring actor Owen Wilson, featuring Wilson in the lead role along with his brother Luke. The debut fared poorly at the box office but became a comedy cult-classic. The writers collaborated again on *Rushmore* (1998), featuring Bill Murray, and *The Royal Tenenbaums* (2001), earning them a nomination for Best Original Screenplay at the 2001 Academy Awards.

Synopsis

The United States, the present. Max Fischer is a scholarship student at Rushmore, a private school where he has great success in organizing clubs and dramatic productions but fails most of his academic classes. He befriends a rich industrialist, Blume, and falls for a recently widowed teacher at Rushmore, Ms. Cross. His attempt to build an aquarium with Blume's money in order to impress Ms. Cross gets him expelled. Max then discovers Blume also loves Ms. Cross and he seeks vengeance. Blume retaliates, war ensues, and Max's troubles worsen. Rescue comes from unexpected places, including his simple but philosophical father, a barber.

* * *

KEVIN CONROY SCOTT: *I believe your father lent you a camera when you were young. So what kind of films were you making back then?*

WES ANDERSON: He gave me a Super-8 camera, and the first film I did was called *Skateboard Four*; it was based on a book I read that I'd checked out from the library. Then we did adventure movies, and a lot of chase-type things.

I know it sounds silly, but since we are talking about screenwriting . . .
did these films have any kind of narrative structure?

Yeah, the structure was usually a scene where some guy gets alienated
by a group of people, and then is hunted by them and killed. That's
basically the structure of almost every movie we did.

Was becoming a filmmaker your career ambition as a teenager? I
understand you were very interested in the theater back then.

I was interested in theater even earlier than my teens. When I was a
teenager what I really wanted to be was a writer. I always had movies
on my mind but I was mostly focused on writing—until I was eighteen
or nineteen, then I got back into movies.

From your teens you were obsessed with the New Yorker. *Can you*
explain what was your interest in the magazine?

I just read a couple of articles that interested me, in my school
library. So when I went away to college I ordered a subscription,
which was one of the first things I did. That's a magazine—especially
then but still, I think, even now—where you'll often find that you
want to read every single article and as a result, you'll get to know
the writers. Also, I was always doing research on everything I would
come across. I remember hunting down the Truman Capote profile
of Marlon Brando that had been in the *New Yorker* and I went and
got Salinger stories that they had printed, and I started reading old
Pauline Kael things so I would always refer to the *New Yorker*s that
were in the library. Actually, the shelves in my office are usually
filled with bound *New Yorker*s. The more I got interested in the current stuff the more I got interested in the earlier stuff. A lot of those
writers, their pieces are collected in books. Like Mitchell, Liebling
and other less-read guys like S. N. Berman or Walcott Gibbs and
dozens of others.

You studied at the University of Texas. Did you take any writing
courses there?

Yeah, I took English literature courses and I probably did a couple of
years of writing classes which were OK; they just gave you some
kind of structure. One thing is, they give these conference courses,
little seminars where you could set your own agenda if you worked
it out with the professor. Those were good. I could get someone who
knew a lot about something that I am already interested in, and get

a lot of information from them. I did a couple of playwriting classes too.

Did you write plays in high school as well?

No, I wrote one in college. Many before high school . . .

So there weren't any "little one-acts on Watergate" written during high school?

[*laughs*] No, it was more like I did a play on *King Kong*; I did a *Star Wars* play, a play of *The Alamo*. They tended to be things that had a lot of scope, but only lasted about fifteen minutes.

You met your co-writer on Bottle Rocket *and* Rushmore, *Owen Wilson, at university. How did that happen?*

We were in a playwriting class together. I don't think he actually ever wrote his play for that class, but I did, and we sort of knew each other from that. Then we had a mutual friend who really introduced us. In the drama department there, they wanted to produce the play I wrote in class during the next semester. I thought Owen would be good for a character in it, and that was actually the first time he ever acted in anything, in that play.

Did the pair of you write any screenplays before Bottle Rocket?

No, but I wrote one. It was called *The Plagiarist*. Since then, somebody wrote a novel with the same title, which seems appropriate, somehow . . . It was nothing describable. That was one of the main problems. I think it would be best described as a screenplay about this guy. Some guy. Which is what I felt was a good idea for a screenplay back then. It was just a rambling mishmash of different influences. There was no hope for it. It was never going to be anything. It was a completely literary object. It wasn't meant to be a movie, it was not even meant to be read, ultimately—just written, I think. [*laughs*]

I think it is safe to say that there is a very unique tone at play in the films that you and Owen Wilson have written together. At what point were you aware that you had a similar sensibility towards life, or at least to your work?

Probably instantly, I think. We started talking about *Bottle Rocket* and then that summer we weren't around each other and I wrote it and gave it to him. He found it interesting but then we made it something completely different. There were a few scenes that made it through, like the bookstore robbery. The problem was, at the time that scene didn't fit with the rest of the piece. It didn't have the tone right. It took us a while to finally realize that neither of us were really suited to doing a *Mean Streets* type of movie.

So it was a straight-up drama back then?

Not really, because it had that bookstore robbery just the way it is. It just didn't know what it was. It definitely had very serious dramatic things but they weren't the right sort of dramatic things. They were like *State of Grace* or something. They were not in keeping with what they needed to be. So we slowly worked our way around to that. I think *Bottle Rocket* came from how our lives were. And if you take the guns and crime element out of it, then it was more or less our lifestyle at the time, some of the places we were around that we were interested in. It was more about the group of friends we had than anything else.

At some point the screenplay was over three hundred pages long. How did it get so fat?

It was three hundred pages because we had written what we thought was a hundred and twenty, but then some people in California kind of formatted it for us, then it turned out it was much, much, much longer. Also, we did a reading that was interminable, so we knew there was something wrong.

The legendary writer-director Jim Brooks helped you with the script for three or four months. At one point he told you to read it out loud. Is this something that you find helpful when analyzing your scripts?

We did two readings of *Bottle Rocket*. One very long reading where Jim and Polly Platt had come to Texas to meet us, and it was a disaster. Then, some months later, we went out to LA, more or less to find out if they were really going to do our movie, for Jim to make a decision. They weren't telling us that, but we knew that was more or less what was happening. For that I had us rehearse it like a play. We cut out lots of description and we rehearsed it and that went much, much better. That also got everyone excited about it.

We didn't do a reading of *Rushmore* but when it came time to do *The Royal Tenenbaums*, we did kind of a half-baked reading up at the house where we filmed. We also did one of the new scripts that Noah Baumbach and I had just finished, *The Life Aquatic*. That was with Bill Murray and a group of actors. That was actually one of the better readings I've had, because we did it early enough in the process; we learned some things about what was working and what wasn't. We wanted the reading to figure out what was working and we definitely got some stuff from it.

How so? Is it just that you can hear that a line is not working properly?

It's more to do with how I am feeling about this character, how are these relationships taking shape, is the story moving? You can really feel when it's moving in a reading. And the absence of feeling like the story's moving—you're made aware of that as well.

Jim Brooks is considered to be something of a genius when it comes to screenwriting. Can you tell me about any rules you might have learned from him?

I don't think we learned rules from him, although Jim will talk about theories and rules. "There's a theory that they will give you the first minutes of a film, that's a theory that some people will believe in." He'll quote you something like that, he doesn't really believe in it, but if you're arguing then he'll make an argument based on a "theory." What Jim really gave us was a whole screenwriting course.

Jim had things to teach us and we had things to learn, and that was a whole big complicated experience of us realizing that we didn't know it all. I was never more confident then when we were about to show *Bottle Rocket* for the first time and I have never been that confident since.

At the time I wasn't really prepared to be told how to do anything, wasn't inclined to hear a bunch of rules, because I felt so confident that we were going to do something that was above the rules—which Jim sort of forced me to realize wasn't the case. He helped us to make the script work towards engaging an audience, maybe in some ways be less esoteric. Once we had shot the movie Jim was working with me on the cutting, and that was another screenwriting course. That was, "How does this work as a movie?" I feel like I got enough from Jim, especially in the editorial process, that both *Rushmore* and *The Royal Tenenbaums* were basically the script, whereas *Bottle Rocket* was rewritten like crazy and then the movie was re-edited like crazy, re-shot. We wrote a new opening, we wrote new scenes, we worked and worked and worked to try and make it function. *Rushmore*, more or less, works the way it was meant to work. The script did that and there was not a lot of reorganizing.

What about your interest in plays? You still read a lot of plays and the theater featured heavily in Rushmore. *Are you still interested in writing for the theater?*

It interests me but I don't know if I am really suited for it. I do know that I would like to produce and direct a play. But in terms of writing, if you're thinking of an idea and then you have a montage that goes with it and the settings are all cinematic, then it is a movie. I just haven't had ideas that I have been thinking of lately where the emphasis is on the words in such a way that you would just want them to just be sitting on stage.

Do you think it also has something to do with plays having this unity of space incorporating long scenes on one location?

Yeah, in *The Royal Tenenbaums* there are only four or five scenes of any real length at all. Most of the scenes are very brief. *Rushmore* maybe less so, but there are a lot of little scenes in *Rushmore* too. The new one I'm working on, there are some long scenes that are longer than anything I can remember having done; but yeah, it's an interesting point. I'd like to write longer scenes at some point.

Are there any playwrights you are particularly fond of?

Just tons. I just found this play *The 5th of July* that Lanford Wilson wrote which is very good. He's the guy who wrote *Burn This*, that's a good one. The ones who were always my key guys, that I read everything of and was the most interested in were Shepard, Pinter, Mamet, Tennessee Williams, Chekhov.

Have you ever read David Mamet's book on writing, Three Uses of the Knife?

No, I guess what I read was *Writing in Restaurants* and there is one on directing that I read. That's like a rulebook. He's very focused on the rules.

Yeah. Three Uses of the Knife *is quite good because it's based on how an object can become a metaphor and embody the change that occurs between characters during the story. I think it goes something like, "You use your knife to go out and cut down food for your lover, you come home and you use your knife to shave to look good for your lover and then you use your knife to cut out her lying heart when you find your lover cheating on you."*

That's real Mamet.

Where did the idea for Rushmore *come from? You described it as "being interested in characters whose ambitions were completely out of proportion to what they could realize."*

I wanted to do a school movie for a long time. When I applied to film school, I had to do these two treatments; one was roughly *Bottle Rocket* and the other was roughly *Rushmore*. It was just a school movie and I only had a vague idea of the character. Before we made *Bottle Rocket* we had some time to figure things out. I wanted to do a school movie and Owen got excited about that too, and we sort of slowly cooked it up.

Somewhere early in the thing, I had written this play that Max in the film was doing called *Shakedown in Alphabet City*—the *Serpico* play. And then when we sat with Mike De Luca, who was running New Line Cinema at the time, to tell him about this, he wanted to do something with us and said, "Whatever you guys want to do." During our description of what we wanted to do, as shorthand we said we did a play of *Serpico* and we got a really good reaction from Mike De Luca. So we kind of adapted *Shakedown in Alphabet City* and put in a few lines from *Serpico*. Most of it was the way it always was because it was this *Serpico*-esque thing. I had written a lot of plays like that but there was also a Fitzgerald story, I think it is called "The Captured Shadow," and there is another one called "The Freshest Boy." Owen and I have always loved Fitzgerald so somehow that figured in.

Do you remember having cinematic influences on the radar during the writing process?

If . . . was definitely one. *Murmur of the Heart*, the Louis Malle film, it's one of my favorite movies, that one. And *The 400 Blows*, of course. I think there is a whole French thing that connects to it. And I guess *Harold and Maude* and *The Graduate* were big movies for us that were somehow tying in.

Have you ever thought about adapting a novel or directing a screenplay that was not written by you?

Not seriously, but at some point I figure I probably will. You know, John Huston's entire career of movies is almost all adapting books and stories that he loved, and he made so many good movies . . .

Does it bother you that so many critics thought Rushmore *was autobiographical?*

No, it doesn't bother me, because there is a ton of autobiographical stuff in there anyway. I'm not really like Max, I never was. But the fact that I wrote plays, which gave us the idea of making those plays in the film, is enough to make them say that.

You have said that Rushmore *is a dream version of the school it was set at. What did you mean by that?*

It's sort of filtered through his perspective of the place. Max sees Rushmore as this great institution with longstanding traditions that will be upheld, and really it's just another school, and he's the only one wearing the blazer with the patch on it. In the way we photographed the movie, at Rushmore everything is warm with all of these rich colors, and when he gets sent across the street to the other school, Grover Cleveland, it's lit like a prison, more or less. We sort of timed it that way, cold, to take out all the colors, and put barbed wire on the fence and things like that.

Bottle Rocket *became something of a cult film with studio executives in Hollywood. How did those people react to* Rushmore *when they read the script?*

We had enough people who wanted to do it where we got to choose. Scott Rudin read it and wanted to do it. The guys at Jersey Films read it and wanted to do it. Joe Roth read it and wanted to do it, and he was running the company. It was originally written for New Line and we would have great conversations with them about it but really the conversation was, "Are you guys going to do the movie?" and they ultimately weren't. That was that. Then when we went to Disney and Joe Roth, and he was ready to do it.

I understand that you and Owen Wilson don't work in drafts. Instead you focus on part of a film and then rewrite it. Are you ever worried that by concentrating on one part of a film that it will make the other parts suffer?

It's not concentrating on a particular part at a time. Noah and I have shown our script to people, we get different notes, maybe we get an actor to read it and when we hear back from her we incorporate it into her part so we think about that part for a while and that is woven through the movie. We think about someone saying, "I don't feel this way about it," then we think about something. It tends to be an element that is woven through it than about working on one scene. That is the way I feel like I have approached them.

Can you tell me something about how you work when creating a screenplay?

With *Rushmore* we started talking about it when we were doing a cross-country drive; we just figured out a lot of things. Then we just started writing different scenes. On *Rushmore*, we were working together closely for the first half of the script, then we worked apart. The kind of thing we would talk about were ideas for events in the story and things about the character and the key relationships and the idea of him having a relationship with this older guy where they're more or less equal. Then I would write something and show it to Owen, then Owen would write something and show it to me.

When you are alone during the writing process and you are not satisfied with your work how do you deal with nagging feelings of self-doubt?

I don't know how you handle it because it is a constant thing. I think what I always try to do is say to myself, "How did I feel about this last one when I was around this point, was I feeling good?" The answer to that is usually, "No, you were feeling terrible. You didn't even know that you wanted to make the movie." Usually I ask somebody else to remind me because I have a mental block and it always seems like it was going better on the last one. There are always times when you don't know if it's a movie. The thing which we are on now is as much a movie-movie as anything, and up until six weeks ago I just wasn't sure if we were on the right track at all and somehow we turned a corner and got confident about it.

When you are doing the physical writing, do you have any tricks to keep yourself engaged like making yourself sit in a seat for a certain period of time?

I use little notebooks. I write out everything longhand first, then I type it into the computer. Back when Owen and I were working together, he would write in longhand also. *Rushmore, Royal Tenenbaums* and *The Life Aquatic* are all in small notebooks like this . . . [*Anderson presents a pocket-sized notebook, and flips through the pages showing carefully sketched portrait drawings very similar to the chapter headings featured in* The Royal Tenenbaums] I create seven of these for each film for some reason.

Is it ideas for characters or ideas for moments in the film that you're putting into these notebooks?

Both. The first notebooks are like this one, and then the fourth, fifth and sixth notebooks; you can flip those open and say, "Well, that scene's in here. This scene's totally changed now. This part never made it in at all." For me, where I start first with a script are these images of the characters. There's usually quite a lot of *that* before there's anything that resembles a page of a script. Then, once we have it printed, I always have a draft on me and I make changes on the page as we're reworking the material.

You wrote Bill Murray's role in Rushmore *with him in mind. I've always been intrigued by how a screenwriter can write something for a specific actor.*

Well, it was written with Bill Murray in mind but we thought we weren't going to get him at certain points. And there were other guys we thought about, in case Bill wasn't going to do it. There's a scene in the beginning of *Rushmore* where Blume gives a speech: I had seen Alec Baldwin giving that speech in some ways. So it was written for Bill, but less so than *The Life Aquatic* was. The central character in that is written for him—I just couldn't see anybody else doing it, period.

That's what I am trying to get to. Is it Caddyshack *Bill Murray; is it* Groundhog Day *Bill Murray . . . ?*

In the case of *The Life Aquatic*, there is a lot of Bill Murray. I've now known Bill for six or seven years, so I just think of him like the way I would draw on someone else I know and put them in it. And this one is a lot more Bill that I know, as well as Bill from the movies. It's really a mixture of all kinds of people—like *Royal Tenenbaums*, the main role was written for Hackman; I didn't know Hackman at all but I just had an image of Hackman and his voice and I just pictured it, I guess. Basically, everyone else was the same way. Luke's character was the first thing I wanted to have in the movie, and he was supposed to be the main character but then it shifted somewhat. Anjelica Huston, I always had in mind. Owen's character is kind of odd. When he read the finished draft he felt that that character didn't belong in there, the character was something that I had written and he didn't see himself playing it at all until the first day of shooting. Then he was totally comfortable with it and brought it to life in a way that he didn't expect to.

Were you ever interested in writing on your own?

Well, for *The Royal Tenenbaums* I was more or less on my own. But I prefer to write with a partner—probably for the same reason I see myself as a director more than anything else. Because I like to have a team together, and work with people. Owen was mostly an actor, and that's what his schedule was shaped by. So to have a writing partner who you meet with every day, and work, and talk about the thing and sort it out . . . for me, making these movies, that's what my whole working life is about, and it's just good to have someone who is completely in it with you. Also, the way that Owen and I would spark each other creatively—I have that same thing with Noah Baumbach, who I am currently co-writing with on my new movie, *The Life Aquatic*. They each have different qualities, but I feel like I can be inspired by my interaction with somebody who's got the enthusiasm and the ideas.

And who has a similar frame of reference and sense of humor?

Yes, one thing about Owen and Noah is that they are both guys who, if we go out to dinner with somebody together and we talk about it afterwards, we're going to laugh about the same things.

Music is a really important part of Rushmore. *Do ideas for scenes come to you through music? Do you also play it while you are writing?*

Yes, I'll play music while writing a specific scene. There's a scene in *The Royal Tenenbaums* where Gwyneth Paltrow puts on a Rolling Stones record. When I was working on that scene, I was playing that record over and over and over. It was a song I had known I wanted to put into a movie for a while, and then I sort of figured it out.

Sight & Sound *said that it was the only scene in cinema history where actually two songs from the same album are played back to back.*

Although they don't actually occur in that order on the record . . .
But we make them appear that way by putting in that "hiss" sound,
making it seem like it's vinyl. If it had played the *actual* next song, that
would have ruined the scene.

*I liked the opening of the film where Max demonstrates his skills as
a maths genius only to wake up in chapel service because you don't
realize you are in a dream until Max wakes up. You withhold this
information from the audience. It's also a curtain-raising set-piece.*

In *Bottle Rocket* we have that too, the way we hold off on telling
them it's his parents" house they're burgling. That to me is a theatrical device more than it's a movie thing. The *Rushmore* scene was
something that we added to the script late in the game. I wrote the
first version of it, then I showed it to Owen and he liked it a lot. But
then Owen made changes to the dialogue to make it more dream-
like. It's a good example of our collaboration, how we took it further by working together. It was also very consciously a scene where
we would really open strong on Max. Previously he had appeared in
the audience at Bill Murray's speech, and we kind of slowly found
our way to him. But then we added this scene where you just land
right on him. Also there's the idea of someone who's able to solve a
math problem; we'll quickly learn that it is far out of Max's range
of abilities.

*Then there's Bill Murray's strong opening where he makes a speech at
the chapel service, telling these students how lucky they are and making
an appeal to the underdogs in the crowd.*

I had an idea of a speech that was like Alec Baldwin's in *Glengarry
Glen Ross*.

"Coffee's for closers"?

Exactly, but it wasn't as strong or as interesting as that. I was trying
to come up with it and I called Bob Wilson, Owen's dad, and asked
him to write a chapel speech, because I knew he was interested in
this kind of stuff. I explained it to him and he sent me a speech—it
wasn't really the speech he would have given himself, it was more
him interpreting what I wanted for the character and then writing
the scene that way. I just phoned him and said, "Just write your
speech." Then he wrote a second speech, and three or four lines of
the one in the film are directly from Bob Wilson. There's that line,

"Get them in the crosshairs" that I heard him say on the phone one time, he was talking to someone about some incredible lawyer. Also, "You were born rich and you're going to stay rich"—that was a Bob Wilson thing. "Take dead aim on the rich boys" and "They can buy anything but they can't buy backbone"—that's him too.

In that scene where Max takes Mr Blume, Ms Cross and her doctor friend, played by Owen's brother, Luke, out for dinner after the opening of his new play, there is a great line. Max is getting drunk and criticizing the doctor, making fun of his outfit, "I like your nurse's uniform, guy." To which Luke says, "They are O.R. scrubs." To which Max says, "Oh, are they?" You probably get a lot of laughs for that line.

That's Luke. Luke wrote that line.

So there are a lot of different people who make small contributions to your screenplays?

Without a doubt. That line is without question something people ask me about. Luke read the script and came up with it. I recently gave my new script to Luke when we were at this bar called Bungalow 8, and Luke left it there. This script is meant to be top secret and he left it there . . . So he got another one sent to his hotel, and then left that one too. He called me and was really apologetic but, I mean, he lost it twice in one night. Then he wanted me to send it to him in LA and I was thinking, "No." But now I'm remembering how good the "Oh, are they?" line is and I'm thinking, "I should send it to him." [*laughs*]

One interesting thing about that scene is where you actually get four people playing a scene at once. Most of the movie is two people, two people, two people; so that is one of the few where it gets to go all around. One of the inspirations for that was a movie Owen and I both love, *My Left Foot*. There's a scene in that film where Daniel Day-Lewis has a total meltdown and that's kind of where this scene was coming from.

Yes, the great thing about that scene is that Max has tried to act so sophisticated and suave and now the truth comes out about how emotionally immature he is. Was the screenplay designed for that rift to happen there?

I think it was more like we just felt at this point he needed to do this. I think we were surprised when we were writing that it becomes a scene where it breaks through his whole act. It might have just been intuitive, and then we just knew we needed it. We used to have another scene after it, outside at the valet, where it went even further. But somewhere along the way we just condensed it—it was redundant.

Do you find that a lot of editing that you do is taking out things that are repeated?

Yeah, sometimes you don't even realize how many times you are doing the same thing, but then you step back and there it is.

Your montages are very effective, and it seems like you enjoy doing them. I'm thinking of the opening where you show Max performing his school activities and all the school clubs he's had a hand in starting: the beekeepers society, the model United Nations, the go-cart team. But that's exposition, which we know is a terrifying thing as far as the rules of screenwriting go. Were you ever worried that this would make the audience a passive participant?

Worried? For sure. At the start of *The Royal Tenenbaums* we tell the whole story of the family, which is absolutely expositional, I guess. Then we introduce all the characters in the present, with their names on the screen, and then we tell what every one of them is doing now. So we've actually spent twenty minutes before we even have the first scene where we can see something happening in the present. The whole first reel of the movie is just setting it up, and that's just not right. It's not the way to do a movie, and it probably doesn't function properly, but I was just really attached to it. Part of the reason I wanted to make the movie was because of all this stuff at the front of it. So I just felt like I wanted to do them anyway and hoped that they would be engaging on their own even though the movie doesn't really start to function dramatically until after that. We also fill in an entire backstory of Gwyneth Paltrow's character, Margot, at one point through a montage to a Ramones song.

There is a real turning point in the film that relates to a minor character, Dirk, especially with the almost gothic music that you use to show Max's younger friend's feelings about being betrayed by Max. It happens when Dirk is told that Max has been bragging about getting felt up by his mom, which is the only reason Max chose Dirk as his chapel partner. You are walking a real tightrope there as far as tone is concerned. His conniving letter to Max is very Machiavellian.

That letter we were having some problems with, and I actually asked our agent to have his son write a letter. So that is another situation where we asked somebody else to do some writing for us! So I explained the situation to Jim Berkowitz's son Jordan, and he wrote a letter, and we used the opening and last lines of that: "Dear Max, I am writing to tell you that I have learned that Miss Cross is secretly having an affair with Mr. Blume." Here Jordan is laying out the exact thing that I have told him on the phone. After seeing the letter, I think Owen had the idea that Dirk was being deeply sarcastic, then we wrote the letter from that. It was part collaboration between me and Owen, and part collaboration between Owen and Jordan Berkowitz.

Dirk has a small but crucial role as far as the plot is concerned. He does bad things and good deeds. Was that something that got cut out at some point?

There was an element of him setting things up behind the scenes, which I think is there in a slight way. I think there is a shot where Blume drives up and Dirk is watching with his binoculars. We went with "Dirk is watching" rather than "Dirk is orchestrating" because it was a little bit too contrived.

Why did you use the seasonal title cards through the film? Was it to give some kind of a structure?

Yeah, and I was also thinking of Powell and Pressburger. It's also tied to Max doing his theater stuff. The one I like the most is when it goes to October; there's a green curtain and then it opens to Grover Cleveland High School. The second it opens, we learn this big piece of information: he's been kicked out of the school.

I think the scene that follows that is where Max climbs through Miss Cross's window on a rainy night claiming to be hit by a car. It's a very daring gesture on Max's behalf . . .

That scene is the scene that is the most like a play in the whole movie, I think. It is one of the longer scenes and a lot plays out between the two of them in it.

Were you at all worried about the audience believing that Miss Cross would let Max get as far as lying on her bed with her? When she goes to the toilet to find some medical supplies Max places some mood music into her tape player and lies down on the bed.

You know, the scene used to be that while she was out of the room he looked around the place and then he found a shoebox and took it out and it was filled with pot. And it used to have that she threw some of his clothes in the laundry and he was wearing a bathrobe. So it took it much further before. I think the thing is, she's drawn to him. She is overstepping something a little bit because she is connected to him.

When they start talking about Miss Cross's husband, Edward Appleby, Max is quite coarse in the way he talks, very matter of fact about her husband being dead. It's kind of insensitive. This is something that also comes up in The Royal Tenenbaums *where Gene Hackman's character calls Danny Glover's character "Coltrane." Where does this edgy stuff come from?*

Owen and I like characters who are capable of some bad behavior. And you kind of want to put them through something. At the same time that we're drawn to showing them at their best, we're also drawn to showing them at their worst. Often something mean is the funniest thing, especially in people who are unaware about how they come across and don't censor themselves.

Was Max meant to be getting somewhere sexually? There are a few moments in this scene where he seems to be teetering on the edge of scoring with Miss Cross.

Definitely, she sort of has a thing for him on some level. I think she does associate him with her dead husband, she can definitely see some connection between the two of them.

At the end of the film you show your theatrical influences by putting all of your characters together in one scene. It's the opening night party for Max's new play about Vietnam. In some way it rhymes with the final scene in The Royal Tenenbaums. *It ties up all the characters together in a large set-piece.*

Right. Part of the inspiration for this came from *The Magnificent Ambersons* where Welles has a great big party scene shot in long takes, moving through the party, from one group to the other. I remember this scene being so easy to write, just because we knew all the characters so well, and they all had outstanding things in their lives, and it was just so easy to plug it in.

What is the trick to getting to know your characters?

Well, probably being obsessed with them for more than a year while you are writing, you're going to know them . . .

New York, New York

Darren Aronofsky

7

DARREN ARONOFSKY

Requiem for a Dream

"Hit them with emotion after emotion."

Darren Aronofsky burst on to the U.S. independent scene with *Pi* (1998), a paranoid thriller shot on a shoestring budget. The film won him the Best Director prize at the Sundance Film Festival and Aronofsky went on to win an Independent Spirit Award for Best First Screenplay. His follow-up, an adaptation of Hubert Selby Jr.'s novel *Requiem for a Dream* (2000), won critical praise for the writer-director with a brave performance from the Academy Award–winning actress Ellen Burstyn.

Synopsis

Brooklyn, New York, an unspecified time. Sara Goldfarb, a lonely widow, learns she will be making an appearance on a TV game show and, determined to drop some of her flab, starts taking weight-loss pills. Meanwhile, her son Harry and his girlfriend Marion start dealing heroin to make some money with their friend Tyrone, in the hope that they can open a clothing store. Each battles their addictions: one lands in the hospital, two find prison, and the other starts a devastating new line of work.

* * *

KEVIN CONROY SCOTT: *Darren, did you get involved in any kind of creative activity when you were a teenager growing up in Brooklyn?*

DARREN ARONOFSKY: When I was a sophomore in high school, fifteen or sixteen years old, we had these things called *Sing*. The different grades, everyone competed and put on a play: the freshmen versus the sophomores. A bunch of girls would come in as the dancers, a bunch of kids who played instruments would form a band, and some kids who thought they wanted to be actors would come in as actors; so you cast it and then you wrote it, and it had a director and a producer. And that was really the first thing I directed, I somehow convinced the producer to let me direct this little musical. I think it was written by committee, so I'm sure I had a contribution there. And we actually made a film of it—I've always wanted to see a videotape, but I have no idea where it is.

So I did do a little directing, but I think I really didn't know what I wanted to do. I was into writing. I wrote a lot of poetry and some prose: more poetry, though, in high school. I was probably better in school at the sciences and math, but I did both. Then when I went to college I figured I would get a good liberal-arts foundation, which was probably a smart thing to do, because you miss a lot of stuff in New York's state school system. The education is haphazard.

You took your undergraduate degree at Harvard.

In high school I never really thought of Harvard, it wasn't a possibility, but my guidance counselor encouraged me, so I figured I'd try. My grades weren't great, but somehow I got in, probably because I did a lot of interesting extracurricular activities in high school. I was involved in a big organization that I'm an alumnus of now. It's called the School for Field Studies and what they do is take mostly college students and some high school students and they do on-site research: science, biology, field studies. And I went with the School to Kenya, south of Nairobi, and did research on ungulates, which are animals that stand on their hooves. And I went with them to Alaska the summer after that, and spent six weeks kayaking around Prince William Sound, studying seals. So, I don't know, I think I spent more time out of school than I did *in* school. And then I got to Harvard, it's a hard place to turn down because of the name and the prestige. I graduated high school early. I had enough credits, so I left in January, when most people graduate in June, and I went to Europe and backpacked around. And I turned eighteen in Europe.

Your Before Sunrise *experience . . .*

Exactly, except I didn't fall in love with a French girl, unfortunately. But I started off in Jerusalem and about six months later I ended up broke and sick with pneumonia in London. I hitchhiked and saw everything.

Outside of your coursework, who and what were you reading at Harvard?

I discovered Hubert Selby Jr. there. I was in Lamont Library, the freshman library, and I stumbled upon it. I also met the guy who started *Pi*, Sean Gullette, who was a big literary guy and he turned me on to William Burroughs in freshman year. So those writers didn't really hit me until university, although I think I had heard of *Naked Lunch* in high school. A friend of mine told me that in the back of *Naked Lunch* they had drug recipes, and it said that if you eat nutmeg you get stoned. I think we all got very sick one day . . . So I knew of *Naked Lunch* but I'd never read it, and then *Cities of the Red Night* was given to me by Sean and I read that, I was pretty impressed. I started writing prose after reading Selby, and I wrote a few short stories in college.

And when did you start experimenting with writing screenplays?

The summer after freshman year, I didn't really know what I wanted but I went to NYU and took a film history class, just randomly, and a drawing class. And I remember watching *Raging Bull* and a bunch of other great films on the projector. Then I came back and I took a drawing class at Harvard that had a great teacher who taught you how to perceive things, how to turn three dimensions into two dimensions of drawing. We learned all these great techniques. And it just kind of blew my mind because it was a new way of using visual meaning to look at the world, a new way of analyzing the world. And then in my junior year I started working on film. It was a documentary course so it was cinema vérité. We had a bunch of film directors who started their own documentary movement, like Ross McElwee, the guy who did *Sherman's March*. It's sort of that school of filmmaking, "personal documentary."

So they started our education by having us do a documentary. And then the second year of film, my senior year, that's when I started doing narrative filmmaking. I probably wrote a screenplay, but not in script format, I just wrote it how I thought it should be written. Then I graduated from Harvard and my film teacher said, "You should go to the AFI because you'll learn a lot." So I took a year off, didn't do anything, went back to Brooklyn and spent the year writing; I thought I was going to write a novel. My parents said, "You're not writing a novel, you've got to *do* something." I was just hanging out with my old friends from Brooklyn, guys who'd never left Brooklyn, which was probably not a good influence, and I ended up applying for film school because I didn't know what else to do. And I got into the AFI and they said, "When you come out of here you should have a few screenplays written," so I spent the spring writing screenplays in Brooklyn. I wrote a screenplay called *Protozoa* which I ended up making at AFI, which is now the name of our production company. I also adapted *The Fortune Cookie* which was the Hubert Selby Jr. short story. After film school I started working on a script called *Dreamland*; I probably spent two or three years on it, and it was a pretty miserable experience because I went round and round. I find that to be a repeating pattern amongst my friends who write screenplays. Maybe it's actually good advice for screenwriters, that your first screenplay sometimes you can't finish because, at least for me and a few of my friends, there's a good idea there but the whole sense of how to structure it isn't quite there yet. I was nowhere near budget or the possibility of having it made, so I was just trying to make it work. In some ways, before you make a film you really don't know what you need to put in there, what it really needs to work. And you find out that, at least for me, the screenplay's really a blueprint. There's an old cliché that if it's not in the screenplay it's not in the movie. You can read my two screenplays and there's barely *anything* in those screenplays that's in the movies, because to write everything visual that's going on in my mind or what we develop as a screenplay just wouldn't make a screenplay. Once we get the screenplay, my team and I just rip it apart. Basically we just figure out how to tell the story with images and sound.

What's the hardest part of writing screenplays for you?

Probably the loneliness of being in a room alone and facing the computer. And then the best part is when you actually start writing, and you forget about time.

What's the easiest part about writing screenplays? Is there something that you find comes naturally?

I don't think there's anything easy about writing screenplays. [*laughs*] I mean, there are easier parts of the process. You break it down; first you start with an idea, then you start to flesh out the structure, and that's a long process. I think that's where we spend a lot of time, just figuring out the structure and figuring out all the acts and figuring out all the beats of the story. And then comes the great leap which is the first draft, I call it "the muscle draft," where we just muscle it out. You don't worry about what you're missing, you just get through it, get to the end.

I think the best metaphor I've heard for screenwriting is that it's like sculpture; in sculpture you start off with a big lump of clay and if you focus too much on the head or on the hand then that head or hand is going to be grossly out of proportion in detail and in size to everything else. And the way to do it, I think, is to carve it slowly, and to go through it over and over again and keep picking at things and getting it better and better. You find that a lot of novice screenwriters will spend years on the first act and it'll turn into the best first act in the world, but you need to have the whole picture. I think I read an interview with George Lucas saying that the best advice he got from Coppola was, "Just get through it." And I think that is really good advice. When you sit down, just go all the way through the entire scene in one pass. It doesn't need to be poetry each time. And sometimes poetry hits when you're going through it, you get like a moment. It's funny because in *Pi* there were things that I wrote in the first draft, the "muscle draft," which I wrote in a cabin up in the woods by myself, all alone and terrified. Those creepy scenes I wrote in that first draft made it into the movie and didn't change at all because they just worked.

Pi was an original screenplay. Can you tell me about where that idea came from?

There are ideas in *Pi* we were probably thinking about in college or right after college. I think when I write original screenplays I always describe myself as a tapestry maker; that's the closest craft I can come up with. I take a lot of different threads from a lot of different places and try to weave them together; so the Kabbalah, and the conspiracy, and the paranoia, and the sci-fi and the *Twilight Zone* elements all came from different places. Even the idea of a spiritual element of *Pi* comes from my high school teacher who taught a spiritual math class.

A "spiritual math class"?

Yeah, it was a weird elective I took, and it was a really cool class—all about Pythagoras and weird math things. More like history of math class but with spiritual elements, because you know if you take the height of a circle and divide it by the radius you get pi, things like that. All those weird things just stayed with me in the back of my head. Then there was a friend of mine who worked at the Voice Literary Center and he started to write on the *Village Voice Literary Supplement*, and he got sent this one manuscript by a totally paranoid guy who just saw all these numerical patterns out in the world. It became a cult book among me and my friends; we would just pass it around. I was also reading a lot of Philip K. Dick at the time. The *Twilight Zone* I grew up on, the Kabbalah stuff came from my trip to

Israel after high school when I met some weird spiritual mystics. And so it all just tied together, and it was Sean Gullette the actor and Eric Watts the producer and me who wanted to make a thriller. So we just structured a very simple thriller, that's the core of *Pi*—it's just a chase film, the guy has a piece of information and two groups want it, and he's dealing with his own personal demons. I think the initial idea of *Pi* was of Sean standing in front of a bathroom mirror digging into his head with a razor blade to plant a microchip. I was into the idea of microchips in the head . . .

When you were at film school, thinking of your future as a filmmaker, did you always see yourself as a writer-director?

Everything I was doing in film school I was writing and directing, and I enjoyed the writing process a lot. But in film school I probably had little sense of what that meant. My heroes probably aren't writer-directors, like Martin Scorsese *seems* like a writer-director but he doesn't really write his stuff. And there's very few who actually write and direct. It wasn't that I wanted to have a voice or something, it was more just like the only way I knew how to do it. And I enjoyed the process, I enjoyed writing the words, putting them in the actors' mouths, and then shooting them.

After Pi *and before you started doing* Requiem, *were you at all interested in directing someone else's screenplay?*

I'm always interested in it. We read many, many screenplays at our production company and there's just been very few that have hooked me; that I can find a passion for. For me, making a movie takes about two or three years of your life and to wake up every day and find a passion to do something, to get out of bed and do it, there needs to be a very deep well of purpose or something that connects to me. I don't know how people get out of bed and do it because it's a very hard job. I wish I could do that, I would make a lot more money, but it's just not for me unfortunately. There's been a couple of things that have come in that we've been into, but usually we're not big enough to get them. Much more established filmmakers usually get the really good scripts.

But what about creating your own original screenplays? It worked very well on Pi?

That's what I'm doing now, and have been for the last three years—writing an original screenplay with the help of friends.

What was your method for adapting Selby's Requiem for a Dream*? How did you physically go through and adapt the material?*

I started off with a great novel so that was the gift. I remember Sean never got *Requiem*. He was like, "Why are you doing this?" I told him that I always had a lot of passion for it. I really looked at the book as a bible, I really believed in it, and I was very true to it. The first four months was taking a 480-page novel and reducing it to a 110-page screenplay. It was more finding out a structure first and then identifying which scenes belong to the structure, and how beat after beat after beat follows.

Do you have a routine that you follow when you're writing a screenplay?

Yeah, I mean it's become a routine to me, I remember the frustrating times of being a beginner, not really knowing the process and really having to invent everything. I was aware enough to know that those Syd Field books were evil. I was always antiestablishment enough to resist those. And I sort of developed a process which is the first job of trying to identify a three-act structure, which I do believe in. I'd love to see if there's anything beyond the three-act structure but I think it works very well as a narrative structure of a film. And for me the narrative is my mantra, it's the one thing I can believe in, that you can create something that works on a narrative level and it can work for almost every person on the planet. So I try to search for that perfect narrative within the material. First I do the large things of just organizing what the general structure is; and then you slowly break it down beat by beat, and then I move on to index cards, which is a very useful thing. And I usually try to order the index cards with color and try to find patterns going on within the index cards, so I can try to understand how the whole thing works. I'll usually take a wall out in my apartment or in my office and just put them across and try to structure them on the wall to make a meaning.

So index cards are scenes?

Yeah, one card per scene. And then when the index cards are in a good place, it's the writing, and I sit there at the computer with the cards next to me, and look at the card as I do each scene.

You and Selby collaborated on the screenplay. How did this work, since he lived in LA and you in New York?

Well, Selby had written a script when the book was published in 1978. It was a hundred-odd pages and I don't think it was a proper screenplay format but this was the seventies when that stuff was a little less known. When he sent it to me I had finished my version of the adaptation, and about seventy per cent of what he had used I had used. There were a couple of themes in the book that I really enjoyed following that he didn't follow, and he chose a couple of others, but we were definitely both going to the same place, the same outcome. So then I just basically fused them together. From there I'd send him each draft and get some notes from him and adapt them and there were a few scenes that needed writing. Those scenes were where I needed some bridges made; I'd cut out stuff and I needed connections made.

So when it came to inventing scenes to help bridge the gaps . . .

I think Hubert wrote a couple of those. He wrote a few things that were original.

How many drafts of Requiem *did you guys go through?*

Official drafts? Three. The official one is the one that goes outside of the family. But how many did I go through? Probably twenty. Oh yeah, it's always about twenty drafts every film, every film from short film to long films. Every once in a while from draft twelve to thirteen it might be just a small change but it is generally decent sized changes between all the drafts. I mean, the script we're working on now I'm on draft twenty-two and we don't have a start date.

You've talked about Hubert Selby Jr.'s generosity of spirit and his kindness. Was there ever a time when you two had creative differences?

You know, I don't think so. Selby really trusted me, and really let me roam with it, and was open to an interpretation. I don't know why, but that's just the way he was.

When you're writing on your own and things aren't going well, it's going to happen to any writer, do you ever experience any self-doubt about your writing?

Oh yeah, self-doubt is a daily exercise and that's why you need to be passionate about the material. You'll wake up many mornings over those two or three years and you'll be totally at a loss as to why you're doing this, what is the purpose. And you have to hate your project.

My dad used to say, "A man without doubt is a man without wisdom." You have to constantly keep doubting yourself because otherwise you'll get cocky and that's what destroys you.

Peter Biskind's book about Hollywood in the seventies, Easy Riders, Raging Bulls, *demonstrated that that kind of cockiness destroyed a lot of careers.*

That's a great lesson for young filmmakers. Luckily for me that book came out right after *Pi*. I think after *Pi*, before I would go to sleep I would write ten times "I'm just an idiot, I'm just an idiot, I'm just an idiot" to just remind myself that it's about the struggle and it's about being a student, it's about constantly learning new things. And that's a great thing about filmmaking, about screenwriting, about making movies — is that you get to just dissolve yourself into a completely new universe every two or three years and you get to see whole new concepts of thought. That's the exciting thing about our work; we don't have to be pressing the same buttons for twenty-five years.

What do you do when the writing isn't going as well as you like? Is there a certain thing?

I think there's nothing you do; I think you just have to understand that it's like manic-depression. There are crests and troughs and you have to be able to cope. And just have to know that when you're feeling it's going well that at some point in the near future it's going to be a struggle and that's just the reality of it. When you're down, just be kind to yourself; go buy a CD, go see a movie, wait until the inspiration comes back.

When you're working, do you ever set yourself a page-per-day count?

I've done that with "muscle drafts," ten pages per day. I did that on *Pi* just to get through it and I think it's totally fine to just push yourself and get through it because, I'll tell you, as you're writing it you can say "This is junk, this is crap," but when you go back and look at it, it's totally useable, and you'll be amazed. You know what? It's filling up the pages and there's something there and it's sort of describing the idea that you're trying to get across. Then you just have to shape it into what you're really trying to say. It's just really working away at it. With the chisel you can't get that fine detail — at first you have to work with the big fat chisel, then you get to the fine work.

You are from Manhattan Beach, the neighborhood near Coney Island where Requiem *was set; however, the novel was set in the Bronx. What's the reason for the change of setting?*

I asked Selby why it was set in the Bronx. He told me the characters were based on some people he had heard of in the Bronx, so for him there was no real reason. I didn't know the Bronx; when you're from Brooklyn the Bronx is the other side of the world. And I just knew it would set really well in the neighborhood I grew up in, there was great translation there. That way, I would be able to show off my neighborhood, shoot places I really knew, and it was once again going back to the root. And that for me is really important, it's a creative root. All these details of your own youth, and all the locations I chose for *Requiem* all meant something to me; and because they mean something to you, you know how to photograph them. So it's kind of like cheating.

So, for example, where Harry and Marion kiss on the beach, you used to go there as a teenager?

Yeah, exactly.

So, thinking of that in your head when you're writing the screenplay, does that help you describe the moment better or is it more to help you shoot the film?

More to shoot the film. I might have chosen the locations in my head but they don't really come into it until later. Like that scene when they're out on the rocks, I've spent many hours of my life out on those jetties, that's what we did. For instance, the scene where they go to the top of the tower and they throw the paper airplanes, that's not in the book, that's just based on something my friends and I used to do. And in fact setting off the alarm and everything was an actual adventure that we had, and it was purely me, it was in those towers that we did that, we got chased by the police and everything. So I was able to see things from my youth, to put in things that I knew we needed in the movie but weren't in the novel.

Music is used to great effect in the film. At what point during the writing process does the music come into play?

Clint Mansell was involved early on in the process of *Pi*, he wrote this overture of Max before we even shot it. I remember the day he came in with it, the whole crew was there and I went into the side office and listened to it and I brought the whole crew in and it was great. It was that slamming jungle music. And then in *Requiem*, before we even started shooting he put a CD of some ideas together and when the film started to get cut he started to create music and it just wasn't working. And I actually got really scared because he was living in New Orleans at the time and I went down to New Orleans to work with him and we went back to the original CD and that's where we found the main part of the *Requiem* score. All those pieces were from that original piece he wrote, so it's interesting that those initial instincts with Clint really, really worked.

And when you were writing did you listen to any music to establish a tone for a scene or was there any stuff you would do while you were writing to help yourself?

When I write I have music always blasting, usually. During *Requiem* I listened to a lot of Sleater Kinney, just because I find they're true artists; they're not pop, they're not trying to sell records, they're just trying to make their music. And every time I see them live they're an inspiration to me just because they're out there doing really good music. But I listen to a lot of different things when I write.

I was reading the novel and there's this great passage where it describes Harry picking his nose while high on heroin and how much he's enjoying it, and I thought, that's great but how the hell do you get the audience to appreciate that?

I had to cut that scene out but the point of the scene was how much he was enjoying the high, how much he was just enjoying nodding, how much he was just enjoying that thing. I didn't think it was too sympathetic. But you could see how Selby paints that inner monologue so it's about how to pull that inner monologue out and showing it.

Knowing that you're adapting a book that dealt with the use of drugs, were you worried about how to dramatize the effects of these addictions?

Well, that was the challenge; that was probably the whole reason I made the film. It's so deeply about addiction and the way Selby captured addiction and the internal struggle, it was about how to visualize that. That was the great excitement of it. I knew there was a way to visualize it, and it worked really well with what we started to develop in *Pi*, which was a form of subjective filmmaking, of really pushing film away from theater and objective camera angles, helping the audience get into the character's head.

So you were thinking when you were writing that if you had a series of extreme closeups, and you were using a lot of visual effects in the film, that you could conquer this problem of subjectivity?

Yeah, like that scene where the food disappears; it was a way of just expressing how quickly it goes away for her character and just how one second it's there and then it's all gone and she's all alone again; there's that emptiness. And it was explained in the book but there was no visual way of expressing that.

Of the four characters, which did you have the hardest time writing?

They were all so well written in the novel, I don't think any of them were hard to write. I think updating a bit of them was hard, like in the book Harry wants to open up a coffee shop and I sort of felt that was a bit outdated because of Starbucks and stuff. I invented Marion having a fashion background, I changed a few things.

This notion of not really being sure whether it was contemporary or period, how did you approach that in writing?

Well, the question was, "Do we or do we not update the dialogue?" And we started to think about updating it and we realized that one of the great things about Selby is his ear for language. It would just be a big mistake to try to change the slang. So we decided to keep it and try to mix when it was. Clearly they're using cordless phones so it is the nineties but we tried to give it a seventies feel with their clothing. That was completely conscious because we wanted to make it a timeless film, it doesn't matter if it's the eighties or the nineties, it's addiction and it could be any time.

Was this also why you didn't see much of the background of the film's locations?

I think the film was supposed to be more wide at the beginning when it was summer and things were a little bit better; there were some landscape shots of Brighton Beach and Coney Island and stuff, but with a very conscious effort to make it more and more claustrophobic as the film progressed and to get deeper and deeper in their heads. In fact, in the third act, what we were really trying to do but didn't pull off was to just have it all in extreme closeups, all the size of an eyeball in the end. We couldn't really quite tell the story that way, but that was the idea to go from wide to tight.

Did it worry you that the novel has four different characters who are all given a subjective point of view by the third person narrator? I guess, in other words, there is no clear protagonist for the audience to get behind in the traditional sense.

While structuring the film I was trying to figure out who the hero of the story is, whether it was Harry or Tyrone or Sara. And while structuring it, I sometimes used a graph to plot the ups and downs of the character, and every time something good was supposed to happen to the character, something bad happened. I started to get this upside-down arc, and then I realized that the hero of the story was not any of the main characters, it was addiction, which is the monster in the movie. Whenever something bad happened to the character, something good happened to addiction, and I started to look at addiction as an outside force that was a character. It was a monster movie, but the monster wins. So what we tried to do always in the movie was always show addiction and what addiction was doing in each scene. Make addiction part of the film.

You said that the novel has an amazing structure and it translates very well into three acts. What did you mean by that?

The novel was written like a movie. In fact, I think Selby said he was trying to write a movie, and then just started writing, and two weeks later there was this novel and that's what it became. But I think it really has the three acts; there's summer, fall and winter, and it really progresses over those three.

You did the character arcs for the screenplay. How does that work?

I do it all on paper. I start by putting the character's name at the top and sort of follow the different beats of the character through the progression of the film. Sometimes I would graph it as I was telling you. I would have a graph with the time on and different events that happen and then where each character was and then I would draw with different color pencils, so I am able to look at where each character was. It was sort of a visual representation of what was going on.

And then you took the screenplay to the Sundance workshop—was that helpful?

Yeah, it was tremendous, because the script was read by five or six established screenwriters who basically gave me notes. The main thing that came out of it was the scene between Harry and Marion on the telephone when Marion cries, because everyone felt that they needed some contact in the third act which doesn't happen in the book; they never talk again once he leaves for Florida. So we had different discussions and there were different responses and it was interesting to see them. I got to sit with Robert Redford, he came down and met with me for two hours, and originally I was like, "What's this guy gonna know? He lives up here in Utah, he's a cowboy." Actually, he's an unbelievably intelligent guy and completely identified with two or three big emotional points of the film. And one of them pointed out a moment that I didn't realize was such a huge emotional point, and it became a seminal moment in the film for me.

Why did you start the film with the closet scene, where Harry steals his mother's television and she locks herself in her closet?

Well the closet scene is the first scene of the book. I think it's a great scene because it introduces the dual world of Harry and Sara being separated. And when I started reading the book and thought about translating it into a film I thought about the split screen and creating that as a grammar in the movie. It was a way of showing characters in the same scene but totally separated.

And where did Tappy, the tacky quiz show host character, come from?

Tappy was a character that I created for *Dreamland*, that screenplay I worked on for four years. TV was a main character in the book, but I realized that getting TV shows to license would just place it too much in a particular time; that's why I used Tappy instead of actual TV footage. When I first read *Requiem* I always put it down because it was something I was thinking about. TV addiction was something I was already writing about. In fact the novel I was writing after college was about TV addiction. So here was a character that came to represent that, and his whole persona is about a way of conquering, getting control of your life, and that sort of became a metaphor for the film.

In the book it's pretty important, this relationship they have where Sara won't give Harry money but he'll come in and steal the television, which is a great hook for the story and a great way of introducing the relationship. But did you ever consider changing it?

A lot of people critiqued it, saying, "Here are your two main characters and they're pathetic in the opening scene; you can't do that." But the hero, once again, is addiction, and addiction is brave and bold in that scene. Look at the horrible things he's making these humans do. But whenever you try to do something a little different . . . I mean everyone was like "No, no" about this movie. Even after it was premiered in Cannes to a standing ovation, the studio wanted to cut it. They barely released it.

Many successful literary adaptations make use of voice-overs. But you decided against that, why?

At some point we thought of voice-over. At one point there was a writer we approached to think about writing this instead of me, a guy we found who was very interested in the book, and he wanted to do a voice-over, and I sort of avoided that. I think it worked really well in *Pi* because the whole idea was to make a silent movie and have all the dialogue in his head. But this I felt was a lot to pull off.

The scene where Harry visits his mother and notices that she is on a version of drugs herself was very powerful. It is a ten-minute static scene in a film that has quite a few inserts and quite a bit of tempo and pacing. Were you worried that this scene would throw off the rhythm of a very fast film?

Well, that is the emotional heart of the film. Probably one of the other major reasons I wanted to make this film was for that scene, because when I read this scene I was just crying. It was such a beautiful scene and it's so human, and even though I've never been a junkie I could identify about that generation gap and about the loneliness of a mother and separation between mother and child. I think that is the scene that gets everyone and it's kind of the center of the movie; it's ten minutes long and I just loved shooting it and watching Ellen's performance, and I knew it would be great. There's just so much going on which keeps you interested, this information that they're not sharing.

Ellen Burstyn made a nice choice in the way she played that scene, because when Harry tells her she's got a TV set in the book she gets really excited and grabs him. But she chooses just a very tender moment and doesn't make it such a huge gesture; it's more like just a nice hug, like, "That was a sweet thing to do for me, Harry." It was a great choice for her, it really humanizes the character and makes her nonmaterialistic.

If you watch Ellen in that scene you'll notice she then becomes very mellow. And I kind of gave her a hard time because it's not how it's scripted in the book. I can't figure it out but I really like the choice she made there. So when he hears something, and in the book I still remember the whole thing where he heard something and couldn't figure out what it was: What is that noise? And then he realizes it's her teeth grinding. So we created a camera move where we went around, crossing the line, and ended up on the other side of their faces. For me, I put us on the dark side of their faces. This is scripted exactly as it is in the book.

That's quite an interesting moment for him too as a character, because that's obviously the path he's going down, the path of drug addiction.

Exactly, but he's just ignoring it.

So he can see it in his mother, but he can't see it in himself.

Exactly. It's one of the only true points in the film where the characters are really saying what's really going on. In fact, I was concerned a little, Ellen and I talked about this, it suddenly made her a lot more intelligent than she is anywhere else, it's almost the writer of the novel writing what's really going on. It's a little like breaking character because it's an incredibly honest real moment but sometimes we have those. And I think Ellen's performance takes you right across any worry about that. It's a beautiful thing, the way a performance can do that to the writing; I always think that, how the blocking just sort of created itself on the set. We were running out of time and we just put the light in between them.

And the empty chair between them is where the father would have been sitting.

Yeah, the three seats.

What's so true about what's going on in his life is that if he was listening to anything his mother was saying, he'd know that the part to pay attention to wasn't the drugs; it's the fact that she was lonely. If he was to take care of that in some way or another the other problems would probably go away.

And that is the big scene that Redford was into, the big, emotional moment there. How lonely it is. It was just about how heroin makes it all right.

Harry has some success as a small-time dealer, but after the drug deal in the limo goes wrong, the film shifts into a very dark mode. That scene also sets up the last half of the film. Were you worried that the shift from good times to bad times would be too abrupt?

Well, I think the hope scene is where the turning point is, you think that things are going well, and then you see the real truth behind Sara and really what's going on with these characters. And then you see Harry in the cab and he's getting high just to get over his sadness, and realizes that it is no longer fun. It is an abrupt moment, everything suddenly changes. But that's how things happen, just one day, that's the whole point. Looking back, I think I would have covered it differently now, I would have given it a bit of a wide shot to give it a moment to establish itself.

Immediately Tyrone's in a scene with a dealer and in a way you don't deal with his apprehensions about getting in that car with the dealer. Is that intentional?

My whole thing is get in late, get out early. In most films, you have to see the car drive, get up to the house, cut to the house. My whole theory is that audiences are so sophisticated now they just want to get to the meat of the emotional story, and you can hit them with emotion after emotion; they're not really interested in the whole setup. And unless you're doing something dramatic with the setup, the audience doesn't need to know where the hell they are or what space they're in; they just want to know the story.

And hopefully not make it too confusing, so that the audience doesn't shut off and put the book down or walk out of the movie or turn off the DVD — that's the balance.

Well, if you're a filmmaker in sixties Europe then that's what you want.

Exactly, graphic novels do it too, where they start off in tremendous confusion and then you slowly piece them together as they go on. Alan Moore does that a lot as a writer. But for me it's just, "Let's get in it." If the apprehension was interesting enough to fill the fear and the tension, if I think we needed it, but that's not where Tyrone's coming from. He's not coming from apprehension, he's coming from cockiness. These guys are going out, they've got the drugs and they're going for it, so apprehension may actually give away the gag, so I probably wouldn't have chosen to do it even if I wanted to. I was going for, "Let's get into the beat of it right away."

In the book, Tyrone is all about the love. How did you update his character?

It was a tricky thing, because Selby wrote the book in the seventies and wrote their language in a kind of Blaxploitation-ish thing. And when we sent the script out to Hollywood and I sent the script out to black actors, I actually wrote a cover letter explaining that this was from Selby's writing and that Tyrone is actually a really deeply human character; that it's just the author of the novel trying to capture the language; it shouldn't be perceived as a two-dimensional device, because that's not how I perceive it. And that got a good response, because there was a big sensitivity to that in America and in Hollywood, which there should be, because there has been major exploitation. I think Selby can sometimes be accused of writing clichés, I think Sara borders on a cliché of an old Jewish lady. But I don't think Selby's making fun of them or abusing them for that. I think he's just trying to find the beauty of that particular culture, Jewish or black. I think prejudice and racism is about intent. You can sit there and make jokes about all cultures and if there isn't an intention to exploit, that's fine. It's just when it becomes about one culture or race being better than the other, that's when there's a problem.

Your use of transitions in this film is quite fluid. Are transitions something you think of a lot as a writer or does that come in with the editing?

I do think a lot of it as a writer, especially in this film: this film is all about transitions and how to get in and out of scenes. And we became very clear in opening up scenes with extreme closeups, and getting you right into the middle of it. Because I'm a writer, there's a definite sense of how it's going to get cut when I make it. When we attack a scene, I picture how it's going to be cut before we ever get to the shooting phase.

I've noticed a lot of Hollywood screenwriters will include expressions like "smash-cut," things that get the rhythm, but then they'll also write in camera angles.

I think there's no need. Unless it's telling something in the narrative, the writer shouldn't really write where the camera is, unless it's *really* important that we're really tight on something, or if he's trying to make a particular appeal for a character, because it has something to do with the material. That stuff turns a director off, I think.

I thought the ending in the book was beautiful.

Yes, it goes something like, "They stared at the gray walls and lifeless trees, and with tears falling from their eyes, they hugged each other. They stayed for an endless hour and then reluctantly but with a sigh of relief, left." It's beautiful. And this is the best I could do as far as a happy ending goes. It's a *delusional* happy ending . . .

It's true to the character of Sara.

The book ends with Tyrone being hugged by his mother, which I always thought was an interesting way to end, because in some ways Tyrone's the one most likely to survive. At least he has all his limbs and he's not a whore and he's not in an insane asylum—he's just in a prison, and one day he'll get out. I kind of liked it, the most minor of the four characters having a private moment representing what the whole thing was about. But it just wasn't enough—I had to put in a scene with Sara.

New York, New York

Patrick McGrath

8

PATRICK McGRATH

Spider

"We don't have to like them, we just have to be not bored by them."

Patrick McGrath was born in London and grew up near Broadmoor Hospital, where his father was Medical Superintendent. His novels include *Blood and Water and Other Tales, Dr. Haggard's Disease, Martha Peake* and *Port Mungo*. He has adapted three of his novels into screenplays, *The Grotesque* (1994), *Asylum* (2004) and *Spider* (2002), directed by David Cronenberg. McGrath lives in New York City and London with his wife, Maria Aitken.

Synopsis

East London, the 1960s and 1980s. "Spider," a deeply disturbed boy, "sees" his father brutally murder his mother and replace her with a prostitute, Yvonne. Convinced that they plan to murder him next, Spider hatches an insane plan, which he carries through to tragic effect. Spider is released into a halfway house. Unsupervised, he stops taking his medication and starts revisiting his childhood haunts. His attempts to sustain his delusional account of his past begin to unravel, and Spider spirals into madness.

* * *

KEVIN CONROY SCOTT: *Patrick, before you started writing novels, how deep was your interest in cinema?*

PATRICK McGRATH: I had an affection for film, an interest that wasn't particularly detailed or knowledgeable—all that came much later, once I'd been writing fiction for some years. But watching movies became very central to my development as a novelist. There was a place in New York in the 1980s called Theatre Eighty on St. Marks Place; it basically showed two movies a night and they were almost exclusively American movies from the thirties, forties and fifties. So I saw a great deal of American cinema, and I was using what I saw as a way of developing my skills as a fiction writer. I was looking at plotting, the way scenes were cut, and the way that behavior on screen was indicative of inner states—how tension, fear and other emotions were expressed physically by actors on the screen. And I was absorbing that into my work in fiction writing.

When did the notion of actually working in film first arise for you?

After my first novel, *Blood and Water*, was published, I had already been in New York for eight or nine years at that point, and my agent called me up one day and said that there was an agent from Hollywood in town who'd like to meet us. That was the first time it occurred to me in any serious way that there might be any crossover. So we all met and this young woman from Hollywood said she'd like to represent me and had I ever thought of writing for movies? I said, "No, but now you mention it, it's an intriguing idea." So I began to teach myself how to write scripts. She got me out to LA and I trekked round the studios.

Did you do any research, read any books?

I went to the Robert McKee weekend. That was one of the first things I did. And it was a very useful first step in thinking about film in an analytical way, breaking down story structure. It's not the only truth there is, but it was useful to get one thinking in that way about how to structure a story and various other insights.

What were your feelings about the screen adaptation of your novel The Grotesque?

That was pretty difficult: it had one of the same problems that *Spider* would throw up, an unreliable first-person narration. Also it may have been that I was a less experienced screenwriter when I did the adaptation, but I found it tough to somehow make a coherent story out of *The Grotesque*. I'm not sure where the problem lay but when I saw the film after some time, it failed to cohere. We were all inexperienced: the director, the producer, and I think the script could have been a lot tighter.

The major character in the novel and the film is Sir Hugo, who is, in your words "a neurotically repressed character." Was it a problem for you that he might be considered an unsympathetic character by, say, producers or financiers?

I always take the attitude that a character doesn't have to be sympathetic but a character has to be vibrant and vital. A character can be a real bastard but if they've got a real force of energy about them we'll be fascinated by them. We don't have to like them; we just have to be not bored by them. I'd say that was the rule.

The Freudian theme of the piece, paranoia in respect of homosexuality, isn't something that's a staple of Hollywood cinema. Did anyone on the production team try to smooth the edges of the screenplay?

No, nor did anybody do a great deal of work on it. We did bring in a friend of mine who's an experienced screenwriter, Guy Gallo, who wrote the adaptation of Malcolm Lowry's *Under the Volcano* for John Huston, and he worked with me to get the thing to flow a bit better; we worked on the narrative line. But the producer signed off on it before it was ready and the director contributed to it by throwing in a lot of wild animals and that kind of thing, and sexing it up a bit and changing the ending. So he added to it rather than modified it, which I think complicated the mess a bit further.

David Cronenberg has said that creativity involves a lot of waste, using the analogy that a spider will lay a thousand eggs and only two of them will end up being mature spiders. Do you think that analogy applies more to your work as a novelist or to your work as a screenwriter?

That's a good question. I think there's a lot of waste either way. Not waste so much as work that is unsatisfactory but at least ropes off a blind alley, gets you to the next thing that occurs to you. Your first impulse to do it one way might not work but there's another idea and you try that. Maybe that doesn't work, and maybe there's a week involved each time but you keep on dispensing with ideas that don't work and eventually that leads to the idea that does work. And I feel the same process operates in fiction and in screenwriting.

Throughout these interviews I've been asking writers about self-doubt and how you deal with that during the writing process, the writing day, even.

I think you deal with it when you're early in your career just by the sheer energy and determination you have to make it; and if you allow yourself to be sidetracked by self-doubt at that stage you'll basically fall by the wayside and cease to produce. You've got to just keep on working even though you know the work is not good enough, but you keep on working because you have no choice, because you're driven, or whatever. And then later on you gain a confidence that enables you, when you have an inability to solve a problem, to get a story on its feet, get a character to come to life. You have the confidence born of experience that you've been in this mess before, and that just by staying at your table, staring at it and trying to make an idea come to you, if you stick with it long enough you'll solve the problem—because your own history has told you that.

What do you find most challenging about adapting your own work?

I suppose it's the same for any screenplay, it's that business of mounting narrative progress, that business of having to build on the scene, or every scene having to work on two or three levels at the same time, giving two or three bits of information about the story and the character, not repeating yourself, sustaining that momentum. It's, I suppose, not being able to drift as you can in a novel, it's the central imperative of the story in film. You have a hundred minutes and not the luxury to waste a single one of them.

Where did the original idea for Spider *the novel come from?*

It's usually the same process for me; all my novels had a similar pattern. First of all, a fairly straightforward story or stretch of narrative comes to me, and in the case of *Spider* it was about a plumber who grows restless and unsatisfied with his wife and takes on a lover, who is a big, blousy, brazen prostitute. He murders his wife and puts the prostitute in his house in her place. And that was going to be the novel, with some variations and developments and so forth.

So at one point it was a rather straightforward narrative.

A straightforward narrative about a murdering plumber . . .

Can you say how the murdering plumber arose in your imagination?

I had a wonderful book of photographs by Bill Brandt called *London in the Thirties*; it's divided into three bits: upper-class, middle-class, and working-class London, as it was classified then. And working-class London was photographs taken of the East End before the Blitz, when the East End was still the East End, and there were a lot of seedy little pubs with men with flat caps, and busty barmaids with missing teeth pulling pints. There were couples in little alleyways in the shadows having a bit of furtive canoodling, there were kids playing football in the streets. There was a sense of a very vigorous working class. But particularly at night, with the narrow streets, there was a very *noir* atmosphere. There was something a bit furtive and shabby and sinister about it. And the atmosphere that came off of these photographs was so strong that it just cried out to have a story written in this setting.

So then stage two for me was deciding who was going to tell this story, and I toyed with the idea of each and any of the characters telling it, before I settled on the idea that maybe there was a child in the household who saw his mother disappear and this horrible woman take her place. And that seemed to be much more charged with pathos and drama. Then I thought, "What if the child is remembering this from adulthood, remembering terrible traumas of his childhood?" So I got to that third stage when it occurred to me that the remembering adult might have completely distorted the past and that his memories of the father, the mother, the murder, the prostitute coming into the house—that this might all be a tissue of delusions that he had somehow created in order to hide from himself the truth of what had happened in his childhood. And at that point I thought "Now I've got a narrator with a really twisted take on his own past. In fact I've probably got a psychotic narrator—a schizophrenic narrator." And that was a challenge that was both rather intimidating and rather fascinating. And I'd say the same about all my books, that there's a scrap of narrative that then becomes in some way complicated and layered through the decision as to which character in the narrative will be telling the story and what that narrator's relationship to the story will be.

When you adapted Spider *you thought it was going to take six weeks. Instead it took six months. Why?*

It's a trick that a writer tells himself. I think what I really meant was that I didn't *want* it to take more than six weeks. I thought it was doomed. I thought there wasn't a movie in this book and if I was going to waste time on this rather fruitless quest I'd rather waste a little bit of time rather than a lot. So I thought I'd do it for six weeks and when I'd proved to myself and my wife, who was the one who was urging me to do it, that this book was un-filmable then I could just say I'd had a go.

And the basic problem was to do with the subjective nature of the narrative?

That was what I saw as the problem: how do you get all of Spider's interior experience on the screen? But what I found once I went to work was that, while that remained a problem, the childhood he describes, even if it's largely invented, was full of dramatic incident and vivid characters. So I was able to take all the stuff with his dad and with his mother and the prostitute and the murder, the aftermath of the murder, the prostitute moving into the house—that was all good dramatic stuff, so I had a spine of dramatic incident into which I had to weave the adult Spider, remembering back. So the problem became more manageable at that point. So basically I just turned all the scenes of his childhood into scripted scenes and then I had a backbone to the thing and then began to develop the adult Spider's activities in and around that spine of a dramatic childhood.

And in terms of conveying Spider's interiority—what did your solutions consist of?

Well, it basically came down to voice-over. In the book he heard voices, and I had that in, he has various hallucinations about what's going on in his own body, bizarre things happen when he's a little boy. There's one point where he cuts a potato open and the potato bleeds. So I put these things in to suggest a disturbance in his mind and I did a lot of voice-over in order to get a sense of the confusion and wildness of his thinking. And Cronenberg said, "Take it all out."

Would you agree that voice-over is good for a screenplay but bad for a film?

I think I would, yes—with exceptions. And then I'd think of all the movies I've seen. I was looking at *Apocalypse Now* the other day and I thought "That's a film that would be much weaker without voice-over"—without Martin Sheen talking about Kurtz and the river and so on, and in that quite exhausted voice with which he does it.

Several directors were attached to Spider *over the course of several years. Can you tell me about this process and how it affected the screenplay?*

There were two in particular; Pat O'Connor was quite seriously involved for a while, I don't really think it was his sort of a movie but he was a very nice fellow and we got on very well. We spent two weeks in LA in the classic way: a producer sent me over and put me in the Chateau Marmont and we'd get together and natter away and go out for ice creams and it was all smashing. And we did quite a lot of work on the script, and it's very hard now to pinpoint exactly what bit of the script evolved at what time and in collaboration with who; but I think we made progress; we got it to the next stage. Then I think Pat—just the expediencies of his career, directors always need to work—couldn't wait around for us to put the money together. Stephen Frears was very helpful; he never committed himself to it but he took a lot of interest and I think that's maybe the sort of guy he is; he's interested in other filmmakers and writers and will give time; he's a generous man. There was one night I remember, he lives in Notting Hill and we were in Kennington, he drove all the way across London, paced about in our kitchen worrying about the script and how it could be improved and so on. His support was very important. Those were the two directors who had the most impact on the script.

Did it bother you that the film wasn't getting made?

It did and it didn't. I had always been somewhat skeptical, I hadn't allowed myself to get my hopes up; I'd been around movies enough to know that a posture of slightly skeptical detachment is the best way to go with movies because nineteen times out of twenty they do fall apart, so you must be able to walk away and say, "Oh well, we tried." But this one was different, in that for a long time we didn't seem to be able to get anywhere with it. Then David Cronenberg suddenly appeared on the scene like an angel and everything is light and progress, and then we moved very quickly. Then I really started to allow myself to believe that the movie was going to be made, by David Cronenberg, with Ralph Fiennes and Miranda Richardson. And three weeks before principal photography all the money fell away, and I'd allowed myself to get really up on it, and then there was a terrible deflation and the thought that we were so close and we'd lost it all . . .

During the course of Spider's *long development process I am sure you got some notes from producers on how to improve the script. How do you feel about notes, how do you deal with them?*

It always depends on the source that they come from and the quality of them, and what surprised me in Hollywood was that people who are in the business of making movies are so astonishingly naïve about the process through which scripts are actually created, so that you could have written a draft where everything fits together—the draft of a feature film is an intricate piece of work and if it's any good at all it fits together with some precision—and you go into the executive's office with all the assistants who are about twelve years old, and they're all allowed to give their suggestions. And because politeness is important to the people who will green-light the thing or not, you have to sit there politely as some teenager comes up with something like, "What about if the guy has a wife and she's dying of cancer?" And you've spent a hundred pages establishing this guy and his relationships and so forth . . . you're talking about three months' work. So you tend to walk away and the minute you're out of the executive suite you turn to the producer and say, "What the fuck's that all about?" And they say, "Don't worry, it's OK, you did good." So it's a farce. Hollywood is supposed to be a profession; they make all these movies and yet you've just been through this farcical event. On the other hand, you then have the situation where a David Cronenberg comes in and tells you what he wants done to your script and you listen with deference and respect, thinking, "I'm learning something here."

One of his notes being to get rid of the voice-over . . .

Which didn't take very long. There was another brilliant suggestion which really made a large impact on the film, which was the notion that Spider could actually be present in one of his memories. So we put this in one scene and it seemed to work quite well; in fact it worked so well as far as Cronenberg was concerned that he told me to put the adult Spider in all of the scenes of his own childhood. And so that was, again, a simple thing to do; every time the little boy's having dinner with his parents, going down to the pub to get his dad out, whatever, Spider is there somewhere watching and reacting. It had the great advantage of very vividly depicting a man remembering his own child-hood, and it also gave us the opportunity to use Ralph in practically every scene in the movie.

In the novel Spider writes beautifully. Were you upset at losing that aspect of his personality, because the prose inside his head is so well-structured, so pretty?

Well, no, I totally agreed with Cronenberg when he said the articulate, literate Spider is incompatible with this shambling, mumbling, confused man that we see wandering through the streets. And whereas I had to give Spider a voice in the book, that simply would not have worked in the film. You know the way Ralph Fiennes shuffles about, the mumbling and the eyes—if you'd had a voice-over where he'd be articulating in nice, well-rounded sentences then I think you would have undercut the power of this almost mute figure. So I thought Cronenberg was absolutely right to say, "Let's get rid of the language."

Surely you must have been nervous, as it's a lot to ask of the audience, to not have a very clear idea of where he's coming from or why he's doing what he does?

Yeah, it worried me but it never worried Cronenberg, he knew exactly what he was doing. And I would ask him exactly that kind of question: "How are you going to let them know that Spider is getting things wrong here, that his father isn't having an affair with this woman?" And he'd say, "Well, I don't ask you how you do your stuff!" And I'd ask: "How are we going to know what's going on inside Spider's head?," and he'd just say, "Leave it to Ralph, that's his job." So he pacified me and then he'd get on with it; he knew what he was doing.

How did you and Cronenberg first get together?

After he got the script in Toronto he came over almost immediately to meet the producer, Cathy Bailey, and Ralph, myself, and my wife, Maria. And the crucial meeting really was between him and Ralph, because Ralph had been waiting for years to attach a director so that chemistry had to be right. I was there, and it was clear in two minutes that Ralph liked David, and David liked Ralph. It was a great relief to everybody when we saw them chatting away.

One of the great things I learned from Cronenberg was that he was very good at saying "Take that out, it's superfluous, we've already had that." And through his eyes I began to see my script full of redundancies, like putting Spider on the Tube after we'd seen him at Waterloo station. I wasn't really telling us anything new, I was elaborating what I'd already established. He was very economical, he'd say "We know that, so we can cut that." The result of which was that the script was down to seventy-eight pages and I said, "It's not long enough." So he then said, "I'll film slow!"

You were on set during production. What was your role?

Nuisance, really, but I was made to feel welcome. Cronenberg is unflappable. I know some directors don't like the writer around, but he was always happy to see me, and there'd always be jokey stuff going on and I just wanted to watch him work. I liked the man enormously, so it was just neat to be around him. And I kind of like film sets; that loose camaraderie, nobody minded me, and here it was, my story, being made.

How did it feel to see your novel in the real world?

Probably the biggest shock is the actual, physical presence of the actor. You've lived for years, in this case with a mental image of the characters and then suddenly you're confronted with the actor who's fleshing that image, and they're not as tall or thin as they should be; and you see all of these ways in which they're not the way in which you imagined; and you simply have to adjust your perception, which with Ralph happened very quickly because he inhabited the character of Spider so utterly and completely that I dismissed the character that had been in my head, which would look something like Samuel Beckett, a great, tall, lanky thing; and Ralph certainly made himself very thin but didn't have the height for Beckett. I'd always seen Spider as gangly and tall, but as I say, after an hour or two on the set on the first day, Ralph was Spider, and so I had substituted Ralph's embodiment for the previous one. But that for me is the biggest shock, and then the same is true of the rooms, the streets, all the physical details which for me are quite vividly visual in my imagination, and all of those have to be adjusted to what the production designer, and the actors, and the director have constructed.

Spider *competed at the Cannes Film Festival in 2002. How did you find that experience?*

Oh, it was great, because I saw very many harried, frenetic people trying to make deals, looking for money or whatever. And all I had to do was basically show up and drink champagne and walk up the red carpet on the night of the screening. Everyone was being terribly nice to me; Cronenberg is very popular in Cannes, so it was just pure pleasure.

You wrote an article about how Spider *came to life as a film, in which you say: "The story of the financing of* Spider *is a baroquely twisted tale of gothic proportions, involving bad calculations, outrageous betrayal, brutal vindictiveness, scheming manipulation, dogged obsession, high moral courage, breathtaking brinksman-*

ship, plus amazing feats of self-sacrifice, loyalty, recklessness and hard work. It would require at least a slim volume to tell that story, for it involves the arcane minutiae of film financing in volatile combination with much that is base in human nature, and much that is fine."

It could be a book—and I could still do it. There were hundreds of producers. And the stories about some of the bastards or the good guys are amazing. The complexity of the film's financing was remarkable, in fact I spoke for two hours at a party with one of the lawyers who worked on it, and we barely scratched the surface, and the intricacies, and the personalities . . . It could be a hell of a book.

The opening sequence in the St. Pancras train station is interesting. Was that a scene that you wrote?

Yeah. I think I had it set in Waterloo, but it's pretty much filmed as I wrote it. I wrote a whole lot more, too, that got left out; Spider's case falls open, I got him on the subway, he lights up a cigarette on the Tube and somebody tells him to put it out, so I had a lot more of him getting accustomed to being in this world.

The novel is set in the thirties, then the fifties.

Right, the movie is sort of sixties and eighties.

Was keeping Spider isolated in the present day something that you were concerned with?

Cronenberg talked about this; that there are always extras and cars on hand but every time that happened the scene wasn't as strong, every time they took something away the scene got stronger. And then it occurred to him that an isolated Spider was the strongest image of all, this isolated figure.

Spider wears numerous layers of clothing. Why?

It's sort of as Terrence says a bit later: "The less there is of the man, the more he needs the shirts." It's something I saw myself when I was growing up; there was a guy who my father was treating—my dad was a psychiatrist—and this patient had several shirts on him because it was self-protective, because if you're frightened, confused, alarmed you would think this clothing is armor.

The journal that Spider is constantly scribbling in is interesting because it's illegible, the viewer is shown what he is writing but it is indecipherable. Was that a big decision?

Yes, because in the novel the journal sort of *is* the novel, what he's scribbling away at is what we're reading, whereas Cronenberg wanted to get away from an articulate and literate Spider and also was interested in Spider as a representative of the artist attempting to make sense, make a pattern out of this confusion of feelings and perceptions and memories. And this hieroglyphic writing Cronenberg sees as the work of the artist trying to somehow render reality in some kind of design.

Also in the novel there's a sense that as long as he's writing he can make sense of things.

That's right, you find that as the story gets more and more disturbed and horrific for him, the more frenzied is his attempt to get it all down and keep it all organized and under control in his journal.

Spider's obsessed with smoking, isn't he?

Oh yes, like many mental patients for whom life is very tedious, smoking is one of the few activities that can be conducted for pleasure.

To me one of the most important scenes, tonally in the book, is the huge threshold that Spider crosses—from the present, into the past— only because he has seen himself in a window of his old house. I was wondering how this came to you?

Well, once we'd decided that he had to be in his own memories, then this seemed to be a way to get to that, to have him approach his house; and suddenly we're twenty years in the past. Once we spend some time with his younger self, I think we get the sense that that's his younger self, nobody can be in any doubt. That convention is established and I think that it is very elegant and economical. And the little boy, I didn't write it, but he gets the little boy picking up garbage, like we'd just seen Spider doing ten minutes before.

The dialogue was very authentic sounding. Was there any research you did on that?

I was reading stuff like novels of the period of working class life, J. B. Priestley and George Orwell, I was looking at movies. I was immersed in the working-class culture of 1930s East End, and I was trying to absorb it and then play it out again in dialogue.

Spider's parents don't have a lot to be happy about, do they?

I always thought they were probably like most couples; they were happy part of the time, they were miserable part of the time. They had a rather restricted life; there was obviously no money and it was a very little house. But they get through by going to the pub, sex, their little boy, the allotment, the garden; it's not a joyless life but there are a lot of stresses in it.

How did you come up with his nickname, Spider?

The weaving of webs is what Spider has always been about, circular structures rather than linear structures. The center of his existence was the death of his mother and he goes round and round and round it, and it takes him until the end of the story to actually get to the center and see what . . .

With all the twists and added twists, were you worried that something like the gasworks as a foreshadowing was going to give away the ending? Because in a way you are building towards a surprise twist.

I don't think so. I never thought anything was giving, I thought we were making the audience work quite hard to see things. For example, when Spider's turning the pornographic photo into the woman in the pub, but the woman in the pub he's already transformed into some sort of version of his mother. So I got the feeling people had to work quite hard just to keep up with what's going on and there's not much room for shooting forward.

What was your internal barometer as far as trying to gauge how far the audience was going to go in being able to pick through these narrative clues?

In terms of the audience I really couldn't gauge it, and I gave that problem all to Cronenberg—or rather Cronenberg assumed that problem. When I first saw the film I simply couldn't gauge whether somebody who didn't know the story was going to get it. I just had to trust that David knew what he was doing and got it right.

I remember there was a screening in Cambridge where my cousin lives and I asked her whether she finally understood what was going on in Spider's psyche. My cousin's not a "film person" in particular but she's smart, and she said, "Yes, at this point we realize that the mother and the woman are the same one." She went on and laid it out beautifully and I thought, "Yes, Cronenberg got it right." The alert audience is getting the information at exactly the right moments. I hadn't been able to gauge that.

In addition to economy, I also learned about subtlety from Cronenberg. In one scene David shot Spider's mother just trying on her slip. It's enough to indicate Spider's panic over his mother's sexuality. I'd written a scene in which he sees his parents having sex, and I wanted to hit it squarely on the head, but Cronenberg thought we could just do it with the slip. I still kind of think we could have done with a cruder, coarser piece of sexual activity than that, but that's the way he wanted to go.

When Spider's father murders his wife we get to the point where the story hinges and turns in the other direction. Did you want to put in those touches of surrealism, like kicking the body . . .

That was when I was writing the novel. I'd done the shovel, the blow; at that point I thought the scene ends there; you end the scene on the murder. But then I thought there's probably more in this scene if you follow the immediate aftermath of this terrible act of violence, so I wanted to show them disposing of the body and walking off. Then in the book I followed them through that night, to him waking the next morning with the hangover and the memory of what happened, just the ghastly aftermath and the first touches of guilt. He goes round the house looking for something to drink while she's asleep upstairs. I played all that out. And some of that made it into the script. I wanted to see the aftermath and at least get them back to the house.

One of the wonderful things I like most about filmmaking is that so much can be undersaid. We see that glass, his eye did that quick glance round, we don't need to see him picking it up and hiding it, that's enough to know and then we just get on with it.

The film's been called a horror film, and your novel has been called something like a horror classic. Which is funny, because in all the direction of the film there's none of the classic traits of horror—camera angles, manipulative score . . .

The best definition I read of horror was emotional horror being a combination of fear and disgust; and horror films set out to arouse both of those feelings. I think some suspense is aroused here but it's certainly not horror in the sense of that definition.

In fact, the majority of the film is Spider trying to piece together this puzzle.

And I hope there's also an emotional sympathy that's aroused with him, so that at the same time as you're busy trying to put together the puzzle, you're also engaged with his plight.

New York, New York

Alex Garland

9

ALEX GARLAND

28 Days Later . . .

"Structure is what I love."

Both of Alex Garland's novels, *The Tesseract* and *The Beach*, have been adapted into films. The latter was made in 2000 by the British writer-director-producer team of John Hodge, Andrew Macdonald and Danny Boyle, starring Leonardo DiCaprio. Macdonald and Boyle optioned Garland's first feature screenplay, *28 Days Later . . .* (2003), a zombie horror movie shot on digital video, which became a breakout commercial and critical success.

Synopsis

London, the present. Jim awakes from a coma to find the hospital, and the rest of London, deserted. He learns that in the past twenty-eight days, a blood-borne virus has been released from a research facility and has swept across Britain, killing many and turning most into murderous zombies. After coming across a handful of uninfected people, Jim and his companions go to Manchester, where they believe other survivors are gathering.

* * *

KEVIN CONROY SCOTT: *Your father Nicholas Garland is a cartoonist for a London newspaper. Could you tell me something about his work?*

ALEX GARLAND: I think his work is really relevant to me, in a way, because he does single-paneled political cartoons mainly, but he also had a huge interest in comic books. So when I was growing up I was reading comic books the whole time. They were just lying around the house, or stacked up and stored. Some of them were superheroes—Batman, Superman, *Marvel,* Stan Lee, that kind of stuff. There were also early *Mad* magazines, and particularly a guy called Harvey Kurtzman who my dad was absolutely crazy about. It became very relevant to me because the construction of comic strips has a lot in common with cinema. Storyboards are the obvious connection, but it meant that from an early age I had a complete way of thinking about narratives that have images, essentially. I can remember when I first got something published, which was the novel *The Beach,* and the reviews said, "This is like a film in the form of a novel." I suppose in some ways that's true, but it's also like a comic strip in the form of a novel. But because the reviewer was more familiar with film, that was the connection he drew. So I think that just growing up around someone who was drawing the whole time — and that's what my father did, every morning, he'd just be drawing if I was hanging around.

He would be reading the papers and thinking of political commentary?

Yes.

So was his line of work something you were interested in as a child, something you perhaps thought of doing?

Yes, I thought I was going to be a cartoonist, from age eleven or something like that. It's strange, because a lot of writers who I've met since writing ended up being my job; a lot of them spent their teenage years writing either aborted novels or completed novels, or poetry or short stories or something. So really what they were doing was working with words. Whereas up until the age of twenty-one, all I really did was draw.

Can you tell me something about some of the lessons you learned about constructing narratives from drawing cartoons?

One of the things I definitely learned was how redundant dialogue can be at times. What you can do is rely on the image; comic books and films do this the whole time. In a novel, you tend not to do that, you'll fill in a period where there isn't dialogue with prose writing that very often will go on inside someone's head — so in effect you're still having a kind of dialogue. With a comic strip, what you'll do is just a shot of someone thinking; but you won't necessarily know what's going on inside their head, and of course you'll get that in a film as well. So what it is, in effect, is an enforced "show-don't-tell." Of course, in terms of writing stories, you're told that it's a good idea to avoid lecturing and trying to keep the authorial voice out of a narrative; because as soon as the reader becomes aware of the authorial voice, something's getting broken, which is essentially their connection with the characters and the plot. I think my understanding of comics made it quite easy for me to do that. Also comic strips are swift in the way that the story moves; they're often too swift, as it's dictated partly by how long it takes to draw something—so it forces a real economy. I think all those things were things I tried to appropriate. I thought, as a prose writer, I was aware of my strengths and weaknesses, and one of the things I thought was my strength was that I was very economical and stripped down. And then I got to screenplay writing and I realized actually I wasn't at all, that there was another whole area of economy that I hadn't tapped into.

Is this also because there's a limited amount of space to actually write the dialogue in, or to write in what's happening?

There's always a restriction in terms of the form, all of the various story-telling mediums will give you one type of restriction or another; the restriction in straight prose is that you can't rely on an image. But I think that in a way it's not so much to do with restriction, it's to do with confidence; it's actually getting to grips with a freedom rather than a restriction and the freedom is realizing, trying to sense, just how quick people are at picking up on something. If you have an image of someone looking sad and they say at the same time "I'm feeling very depressed" the words just aren't adding anything, in fact they're probably detracting. I think it's one of the hardest things to figure out when you're constructing a story, what people will absorb, what people will take and I still get very, very surprised by that. I get surprised that you can put a line, subtly, one-third of the way through the story and reference it again near the end and people will almost always have remembered the thing that you're referring back to. There's a terrific urge to overstate because you're afraid that people will miss something, and when I look at *28 Days Later*, for example, which is the only screenplay I have ever written that went straight through to being made into a film, one of the things I think is tonally wrong about it is that it spells stuff out at times when it really doesn't need to.

People have already made the connection.

Yeah, they're ahead of you. And it's very dangerous because a lot of times a point you're trying to make in a story—if you present it in a very bare way—it may well be quite trite. A point can be a good point if it's presented in a subtle way, it can be an embarrassing point if you present it in a clumsy way. The point is the same. It's just in the execution of the point.

Isn't it having an instinct about when your audience needs some information and you don't want to insult their intelligence?

You certainly don't want to do that, that's a key part of the equation. The difficulty you get is, as far as my experience is concerned, I've never worked on any "book or film" that's taken less than two years from start to finish. Two years as a solid block when you are only working on that thing. What always happens is that towards the end you completely lose track of any objectivity, you don't know how your reader or viewer is going to respond; suddenly you're really winging it, totally winging it. It was very interesting to me to work with very experienced filmmakers to realize they're winging it too.

One of the big revelations to me about cinema really was that getting together a group of people who are talented in no way guarantees that you'll get a good film at the end of it. All those frustrations I've felt with making films in the past, I suddenly began to understand why they might not have worked in the way that I might have expected them to work.

I read somewhere that you were interested in pursuing the comic book work but it took too long to create. Is that true? Is that the reason why you didn't take it to another level professionally?

You rationalize things afterwards, but before I started ever trying to write a novel I wrote a comic strip. It was sixty pages, the longest one I've ever done. The drawing side of it took just over six months and I remember afterwards I sat down and read it from start to finish— which of course you're doing constantly while you're creating it, I read it as a completed thing; I'd give it to friends and my dad to read and often sit in the room while they were reading it just trying to figure out how they were responding.

There's a very large crash-and-burn potential in that experiment.

Yes, but also it's a very good way of finding out what they think. People betray themselves quite easily by fidgeting or by whatever happens while they are reading or watching something. It would take the person about ten minutes to read it, and I thought, "I've worked six months on this thing, just on the drawing side of it, and people just fly through it." Then I sat down and read it myself and I thought "this is really insubstantial, it's like a short story, it doesn't have any of the weight that I hoped it would have," and I felt so dismayed by that I just abandoned comics on the spot.

How was your drawing? Were you OK?

For a twenty-one-year-old I was fine. About six months ago, I did an eight-page strip for a *Batman* comic which was illustrated by a guy called Sean Phillips, and when his drawings were e-mailed over and I saw what he'd done I realized I was borderline OK back then, but having spent ten years writing instead of drawing—and this guy's spent ten years drawing instead of writing—I'm way behind the standard that I should be at in order to pull it off. The long fantasy I've had—returning to comic strips and drawing them myself—I suddenly realized that I'm never going to be able to do that. You just need to be better, and I've lost ten years of practicing.

As a teenager coming up to university, were you drawn to classic literature, or contemporary classics? What kind of stuff were you reading?

I've only ever read people that I find easy to read and I'm not as well-read as a novelist should be. It's something I've sometimes felt self-conscious about. On the rare occasions I've been in a room with a bunch of novelists, I'm quickly left behind by their conversations. Actually, I think it's a good thing for me because it means that I've got a different set of references and I'm capable of exploiting them. But yeah, I did read a lot, I tended to read more non-fiction than fiction as a general rule. Unless a fiction narrative is constructed quite well—particularly after I started being interested in narrative construction, there would be certain things that, if I detected them I'd just stop reading and not go back. One of them was the author's voice, I always hated that.

You mean the first-person narration?

No, I mean if you're reading a book by Salman Rushdie he never lets you forget that it's by Salman Rushdie. I say that, by the way, never having read anything past the third page of Salman Rushdie, and so I could be wrong, but I don't really care if I'm wrong or right. It's useful to create a set of rules; you sort of say, "Well, this is the way I'm going to do something" and something about that is going to be reacting against the way other people do things. It's not exactly judgmental, it's personal.

I understand your mom is or was a psychoanalyst; do you see her as a helpful influence in understanding human nature? I was thinking that being around her might help you understand people and draw characters.

Maybe. My mom's specialist area is trauma, that's her field really, so it's people who've had something very tough happen to them in one way or another. I remember giving my agent 28 *Days Later* to read and he said, "Oh you've just done what you always do. It's a bunch of characters who are stuck between a rock and a hard place." So if I look at what I do, in some ways it's very visual in that I always looked to comic strips, and that would be because of my dad. And then there's also the very extreme situations that the characters I write about are in, so I'm sure there's something there to do with my mom. But lots of writers write about the unconscious or have unconscious motivations for doing things, so it's not like you need a mom who's a psychoanalyst to propel you in that direction. Having said that, while I was growing up I was always hearing about the unconscious. I got packed off to a shrink when I was about twelve. I was there till I was seventeen. I would have thought that spending a couple of times a week talking over various sorts of stuff when you are a teenager . . . it's a formative age, so it's going to find its way in there.

You went to university in Manchester. How deep was your interest in cinema then?

I've always had an interest in cinema, and when I'd go out often it would be to see a film. The true way to describe this, I've just realized—to describe this era of my interest in film—was that aged sixteen or seventeen I knew there was this film *Taxi Driver* that I really should have seen, and that I wanted to see; and I think probably if somebody had asked me at that age, "Have you seen *Taxi Driver*?" I would have said, "Yeah, yeah. Brilliant film." But I didn't actually see it until I was at university. It was a long time since that had been on the cinema circuit, and I didn't have a video player, so I missed out on the opportunities that would have provided me. But I had an interest, and then I explored it, and I got really stuck on films.

When I left university, I moved back home to my mother's house. She had then got a VCR and for about three years, while I was working on *The Beach*, I would go to the video shop pretty much every day and rent one film, quite often two and sometimes three. And looking back on it, it's odd, because what I was doing was trying to write a novel but what I was actually doing was watching hundreds of films, everything I could, till very soon I got to the point where I couldn't find anything I hadn't seen in the video shop.

It's not like films hadn't been a big part of my life beforehand, it's just they'd been restricted. I think one of the reasons why George

Romero's films, *Dawn of the Dead, Day of the Dead* and *Night of the Living Dead*, had an impact on me was because there was a guy on my street who did have a VCR and one of the bunch of films we'd watched had been those Romero films. This was when I was fourteen. Also, this is something to do with my age, I'm thirty-three now and in my teens it wasn't the case that everybody had a VCR like everybody does now. But these films were talked about at school. Everybody talked about *The Evil Dead* and you could get away with not watching *Taxi Driver* but you had to see *The Evil Dead*.

When you were writing The Beach *and you were seeing all these films, did you have any concrete ideas about one day becoming a screenwriter?*

Yeah, I did. I think it had something to do with the comic-book background that I used to see everything storyboarded; when I was imagining a chapter, I would see it as a series of images. I always listen to music when I'm writing and I'd choose a piece of music that would effectively score or soundtrack a chapter. I was aware when I was doing it that it was something that belonged to cinema and not to comic strips. I remember when I sold the rights to *The Beach* I wanted to say, "This is the track that goes here, and this one goes there."

I guess, in a way, writing comic strips—where you're creating a whole new world full of characters, sets and dialogue. It's like being a film director, in a way, because you're in complete control of the universe.

Yes, it is, and the substantial difference between writing and drawing a comic book—or certainly writing a novel, compared to film work— is that film work is collaborative and that makes it different.

You did some travelling before university?

Before and after, in a way separate to all this comic strip writing and stuff. Really, if somebody at that point had said, "So what is it you're really into?" I would have said, "Backpacking." Again, that's a lot to do with my dad. When I was a kid, my dad would go off to India for six weeks or something on his own, quite extended periods of time, and come back with lots of stories and drawings. And when you're ten that has a huge effect on you. The first opportunity I had—which was when I was seventeen—I went to India and just got stuck into a whole backpacking thing, which really dominated the next ten years of my life. A lot of what I was concentrating on was how I'd get money to get another ticket. That didn't really stop until I was writing my second novel and I reached a point where I thought, "OK, I'm done with that."

Your first novel, The Beach—

It's just a backpacker book, basically.

Can you tell me how you went about creating it? A lot of times, first novels are aborted, it takes a while for writers to get going.

It came out of that aborted comic strip which was set in the Philippines but had some storytelling similarity; it was set on an island. It's the place I used to go to most.

It's where your second novel, The Tesseract, *is set.*

I'd been going back to the island for eight years. One of the things about backpacking was that most of my friends were backpackers too, but we never really used to talk about it. We'd go away separately and come back, say where we'd been but you wouldn't really talk; people just hate hearing backpacker's stories and not without good reason, they're boring and narcissistic usually. I remember the first time I sent *The Beach* to a publisher to try and get a deal, I was about halfway through it. The publisher wrote back—I kept the letter—and said, "It sounds like one of these backpacker stories that nobody wants to hear." It really struck a chord with me because I was thinking, "It probably is, because that's what backpacker stories were like." I was very concerned about that.

Can you tell me something about how you constructed the novel?

Just chapter by chapter. I always write prose the same way. I don't really rewrite the whole. I'll write a chapter and rewrite a huge amount while I'm writing it but then once I've printed it, it's done; then I move on to the next chapter. With *The Beach* it meant that the story is incredibly A, B, C, sequential, it's completely linear, it doesn't really look back, it doesn't jump around; also, you don't get a back-story, you just get a little look into a window of time; there's not much about what happens before or after that time. That's because I was really learning on the fly about how you write a novel. I would constantly take books off shelves wondering how you differentiate between three different characters talking at the same time. Do you keep saying "Joe said, John said" or can you attribute the dialogue in other ways?

So you're learning all that stuff for the first time.

Real nuts and bolts, grammar and commas and things like that. I hadn't really been writing prose. I didn't really know how you use a colon or where you put a comma in a sentence. J. G. Ballard and Kazuo Ishiguro—I was always referring to stuff by them. I'm a big fan of Ballard.

The Beach became an international bestseller; it was one of those books that you saw people reading on the London Underground. Did you feel pigeonholed as a novelist, an author of a book for backpackers?

I didn't feel it back then, but I felt it later, because when I then went on to write a film—which was something I'd wanted to do for a while—suddenly I discovered that it didn't count as writing. In Britain I got this weird tag of having writer's block because I haven't written a novel since the second one, which is essentially like saying screenwriting doesn't count as writing. I would have thought that you can't have writer's block *and* write a screenplay, you just can't do both at the same time. So I realized, at that time, I was pigeonholed but it wasn't by the thing I thought it would be about, which was "that guy who writes backpacker fiction," it was something much vaguer than that, more insidious in a way.

In either one of your novels, were you ever interested in adapting your own novels for the screen?

Well, I gave it a crack with *The Tesseract*. But when I sold *The Beach* to Andrew Macdonald, Danny Boyle and John Hodge, I was aware that this was a trio: John wrote, Danny directed and Andrew produced; that was the way these guys worked. So I wasn't expecting to have a crack at writing the screenplay for *The Beach*. In a way I wanted to but in another way—at the point I sold it I was a third of the way into *The Tesseract*—and in real terms I knew that I had to finish that story. Partly I had a contract to do it but I also thought that if I don't do this I'll be putting myself in a bad situation. *The Beach* was working as a novel, it was selling, and I was aware that there was going to be this pressure that comes about from having a first novel that does well. I thought, "I've just got to plough through the second novel so I don't get distracted."

You probably knew there are a lot of distractions because of the novel's success; it makes a lot of demands.

I'm always surprised by rock stars who earn a lot of money and then blow all their money and are surprised they've done that. It's such a cliché, but surely everybody knows that this is one of the things that can happen. If you get a lot of money for your first album, don't spend it all on a Ferrari because your second album might not do so well. That same cliché exists with first novels; your first novel goes well and your second novel tanks. Or you write a successful first novel and you feel you can never live up to it so you won't write anything again. I knew that existed as a cliché and I thought I'd got to try to sidestep it somehow.

So can you tell me about how you got into writing screenplays?

I finished *The Tesseract* and at that time *The Beach* had just gone into production. I had literally no involvement in the making of the film but I did go out to Thailand and just watched them doing it for a couple of weeks, just to see what happens. I was doing it in a very calculated way; I had a big interest in films, I wanted to get involved and I thought this would be a good learning experience. So I went out there to try and learn as much as I could in that two-week period. One of the things that really struck me about it was that it felt like it was just fun, it looked like how I imagined it to be, which was the sense of being in a big undertaking with a group of people and everyone pulling in the same direction, that sort of thing. Novel writing, you're stuck in a room on your own, that's what it is, but film is a whole enterprise with a large group of people. I've always been fascinated by behind-the-scenes stuff, I always loved documentaries about how films were made. When I was a teenager one of my favorite books was the Industrial Light and Magic corporate book, which is all about how Industrial Light and Magic came about and how they did special effects. I didn't have any particular interest in special effects, I just loved all the behind-the-scenes stuff.

When I got back from Thailand, I thought it was the right time to write a screenplay. I thought John, Andrew and Danny had a brilliant setup: writer, producer and director. It's a fantastic way to go about making a film. I could see that quite clearly. A couple of times I'd sit in on a meeting the three of them were having and you could tell that this was the core area where this film was being made; it was really being made by these three people. There was all this other stuff going on around but if you wanted to get to the heart of it you had to be in that room. I knew two guys, Nick Goldsmith and Garth Jennings, who are a very successful producer/director team and I thought maybe the three of us could work together. So me, Garth and Nick would sit down together to work on this spec script, *The Silver Stream.* A funny little thing about Chile and Russia, all a bit weird. We were completely innocent and didn't know what we were doing. One of the difficulties we had, though, was that there were two writers on the project. Now with Danny, Andrew and John—Danny and Andrew are not writers, even though they have a very good understanding of storytelling. Garth is a writer, he wrote some scenes in that screenplay and we worked on it together, and very well up to a point. And then Garth suddenly turned up at my flat one day saying, "Listen, I just can't work with you because this is really dark and violent and I just don't want to work on a film like that, it's not the kind of stuff I do." He was absolutely right. But it was quite hard for me because I was being fired, essentially. Well, he was saying he didn't want to work with me.

The Silver Stream *revolves around an official who works for the Communist Party whose job is to interrogate soldiers, then finds himself interrogating his own son.*

Yes, that's part of it, and then the other part goes to Chile. Because of the interrogation sequences, it sometimes got very dark and violent and grisly. Garth said this thing to me and I felt quite hurt and shocked at the time. But then I went off and wrote *28 Days Later*—a weird zombie film.

How did you prepare yourself for writing your first screenplay? Did you take Robert McKee's course or read Syd Field books?

No, I always felt distrustful of that. Maybe that McKee guy is terrific, I don't know. And, actually, I do write in a three-act structure sort of way. But really what I did was, in effect, take a course because I said to Andrew Macdonald, "Can you give me a bunch of screenplays so I know what they look like?" I didn't really know what I was doing, I don't think I even understood that I had to specify interior or exterior. It was right back to writing *The Beach*: how do you do this? Just nuts and bolts and inventing it as you go along. I haven't been able to bring myself to look at *The Silver Stream* for ages but I know if I did I'd probably see that there are some strong sections in there but in other ways it would be hopeless.

What I was trying to do was learn. I think that there are some writers out there who can just pick it up and do it, but I've never been like that. Before I did *The Beach* I wrote another whole book, which I didn't mention. When I said to myself I was going to write a screenplay, I expected to write at least one before I ever wrote one that could be made into a film because that's just the way it tends to be. You've just got to learn. Writing is so mechanical in so many ways. I just got sent a treatment for something, full of typos, and it was borderline illiterate with incredible misuse of apostrophes—which is sort of a *bête noire*. I read it and thought, "I don't really care what this fucking treatment is like, it's not even spelled properly." So I'm a big believer in nuts and bolts.

Even though your books are very cinematic with sharp, short scenes, I would think that writing a screenplay is a more different exercise for a variety of reasons. What were the hard lessons you learned between writing a novel and writing a screenplay—was there anything you thought would be easy and was actually very hard?

Yes, it was *all* hard. I thought the dialogue that I wrote was quite good, I thought it was one of my strong points—until I started writing a screenplay and realized it wasn't. It's actually one of my weak points; my strong point is probably keeping a story moving. I thought that I was an economical writer and it turned out I wasn't. I remember getting script notes on *28 Days* from John Hodge and I remember John saying, "This scene; why don't you just stop it there? Why have you got all this other stuff? Just cut it there, lose the scene afterwards and cut to there." As soon as he said it, I could see yes, he's absolutely right, I just wasn't able to see it myself initially. In terms of the struggle, the truth of it is— if I can explain this properly—I'm generally amateurish and clumsy as a writer and I think when people react against something I've written, when people say, "Why is this guy a bestselling novelist?" or "Why did *28 Days Later* get made as a film?" what they're doing is seeing all the amateurish crap that's in there and correctly identifying what it is.

Is this something that's always at the back of your mind when you're writing?

Well, it's something that I realized subsequently. When I'm writing a scene, I sit there and think "Yeah, this is great, I can really do this" and then subsequently realize I can't. But somehow I've adopted a way of almost using it to my advantage . . .

Can you try to explain that?

It's really hard to explain. People's first films and novels have a kind of energy in them, I think, which is to do with how hard they're struggling against technical problems. It's the tension between what you want to do and the limits of your ability to achieve that thing. I think that this energy makes first films and first books often very attractive; there's something very rewarding for the reader or the viewers, it's got a kind of life to it, it's got rough edges. The thing that I've managed to achieve is holding on to the rough-and-ready feel of that first project. It is because of limitations of ability, I freely accept and acknowledge that, and I know why it frustrates people who really don't like my stuff because what they can do is correctly identify that "this guy is limited by ability." But lots of other people, I think, respond to the plus side of it, which is something to do with energy and a space that is left for the reader and viewer to fill in gaps. It's not slick—one thing *28 Days Later* is not is slick; *The Beach* is not slick either; *The Tesseract* isn't slick. It's got whole gaps and things that don't fit and it leaves space for the imagination. It makes it like an act of participation for the person who's receiving this thing. As long as there's an internal coherence to the overall story, as long as it's consistent to itself, the viewer or the reader will be able to figure out what happens in those spaces.

And probably thank you without even knowing it because you've given them the credit to figure it out themselves.

Except, for the most part, it's not something I do deliberately, it's something I do helplessly. Although sometimes what you do is you start to play to your strengths and I think what I was doing from an early point was playing on my strengths. I thought, "Well, I haven't spent my teenage years writing, I'm not as adept at this as I could be." I remember when I was writing *The Beach* I made a decision early on. There was a character, Françoise, a pretty French girl who I could have described but I didn't; I think I gave the color of her hair and that's it. I knew that every reader would be able to provide an image of what that girl was like and, in a way, it was to my advantage not to provide the image too clearly in case it clashed with their idea of what a pretty French girl was. I think one of the reasons I worked well with Danny on *28 Days Later* is that Danny is very similar. I think Danny tries to hold on to a sense of clumsiness. Whereas Spielberg wouldn't want to do it because he's got all the technical ability you could dream of. He did that thing, I suppose, of learning how to do it when he was young.

About The Silver Stream—*I was wondering what kind of things you learned about the film business working on this script.*

I learned that actually getting a film made would be really, really hard and what you have to do is limit who you talk to about it and just stick to meeting people who can get things done. I was amazed by how many chancers there are in the film industry, how many people there are who say "I can do this" but just can't; they don't have access to money, they say they do but they don't. So I realized that ultimately what you've got to do is you have to talk to the right people because at some point somebody's going to have to write you a check for a hell of a lot of money and not many people have access to that. Thick skin too, that's the other thing—against people saying it's not going to work. Because you're going to get a lot of that. One part is important, which is the self-critical facility, but some kind of bulldozing arrogance has got to be there too.

Don't you think you need that kind of naiveté to get it made because otherwise if you think about all the roadblocks and all the land mines and how long it's going to take and how long you might not get paid, don't you think you might not do it in the first place?

I know what you mean and I think there is a big element of naiveté that is useful to have. It's useful if you don't know how hard it's going to be and then you don't get dissuaded at an early stage. But at a certain point, it is going to get hard, and then you've got to keep going and the people you're working with have to keep going too, and at that point naiveté is not doing you any good at all; you've got to draw on something else. In a way, the thing to hold on to is not so much naiveté but that it's possible; it's clearly possible because lots of people do it, so if lots of people do it it's got to be do-able.

Stanley Kubrick said that the only thing that kept him going was that when he was younger he went to a lot of bad movies and he said, "Well, when I come to make my film I know it won't be that bad."

That's a really interesting thing because you develop all these pet theories about filmmaking or writing or whatever it happens to be. One of my pet theories about a film is that a film's natural state is bad, that any given film left to its own devices will be a bad film and that what you're doing—or what I felt I was doing—was not struggling to make a good film but struggling to make a film that wasn't bad. That was its natural default position: unless you become obsessed with all the things that can go wrong, they'll get you.

Can you tell me something about how you go about writing a screenplay? When you get the idea, do you do an outline, do you do note-cards and all that kind of stuff?

The first thing I do is on a sheet of A4 paper I'll write it down. I'll be somewhere and suddenly a story will start to form and as quickly as possible on a sheet of A4 paper I will write it down. It's the only bit I do as handwriting, the beats of the story really, this happens; then this happens, then that happens. So the whole story would be maybe seven lines or something like that—a guy wakes up in a hospital, the world's destroyed, meets some other people, that kind of thing. Then, ideally, later that day or the next day, I'll just start writing it and I'll aim to get about a quarter of the screenplay written in about twenty-four hours. And if I fail to do that, which is usually the case, then I'll stop working on it usually.

I've never heard anyone work like that.

Well, I just think the difference between screenplay writing and prose writing is that you can write screenplays incredibly fast because you don't have to worry about any sense of sentence construction or how it reads; you don't have to give a shit about any of that stuff except where dialogue is concerned, all you're really concerned about is dialogue and structure. Screenplays are much more fluid than prose writing. So I'd aim to get, in a day . . .

About twenty-five pages?

Yes, something like that. I'd aim to get that done, not feeling as I would with prose writing that this is now set in stone but that these are the scenes, this is roughly what's happening with the scene, this is roughly what they're saying. I'd aim to get the whole first draft done in about four days.

Really? Do they just come to you whole, these characters? The idea? Isn't there so much you have to do before you sit down? How do you know that you're not going in all sorts of directions if you haven't thought it out?

Well, you've got your sheet of A4 paper which is stuck next to your monitor so you can keep referring to that. I can tell you another thing that happens is that about a third to half of the way through, it then begins to veer away from what you have on the paper, that's true of books as well for me. The thing I thought would be the end of the book turns out not to be the end of the book. The thing about it is that I think you don't have to worry about how it reads because it's completely private, you're not thinking at that point of showing anybody, you just want to get to the end and see if it holds together. Many times I've had the experience of writing the first quarter or the first third and then suddenly hitting a wall and thinking it doesn't work, that's it. That probably sounds more impressive than it is, speed sounds impressive in a funny way; so to qualify it heavily, I almost always work in a genre, apart from *The Tesseract*. The thing with a genre is you've got a pretty shrewd idea what's going to happen next because the genre dictates. If you're working outside a genre, like Charlie Kaufman, you have to invent all this stuff. I don't have to invent it because it's being supplied by the twenty or thirty people who worked before me on that kind of thing.

So in a way the road map is there, it's just a matter of subverting the rules as they stand.

It's what I love about genre, it gives you a structure and a whole lot of rules. I'm a big structuralist. Structure is what I love, to tell you the truth.

I would say that's your big strength, wouldn't you say?

Well, you've got to have one so that might as well be it! *The Beach* is like an action adventure sort of *Boy's Own* story, so you've got a triangle with the protagonist and a pretty girl and the pretty girl's boyfriend. Genre or storytelling would pretty much dictate that at some point your protagonist and the pretty girl are going to get together and that just gives you an easy lead. Just don't do it—and suddenly you've subverted it. Actually one of the things that we've been taking a bit of stick over in *28 Days* is for being predictable, providing a sort of happy ending.

A hopeful ending.

Yes. In a way I saw that as being a subversion of genre because what would tend to happen at the end was a hand would shoot out of the grave or a zombie would rise out of the grave, to give your audience a sting—let them know that they're still fucked.

Getting back to the writing process: you've got this loose first draft, then what happens from there? Do you give yourself a few days? Do you show it to anyone?

I showed *28 Days Later* to Andrew.

And you'd written it in only five days?

Yeah, because by that point I knew Andrew really well, we'd got to know each other while he was making *The Beach* and we had socialized. What we'd do was go out to lunch and I said to Andrew before I wrote it that I'd had an idea for a zombie film. The idea I had was these running zombies and it would all be shot on these bleached hot streets, which in retrospect I can see is connected to the opening of *The Omega Man* where you get this amazing city and this hot California sunshine. One of the things that has often bothered me about British film is you never get blue skies, it's always slate gray; actually, of course, you do get clear skies but the problem is you can't rely on them for filming purposes. But I said to Andrew I had an idea and I was going to try to do something, and then gave it to him about a week later.

Really, you felt confident enough to give it to a successful producer after only spending five days on it? Weren't you worried about first impressions being the most important?

Well, it is important but if something's got any merit—and someone like Andrew has any merit as a producer—then they're going to see there's something there worth pursuing. If I hadn't known him, I would never have sent that script in that state to Working Title or Warner Brothers or try to get an agent. That would have been suicide.

You said when you're writing you listen to music, do you still do that?

Yes, all the time.

What does that do to you? Does it help establish tone? Does it help get inside the character's head?

It helps establish tone and if I'm writing a certain kind of thing and I put the wrong music on, it will work to the detriment of what I'm trying to write. That's another good thing about working with Danny—Danny's really musical. My fantasy of telling him what *The Beach* soundtrack would be was insane because the one thing that Danny keeps a real grip on is what the soundtrack is and how the score works. Quite early on Danny gave me and Andrew some CDs of a band he felt were the musical tone for the film and I used to listen to that stuff just on repeat play.

This is a question I've been asking everyone, it's kind of personal but interesting nonetheless: when you're writing and things aren't going well, you realize there are flaws, how do you deal with feelings of self-doubt that arise?

That's an interesting question. Basically, my response to these feelings is that I'm in no way afraid of them, they don't freak me out because I'm completely aware that if they weren't there then I could feel really sure what I was writing was crap; if I didn't have those feelings then that would be a problem. What I tend to do—I work at night generally, and I'll work until very late until I'm very tired, and you slip into a funny twilight territory where suddenly you'll loosen up. Listen, if I'm going to be completely honest in my answer to the question, what I sometimes do is smoke a joint. Personally, I don't find writing when I'm stoned helpful. I'm never really stoned when I'm writing, except at certain times when you can use it to distance yourself.

To get you out of a rut.

Yeah, it definitely gets you out of a rut, it just pulls you away from what you're doing, and suddenly what you'll do is try an idea you wouldn't have come up with otherwise.

So it helps you make associations in your mind that were very hard to come by.

It helps you make associations. Also, sometimes by trying something which is wrong, it allows you to see what's strong about the thing that you were trying. It's really important to be able to figure out what's wrong in a scene, but it's also really important to figure out what's right. I suppose what I try and do is figure out what's right, but an oblique approach can be a good one. There's a scene in *28 Days Later* where the hero kills a kid with a baseball bat and that came very late in the day. There was a problem in the third act which was a thematic problem. We all knew that the protagonist had to get ejected from the house and then come back; it just felt like what had to happen. He had to be thrown out to the dangerous outside and then come back in and bring the infected with him. There were all sorts of problems about how you bring this about, and we were all struggling with this for ages and it turned out to be that he kills a kid earlier on and then this leads to a conversation between an army major and the protagonist, Jim, where he's asking, "Have you ever killed anyone?" and yes, Jim has, he's killed a kid. That came about through me being completely at a loss how to solve his problem, getting stoned and coming up with a deeply unpleasant idea, but one which is useful for the story.

In other ways it foreshadows the kind of violence that was to come, what he has to do and how grisly that is.

Yeah.

Starting to talk more specifically about 28 Days Later, *in the introduction to the published screenplay you mention some very interesting references for the film—you talk about Stephen King,* The Omega Man, *David Cronenberg—I was just wondering if you could take me through where the idea came from, how you incubated it and where these influences came from, their roles.*

They're all complimentary in a way. Ballard is the big one, on this film he's the biggest. It's partly because he wrote these post-apocalyptic stories and that's what this is, but it's also to do with atmosphere. Two guys on that list, one is Ballard and the other is this comic strip writer and artist called Daniel Clowes, both of whom have written surrealist stuff. He did *Ghost World* too, which is less surreal but it still has a surreal feel. I always saw this as being a surrealist film in some ways so its logic gets very broken in some places but for my part that never really concerned me. I think what I got from those guys was about how you can execute surrealism without having to resort to a fish suddenly landing on your table and a train crashing out of the fireplace.

When people think of the big surrealist directors, like Luis Buñuel, in contemporary times they think of David Lynch, which he is without question. But just on the surrealist front David Cronenberg pushed buttons. I mean, *Dead Ringers* seems like a perfect example; you know it's based on a true story and it's never that explicitly surreal, apart from the strange instruments that these gynecologists produce. There was just something about the atmosphere the whole way through. I was just trying to approximate something like that.

You mentioned George Romero—were you thinking of a modern version of a George Romero?

I was never thinking of trying to update a Romero film, I was never thinking in those terms. It's more like this: I'm thinking about what I like and what I don't like; I like the fact that in any science fiction story or fantasy you've got an easy gift of social commentary that you can slip in there, that these films provided a really good template of how you could do that. Not just films but comics and books too.

I always think that's the beauty of making a film because you get all these interpretations or all these readings that you never thought of, and then you realize that maybe you did intend it but it was something that was coming from your subconscious; it wasn't something that was planned.

It's very true that, and the point at which I really realized that was with *The Beach,* which had elements of social commentary in there as well as things that weren't there but were seen to be. There's a whole thing about video games; I just happen to play video games and I really liked them. When I used to be a backpacker I used to take a Nintendo Gameboy because it used to eat up a long bus journey or plane journey just playing this thing. So I just put it in this book and suddenly it's this thing of "Oh, these people, even when they go to Utopia they have to take these video games!"

You talked in your introduction about your collaboration with Danny Boyle and Andrew Macdonald. I think you said you went through nearly fifty drafts together. I was just wondering why there were so many versions of the screenplay?

Well, on the one hand Danny and Andrew were working with a screenwriter who had never had anything written, who had then appeared on the screen, in terms of his own stuff. So very often they would be asking for changes—normal script development stuff—and I just wouldn't be able to execute them because there was a gap in my knowledge that didn't get filled until we were filming. For a long time Danny wanted the film to return to the laboratory, so it had a full circle quality, it begins in this lab and it comes back to the lab again. I just couldn't find a way of making that work which didn't feel like a contrivance; I tried to make it work, but it still felt like a contrivance. Maybe ten drafts are occupied with trying to do this thing that I just can't pull off so it ends up getting abandoned, that's partly it. But the other thing that happened was that Danny keeps the writer involved at every step; during casting, read-throughs, shooting and editing, you're always part of what's happening.

Were you there constantly tweaking too?

Exactly. So I'd sit in the read-throughs and suddenly realize a scene didn't work when people were talking it out loud—this line is redundant, this scene needs to be enlarged—so I'd make a bunch of changes. That happened even more so when we were filming. The film was shot in sequence so I was able to watch the first ten minutes of the rushes, loosely cut together by the editor, and suddenly I would see actors on a screen in the way that Danny was going to compose the shot and the cameraman was going to shoot it, all these sorts of things.

I think there were so many drafts initially because all of us—that is to say me, Danny and Andrew—were feeling our way through certain parts of the plot, structure and themes. We hadn't actually worked together before and I think that if they'd been working in this process with John Hodge—who had written Danny's previous films—there'd have been a lot less drafts because they'd have had a shorthand way of talking and they'd have been able to get to what was at the heart of the problem much quicker. In terms of shooting in sequence, I think it was the single most useful thing that could have happened to me as part of an education. As a screenwriter, if your first film is shot in sequence it's the best thing that can possibly happen because up to the first day of photography everything is abstract. You've watched a lot of films and you've written a screenplay but you've never really seen how a screenplay and a film really mesh and come together. You haven't seen what comes out of a screenplay, what it produces on screen. Within a few days of watching the edited rushes, I could see huge problems which I hadn't anticipated with the screenplay. I think it would have been impossible to anticipate them without seeing them on screen. You just don't know why a bit of dialogue will work on the page and not work in an actor's mouth without seeing it happening—suddenly, you see it happening and it's the clearest, most stark problem you could possibly imagine.

Can you remember a specific example?

The scene where I had a terrible, chilling revelation that the film would categorically not work in the way that it had been written was very early on and it was between the three characters—the two protagonists Jim and Selena and a third guy, Mark, who's shortly going to get the chop, but the audience shouldn't know that at that point. They're sitting in a newsagent's discussing what has happened to the world and the country. The scene is full of exposition, it's bringing your lead character up to speed and it's bringing your audience up to speed in a way that hopefully feels organic and part of the plot. Exposition is always tricky and you've got to try to misdirect as you're giving it—you have to do that in a novel in exactly the same way. But, essentially, the problem was as soon as you heard these people talking, it felt too expositional. It was clunky in a way that was like anvils dropping out of the sky and landing around you. I watched it and my blood ran cold. I just thought "Christ, this is a catastrophe." Not only that, seeing the way that scene worked when the actors were saying the words, it's very interesting that this did not appear to be a problem in the read-throughs; it was only a problem when you saw it on screen. I knew two things instantly: the first, without question, was that we'd have to reshoot that scene, it would have to be rewritten because what we had filmed at this point was useless. And the second thing was that there was going to be four or five scenes—or probably more—coming up through the film that would certainly hit exactly the same problem. I just had absolutely no doubt about this in my mind at all. Andrew also had no doubt as the producer, but Danny who was deep into the process of shooting day by day—in a way, I think it was particularly hard for Danny to step out and to observe and say "Oh yes, hang on, we do have a problem."

Anyway, if we hadn't been shooting in sequence and if I couldn't have sat down and watched the first ten minutes of the film unfold, I don't think that problem would have asserted itself in that kind of way and, crucially, I wouldn't have been able to start changing stuff later on. That said, it led to huge problems.

So how much of a panic were you in at this point?

I was in a panic, I was in a rage, I was absolutely furious.

With yourself?

With myself, with also just sort of realizing this thing that we have talked about already, which is to do with the fact that expertise and surrounding yourself with very talented people doesn't protect you against making elementary mistakes.

It's not an elementary mistake if the professionals you're working with haven't spotted it either, is it?

The thing about it is that what went wrong at that point was the responsibility of the screenwriter. You could say, "It's not my fault because there should have been people around me who were providing checks and balances." I just think that would be wrong because those people who are providing the checks and balances, they've got their own job to do and you've got your job. If in script meetings previously I was saying to Danny and Andrew "I'm not going to change this scene, this scene is the way I want it and this is how it's going to be," then you have to stand or fall by that. What I could see clearly was that I was going to fall and I had to do something very quickly. I certainly don't see that as being anyone else's responsibility.

Most directors don't involve the screenwriters in the production, so there are two key elements to your education: Danny involving you and the film being shot in sequence. What do you think would have happened in terms of your own development if those things hadn't happened?

I don't think I would have had that aspect of my development and education. So it was a huge learning curve and, of course, like all these things, it never really stops; it never feels like the curve is flattening out, it just turns out there's something else you weren't realizing, and then something else, and then something else. I think it's an endless process. It's endless until you just get worn out and tired of learning and at that point that's when your work becomes stale. I suspect that's the process that happens. You just stop caring. And there'll be some parts of writing where I've definitely stopped caring about things, things that used to really bother me and I'd try and get right. Now I know how to do them I've just stopped caring about getting them wrong.

It's like the point at which you leave one sentence or one scene and move on to the next is where, in some ways, you just get fed up with it; you just want to move on to something else. I think what happens is that I reach that point quicker now. It's not that you think to yourself it's as good as it's going to get; you just think it's as good as you're going to get it tonight, and that will do.

Looking back on 28 Days Later, *can you think of anything you'd like to change?*

One of the ways that one of the key problems was addressed was by introducing the idea that the country was quarantined. When we started shooting the country was not quarantined because the infection had spread around the whole globe. By the time that part of the filming was over, it was because this infection only affected Britain and that Britain had been quarantined by the rest of the world. It was a terrific idea in terms of paranoia and it came out of problems that were identified earlier on, and trying to fix those problems led to an elegant solution. The problem with it was that with an idea as substantial as that, you can't really just apply it late in the day entirely. I think we did it with eighty per cent success but not to a hundred per cent. By the time we got to the closing five or ten minutes of the film we reached a point where we did not know what to do. That is not a desirable state of affairs to be in when you're trying to sort out the last ten minutes of a story.

I think the reviews were very good. There's lot of respect given to your screenwriting, there's a lot of respect given to the fact that you're making a B movie that is doing much more. But there were these questions that came up such as, "If they're zombies, why are they moving fast? If they have this virus, why aren't they now dead?"

None of those problems bother me even remotely, didn't before, during or after. I had easy precedent for that as well. If you watch *Dawn of the Dead*, you don't know what's going on, you don't know why there are zombies everywhere and you really and truly don't care. I don't, anyway. So if I didn't care about it then, I don't care about it now. I really seriously dispute that audiences care as much as the industry often seems to think they do about that kind of explanation.

It's a suspension of disbelief.

Exactly, the audience will make a decision pretty early on about whether they're going to stay with you or not. If you want to know why that kind of concern is bullshit then go to the Internet Movie Database and look at viewers' comments about these films, because what they do is discuss between themselves why, say, the zombies run and they come up with these incredibly elaborate explanations which they seem to think are built into the fabric of the film but they're not, they're built into the fabric of their imaginations. That's who's created this because it certainly wasn't me, it certainly wasn't Danny or Andrew. I have no doubt in my mind that if the audience is engaging their imagination in that way with the film, that makes it a better experience, a more intimate experience.

There were other kinds of criticisms that bothered me a lot because they were true. They would say things like, "The dialogue is bad here, the plot is bad here." Those kinds of things bother me. If it's "Why do these zombies not attack each other?," it's because they don't. You can see on the screen they don't, so that's it.

Speaking of the ending, you said that Andrew, Danny and yourself discussed different endings for the film. Jim, Selena and Hannah are living in the countryside together as a surrogate family. Mankind has won in a way, then a fighter jet flies by and they wave up at it. It's interesting because Roger Ebert came up with an ending that . . .

He had a really good idea for the ending—the fighter jet dropping a bomb instead of just passing by and seeing them living there. As soon as I heard that I thought, "Shit, it's so obvious, that's what we should have done."

That leaves it open-ended in terms of who's controlling the outbreak of rage.

But as an audience member, it's exactly the right kind of bittersweet moment for the closing few seconds.

They've made it but there's still someone there to say . . .

It's infuriating, it could have been so simple, we had the budget.

Infuriating?

It drove me crazy.

It was a great idea.

It's elegant, that's the thing about it, the best solutions are always elegant. What I was always thinking in my head was the John Carpenter ending of *The Thing*, where Kurt Russell and the other guy are basically going to freeze to death in the snow, but they've saved the world and there's something kind of bleak but uplifting at the same time. It's a great genre ending to a great genre film. That's what I wanted and it's really not what we got.

What was your ending motivated by? Was it something that you thought fitted into the film, was it something that at the time you thought worked or was it something that you thought needed to be done in terms of making the film work for the audience?

All those things were going on at once. There were big pressures about whether the film would work for an audience. Before we'd shot any of these endings, we'd shown the film to test audiences up to the point where our heroes escape from this mansion full of soldiers where they've been stuck for the third act of the film. You can end the film there and it makes total sense as a narrative; you leave it open-ended, it worked totally. The test responses were pretty terrible, so there was a lot of concern at that point about why the film didn't work and how to fix it. That pressure comes from everywhere: it comes from yourself, it comes from the people you've been working with and it also comes from the people who've been financing the film. So that certainly played into what we were trying to do, what we were trying to fix.

Why did you change the ending from what you had originally?

This exactly ties up with what we were saying before in terms of quarantine. The ending of the film—when we started shooting—was that the three of them set up as a kind of family in a little cottage in the Lake District. There's a mom, a dad, and a daughter in a way—Jim, Selena, and Hannah—but none of them are related. Jim's not Hannah's Dad, Selena's not Hannah's mom, it's a fake family. That was the idea. Then we introduced the idea of quarantine in order to fix a problem early on and suddenly that's not the problem anymore because you know outside the boundaries of this country the rest of the world is OK, so you have to address the fact that these people are isolated here but the rest of the world is continuing as normal. So the ending that we had to begin with worked for the film that we had, but it stopped working halfway through.

You told me earlier in this interview that you aren't interested in back-story. Why?

I don't care about back-story. Sometimes back-story is truly necessary for plot reasons and it's a satisfying, crucial revelation that the reason the guy did this at this point in the film is because years ago this other thing happened to him. But I would say almost the whole time that's not the way in which back-story's used; back-story's used in a formulaic and talismanic way to make the audience feel that they understand the character. It's a shorthand for motivations; you don't really know why that motivation exists, you can interpret or imagine why that shorthand exists and be allowed into the storytelling part of it. I think that people do that unconsciously; you don't have to ask them to do that, they just do it anyway.

Back-stories are a version of exposition really.

Well, they are, quite. Very occasionally you need back-story and almost always you don't; if you just cut it all out I think the film becomes more interesting because you will understand the film totally but you won't feel like you've had every single jigsaw piece. It's a personal thing really, back-story doesn't interest me and tends to irritate me. If I'm enjoying a film and then suddenly there's a bit of unnecessary back-story at that point I have to sort of close my eyes and pretend it's not happening and then rejoin the film.

Talking about character motivation, does an idea drop out and that's where the character comes from or is it something that you're a little bit more pragmatic about?

At the front end I think, "Who is Jim and what's his character?" And I think he's a normal decent guy and in the normal sequence of events he's not going to kill anyone with a baseball bat, and that's pretty much what I think about Jim. Selena is tough, she was harder edged than Jim to begin with and she figured out very fast, independently, that in order to survive she needed to kill people with machetes. The way I see it is that if you have a scene where the three people, Jim, Selena and Mark, all get attacked and during that attack Jim sits on the floor quivering and getting covered with blood and being generally helpless; Selena kills everyone in sight with a machete and ruthlessly dispatches her friend Mark who's been infected; you know everything you need to know in terms of making the story move on from that point at that moment. Jim's scared, Selena's tough; she'll kill Jim too if he gets infected, and that's all the tension you need between those characters. Past that point a lot of it's just about how they talk to each other, what sort of things they say. Personally, I tend to discover that during the scene, as I'm writing.

It's not something you plan out, like this character needs to go from the beginning of the story where he says he wouldn't kill someone, to now he's someone who is?

I'm not really thinking about character arcs or anything like that. But this comes into the whole thing about influences and whether you do things consciously or unconsciously; I've seen so many films and read so many stories that I'll start shoving in character arcs without meaning to. One thing about not having been, as it were, formally trained by that scriptwriting guru guy about how to write the script: all my stories have three acts, I've got no idea why. I don't think to myself "Time to construct a three-act story," but when I look at it I can see the first act, second and third. It happens every time.

The other thing is that I'm working usually within one genre or another and genres have their own structures. You have a bunch of people, you know that some of those people are going to die; I know, and I think the audience knows, that a certain guy's not going to stick around long. They know that, I know that and you just have to get on with it.

Going back to that problematic scene in the shop. Selena, after killing Mark, explains to Jim that if someone becomes infected by coming into contact with a zombie's blood you've got twenty seconds to kill them before they try to kill you. Roger Ebert said that rule does three things: the first is that it has you counting down to a crucial moment, you know that something is going to happen; the second is it eliminates the standard story device of keeping the infection secret; and the third is the quick elimination of likeable characters.

A memory just popped into my mind, a film called *Under Fire* with Nick Nolte and Gene Hackman. In it there's a sequence where Nolte and Hackman are driving along and they get stopped. Nolte's sitting in the car and Hackman is led away and he's just talking to a bunch of guys with guns. And suddenly one of those guys lifts up a gun—you can't hear the exchange between Gene Hackman and this guy—but he lifts up the gun and shoots Hackman dead. You see this from Nolte's point of view and it's completely shocking. It also felt to me exactly what that moment should be, it should really surprise you. It doesn't have a long buildup. It always stuck with me and unconsciously I'd have been trying to replicate that atmosphere of a death that is shocking in a particular kind of way.

In many films there are scenes when people are dying and it's prolonged, but you're taking the element of surprise.

In my experience, violence tends to be shockingly sudden, you didn't quite anticipate how serious it was going to get, and there isn't an extended buildup. The extended buildup is a kind of sadism, and in the context of a film it's a sadism with regard to the audience. It just doesn't push any buttons with me. I find it kind of boring, actually, because you get too far ahead of the narrative, I suppose. It's an odd thing for me to say because in many ways I'm very bound in genre and a lot of what I like is the fact that the audience is slightly ahead of you and you're all on familiar territory. But when it comes to that particular issue—that kind of teasing relationship with violence and the audience doesn't do it for me.

Where did the idea come from to set the rules about the infection, the rage?

The genesis of the film was me and Andrew Macdonald having a pizza, and he said, "What kind of film would you like to make?" And I said, "I'd like to make a zombie film where zombies run. And it will be quick and brutal and pacy." For me the twenty-second infection just came out of the idea that the zombies run; it's a different speed, everything's quicker. There's nothing more sophisticated to it than a pitch over a pizza.

How did you handle the romantic side between Jim and Selena?

I didn't.

There's a peck on the cheek. Did you write anything into the screenplay?

I tend to really subdue that kind of thing between the boy and the girl. That's one of the expectations that I'm keener to subvert rather than just play into. There are some genre conventions I love, and some that I find less interesting. Exactly the same as *The Beach* novel—I had an unresolved thing, an attraction that was more on the part of the boy than the girl, maybe because of my own life experiences! It works for me. I quite like the idea that there are incredibly beautiful girls who these rather normal guys just kind of pine after. So again, as with *The Beach* film, Danny made the boy and the girl get together, which they don't in the book. I had less control over that. In this instance, Danny wanted them to sleep with each other, I didn't want them to sleep with each other, and what we ended up with was them having this peck on the cheek. The only way I could do it in a way that would satisfy me was to do it in a really weird way. And so their real kiss is after Jim has just killed this guy in this terribly beautiful manner and his hands are covered in blood and it's a really blood-smeared kiss. And for me that made it funny.

A lot of this is just about "Does this interest you or doesn't it?" And the things that don't, I try to resist. Sometimes I can see they should be in there for a good reason. And in this case Danny was right; there should have been more of a thing between these two. The audience would respond to that, Danny responds to that—just because I'm not interested, it seems like an arbitrary reason in a joint project to refuse to let it happen, you've got to understand it's a collaboration and go with that. Now talk about film-making as a collaboration, but it gets marketed as "a film by."

London, England

MICHAEL TOLKIN

The New Age

"Most of the time we're making bad decisions
and running out of money."

Michael Tolkin is probably most famous for adapting his novel *The Player* for Robert Altman to direct in 1992. Tolkin's novels, such as *Under Radar* and *Among the Dead*, have earned him a legion of admirers in the literary world and have been translated into several languages. He has enjoyed great success working as a screenwriter for hire, co-writing films like *Changing Lanes* (2002) and *Deep Impact* (1998). He has written and directed two films, *The Rapture* (1991), starring Mimi Rogers, and *The New Age* (1994) starring Peter Weller and Judy Davis.

Synopsis

Los Angeles, the present. Peter and Katherine Witner are Southern California super-yuppies with great jobs but no center to their lives. When they both lose their jobs and embark on marital infidelities, their solution is to start their own business together. The store fails and they find themselves out of work. The Witners turn to a series of gurus whose prescriptions run from meditation in the desert to all-night pool orgies.

* * *

KEVIN CONROY SCOTT: *When you were a teenager, did you imagine yourself writing for a living one day?*

MICHAEL TOLKIN: I think from before that I knew I was going to be a writer, from when I was about eight or nine years old. When I was in seventh grade I did one of those "career day" reports on being a director. I was always writing . . .

You went to university in Vermont. What influenced that decision?

I started at a place called Bard in upstate New York and spent two years there, then I dropped out and spent a year working with disturbed

children. My girlfriend transferred up to a school in Vermont and I followed her.

And what sort of stuff were you writing at the time?

After I dropped out of college I wrote a screenplay about a town that
dies when a freeway goes by and it doesn't have an off-ramp. I turned
twenty-one after it was done, and I remember being excited by it. In
some ways it was a spiritual sequel to *Two-Lane Blacktop*, especially
in terms of the Harry Dean Stanton character in that movie. It
involved incest and it was very complicated. My father's agent gave it
to Steven Spielberg because I had seen *Duel* and really liked it. It took
a while for Spielberg to get back to him, but he sent me this very
encouraging note. So, that gave me some energy. But that was before
Vermont. There I studied under an American writer called Barry
Hannah, who never really gets his due. Then I got out of college and
went to New York, and I didn't know quite how I was going to do it,
but within six months or so I had sold my first article to the *Village
Voice*. Then for about four years I freelanced as a journalist, until
1978. By then, what I had gone into journalism for was changing:
People magazine had become too powerful, *Rolling Stone* lost its edge,
Esquire had lost its New Journalism cachet. The kind of stuff people
wanted me to write were character pieces about well-known people.
The stuff I had *written* was about comedians and late-night cable television and directors and commercials, oddball stuff. So I didn't make
much money but I learned something about New York, something
about life. While I was doing that I made friends with a guy named
Noah Goldwasser, who was a publisher of *Film Journal;* he knew an
English producer named Don Boyd, and Don and I had an idea for a
movie about a gossip columnist in New York. I met Don in New York
and kept in touch with him, I came out to California and wrote—my
brother and I were working together.

I didn't understand what movies were, I didn't really like them. If I
came to California with a goal, it was to create some sort of marriage
between Fassbinder and Spielberg, the idea for *The Player*—I knew it
was a book. And also at that point I wanted to see whether I was a real
writer—if I could do this thing by myself. I kept it secret, though. By
the time I finished the book only four people knew I had been writing.

How long did it take you to write the novel?

Three, four years? After I sold a script called *Gleaming the Cube*, I had
enough money and I didn't have to work too much. I took about four

meetings in one year and just worked on the novel.

Would you say writing The Player *was a reaction to what was happening to you in your meetings in Hollywood?*

Yes, but *The Player* was also a reaction to what I was reading at the time, which was a lot of James M. Cain and Patricia Highsmith. And when the idea came to me, it started as a joke. The original idea was to kill a number of writers, and no one thought it was a serial killer at work because there are so many unproduced writers. But that was a joke. And after I got to the murder of the first writer, I thought I could go around and concentrate on five or six people as potential killers or I could just concentrate on this one. It became for me, and still is, a story about guilt set in Hollywood, not a story about Hollywood. There was an Assistant Secretary of State in charge of Latin American affairs who had been involved in the Iran-Contra scandal named Elliot Abrams. He went before Congress, testified, and was lying. I knew he was lying when I was watching him. He wound up getting caught, and I think he was disbarred—he pleaded "No Contest." But he sat at that long table facing Congress, with his hand in his chin, like you had never seen anybody, with such contemptuous decorum. Watching him, I used to wonder how he could sleep at night. What was his conscience? Did he feel guilt? And I decided that he didn't. Tim Robbins's character, Griffin Mill, is much more based on Elliot Abrams than on anyone at any of the studios.

A film theorist once wrote, "All of Tolkin's characters abandon or fall from the mainstream and enact dramas of self-redefinition." Do you agree with that?

I don't want to be the centipede that tries to explain how he walks because then I'll trip. Is it true? Probably. Here's why. If you think about it in terms of *The New Age*, when you take everything away from somebody, then they have to find out who they really are. Let's say you commit a crime and you deal with the consequences of that, or, as in this movie, an act of over-confidence, of hubris, throwing themselves into the chaos of an economy at a time when people have to be mindful of making a living. The movie, in part, is about a dying, collapsing economy, and that was what I was specifically interested in: what happens when the society collapses economically? What happens to people? I was watching it around me during a small recession.

Ingmar Bergman once said—

About me? Oh, that's good because I talk about him a lot.

He said that cinema was his wife but the theater is his mistress. Do you think of writing novels as your mistress and screenwriting as your wife?

That's such a straight line. [*laughs*] I'm a bigamist. I don't have a problem having two wives.

But can you compare the process of writing a novel to writing a screenplay?

A screenplay is a very demanding form. It's like a sonnet. You're limited to length, you're limited to budget, you have to write something that will appeal to a bankable actor, and that people will think is commercial, and can be marketed. And you have to be realistic about that and how it relates to the way you work. In the novel, you can do anything you please. The novel is the last place that I know in Western civilization where you can be free, both as a reader and a writer, because a novel exists in the reader's mind as well as it exists in the writer's mind. The movie exists absolutely in the film's mind, although technically because of the DVD or the recorded film, you can control the speed of the film *somewhat*. But a Woody Allen movie takes ninety-two minutes to watch whether you watch that over a month or whether you watch it one evening. There's no time in a novel. Both of us could read the same book and it might take me three times as long or you three times as long just with the book in front of you. So that's not a small difference because that relationship, that *private* relationship with the book, is something that only you can have.

When you get stuck or discouraged when you are writing, how do you deal with self-doubt?

Well, you know there's that line of Beckett, "I can't go on, I'll go on." And I think that past a certain age or point in life a writer has to have the discipline to keep working at it whether they like it or not. But there are times when you just get lost in a particular piece of writing and you don't really know how to dig yourself out of the hole you've dug. I suppose you could talk about character? With self-doubt, you just have to do your best not to listen to it. Cowardice is a much greater threat than self-doubt. Self-doubt's different from cowardice. Cowardice is: "I think I know what I've got to do, but I can't. I don't want to sacrifice what I need to sacrifice in order to do this. I don't want to do the work I need to do to finish this." Self-doubt is just: "I can't." Cowardice is: "In order to do this I have to do something that I know may be beyond me, but I won't know that unless I really attempt it." Self-doubt is maybe a weaker form of cowardice. Self-doubt is also right sometimes; you are right to doubt yourself sometimes. But is self-doubt about the quality of the work, or the general abilities of the writer? And that's why God invented alcohol . . .

How does your day of writing go? Do you have a certain kind of pattern?

Oh, I'm a banker. I get up early, take care of family business, have breakfast and between 8:30 and 9:15 I'm in my office, and after that I finish at about 6 o'clock with a small lunch. I like to eat lunch starting around 12:15 so when people are making their end of the morning calls, I can take the call while I'm not writing; and then while everyone else is having lunch, I'm back at work. So nobody is calling me and I own that hour.

Is there a certain amount of pages that you aim for?

There are some novelists who make a five-page-a-day or five-hundred-words-a-day quota, and they write that every day. And when they finish one book, they start another and just keep to it. The page count is what defines them; they go to work for that. I've written some scripts very quickly. I've had twenty-five-page days. But I've also had two-page days and no-page days. Usually when I'm really working it's not so much the pages as not getting up from my desk until a certain time. So if I am stuck on a scene I won't let myself get up; it's like "I cannot leave this chair until noon. Not even to pee."

Really?

You don't really *have* to go to the bathroom; it's just nervousness, don't go. Just keep on writing. Then at noon, if I'm still writing, well then, obviously I keep going.

You've had great success improving screenplays that were written by other screenwriters. Can you tell me a little about how this rewrite process works?

Well, I've only gotten a credit on two. I've done a few uncredited jobs. The uncredited jobs were really assembly-line work. I was one of a number of writers on *Mission Impossible II* and *Road to Perdition*; I think there were five of us on that one.

How do you get contracted for this kind of work?

You sign a contract, a two-week contract that sets a boundary for your job. You just keep working past it. For example, I had a two-week job where the structure was pretty much what it had to be, but it came down to speeches and dialogue within scenes. That's the way the movies have been written from the very beginning. They've been almost always written by an assembly, with an assembly-line model. There was always a group of writers. The writer was never at the center of the film. Some movies may have one or two writers. In the thirties they had writers' *buildings*. F Scott Fitzgerald plugged himself into that and got a few credits, as did Faulkner at Warner Brothers. So it's not like the theater or the novel where the writer really controls it. I think it's because you take the camera on location. When you're writing a play, a play's in only one place, and you can sit behind the director and the director has to listen to you. But once you get outside of that and you start struggling, then technically it becomes something that has to be done by the director and the actors on the set, simply because there's a certain reality that demands a spontaneity and that spontaneity may mean that you have to ignore the script. There are some times when the script doesn't make sense for a particular moment because you're working so quickly and not rehearsing the way you do in theater or rewriting like in a novel, so you just have to make the changes there.

The two films I got credit on were *Deep Impact* and *Changing Lanes*. On *Deep Impact* Steven Spielberg asked me to do it. Originally Bruce Joel Rubin had been hired to do it — it wasn't his original idea — and he worked on it a year and a half, hit the wall because he didn't quite know what to do, so I spent a couple of months working on it with Spielberg because he was going to direct it. Then he couldn't, and they brought in Mimi Leder and I worked with her. So I was on that for over a year, and it was a big chunk of my life. With *Changing Lanes*, Scott Rudin had the script which Chap Taylor had written and I think they'd had it for three years, maybe more. And they showed it to a lot of writers and no one could quite figure out what it needed because they wanted to make it a high-concept comedy or a comedy of revenge. The basic setup is that two guys get into a car crash in the morning and spend the day screwing with each other, which is how it was presented to me. So I went and had a meeting with the producers and there was something about the idea that appealed to me. I think I sent Chap Taylor a note—I hope I did—saying that I was working on this and hoped that it would work out. The movie wasn't getting made anyway. He lives in New York and we got together and we traded and sent each other stuff. Initially, I don't know how easy it was for him, because it's painful and because it wasn't the movie he set out to write. But in the end, whether he was rewritten or it was a forced serial collaboration, I always liked his idea. I even had to rewrite myself at one point. I finished a draft. Rudin liked it, I liked it and then the studio balked at it and then it was three months before he called me and said, "Let's try it again." We had to rewrite the last ten pages which turned into rewriting the entire script and so I did it *completely* from the beginning. He could have hired someone else to rewrite me but he kept me on.

Your directorial debut The Rapture *has been described as a "low-budget, fundamentalist variation on* Close Encounters of the Third Kind." *Someone also said, "It seriously contemplates spiritual matters rarely dealt with in Hollywood films."*

I prefer the second one.

Where did the idea for The Rapture *come from?*

In 1984 I'd finished my first completely original screenplay in years. It was called *Cowboy Heaven*. The pitch of it is in the novel of *The Player*. It was the first thing I had promised myself I had to finish, and I did, and it was good. And it was winter and I remember that I had gone crazy. I was driving a little Datsun V210—it's a lawnmower, such a crummy car that there are literally none on the road anymore; they either melted or blew up. And I read an article in the precursor to *LA Weekly* written by someone who had been stuck out in the desert and found this little inn where they make the greatest martini of all time. But he said, "The people who make that martini don't want the whole world to know where it is so I'm going to give you a riddle." And the riddle had to do with boundaries of freeways and names of mountains. It was like a treasure map. To me, it was like a grail I was looking for. So I went to the library and looked at some detailed geographical maps and figured out where it was. So when I finished that script, I drove out to the desert—got a speeding ticket from a guy named Officer Foster and he was sort of surprised I could go eighty miles an hour in that Datsun—but he gave me the ticket anyway. I got out to the town, then I got to the road and it was sand and it was three o'clock or four-thirty in the afternoon and I thought "This is probably not a good idea." This wasn't Route 66 but a godforsaken road, no other cars around at all. So I got to a gas station where they told me that a few other people had come out here looking for that place. And the guy said, "That writer's going to get someone killed." So there was that. And then on that same trip, I saw a bumper sticker that said: "Warning! In case of rapture this car will be unmanned." And I knew what that meant. I was driving through the desert; I was insane and I was looking for some kind of high I wasn't able to find and I could have died and the desert was opening up to me and this idea came. Oh and I was also listening to a lot of Christian radio and watching a lot of Christian television at the time, and on that trip something opened up. So, it's a long answer . . .

Why do you say you were "insane"?

I'd bought a windbreaker jacket at Abercrombie & Fitch, which back then was still more of a gentleman's store. Forty-five dollars, I think. And as I was driving I kept on thinking "It's the wrong size, it's one size too big, I have to get one size smaller." That's crazy. The fact I can even remember that I was plagued on this trip—whatever else was going on in my life—by the thought that I had gotten the wrong jacket. I was obsessed with this so I knew I was nuts. I also could not choose, I couldn't decide where to sleep. I'd drive forty-five miles to one motel and then think "No, I want to go back to one I saw earlier." And when I got there, I said, "No, I don't like this one, I want to go to another one." I don't know why. I could not make a decision. And then I finally got home. I drove the longest I'd driven in one day alone in a car. I drove about four hundred miles into the desert, around the mountains and back to LA which is an eight, nine-hour haul. That, to me, is a sign of insanity.

The Player *is full of characters who have a grandiose idea of self-importance and fantasies of success, power and even spirituality. Is* The New Age *a natural sequel to* The Player?

Of course. I think any subsequent work by anybody is a sequel to the previous work.

How did the idea of The New Age *come to you?*

I was living off Melrose. Since 1978, I've lived within two blocks of Beverly Boulevard and no further west than Fairfax, so I've lived in this area a long time. Up until 1978 or 1979, there had been nothing there on Melrose—then it became very chic and for a while it was the most exciting street in the city, and I just happened to live near it. There were fashion stores and interesting restaurants. It was fun. I could even go window-shopping, which is an unusual experience in LA unless you live in Beverly Hills. So I would take a walk every evening. I started to notice that if a store had a sign in the window that said "10% off!" and it wasn't sales season, it was a bad sign. When the sign disappeared, you'd know they'd solved the problem. Once you saw "30% off!" you knew that the store was doomed. There was no way they were ever going to recover. And when you saw "70% off!," you knew it was going to be closing in a matter of weeks. That's one piece of it. The other piece was there was a guy who I used to see selling clothing at Fred Segal. That store has gotten very expensive, but it was less exclusive, less pretentious and less fashionable than it is now. Then there was a clothing store opening up on Melrose, and this guy built it—but it was so cool that he didn't have display windows, he just had the name of the store. He was so cool he thought he didn't even have to advertise. And it lasted the shortest time. As soon as I walked in, I realized he was desperate and knew he'd made this huge mistake. No one was in the store. I then just got interested in what would inspire someone to make so many mistakes from the beginning; and, in some ways, what was he paying for? What earlier mistake was the storm that caused the punishment?

Around the time of The New Age, *didn't you begin to study Jewish tradition?*

I was actually cutting the film when I started studying with rabbis. You can probably see it in my novel *Under Radar* more than in the movies. And in *Changing Lanes* and even some of *Deep Impact*. It's certainly in some of the dialogue. But I wasn't looking for personal salvation and I wasn't—and I still am not—interested in the existence of God. I *was* really interested when I saw that, by studying the Torah, I was looking for a narrative tradition that did not descend from the Greeks. In the *Odyssey* Ulysses gets everything back and that closing of the circle is Greek and Christian. And at the end of the Torah, Moses does not cross the river—he sees it, and sees the promised land, but he can't go. And that moving forward into space was something I was really interested in. I haven't quite figured out how I could do that in a movie—the problem is it might not be *possible* to do that in a movie.

How do you deal with notes on your scripts from your financiers?

You have to listen to them, because they've got the checkbook. You have to answer them. This is just the practical part of it. Someone's investing a lot of money. They're not stupid—they may have some stupid ideas but they are not stupid. There are very few truly stupid people in the movie world; there are a lot of really smart people out here. The product may not reflect that, because there are also a lot of frightened people out here. Fear makes you stupid. And also some of the stupid product makes a lot of money and it turns out they're not stupid and they have some idea of what the audience wants. *The New Age* is already such a violation of all the rules that there are no notes on it.

I found The New Age *in the comedy section in my local video store. Would you agree it was a comedy?*

I'm glad you found it! Yes, that's true. I'm sure it is.

A few critics compared it to European films of the sixties such as La Dolce Vita *and* L'Avventura, *films that lured the audience with the idea of a decadence that can also be condemned. Were these films reference points to you?*

Yes. But only in this way: neorealism interested me because they tried to turn the cameras on themselves. I wasn't interested in doing a movie trying to find Italian-style decadence in LA. I was interested in, and am still interested in, underground, subterranean communities and the way stuff goes on and nobody talks about it. *La Dolce Vita* is really the only reason why the movies exist, it's my favorite movie.

What about the famous ennui of L'Avventura?

It's the cinema of sophisticated urbanites. It's true, that Italian cinema is really about boredom and stasis. *The New Age* and even *The Player*, at their core, they're about an economy which is not collapsing but doing great, and everyone's doing really well. And one of the things we can't quite grasp now about those movies made in the late fifties and early sixties is that they were made only thirteen to seventeen years after the Germans left Rome. The Italians went from the ruins of the war to success very quickly, and there's no reference to what happened. It's completely repressed. I think that that repression is what drives a lot of these movies, the absence of reality.

I guess what I am trying to get at is that Peter and Katherine, the married protagonists in The New Age, *are grotesquely materialistic but it's hard to work out whether you're satirizing them because you don't give the audience any clues, like voice-overs or ironic music. You don't give the audience an easy way out and neither do those Italian films.*

Because I like movies that make you work.

I want to ask you some questions about some specific scenes in the film . . . out of curiosity, who is the woman dancing at the beginning of the film?

Her name is Rachel Rosenthal and she was a performance artist. Years before I made the movie, she had a class, a two-and-a-half day intensive workshop on spontaneity called D.B.D., "Do by Doing," which has helped me for the rest of my life. It was like, "Make theater right away; you have to create something right now and without too much rigmarole around it." She gives you an assignment and then you have fifteen minutes to organize something with a few people and put something on. And it works.

A lot of the dialogue in *The New Age* is deliberately clichéd and so part of the story is what happens when you speak in a language of clichés and then follow that cliché.

The beginning of the movie shows Peter and Katherine in separate worlds. Was that very deliberate?

Yeah, because you don't know his connection to her, and it's important that you see him with another woman before he goes home. For the scene to end properly, you have to know with the smile that that's what he wanted. He's very happy.

Peter and Katherine are really self-involved. Did you worry about making them unsympathetic characters?

No. It's the stupidest comment that people make, but it's also the one you have to pay the most attention to. Because these are not unsympathetic people, this is what people are really like. So what do you want? What people unfortunately want from the movies and from the culture is a character they can't identify with but a character they'd like to be. There are times when we'd all like to be Dorothy, and just follow the yellow brick road. Or be like the Terminator and rip the shit out of everything. But most of the time we're making bad decisions and running out of money. It's the plague of my existence, the notion of sympathetic character. Why is a redeeming quality something you should have in a character? The only thing you want in a character is that they *want* something. Peter and Katherine want to change, they want to get better, that's their redeeming quality. And they make some mistakes. She, at the end, makes the right decision.

Did you do a lot of research?

I did. I went to a yoga meditation retreat which was very helpful because everyone was speaking New Age meditation talk, a vocabulary when every thought is frozen. Everything the guru says, although it sounds true, leads them to disaster. He says, "Follow your bliss." It's Joseph Campbell advice, which sounds good except you can hurt yourselves that way. People in this film rarely speak honest language except Katherine when she says, "It's not fair. You neglect me, you're not being real." *She's* being real at that point. She's real almost all the way through. She says, "You shouldn't have quit." The economy happens to her, she's a victim of the economy. Peter is being offered concrete opportunities but Peter doesn't know what he wants, just some vague notion: "The best of me." The film is just filled with a lot of mistaken manuals on how to live. *The Hero's Journey* comes from Joseph Campbell. The script was easy. It didn't take a long time, just a couple of months.

Did you have any problems keeping a certain level of realism in the script?

I can tell you this: the house we're sitting in I bought after the movie from a couple. She was living over in one part of the house, and he was living in another. He'd been an investment banker who had fucked up because of cocaine, and she was a graphic designer. That movie, that story paid for a house that was for sale because of the same story.

How do you feel about The New Age *now?*

I haven't seen it for a long time. But now that I've recently revisited it I realize it's much better than I thought it was. It didn't do well at the box office and I tried to figure out why. I was right and the box office wasn't. It was ahead of itself. People don't want to think about themselves like that and it was made just as the nineties bubble was beginning and now, with the collapse there's nothing here that doesn't make sense. At the height of the dot-com boom, it looked like ancient history. But it's completely true now. I could show this film in San José or somewhere near Silicon Valley and they'd know exactly what it was talking about.

Did you find the scene where Peter and Katherine watch their friend dying hard to write?

No, again it's really almost a collage of pop culture references, pop psychology, pop philosophy, pop theology, some of which may be true.

There's a biblical injunction against tattoos because it's what the other people do. You're supposed to scar yourselves with grief, not do something to your body. The easy answer to that is God gave us our bodies whole and we should return to him in that way. The other is that if you keep yourself unmarked and look around and you see who's getting marked that teaches you something about the world. It helps you divine what's going on in the world. Which is what this scene's about. It's not just about marking your body but it's also about being careful of a time when a lot of people have tattoos.

What's interesting about *The New Age* is it's the biggest character study and the least plot-driven story I've done; which is probably part of the reason why it didn't do that well, because people go to the movies for a really good plot. But every scene follows every scene in exactly the right way, there's a progression for all the characters. It's about what happens when people look in society for spiritual answers and there's no traditional spirituality—not once do they see a church, or a rabbi. The cross you see is the cross in the pagan water, she drowns the cross. All the ritual is what people have invented to cope with a world that's collapsed.

Los Angeles, California

Scott Frank

SCOTT FRANK

Out of Sight

"It should always feel like play."

Scott Frank has written many successful screenplays featuring Hollywood stars like Jodie Foster, George Clooney and Tom Cruise, while working with directors like Sydney Pollack and Steven Soderbergh. He specializes in literary adaptations and has been particularly successful with the crime novels of Elmore Leonard, *Get Shorty* (1996) and *Out of Sight* (1998), for which he was nominated for an Academy Award for Best Adapted Screenplay. He also cowrote the adaptation of a Philip K. Dick novel, *Minority Report* (2002), for Steven Spielberg.

Synopsis

Florida, the present. Jack Foley, a career bank robber, escapes from prison with the help of his friend Buddy, and kidnaps a U.S. Marshal, Karen Sisco, in the process. She escapes but not before falling for Foley. When the two cons head for Detroit to do a job, Karen is put on their case, but she has second thoughts about bringing them in.

* * *

KEVIN CONROY SCOTT: *I understand you're a voracious reader. Who are the writers you love? And what have you been reading lately?*

SCOTT FRANK: I love John Fante. Ian McEwan, he's one of my favorite authors. I loved *Enduring Love*. I wanted to adapt that—just for that opening scene with the balloon. I love John Gregory Dunne, John Updike—his *Rabbit* series had a big effect on me. Recently, I loved Richard Russo's *Empire Falls*—it's great. I love pulpy crime stuff, I read a lot of that. All different kinds of things. I love great stories and don't limit myself to any one genre. I don't read much non-fiction. The one non-fiction thing I'm reading now which I really love is a biography of Tolstoy. It's fucking great. It's like reading a great Tolstoy novel.

What kind of pattern does your week take in terms of reading?

I'm a very slow reader. But usually I always try to read something, and finishing a novel takes me two or three weeks. I read the paper as much as I can. I fix the kids' breakfast in the morning so it's a bit insane jamming the world news into fifteen minutes. Then Sunday I read the book review and often grab a book based on what I read there.

I believe you've been working on a novel yourself?

Yeah, I haven't had time to get back to it. I work on it in fits and starts. If I have some time I'll do a sprint and then put it aside. It's really quite bad, so I don't have enough incentive to finish it. I've just been working on it forever and it's so much fun—knowing it's not any good, and that no one is waiting for it and there's no pressure. It's a place to go. When you write scripts, you hear so many voices, especially if you work for people who are smarter than you. You can trust these people, and their voices seem to replace your parents in your head—you hear them when you're working and they seem to be editing you, and they encourage you, or start to discourage you sometimes. So I started the novel just to get the voices out of my head, to try and locate myself and my writing process.

Are you interested in sharing the novel with others once it's finished?

Yeah. I'm more inspired by novels than films. Films have ceased to inspire me. I don't even go that often anymore. I certainly love writing them, and the process of writing them, but they just don't tell stories anymore—they've become so conceptual, more about ideas than real stories, more about attitudes than real character, and I find that frustrating. Also, they pay the least attention to the writing part of the process and spend more time in post-production, and that's frustrating.

You've adapted a lot of novels into screenplays. Do you have a method of operation?

What I do is read and re-read the book, then read it again, only this time marking it out with thoughts as to what I want to keep and what I lose, and how I might change things, or dialogue I absolutely must have. And I cross things out I know I'll never use. And after that I usually don't create an outline, because then the book itself is an outline for me, and I try to realize a screenplay based on that. Then I look at the script, and usually the first draft is just a flattened version of the novel, so I then try and figure out mostly what it's about for me. I really have to decide what the issues are, what themes and which parts of the narrative matter to me. Then I tell my own story and filter it through my own point of view and my own voice, and see how it comes out, while solving the problems that arise. There are often problems that you don't notice in the book that come out when you are writing the script. The character can be more passive than you originally realized. The narrative can be much more internal than it appeared when reading the book.

Do you find that you have a perspective on an adaptation through the eyes of the producers who hired you?

Very much. I intend to work with the same producers over and over again, and I get an enormous amount of help from showing them the scripts and from the initial conversations about what the book is really about, what the focus is going to be on, just to point me in the right direction. I'm a pretty needy guy in terms of getting the work done so I tend to have numerous conversations about "what it's about" or "what's going wrong." But I take a long time before I show it. It's not that I don't like collaborating, it's just that I'm so insecure about the material.

When you were studying at UC Santa Barbara, would you say you were more interested in being a filmmaker or a novelist?

I was more interested in writing screenplays. That was the first time it had ever occurred to me that it could be a career. I was spending a lot of my first year or so there thinking what kind of job I could earn money at. Then I met Paul Lazarus who was teaching screenwriting there and had worked under Harry Cohn at Columbia Pictures. And he was the first one to say to me, "If you're twenty years old and you have a fallback already, you'll fall back. If you're good at this, you should pursue it, but first, you need to know if you're good at it." So he had me write a five-page scene called "The Confrontation" just to see if I could write something. He said it could be about anything I wanted. So I wrote that and I remember looking at it and in five pages there were about thirty spelling mistakes but at the top, in red pen he had written, "Damn good. Write more." And then he told me the next time I turned something in, I should have a seven-year-old proofread it for me.

You made some short films too. Did you write and direct?

Well, some of them I wrote and directed, some I just wrote for other people. They were really off the wall, strange, a lot of them involved death and graveyards. Surreal comedy. In fact my first draft of *Little Man Tate* was much more surreal than the finished film was—a very surreal, dark comedy.

You've mentioned that you've been stealing from Elmore Leonard for a long time. How did you first come across his work, and what attracted you to it?

I may have read him in college, but I think I really hooked into him when someone sent me a novel of his to adapt when I first started in the business back in 1985–86. It was *Gold Coast*, which was subsequently made for Showtime. I was working on a film at Paramount but was still looking for other work. And I remember loving the book, the dialogue, and the fact that everyone in it was so the way I'm not and wish I was. They were so clear and direct and knew what they wanted. I loved the way they spoke and the rhythm of it. So I went to a meeting and they told me I just wasn't the right guy for Elmore Leonard, and that was that. They didn't think I was dark enough, edgy enough, tough enough, any of those things. But I started to read his books, in quick succession. Funnily enough, I never read *Get Shorty* when it first came out, because I'd read a review that I took to be negative, sort of dismissing it as a Hollywood book. Then they offered it to me and first, in fact, I passed because I wasn't interested in that kind of thing at the time. They tried to get someone else to adapt it and couldn't. And Stacey Sher said to me, "I'm going to come back to you on this. You're exactly the right person on this." She was very tenacious, just wouldn't let it go and I finally read the damn book and just loved it. I didn't get that far until I called her and said, "OK, I'll do it," not realizing how difficult it would be. It just hit me, and I was in the mood to have fun. I had just been fired off a movie I'd been working on for a long time, so I was more cynical at that time, because that had never happened to me before. And I think that may have played into it . . .

How did you get involved in Out of Sight?

Because of *Get Shorty*. Elmore sent me the book, and sent it to Jersey Films at the same time. I had no desire to do any other Elmore Leonard adaptation. I didn't want to become the Elmore Leonard guy and I felt that *Get Shorty* had come out so well that I could only fail the second time. I started reading the book and got to page twenty—the scene in the trunk—and phoned up and said, "OK, I'll do it."

How had your relationship with Elmore Leonard developed to that point?

We had lunch before *Get Shorty* got started, and the lunch basically consisted of two hours of him telling me all the horror stories about people who had fucked up with his books, one after another. I left that lunch and all I could think was, "Oh God, I'm going to be another story at someone else's lunch!" The last thing he said to me at the lunch, by the way, was, "Have fun." So I sent him drafts, called him every now and then, and saw him when he came to town. And he was always nothing but positive. I think he had one note on *Get Shorty*: "This line, he wouldn't say that." He was really good. Everything he would say was positive: "You've done something really good and people don't know how hard this is. You're not going to get any credit for what you've done." He kept on saying that. It can be a really difficult thing, adapting someone else's work and talking to them about it, and he was really supportive, so it was terrific.

However, on *Out of Sight*, he didn't like my early drafts of the script because he didn't like Ripley, Albert Brooks's character in the film. Ripley's just mentioned in the novel, but I made him a whole character in the film. I felt that we needed him. Elmore just didn't like him. And he also felt that it took too long and should just open with the bank robbery and go from there. The flashback wasn't going to work. So I said, "You open with the bank robbery and then you have sixty pages of history." But he didn't like it. But he did love the finished film and he left me a great message on my answering machine after he saw the film saying, "Scott, it's Dutch. You were right. We needed Ripley." He was very nice about it. But he also helped me with the ending because I couldn't figure out how to end it. You can't have them together, but you can't have her just bust him the way she does in the book. Also the book was about her and the movie was about him. She's a great character but she doesn't really change in the book, you can't really explore anything. Whereas in the book he's older, about fifty, and there's my favorite, favorite theme—the road not taken, it's too late, I wish I'd led my life differently. It's much sadder. I thought that was great, and George Clooney really got that sadness. This was a man who wanted to live another life. A man who truly, truly regretted the life he'd lived. It was just sad. I had never felt that way about somebody who was essentially a criminal. And in the book I also found him to be mildly suicidal. He really goes into this thing at the end not knowing anything; he doesn't know the guys who are going to rob the house, he's had no history with them whatsoever, knows that it's going to end up with a murder—but he goes anyway. He knows he's either going to get caught or killed, and he doesn't want to do what he's doing. He has no motivation. At one point he's asked why he's doing it, and he says, "It's something new." In a film you just can't do that, but I thought the solution to that problem was really interesting and that intrigued me.

I was wrestling with it because I'd written a couple of first drafts and it was still ending like the book. I was on the phone with Elmore one afternoon and told him I was wrestling with it, and during the conversation he said he'd been reading a script from a guy out of jail who he'd been mentoring. The guy had broken out of several different prisons. And we were talking and we agreed that it would be great if we put that guy in the van with Jack. And so I just thought about what that guy could be like, and started to think about a guy sitting back there who likens his whole experience to the flight of Mohammad. And it just came to me and was written once and changed very little. It was one of those things that just happened in a nice way.

How would you compare Out of Sight *with* Get Shorty?

Out of Sight is a more serious film. It's about more, I think. *Get Shorty* is a little more gag-funny, it has a broader sense of humor. *Out of Sight* is more like a film of the seventies; it does have that intimate feeling. There are no buffoons in *Out of Sight*. There's only really one real gag in it which is when the guy falls on his gun.

I heard that Barry Sonnenfeld, who you worked with on Get Shorty, *was at one point going to direct* Out of Sight. *What happened to that partnership?*

In my mind, I didn't think Barry was going to do it because he kept on asking one question which I think is the telltale sign that a director isn't going to do a film, which is, "What film is this like? I can't think of another film this is like." He was really having trouble referencing movies that he understood, but he was very smart about the script and story, and enormously helpful in the initial writing of it. But ultimately when it came time for him to make the film, he didn't know how to apply his own point-of-view to the material. It didn't match. I've always thought of *The Last Detail*. And, in fact, when we met Soderbergh the first thing he mentioned was *The Last Detail,* which is why I knew we had the right guy. *Out of Sight* is that kind of movie.

The emotional heart of Leonard's novel is this trust between an outlaw and a law enforcer who spend little time together but spend a lot of time thinking about each other, which, as we all know, is something that's very difficult to dramatize. Can you take me through the thought process behind your solving this problem?

Probably the biggest problem in the book is that they fall in love after being together once, and throughout the novel they think about each other. Then they're together again and they sleep together and have thought about each other so much that they've worked themselves up into a "What if?" frenzy. You buy it in the novel, but you can't do it in a movie because they're never together. So I did a couple of things. I thought, "It doesn't take a lot, and it's cheap . . ." I have her dream about him, a whole fantasy thing, just so we know—and I made it into a bit of a joke so it was funny. He was on her mind in spite of herself. I thought that was key. And I had him call her and had them talk on the phone. So everything kind of built—and then he waves to her, which is in the book, but now it comes after he's seen her twice.

That dream sequence in the bath—how did you structure it? Because for a while the audience believes it's really happening. How soon did you want them to catch on?

Immediately, I hoped. I hoped they would say as soon as she walks in, "How did she find him so quickly? Come on!" That they would be mad at the film. I also hoped that when he pulls her into the bathtub and she starts kissing him, then they would be even more upset, because it then makes the realization that it's a dream such a relief.

In the deleted scenes on the DVD, there's a bizarre scene, part of the same dream, I think, where Jack and his buddy are talking about lavender and different kinds of soaps.

The joke was from a woman's point of view. So it's a woman thinking about Jack and having a dream or a fantasy about what two guys would talk about when coming in after being out in the mud all day. It's all mixed up, whether it's her voice or their voice. But it played so gay that it gave the joke away too fast—it became a hat on a hat, and we really had to lose it.

What does "a hat on a hat" mean?

It means two jokes piled on top of each other on the same thing.

The intricate flashbacks mark out the film. In those that you invented yourself, you also change details from the book, such as making Ripley meet Jack in prison. Why?

In order to make the end work, and understand why he's there at the end. Also to give it a different level of something at stake for Jack besides "Will he get caught?" I wanted it to be more emotional. I wanted it to be tied to the humiliation of when Ripley offered him the job of a security man. I just needed it to be freighted with more character issues than it was.

There's a scene which takes place in Lompoc, where Don Cheadle's character, the boxer Snoopy, crushes Ripley's goldfish in the library and Jack stands up for him. You invented this. Can you take me through the process of making a scene from scratch using the words of characters Elmore Leonard has created?

Actually in *Get Shorty* there are even more scenes which don't happen in the book. I don't know what the process is other than I feel very connected to his writing. I feel like I understand it. I couldn't mimic it in a novel, but I could certainly infer from it in making a screenplay, telling the story through his characters, and it wasn't that difficult for me. Sometimes I messed it up; sometimes I cut it up too much and rearranged the words that wouldn't work right. In terms of creating something from scratch, he's given me such rich characters that I so understand their patterns and points of view that I don't know if I'm that conscious of what I'm doing.

How involved were you in production in relation to the writing? I'm thinking about your role during rehearsals and how you incorporated that feedback into the script.

My role during rehearsals was to answer questions, and to ask questions, and to see if things could work better, to see where there was too much dialogue, where there wasn't enough dialogue and things weren't clear, where there were better ways to say things, whether lines were a mouthful for the actor, to just make sure things are working. It's a great way to workshop the script. I scribbled notes and I was careful not to rewrite the script right away. I would kind of live with what happened in rehearsal and then do it in stages.

Do you find when you write dialogue, you have to speak it out loud?

Yes.

And then as far as the rehearsals went, were you nervous at all?

They were such respectful, unbelievably nice people and were all busy asking about the material and they were all appreciative of the material, enormously collaborative, and they all were just trying to find ways to make it better. If they challenged the material it was just so they could try to understand it better. Nine times out of ten what they came up with in rehearsal was helpful.

You and Steven Soderbergh talked a lot on the phone during the shooting of the picture. What would you talk about?

We'd talk about dailies and he'd tell me about problems that were coming up which we needed to solve. We hadn't really solved the scene in the house at the end so I flew to Detroit to talk to him about that. We didn't know what was going to be in the safe and things like that. I didn't bother him that often. I'm not one of those writers who have to have their dialogue said exactly the way I write. However, if you miss the intent, I get all upset. So there were times when we would have discussions about that, or he was just worried that something wouldn't work, or that he would have to cut something.

At the beginning of the film you show Jack Foley robbing a bank. Did you ever consider playing around with the structure?

I always played around with the structure. Then after Steven came on, I panicked at one point and straightened it all out and he told me, "No, no, no! Don't do that, go back to it." I wrote it all linear, all in order. I thought no one was going to follow this. But we were always rearranging things.

The bank-robbing scene is very close to what is in the book.

Yeah. Steven had seen a thing with the lighter one day and we added that. I just added little bits here like the dialogue with the bank clerk. George Clooney added, "You have a very pretty smile."

Immediately you have sympathy for him.

Yeah, you love him. I had to make it clear that he didn't know the guy, that little twist.

Now in the book, he gets into a car accident instead of the cops grabbing him because his beat-up Honda won't start.

I had written versions of that. I just thought it was funnier that he has problems with cars. You like him so much now. The only thing that's different is that in the script they say the lines here but they're a little more casual.

The scene where we are introduced to Karen by her having lunch with her father wasn't in the book. He gives her a gun as a birthday present.

She got the gun from her father—what a great scene to see!

Yeah, and you use it as a beat throughout the rest of the story. Do you find it helpful to use these objects, such as the gun, to embody change throughout the story?

Yes, absolutely.

How did you handle the trunk scene where you have two characters in a static position for ten minutes and a lot of get-to-know-you exposition to get out of the way?

Now, this is a whole discussion. In the second version of the script, I rewrote this whole scene. Originally, we shot it all in one take. There was just no cinematic punctuation whatsoever in the scene and watching the movie I learned there was some information that we could set up that would help us here; a little more about his ex-wife and other things. There's none of him over her shoulder.

But you never changed the way you wrote it.

No, it was just shot differently.

When you talk about cinematic punctuation, what do you mean by that?

Cutaways. Things that give it a rhythm, give it a feel, give you a body in a car. In the book, there's no flashlight but he has to find a flashlight, otherwise there's no movie. I have him find his flashlight so he can see. Again they're talking about Buddy while he's there. He's got her— "How many banks did you rob?" We also found a lot of ways to shorthand a lot of dialogue from the other version.

Kind of distill it.

This is all about them. I rewrote it to be all about them. None of that was in there. His hand on her leg. None of it was there. None of it. It could almost be a hotel room.

After the scene in the car there is another flashback, which is tricky because that flashback used to come in a different place. You think Jack and Buddy have gone back to prison but in fact they are in a different prison. They got busted two years ago so you have to say, "Wait a minute, where are we?" There's a different color scheme for every prison. And then I used this to get all the back-story on Snoopy, I rewrote and reorganized all the material so that we would learn about it.

And Snoopy's character is interesting. At first he's depicted as cartoonish but literally two minutes later he's stabbing someone to death. That's too different extremes . . . as a scene which contains exposition on Snoopy like this, how do you do it?

I'm just conscious of it when it sounds like exposition. I just keep on rewriting and rewriting it and come up with new stuff.

Can you tell me how you and Steven Soderbergh collaborated?

I would do work and then we would talk about it and I would show him stuff. Or sometimes with certain scenes, he'd come into Pasadena and sit at the desk and type dialogue and run it back and forth and talk it out, write speeches together and just sort of say it out loud.

How much rewriting was done once he came onboard?

Quite a bit, I think. He touched everything. We had such a long prep time waiting for George to finish *ER*, we had a long time to work on the script, which was great. I would say we wrote a third of it.

He's very similar to you. He's got literary sensibilities . . .

Yeah, and very willing to try and probe something new.

Getting back to Snoopy's character . . . you don't dwell on the fact that he murdered someone in prison.

I wanted to set him up more than what was there. In the book, they set him up more in the murder scene and that's just a guy who's just gross and disgusting and completely out of place. It takes you out of the book and you don't understand why Foley and Buddy would ever go with the guy.

Karen's father uses the newspaper article to tell his daughter some-thing. What was not clear to me was when I watched the film it said the article was about Chino, who escaped from prison with Jack but felt betrayed by him. Was that something that worried you?

Yes. It's a problem that was not really solved. It wasn't clear. I was trying to keep Chino alive and the Chino part of this movie was the part that got really sloppy for me.

Why is that?

There's always something that slips through the cracks and for some reason it's never strong enough in the first place, so you kind of pare it down and you don't really protect it. There's too much stuff to do in the movie and the Chino character suffered as a result.

I thought Chino's motivation in the book was very weak. Why in the world would he ever go to hunt down a woman when he's just escaped from jail?

What happened is that in the actual scene where Karen busts him we have some guy come in and it became a joke. In the book, it was much better with his gun on her and her gun on him, which became about her ability to talk him out of it.

This thing about Ripley's diamonds . . . it wasn't pounded home as much as it was in the book.

I think that there is a subtle thing happening here that even if you couldn't articulate it, you're not going to question the fact that they're going out to Glen. They're going up there. They know he's on to a score. It wasn't that it was so ridiculous. There's something subtle that happens when you set up a character, so when you go back to meet the character, you have a tendency not to question why. But it's not really spelled out.

We cut a lot of stuff. Those scenes were some of the best in the script and they started ad libbing on it. Some of those ad libs are awesome and in fact to make room for it we had to cut stuff. I really missed the bit about the guy leaving his wallet inside the house. We moved it here because it was too long and they shot it but we cut it.

They're going to commit a really horrible murder and it's only dealt with in an obtuse way.

We shot the murder but cut it. There's a lot more of their story in the long cut of the film; we saw them on the news, their escaping. We shot all of that stuff. Steven cut it right away because he knew he had to lose it.

But with seeing Snoopy's gang murder someone, you've been away from Buddy and Foley on their way up to Detroit. Was that something you were worried about?

No, I never thought about it. Those kind of things for me it's all feeling. If I feel we've missed something, then I write something, but as a rule, I don't think of that. In fact, it makes it all the more dramatic when they do appear.

The trick with that is that you've got to show the scene with him killing and raping that girl within a comedy.

You'd be out of the movie. It'd be dead. The movie's dead. You see it happen. I have to be honest that most of this is feeling my way and making mistakes and seriously happy accidents in respect of things. I just would feel I knew that the structure had to be better organized. The three mandates were one, it had to better organized to happen faster; two, you had to understand why they slept with each other and how they thought of each other in a certain way; and three, you had to motivate him so he won't go to the house. Beyond that I don't know how conscious I was in terms of strategy.

How do you deal with notes?

I never got any notes from George. He was always very happy.

Did you have a strategy for writing a love scene between George Clooney and Jennifer Lopez? They meet in the hotel bar and then it cuts away to them in the room together . . .

That scene is interesting because when Steven and I first met to talk about the script the very first time, he wanted to cut all that dialogue. He wanted to try all the stuff about when you see someone and this stuff about love and missed opportunities and I probably did cut it once and probably did a version of it. And then I had this idea that it would start with them talking and then you'd start to see the hotel, the elevator, the whole scene as you do now but they're in motion, so by the time they get to the hotel in Florida, they're kissing. He said, "Write however you want, I'm going to chart it out." Right from the beginning, he was going to make a mean model of the movie right here. Because if you notice that from right here from this point on, it's played straight and there's no more flashbacks. So he'd always had this in his head, and it's a sort of "don't look now, jump back." And it was a great way to solve the problem, to get all the talk, because you need all the talk, you really do.

I heard that you criticized Soderbergh about the sex scene.

No. I remember seeing dailies and thinking this is going to be so boring and unsexy, but you know what, when I saw the dailies for the car crash, I thought, "Oh my god, they're going to have to reshoot that, it doesn't look like they crash." It's all about editing and music and when I saw this in rough cut, I was absolutely amazed.

We almost cut the beginning of the scene in the hotel room. The studio wanted us to because it was long and talky and we fought hard to keep it because it's all about her, and how she feels about it. Suddenly she's worried about it and she's vulnerable for the first time in the movie and it's great. The story he tells her about the dummy is great. He's so good the way he does it. He's so honest about who he is and it makes her sad. It's really a sad scene.

How did you go about writing the scene at the boxing arena in Detroit?

This is all not in the book but the scene is here just to make sure you know why they're doing it. It's not so much summarizing as making sure that you make sure you've reset their agenda: they're going to try and get the diamonds before he does and they know that Maurice is going to set them up.

You talk about the rule of three. What is it?

It's just a rhythm thing if you're going to set something up like that. You make sure it's a setup: you state it, restate it, then pay it off. That's really what it is. And then it's just a feeling, if he's slipped once and then slipped again it wouldn't feel right, but if you make a habit of slipping on the stairs . . .

When they are in the van on the way to Ripley's house for the climactic set-piece there is a lot of dialogue missing from that van scene.

We chopped all the stuff in the back of the van out, which I really miss. We needed it for pace. We were running for the finishing line at this point in the film.

The end of the book is really different. Buddy gets shot with a shot gun, it's really brutal.

At what point did you realize that you had to tie all the threads together, with Ripley's diamonds being in the fish tank . . .

From the beginning. Snoopy and his gang should have been a little scarier. But it still works. It's one of those things that you can't try for; it just comes out that way. And luckily it comes out in the script but even more importantly, it comes out in the making of the film; everyone understands the movie, they're all humming the same song. These actors were so in tune with one another.

When one of Snoopy's gang, the tall, overweight man, slips on the stairs for the third time and shoots himself in the head, that gets a great laugh from the audience.

It's a laugh but a shocked laugh.

And that's why this movie works.

It's a fundamental thing.

What about when Karen has Jack in her sights, her backup will be there any moment and she either has to arrest him or kill the man she has fallen for . . .

Put it this way, it didn't occur to me until I watched the finished movie but it is something I wished we had done. I don't know whether I did it in the script. He's got to point a gun at her in order for her to shoot him in the leg.

Steven Soderbergh thought that she would be made to shoot him.

I wished Jack had lifted the damn gun. When he's lying on the floor, he's so sad in that scene, it's great. This was a reshoot shot at her looking. I love that shot. Such a beautiful shot. The look on her face.

It's a great film. A great screenplay too.

There are days when you're on set and you walk up and see fifty trucks and what I think about is not the marionette aspect but the journey. Like, four years ago I was sitting and writing this thing; I remember the day I was struggling with so-and-so. I marvel at the journey and how if I were to look forward it seems such an insurmountable gap you have to cross to get there, but looking back it feels like just a blink. And that's what I marvel at when I'm on set. *Minority Report* was the most painful, difficult thing I ever wrote in my life and so hard and so frustrating; when it was finally made, I couldn't believe it was happening. With any movie it's the whole idea of how far you've come, less than the idea that you've made it all, because I get so much help and I feel so inept throughout the process. I really do believe that for me good writing is the result of a series of happy accidents. And eventually I just get it right. I fall in a hole and it tells me what kind of movie it is. Sometimes it's so overwhelming that I can't be on the set. I'm alternately overwhelmed and bored on the set.

When you paint yourself into a corner when you write, how do you cope with the pain that things aren't going well?

It's hell for me usually because of self-doubt. I try to trick myself. What gets in the way for me is a very strong inner critic and powerful, powerful feelings of self-doubt and voices that constantly identify me as a fraud and inadequate to the task. So what I do is I try very hard to mute the voices as much as I can. I know that they'll never go away, but I can make them like the radio in the next room where you can hear them but they're not bothering you. They're there and I'm aware of them but I have some sort of arrangement with them. The best writing is also subconscious where you don't know that you're doing it, and you don't realize you've done it. That's a few seconds and the rest of the week is using the other half of your brain manipulating what you've come up with in those few seconds. The only way you can get to those subconscious places is by having a sense of play; it should always feel like play. That's how I try to do it. If I'm not having fun, it's wrong. Sometimes it's not fun but even when you're under a lot of pressure, you need to try and have fun and try to be excited and exhilarated and that's the hard part.

Directing, is that imminent?

I haven't found the thing I want to do. I've waited such a long time because my kids are so young; it's a very disruptive thing to go do that. I've just been waiting because I don't want to go away. I'm ready for it now. I don't know what happened because there was a time when I thought I could be happy not doing it. John Gregory Dunne wrote a great book that said that just wanting to be a screenwriter was like just wanting to be a co-pilot. And that haunts me! What he's saying is that there is only a limited sense of satisfaction. I'm proud of the work I've done but at the same time, I'm the co-pilot. And I don't want to direct because I feel my work has been compromised, mistreated or I want control as a loser. What's frustrating as a screenwriter is that you have a voice but no say. At least as a director you'll have a say. Sometimes trying to exercise your voice on the set and say something without violating the politics of the production is like picking a lock with a wet noodle. You're trying to do it, but you don't want to intrude, don't want to insult and threaten anybody so you have to be very careful. And I'm tired of it, tired of being careful and writing it once for myself, writing it again for the studio, writing it again for the director, writing it again for the actor, all that Rubik's Cube you have to go through. So tomorrow I'm craving a new kind of process, a different experience. I have a great career and I truly enjoy my days.

You don't seem to have an ego.

It's just about having a different adventure and being fed in a different way. I may fail miserably but I'm just ready for something.

Do you know what scale the film will be?

The material will tell me. I haven't found the material, the thing I really want to do. I'm looking aggressively but there's nothing.

Pasadena, California

Alexander Payne and Jim Taylor

ALEXANDER PAYNE AND JIM TAYLOR

Election

> "We try to begin with the raw materials of life,
> not the raw materials of other movies."

Alexander Payne and Jim Taylor have co-written (with Payne direct-ing) four movies together: *Citizen Ruth* (1996), *Election* (1999), *About Schmidt* (2002) and *Sideways* (2004). *Election* was nominated for an Academy Award for Best Adapted Screenplay and *About Schmidt* won the Golden Globe for Best Screenplay–Motion Picture. The writing team have also collaborated on Hollywood rewrites such as *Jurassic Park III* (2001) and have worked with a variety of interesting actors such as Laura Dern, Matthew Broderick, Reese Witherspoon, Jack Nicholson and Kathy Bates.

Synopsis

Omaha, Nebraska, the present. Tracy Flick is the most ambitious student at Carver High. Her teacher, Mr. McAllister, is in charge of the student government. Elections are coming up and Tracy Flick is the only one running. Annoyed by Tracy's overly ambitious ways, Mr. McAllister convinces the popular football player Paul to run against Tracy. Meanwhile, Tammy, Paul's lesbian sister, decides that running against her brother is the best way to avenge being dumped by her ex-girlfriend who is now dating Paul. Mr. McAllister makes a bad decision when counting the ballots, causing a scandal that mirrors a real political election.

* * *

KEVIN CONROY SCOTT: *How did you two come to work together? I read somewhere that you lived together in Los Angeles for a while, so I'm wondering how the friendship started.*

JIM TAYLOR: We were only acquaintances through mutual friends, until I moved into a room that Alexander had available in his apartment.

Although I'd been working in film-related jobs for many years, I had recently started to temp in law offices so I could have more time to write. After I moved in, Alexander and I gradually became friends and we ended up collaborating on the scripts for two short films. That experience was fun and went well, so it seemed like a good idea for us to write a feature together, and we wrote the first draft of *Citizen Ruth* before I moved to New York.

What had been driving you to write on your own before meeting Alexander?

JT: I had wanted to be a filmmaker since I was thirteen, and I was working in the film industry, trying to figure out how to connect my work experience with becoming a filmmaker myself instead of helping other people make their films. So it seemed like the best way for me to do that was to write scripts.

Alexander, what were you doing when Jim moved in?

ALEXANDER PAYNE: I was finishing up my thesis at UCLA film school. Jim moved into the house in around 1989, my last year at UCLA, and my first two years of trying to get a film made. The last eight months of Jim's living there were spent writing *Citizen Ruth*.

At what point after you met did you two know that you would work well together?

AP: It was more a shared sense of humor that was responsible for why our friendship was growing.
JT: It probably had a lot to do with how we enjoyed talking to each other about articles in the newspaper. Our first script was inspired by some of those news stories.

Alexander, can you say something about The Passion of Martin, *your thesis film?*

AP: It was about fifty minutes long . . . If you check it out you have to be very, very forgiving. There's a lot of amateurish stuff in there. It was loosely based on an Argentine novel, and I spent a lot of time making it, and after I graduated in 1990, I had an agent who got me a writing-directing deal for a studio. That's when I wrote *The Coward*, which later became *About Schmidt*. It took me a long time to write. During that time I also co-wrote two shorts with Jim that I directed.

JT: Writing those shorts was a test. Not intentionally, it just sort of happened that way.

AP: So by late 1991, early 1992, I finished *The Coward* and was trying to figure out what to do because the studio that hired me said, "We're not making this." I was maybe going to try to rewrite it and raise money to shoot it on 16mm or something. Then in February of "92, Jim and I came upon the idea of *Citizen Ruth*, so I abandoned *The Coward* for many years.

When you guys were writing, what were you doing to make ends meet financially?

AP: I had that money from Universal. And I never changed my lifestyle from the one I had as a student until after I made *Citizen Ruth*. Until the year 2000, I never paid more than $800 a month in rent.

Which leads me to a question, Jim, about you and the host of Wheel of Fortune, *Pat Sajack.*

JT: Oh, right . . . [*laughs*] In the years before I moved in with Alexander, I had been working in a lot of film jobs. If I wanted to be a creative executive at a studio I was well on my way, but I wasn't interested in that, so I stopped doing that kind of work. I went to a temp agency and I said, "Don't send me to entertainment companies." I started temping in law offices in downtown LA. It was depressing, putting on my tie—

AP: Jim hates wearing ties.

JT:—and you know, packing my lunch and getting on the bus and going down there and doing word processing, mostly. So we had to carve out time to work around my temping schedule. I had been working with the director Ivan Passer for a few years, which was great, but it ended up being that the project that was driving our little company along fell apart. I hadn't been paid for a few months and I was already in debt. Actually, that's why I ended up living with Alexander, because I couldn't afford to live in my own apartment. So I guess it's an example of how bad luck can often lead you somewhere good . . .

The thing about *Wheel of Fortune* was that I needed money and I knew people who had been successful on game shows. *Wheel of Fortune* was, at the time, the only show where you could get a good chunk of money. Except for *Jeopardy!* of course.

AP: He wasn't smart enough for *Jeopardy!*

JT: But I thought I had a chance of winning on *Wheel of Fortune*. The process took a long time and I was very serious about it. I trained with Alexander, do you remember that?

AP: I participated in many training sessions. It's like practicing for your SAT tests.

JT: I trained because a big factor in winning is getting used to spinning the wheel while you're trying to solve the puzzles . . .

It sounds like something you guys could make a short film about.

AP: He was going to.

JT: As I was preparing for the show, I realized that I really needed to get something out of it—it wasn't for fun, I desperately needed the money and if I didn't win I was going to be very depressed. So I thought, "OK, maybe if I lose I can make a short using the footage." So I came up with a scenario for the film, but in order for it to work, I had to change what my character would be when I was introduced on the show.

AP: It was about a third grade teacher who is engaged to be married and loses on *Wheel of Fortune*. After the show, not only does his fiancée leave him, but his third grade students make fun of him for being such a dope on the show.

JT: So I went up to Pat Sajack before we started taping the show and I said, "Actually, I'm not a writer. I'm a third grade teacher." Which was partially true since I'd recently been substitute-teaching in the Pomona school district. Pat crossed out "writer" on his card and wrote in "teacher." Also, during my introduction I made sure I had a chance to say, "I'm engaged to be married to my lovely fiancée Beth," because she was going to be an important character in this short film. When the show aired all of my extended family thought I was getting married. People who didn't know me well were very confused . . .

So what happened with the project?

JT: I ended up using the idea for some directing exercises, but I never made the film.

AP: And you won, too.

JT: True, I won one show but then I lost the next one so I did have the footage I needed of me losing. It just didn't end up being something I wanted to make. Besides, by the time I got around to really thinking about it, I'd aged and put on weight so any additional footage I'd shoot wouldn't have matched . . .

AP: He won a boat, and at the end of the show when everyone is applauding and the credits were rolling they cut to the grand prize, the boat that Jim just won. Jim ran over to the boat and climbed up on to it and went into the front and stood there, one foot in the air behind him with his hand to his forehead and his other hand behind his back like he was looking out to sea. It's the funniest thing in the world . . .

JT: I don't think Pat Sajack liked my attitude very much.

AP: Do you still have that tape?

JT: Sure.

AP: Can I show it to my wife?

JT: Sure.

Jim, your short films, Memory Lane *and* Living Will, *are they close in tone to the stuff you write with Alexander?*

JT: Pretty much.

AP: But I think if you see them you will find, in distilled form, an absurd streak which you see in the things we have co-written. There is an isolated deadpan absurdity that is very distilled in those two shorts.

JT: We're lucky that our sensibilities are very close.

How did the two of you work together when you were writing Citizen Ruth?

AP: I think we wrote downstairs in the dining room a lot. I went to the city where the original story happened and did research for a week. I think we were already well into the first draft at that point, and I found that the research was confirming things that we had invented.

JT: It was very organic and it's probably why our partnership works. We just talked and then wrote some stuff. But of all the scripts we've written, I think *Citizen Ruth* changed the most from the first draft to the shooting script.

You managed to get paid for writing the first two short films you did together, didn't you? Which is unusual.

AP: It was a job. The film was shown domestically on the Playboy Channel.

JT: [*laughs*] It was interesting, actually. It was a show that Propaganda Films produced that was trying to be something "new and different." Actually, a lot of Alexander's filmmaking team came out of that short.

AP: Rolfe Kent the composer, and Jane Stewart the production designer.

How did this Playboy job come about?

AP: I met producer Alan Poul at Sundance in "91 and he hired me there. I thought I would do it because no one would ever see it and I could just practice directing. Of course, now one of them is out on DVD . . .

JT: But the second one we did, Playboy hated. It only aired once and since then they've buried it. I'm proud of it because it's truly subversive, especially considering where the money came from.

AP: It was anti-Playboy. It shows at one point a very lonely fifty-eight-year-old Czech plastic surgeon in his study watching 16mm footage of a dead girl from his youth, and he's masturbating watching her. It was called *The Hands of God*.

JT: What did that executive from Playboy say? "What is this auteur shit?" First we did one that they loved, then when it came time to make the second one they said, "What is this? We don't understand it." And we said, "Don't worry, it's funny. Just like the first one."

I think this kind of ties into another job that you guys did. You were hired to rewrite Jurassic Park III. *Can you tell me something about that experience?*

AP: It was a job. Four weeks. We also did *Meet the Parents*, the last draft before shooting, uncredited. We made enough structural changes in *Jurassic Park* to get credit but we didn't make enough changes in *Meet the Parents* to get credit.

JT: It's weird because there is much less of us in *Jurassic Park* than in *Meet the Parents*.

AP: They hired us for character and humor.

JT: And Bill Macy was going to be in the movie, so we thought it would be fun to write for him. Also, I like the *Jurassic Park* premise. I find it really compelling as a nature-bites-us-in-the-ass story.

AP: When we started, I talked to the director a lot about how it should have elements of the original *King Kong* and *Wages of Fear*. They hired us six weeks before they started shooting, and we had four weeks to write a whole new script with new characters while maintaining the five set-pieces they had already built. It was a challenge and an exercise.

JT: It was really hard work. But these rewrite things, as much as they're lucrative, they give us a chance to write something very fast—because we usually write very slowly.

You could also argue that the restrictions that genre movies provide can actually bring some creativity to your writing. Did any of that happen with Jurassic Park III?

JT: It was too rigorous a deadline, and there were too many obstacles in the way of doing great work. The last rewrite we did—they often pay you by the week—we were contracted to do a two-to-three-week polish, and we took three months to do it because we just couldn't limit ourselves to a polish. In that case, there wasn't a production date looming, so there was room and we took it. [*laughs*] *Jurassic Park III* was an interesting lesson for us. But ultimately the realities of producing an effects-driven movie almost always get in the way of telling the best story.

AP: It's a ride. My phrase when taking these jobs is, "We might be highly paid but we can't be bought." The biggest obstacle in the rewrites that we've done is that you really have to follow the orders of the producer and the director. We do this to a certain point but then after that point we say, "Well, you hired us for us and this is what we think it should be." So from time to time there has been a tension between what we think the good movie version should be and what they want to do. For example, on *Jurassic Park*, there were things they wanted us to write into it but we refused to because we thought they were too dumb.

JT: I think most writers would agree that it's almost impossible to do a decent job writing scenes that the filmmakers don't support.

So then how do you deal with notes from the studio—on both your writing assignments and your own films?

AP: In the rewrite deals, it comes written in the contract that we're going to get notes. In fact, we *like* to get notes from the director because we trust the director; at least that's whom we have to serve. Fortunately, the three movies that we have co-written and I have directed, our scripts have largely been left alone. We have been really lucky in terms of studio notes. *Citizen Ruth*, no one ever said anything. *Election*, we had a little bit right before shooting in one scene; and then *About Schmidt*, zero.

I remember reading you quoting Mel Brooks to the effect that studios tend to leave you alone when you write a comedy. Why do you think that's the case?

AP: I read that in Kenneth Tynan's piece about Mel Brooks that was printed in *The New Yorker* in the seventies. Mel Brooks thinks that when you direct comedies they leave you alone a little bit more because they think it's harder to talk about—

JT: When we were doing *Election* it had all these voice-overs, and all of these convolutions in the story. It's kind of hard to tamper with that. If you've moved far enough away from what is the norm then it's difficult to force the script into a normal form because it's not even close.

So it's something about the tone of the film?

AP: In interviews after the films I get so many questions about the tone. "How do you ride that balance between drama and comedy?" I don't know how to answer that because the tone simply comes out of us.

JT: One good thing is that now when someone asks us what a future project of ours will be like, we can just point to previous movies of our own as examples . . .

When you are doing polishes on these rewrites, how do you approach it? Do you look at what is there and then it's just a matter of tweaking it?

AP: Usually it starts with, "Do we think we can help this along?" Because these things are very highly paid, and we would never want to not give them their money's worth. Even though we took three months on that project that we were hired for two to three weeks, we only charged them for three weeks.

JT: On the one hand we're doing the job for the money, but on the other hand we care far more about doing something we're proud of than how much we're getting paid.

AP: We have to be honest contractors. It's like, "We gave you this estimate, and we should have tested that wall and seen that it was all rotted inside."

How did you come across Tom Perrotta's novel Election?

AP: Albert Berger and Ron Yerxa sent the book to us in January of "96 but I didn't read it until April—because I was not remotely interested in anything set in high school. But as a favor to Albert I went to Palm Springs for a weekend and read it, and I got sucked into it. Then I sent it to Jim and he agreed that we should do it.

JT: And Alexander didn't set it up for me by saying it was great. But as soon as I read it, I realized it was great material for us.

How did you go about adapting Election *from the novel? The novel is told from multiple points of view.*

JT: Using multiple voice-overs was a decision we made from the outset. Thankfully it was a decision that the studio supported us on.

AP: In fact, one of the main reasons I wanted to do the film in the first place was because I wanted to do multiple voice-overs. I thought it would be a cool thing to try.

Election is set in New Jersey but the film is set in Omaha, Nebraska, which is where Alexander is from. How important was it in the writing to have a location that you could identify with?

AP: I think *Election* could have been set anywhere. It's not that "Omaha" is in the writing or structure of it but it is in the production design and the photography and the casting.

How long did you work on the screenplay?

AP: It's always about six months.

For just your first draft?

AP: Yes, but our first drafts are always very much within striking distance of the final draft. They're usually about eighty-three per cent there . . . Then we'll let a month go by, and we may do another two or three weeks and that's pretty much it, but with constant tweaking after that. It never stops. It's there structurally, but we never stop thinking about it. That was the case mostly with *Citizen Ruth* because it took such a long time to get made.

Jim, since you are not behind the camera, do you help out with suggestions as far as directing goes?

JT: In one sense, yes, because when we're writing I'm working with the director, and together we're talking about certain things that he wants to achieve when he's directing, so we're trying to write them into the script. But when he's on the set? No.
AP: But I consult with you about casting sometimes.
JT: *Citizen Ruth* I was there on set all the time because it was our first movie and it was exciting. *Election* a little less. It's really dangerous if an actor is looking to someone besides the director for guidance.
AP: On one of my films I had to ban one producer from speaking to any of the talent because he or she spoke to the talent in a way which made that actor insecure and uncomfortable. It was just wrong.
JT: If I'm around during filming—and I am around less and less on each film—people know that I probably have a good idea as to what Alexander is thinking and they'll ask me questions. My response is always, "You have to check with Alexander but I think . . ." There's one person on the set who everyone should go to if creative decisions need to be made on a film Alexander is directing, and that person is Alexander. When I'm directing it will be me.

AP: Jim did do second-unit directing on both *Citizen Ruth* and *Election*. Actually, Jim just finished the first draft of a script for the first film he's going to direct. I cowrote some of it but I didn't get quite as involved with it as he's done with what I've directed. I had the same experience working with him as the co-writer—not as the director— and then trying to listen to him about how he wants to direct the film so then we can write it accordingly. I liked that experience of having the tables turned very much.

So you have a generous relationship with each other.

JT: Yeah, it keeps getting better and better . . .

Now that you are both directors in your own right, is there any way either of you can write on your own?

JT: We can but we hate it.

AP: And I think the work wouldn't be as good. The thing that Jim is going to direct is very much him—his sense of the absurd, and making fun of the pretentious. When I was writing with him I was able to bring it out of him even more.

JT: Absolutely, we are such a good audience for each other. I'm not into being a solitary writer, sitting in my room, alone. It takes me forever to write something on my own.

AP: It helps to be writing with a director. The polish we took three months on, the job-job, we didn't have a director. At least with *Meet the Parents* and *Jurassic Park III*, even if we disagreed with the decision, the director would give us a reason. The length it takes to write something is all about the speed with which you make your decisions about the overall story and then getting from A to B and B to C. You can execute any decision quickly, but it's about making sure which decision is the best that will lead to the next set of choices that are best for the material. So when we were writing Jim's directing project, because he is going to direct and knows the film, he's able to make decisions on the spot based on his own feelings.

JT: It's a really important distinction between directing and writing. I know there are all of these co-directed films, but I think that directing comes down to one guiding instinct. When we are writing in our early drafts, we are strictly co-writers. Alexander becomes more and more the director as the drafts go on. Ultimately the script is finished because he *says* it's finished and he feels that he can direct those scenes. I can't tell him that it's got to be a particular way if he doesn't feel comfortable directing it, because I'm not the one who is going to be standing out there trying to get the actors to do it.

How do you guys communicate with each other when your ideas are not working or you think something that one of you has come up with is just bad?

JT: That's where a lot of partnerships don't work, when you have to endure the criticism of your partner. We work very hard to listen with an open mind and not take offense.

AP: We generally come to a point where we agree.

JT: Or—we just have to move on. I think both of us try to keep the good of the film in mind and not our egos. Neither of us is trying to keep something in just because it is "ours."

AP: When we have disagreements about the direction of the script, at a certain point we can argue and argue but whoever has the stronger instinct, the other one will trust him unless he feels very, very strongly as well.

Staying in the realm of the uncomfortable . . . how do you guys deal with self-doubt during the writing process, when you question the whole project and your abilities as a writer?

AP: When are you not dealing with self-doubt?

JT: As a matter of fact, what we have been working on in the last few days has been going through this doldrums period.

AP: But we know we'll break through it. You *have* to break through it, because you want to make your movie. Also, since we've already been through the doldrums before, we know it doesn't last forever. That's the only thing that helps from experience, knowing you've been there before and that you got through it.

JT: That's one of the advantages of partnerships. If you are on your own your doubts can deepen and linger whereas in a partnership there is someone there to tell you to move on or to reassure you. That's tremendously helpful.

When you were adapting Election, *how did you know when you had established authority over this high school world that you hadn't created?*

AP: From the get-go, because of it striking chords inside of us. The great thing about adapting novels is that they become immediately personal, because of the dialogue between those concerns in the book and how they echo with your own. Most of Kubrick's films are adaptations and he obviously had the same experience, finding things that struck a chord in him and he then took complete authority in terms of making it his own.

Did you have any contact with Tom Perrotta during the writing process?

AP: We didn't have our first contact with him until we finished a draft or two. He read a draft and then it was communicated back to us that he kind of liked it.
JT: I think that is fairly routine. If someone besides the author does the adaptation, they usually don't bring the author into the process until much later. But he came to the set and we liked him and I think he liked us.

Were you at all nervous about showing him your work?

AP: When you adapt a book, you're not making another book—you're making a movie, which operates grammatically very, very differently. The better the book is, the more you have to change it. A good book succeeds with literary effects, but you need cinema so you have to just treat it as raw material. Anyone who expects a movie to be faithful to a book is not really giving the proper respect to cinematic form and literary form.

Tracy Flick's sexuality was much more overt in the book than in the film. Why did she become less of a Lolita and more of a busybody?

AP: Because it seemed more interesting for her not to be more overtly sexual—even though she really is.

Do you worry that it might be harder for the audience to believe that Mr. McAllister would be attracted to her if she were not as sexually overt?

AP: No. We're in New York. Go to the subway and look around—all of those people, they fuck. If people were only attracted to other people who are themselves attractive then we wouldn't have an overpopulation problem on this planet. The notion that people have to be pretty or sexy to be attractive is bullshit to me, because that's not how the world is.

Election *uses four points of view for narration. Did you have a backup plan if the studio didn't go for it?*

JT: No, it was the only way we wanted to do it.

The voice-over works really well in the film and I think it's wonderful. Why do you think Hollywood screenwriting books are so against the technique of using voice-over?

AP: It seems that there are two schools of thought against voice-over. The first is that in cinema you are supposed to show, not tell. The second is that if a film is perceived to be bad or is incomprehensible you slap voice-over on it so you can at least release it. I don't know why some people take those examples of voice-over badly used and translate it into a blanket statement against all voice-over work. You can point to all the great directors and great films that have used voice-over.

JT: How could you watch *Sunset Boulevard* and say, "You should never use voice-over"?

AP: What about *Clockwork Orange*? I really think it's tantamount to saying that in a play you shouldn't have a character speaking a soliloquy all by himself: "I feel this, I aspire to do this." But I saw *Uncle Vanya* last week and three or four characters have moments when they express their inner thoughts on stage. I can't conceive of *Election* without voice-over. That is where form and content are very much united.

So then, if there are four voice-overs, whose movie is this? Is it Jim McAllister's?

JT: That was an evolving process. We really wanted it to be all four, and then Jim and Tracy came to the forefront with Jim being first among equals.

The music is very good in the film. Was the music suggested during the writing?

JT: Music is very important to Alexander. He has a musical sensibility that's unusual and particular to him, and it's really evident in his films, especially in *Election*. He'll often play something while we're writing to help us capture a certain tone.

AP: In terms of the directing side, one film I found inspiring to watch in terms of music and in some degree of multiple voice-overs was *Casino*. *Casino* is an influence on *Election*, directorially. Kevin Tent and I watched it a couple of times while we were editing *Election*.

JT: I didn't know that.

It's funny you mention Scorsese, because when I think of the day of the election and what Jim McAllister goes through: the botched affair, the bee sting, etc., I think of Ray Liotta's day in Goodfellas *where he's being chased by helicopters while trying to sell his guns and make a homemade pasta sauce for his little brother.*

AP: When Jim gives the pop-quiz he looks at the clock twice—that's stolen from *Goodfellas*, when Henry Hill is stirring the sauce and looks at the clock in the kitchen twice . . .

Also, you've spoken elsewhere about how Scorsese talks about a film being composed of five sequences rather than three acts.

AP: I think it's good to get away from thinking about three-act structure when you're writing films. When you see Scorsese movies or Fellini movies you just see episodes. At the same time, you know that Robert McKee could go and say, "Yes, but it still responds to the three-act structure and here's how . . ." Howard Suber, who taught film structure at UCLA and is a proponent of the three-act structure, used to say that in pretty much every film, no matter what structure, at the one-hour mark there is usually a major change. I've kept that in mind when I have watched films and you can almost set your watch to it. Within plus or minus three minutes of the one-hour mark there is some major turning point, a reversal or something. But that's more about making an observation than it is about making a film.

JT: You just instinctively know when things need to move on. It's a lot like making love. If you're looking at the clock thinking "OK, we've been in foreplay for fifteen minutes and now it's time for the inciting incident" . . . then you're not going to have very good sex.

AP: When I give screenwriting seminars or classes and they ask me, "What advice do you have for young screenwriters?," I say, "Don't read any screenwriting books." I actually think the whole three-act structure is so deeply ingrained in us from living in this culture and watching movies that in order to come up with new movies, which is what I want to see, you really have to fight what you have innately learned. When you're writing, you will find yourself being drawn naturally by gravity into doing something which corresponds to all of these things that you have seen. You have to fight that instinct in order to come up with a new movie.

JT: One idea I had for titling the chapters on the DVD was to use McKee's definitions for where we're at—"Chapter 18: The Point of No Return."

Both Election *and* About Schmidt *start off slowly and then pick up steam, passing along information about the characters very quickly.*

AP: Both films begin like a lawyer impassively presenting a case in court; the facts are presented blandly: "There's this, there's this and there's this." Only later, once you have all that stuff submitted, can you start drawing conclusions from it. You can watch those two movies and say, "Well, nothing happens for a long time." In fact, only when you reach a certain point you can realize it's all been happening but just in a different way than you expected.

You create a visual motif of Jim McAllister moving in circles. We open with him running around the track at his high school's athletic field. Where did it come from?

JT: It wasn't in the script. That's production design and directing. But there were similar ideas, like how Jim McAllister is constantly throwing things away, which we were aware of when we were writing. It begins with him cleaning out the fridge at school.
AP: Oh yeah, but then directorially I went hog wild with it.
JT: True. It's very important that he's introduced this way, cleaning other teachers' leftovers out of the refrigerator at school, because it sets up his character. Jim's somebody who is trying to control the messy parts of life, which he does mostly by blaming other people. But then his own messes spill out and he has to face the consequences.
AP: What was also important was to have Jim and Tracy meet at the beginning of the film. We introduce antagonist and protagonist. I don't know which is which . . .
JT: We also needed to establish the multiple voice-overs. As soon as possible, we give Tracy and Jim each a little voice-over of their own so that right away you get the idea that this is not just going to be one person's movie.

I have to say, the way the school is shot reminds me of my own Midwestern high school routine. Did you look at a lot of schools?

AP: Yeah, I went to every high school in Omaha, Nebraska.
JT: But also it comes from our experiences, because we feel like high school is a universal experience.
AP: Yeah. I was surprised how similar it was to my own high school days, how things hadn't really changed that much.

One of my favorite moments in the film is when Jim McAllister asks his class what the difference is between morals and ethics . . .

AP: We just came up with that dialogue as a joke.

JT: It's a joke, but with a purpose. Jim McAllister is someone who wants to create clear distinctions in the world, and between people, but that's not such an easy thing to do. When we wrote that line, we had *no idea* ourselves what the difference was between morals and ethics — and we still don't.

Neither do I. It made me feel like I was a kid in the class who didn't know the answer.

JT: Right, it's an unfair question — which makes Tracy's certainty about the answer all the more revealing. In a way, she and Jim are both people interested in simplifying the world into easily controllable elements.

How do you handle an expository montage like the yearbook sequence where we see Tracy Flick doing all her extracurricular activities?

AP: David Russell told me he loves this yearbook thing. I told him the idea of it was to give the impression of someone who is so excited about how many pages she appears in, in the yearbook — "Oh, look, I'm here and I'm here and here."

It seems like the film really gets going when Jim McAllister reveals to us that Tracy Flick has been having an affair with his colleague. We are introduced to his fellow teacher by him saying, "Her pussy gets so wet."

AP: That's the inciting incident . . .

In the book the revelation about the affair comes much later.

JT: That was kind of tricky, unravelling the chronology of how that story is told in the book and how we wanted to adapt it to the screen. It took us a while to figure out. Walter Murch says in his new book with Michael Ondaatje that *Election* is one movie that successfully uses flashbacks within flashbacks. But he still advises against trying it.

At one point Jim and Tracy have duelling voice-overs, talking about how much they dislike each other.

AP: Yes, that's when I freeze-frame each one of them as they present their case about the other.

JT: Again, it's about the control thing. Even in the world of the movie they have the ability to stop things.

Do you think a lot about transitions when you're writing?

AP: Always, about how to link them and to make them clever or fun. We write a lot of directorial stuff into the scripts like fade-in, hard cut, dissolves, visual wipes.
JT: Working with the director makes that easier, but it's just good screenwriting to be using cinematic tools to tell the story.

You made an effort to show that Tracy is not as well off as Paul. She takes the bus and he drives his brand new truck to school. How important is social realism to you guys?

JT: We think a big reason many movies are not successful is that the writing and directing, often unconsciously, aspire to create by the "movie version" of the story. "What would happen in the movie version? What would it look like?" And the end result seems fake. When we're writing, we do our best to ignore how we've seen a situation play itself out in movies, and think instead of how it would really happen. We try to begin with the raw materials of life, not the raw materials of other movies.
AP: I always get the question "Why are you shooting in Omaha?" I think one of the reasons is precisely this: we're declaring that this is a real place. Since it's so specific it feels exotic to a lot of people. So that puts pressure on us as filmmakers to be specifically real, not just real.

Can you give me an example of this?

JT: When Jim gets into his car, Tracy approaches, waving her petition. Jim is caught in his seatbelt, which slides up the door's frame as it closes. That's a good example, on the directing level, of what we are talking about. On a lot of movies they would rig that seatbelt so it wouldn't come into the shot because it's distracting, but it's actually one of the best things about this moment.
AP: Here it was perfect that it just so happens that the Ford Festiva has that feature. It was funny and thematically appropriate.

Where are you picking up your dialogue from if you are not getting it from overhearing conversations at the local high school? For example, when Jim says, "When things went all haywire with that election."

JT: I think that's more of a Midwestern construction. Tracy sprinkles a lot of SAT vocabulary words into her speech, which she usually misuses. Things like "unconscionable travesty." Or getting her expressions mixed up like "He's had everything handed to him on a silver spoon."

AP: Or like in *Citizen Ruth*, "We're committed to the afterbirth. We're committed to her afterbirth too." [*laughs*]

There is a funny moment when Jim is frantically running around, trying to prepare his hotel room for an affair while his students take a pop quiz. I like how he goes to his local Walgreen's to pick up his romantic knickknacks, sparkling wine and Russell Stover's chocolates.

JT: In the script it was Whitman's.

AP: There's another scene that we cut out where he goes to the library and picks out this special poem that he wants to read to her. The only thing that remained of that was the shot of that book in his hand.

JT: Which is kind of great because you don't really know what he was thinking. But it was a beautiful poem, actually.

AP: An unpublished Elizabeth Bishop poem.

Was Jim's bloated bee sting meant to be a physical representation of what is happening inside of him?

JT: It just came from an impulse to have him get injured, but without any idea about what it would represent. When we thought about it later we realized that it worked on a lot of levels.

AP: But we didn't think, "We should find a physical representation of his interior malaise." Jim just said, "Something should happen to him here. How about he gets stung by a bee?"

At the end of the film Jim McAllister moves to New York City and he gets a job at a museum. Can you tell me something about the ending?

JT: We shot a new ending several months after the film was finished. We all agreed that the original ending, which was straight out of the book, was adequate but it didn't work as well as it could have . . . it's strange, because two days before shooting, the ending was the one thing the studio said we needed to rewrite. They wanted it to be more explicit. Against our better judgment, we changed it and it ended up being too schmaltzy. Not horribly so, but we'll never know how our original version would have worked.

AP: The rest of the movie turned out so funny that a poignant ending seemed odd to many viewers.

JT: So we set about writing a new ending which would be more in keeping with the rest of the film. It was a tortuous process. For some reason there was this mandate from the studio that Jim McAllister had to become a teacher again. First we made him a park ranger but they demanded that he had to be a teacher. It was bizarre to us, we couldn't figure out why that was so important. I had just been to the Museum of Natural History and I love all of these dioramas. When Alexander came to New York to work on the ending I said, "Why doesn't he just get a job working at the Museum of Natural History?" So when he says in the voice-over "That's right, I'm teaching again!" it's specifically in there so the studio would approve it.

And what about taking the ending further, so that Jim McAllister sees Tracy Flick step into a limousine while on holiday in Washington D.C.?

JT: In a way that sequence really tells us that it is Jim McAllister's movie.
AP: We also shot her looking out of the limo, thinking her thoughts about him.

Why did you omit that?

AP: It just didn't feel right.

New York, New York

Lukas Moodysson

13

LUKAS MOODYSSON

Together

"It is like having a child inside of you."

Lukas Moodysson has written and directed three feature films, *Show Me Love* (*Fucking Åmål*) 1998, *Together* (*Tillsammans*) (2000) and *Lilya 4-Ever* (2003). He is the only Swedish filmmaker to ever win four Guldbagge awards, the Swedish equivalent of the Oscars, which has been running since 1964. Moodysson wrote five poetry collections and a novel by the age of twenty-three. He lives in southern Sweden with his wife and two boys.

Synopsis

Suburban Sweden, 1975. Elisabeth tires of her abusive alcoholic husband, Rolf, so she packs her bags, takes her two children and lives with her brother Göran in a hippie commune called Together. Inhabiting this house share are a recently realized lesbian, her jealous ex-boyfriend and a gay man with a bob haircut. The new arrivals make everyone question their values and test the nature of the hippie ideology, with surprising results.

* * *

KEVIN CONROY SCOTT: *You've described your upbringing as one of "an average, normal Ikea kind of family." Were you encouraged to be creative in this "normal" household?*

LUKAS MOODYSSON: I think I described my *environment* as normal, rather than my upbringing. I grew up in a very normal small town, with very normal surroundings—everything was very normal. Personally, I always felt like I wasn't very normal, but that I was very strange. Well, not strange, but special or something . . . I think what I meant was that I didn't grow up in a very cultured environment. My mother was a librarian at the time so we had a lot of books in the house and so on. I think friends of mine who grew up in less average places sometimes have more difficulty relating to normal human beings, whereas that has never been a problem for me. So I think I had both the feeling that I was special in some way and very normal as well.

Did you spend a lot of time doing creative things at this stage?

If I wanted to analyze myself I am sure that I could sit down and talk about how I wrote these things to come to terms with certain things that had happened but I don't think I am really interested in that.

There are a few important things that happened in my life when I was young but I am not sure if I want to go into that because, partly, I am writing things instead of going into therapy. One thing that I learned when I stopped writing poetry was that I didn't have to be completely personal and autobiographical to be personal with my writing; I didn't have to be private to be personal. That was an important revelation for me; that I didn't have to write about myself, that I could still write about myself even though I didn't write about me. I wrote about myself reflected in other people. As a starting point for my writing I think it is very difficult to know why you do things. It's like falling in love with someone. You can't really analyze why you fall in love with a person. I never felt that I made a choice to write, but it was more that I had to write.

Can you tell me something about how you got interested in writing poetry? Being a poet isn't an obvious hobby for a teenager.

I'm not really sure if this is true but I have started to think about writing more and more that it is something that someone pushes me to do, someone forces me to do it. Not that it is against my will, but it's someone who puts me in situations that I can't really escape from or someone that tells me what to do. It feels like it's my duty to do that. For me that's how it all started. I think I was forced into writing for some reason. I think I felt like it was very interesting to build some kind of universe that existed. I remember having a microscope when I was a child, and in some way I can relate writing to that kind of feeling you get when you look down a microscope. That you can put a small, small slice of something into a microscope and see all of these things. I can also relate now to the way my children play with Lego. They make things that are very strange but fantastic.

You were saying that you build very practical things, and they build things that look like castles in the sky.

Yeah. I try to build things that are like castles in the sky, but they turn out very symmetrical.

Getting back to poetry . . . did you have any personal heroes when it came to poetry?

I think the inspiration was mostly Swedish poets. Bruno K. Öijer, Lars Norén, Gunnar Ekelöf and Michael Strunge, but he's Danish.

I think I remember you saying somewhere that you felt that writing poetry was self-centered. Did you mean that it was self-indulgent?

It is very self-centered. It's very much like looking into a mirror and trying to see what is inside of you. I am more interested in letting the world flow through me and let myself be some kind of filter or something like that. Poetry is something that is very special. I read a lot of poetry and I have also started writing poetry again, but it's very difficult to talk about because I don't have control over the process I am involved in; this is the way for all my creative processes. I have the least control over poetry, and therefore it is very difficult for me to talk about it because it is what it is and it is very difficult to describe what it is. In some ways I think what you try to achieve when you are writing is to try and find your innermost authentic voice, and at one moment in my life I stopped being interested in going inwards and trying to find the center of myself, so I started looking outside instead.

Can you explain the transition from when you went from looking within yourself to looking outside yourself when writing? How do you make the outside world personal?

When I was twenty-two I really felt the need, subconsciously or unconsciously, to change my life completely. I just wanted to turn it upside down because I was very bored with my life, dissatisfied, and I just wanted something else. I didn't really have a direction, I just felt like I needed to change. That was the time I started thinking about maybe doing films. But I also had different plans, like being a lawyer. There were many different things; I wanted to be a chef, I wanted to move away from where I lived, I wanted to break up with my girl-friend. [*laughs*] It just felt like I was stuck in some little corner of life. I think you understand these things a long time afterwards, why you go in those specific directions. I can understand that now. I can understand that I was tired of the fact that my world was very much spin-ning around in my own head. Because of the way I was writing, my world was getting smaller and smaller; it was slowly imploding and as a result I wanted to explode, but I couldn't put that into words at that moment. Then I went to film school and tried to make films but I still had a problem. I didn't realize the changes that I really needed to make, which was the change of going from looking inside to looking outside. So I started to make films that were very, very strange and didn't make any sense. My first film was seven seconds long, and it included one dead woman and one hen. So I didn't have a clue as to what I was doing. I still tried to learn to be a film director, to learn craft. But everything I wrote was very, very bad. Film is an open medium, and I was trying to do it in a closed way so it didn't work out at all. It started to work only when I had my first child, because then I just existentially realized that I am not the center of the world. That's when I first got a grip on what I was trying to do, and I figured out what I was interested in. It was also the time I started to become extremely interested in all the things that happen in life, all the small details. I was starting to look at not only myself with a microscope, but look at everything else with a microscope.

I've read quite a few interviews with you where the journalist described you as an outsider as a teenager. Do you agree with this?

I am not trying to make this sound like I was in any way unique, because I think this happens to a lot of young people, but I think I had a mixed position which has become very useful in my life, because I had an opportunity to go to different places. Like being inside and being outside, being alone and being at parties, and also being from a very normal environment and at the same time being very strange in some ways. Teenage years are long and they can change from day to day. You are either popular or strange, you can be both and it can change from day to day.

Were you writing any short stories around the time that you were writing poetry?

I wrote a novel. Aged twenty, I think.

Can you tell me what the novel was about?

It was about myself but about myself in a fictional way. It didn't really have a story. It's really very bad, I hate it. There's this one scene that takes place at the Central Station of Malmö. It's something like a dream where the asphalt is melting and there is a comet coming towards the planet. It's the story about lost love. I wrote to try and get a girlfriend back. The whole novel is a long letter to her. It's very bad. [*laughs*]

Can you tell me something about film school and what you learned about screenwriting there?

It felt like I didn't learn anything, but afterwards I realized I must have learned quite a lot because I realized that I knew how to do some things. But about writing, I don't think I learned very much about writing. You can take the screenwriting course, but I was on the direction course. I went to Dramatiska Institutet in Stockholm and it is the only real film school in Sweden. I think the school is more about the art than about the craft. I think there were things I wanted to learn about, like special effects or something, but I never learned that. There was a very personal communication between the teacher and the pupil. There were a few occasions where that really worked out for me. I had quite a good teacher in my directing course, and I think I learned a lot from him, most of which I didn't realize until later. Maybe I am slow or something, but it took a long time for me to understand things. All the other students there were quite experienced when they arrived; they had made short films and other things, but I was a complete amateur. I'm not even sure why they accepted me there. It's one of these schools where they only accept two or three pupils every couple of years. It must have been partly on the merit of what I had written and partly that I had an enormously strong will for something, because I didn't have any idea how to make films. I was really surprised to learn that you had to edit them, to cut them together. I was enormously ignorant at that time. So it was very strange for me to start from nothing, which is probably part of the reason why I was making films that were seven seconds long. I remember the feeling when I was sitting in the editing room and I was supposed to edit the film; I was just so amazed by the fact that you could put this picture after this other picture. That made me want to just edit faster and faster until it was seven seconds long. I was just experimenting for a while. It was also during a time when I was learning a lot by watching movies; I hadn't really done that before. That was really the only part of my life when I saw a lot of films. Before that I didn't really see a lot of films and now I don't see many, so I had three years when I saw a lot of films.

What kind of films were you interested in during this period?

The first thing I saw where I felt there was something very interesting in the visual media was before film school, when I saw *Twin Peaks*. I also remember one or two Tarkovsky films and one or two science fiction movies like *Alien* and *Blade Runner*. Then at film school I started to see the American films from the seventies, and for a while I was really interested in Scorsese, Cassavetes and those guys. Then I saw *Ladybird, Ladybird* by Ken Loach and that affected me. I remember feeling that I would never be able to make something like this because there is too much real life in it; I had no idea of how to make something like that. So I remember being uplifted and depressed by seeing *Ladybird, Ladybird*.

You've spoken also of Mike Leigh's Secrets & Lies. *And your work has been favorably compared to his on different occasions. I wondered if you are interested in his working methods, the way that he casts and rehearses and so on?*

I work without rehearsals. Because for me it takes away from all the spontaneity, the presence and the insecurities of the actors, and the director, and even the camera. I am very interested in the insecurities of things because if you are safe and you know exactly what to do you lose quite a lot, I think. Because as a human being, in real life, you are very insecure and you don't know what is going to happen. Often when an actor rehearses they lose that insecurity. I think that is something I try to keep in my films. I am interested in the method that he has, and I would like to use more improvisation, and I would like to work in different ways. I am planning to use some new methods the next time I make a film, but so far I have tried to avoid rehearsing.

So if you want them to be spontaneous you encourage your actors to improvise?

When I have the courage, yes, when I don't have the courage, no. It also depends on what you mean by improvisation. You can use the exact same words, but you can change where you are walking and where you are standing; that's another form of improvisation. That kind of improvisation I do a lot. Sometimes I have the courage to let them lose the script and say whatever they want to say. Unfortunately, quite a lot of the time I don't have that courage, so I try to stay as close to the script as possible when it comes to the words. But when it comes to the movements I have a bit more confidence and courage. I guess it goes to my background as a writer, I still see myself as a writer, not really as a director.

When you were at film school did you always see yourself as a writer-director?

I'm not sure, maybe.

Let's put it this way, would you ever direct someone else's screenplay?

I don't think I could find a script and direct it. It would be more likely that I would find a novel or a theatrical play, something that just spoke to me in a very special way. When people send me scripts, I really can't see myself directing them. Because directing for me is not about going out there and finding something, it's about things coming to me. If you gave me a script, there would be one million directors in the world that could do it much better than me because I am not really a good director. I am a person who, my whole life and my whole work is based on keeping my eyes open and letting things flow through me. I don't ever know where to put the camera, I don't ever know what to say to the actors, and I don't know if I need a close-up or a wide shot. I tried to use some dramaturgical methods once; I was reading some book by Syd Field when I was writing *Fucking Åmål*. Basically I didn't really know how to write a script, so it was interesting for me at that moment just to try and be as simple as possible in some ways. It was interesting to just find some skeleton to put all the muscles on, but apart from that I have never really understood anything from all those theorists.

You don't know what plot points are? Character motivation? The rising action?

I don't know what those things are, I really don't. I think it's a good thing to learn the shortest way from this point to that point. I think that is what you can learn from all those principles and theorists; I think that is a good thing. But after you learn those things you should just learn to walk away in different directions.

Getting back to the whole writer-director thing, David O. Russell told me that for him, the only reason he is in charge of the film set and the real reason he feels like he is in control of all these talented people working on his films is that he is the one who has written the screenplay, so the story is in his bones. Do you agree with that?

That's true, yeah. Absolutely. It would be a real problem if I didn't direct my own script; then I would feel like I am just an amateur and that anyone could do it better than me. I don't feel like I am in complete control, but I do have some small security that I have been sitting in my room, writing this script. But then if someone asks me "Why is this person saying this?" then I feel completely lost. So it is like I have security but it is a small security.

Do you have a trusted group of friends that read your screenplays and offer you advice?

Well, I listen very carefully to what my wife says. She's an artist, she makes different things, cartoons and all kinds of different things like painting. Last year she published a collection of comics. I also listen to my producer quite a lot. With my wife it almost always turns into bitter fights and that can be really painful.

Why, because she is telling you things you don't want to hear?

Yeah.

And you know that she is right and you don't want to admit it?

[*laughs*] No, I know she is wrong. I trust her very much, but when you trust someone very much it is very difficult, because there is always the possibility that they might be wrong. But then I trust her so much that I believe that she is right when she is sometimes wrong, although most of the time she is right.

What about your film financiers, outside your producer? Do you take notes from them?

I only get notes from my producer and he deals with the financiers. On the few occasions I have discussions with them, they were more interested in talking about the script. They can always say no to doing the movie but that's different. *Fucking Åmål* was a difficult film to finance. Of course the financiers had a lot of different opinions on how to do things but we won in the end so . . .

What kind of a living can a screenwriter in Sweden expect to make?

People who are making the most money here are the ones working for television. It is a very small industry in a very small country, so few people can really make a living at it.

When you have gone out to Hollywood, have you ever been asked to write anything for the studios out there?

I've been asked to direct a few scripts, but I am not really interested in Hollywood. I see Hollywood as a bit like the opposite of what I am trying to do. Hollywood is not about expressing something, it's about making money. I'm not really interested in that.

Can you tell me something about your writing process, from original idea to finished screenplay?

It has changed from script to script. I don't have a very good insight into what I am doing; I don't know where it is coming from. I see myself as some kind of Ouija board. It's a very strange process. With *Fucking Åmål* I tried to be a good boy and write it the way that you should write a script, and it worked out very well for that script. I had a computer at the time that I borrowed from the person who wanted me to write commercials for him. But I didn't really write any commercials, so he took the computer away from me; so then I just had my old typewriter. So I wrote the script by hand and on the typewriter; so then from version to version and draft to draft it would change, then I got a computer. I would like to try and write on a typewriter; sometimes it is difficult because you get used to the easiness with which you can write on a computer and how you change things so easily. I would like to just try it on a typewriter from the first word to the last word.

Why, because each word has so much more significance once committed to paper?

No, because it sometimes gets too easy when you write on a computer, and also because it looks finished because it looks so professional. When you are writing on a typewriter there are these "xxx's" and it looks like it is not really finished. Also, I think that you get a closer connection, spiritual or something, because the paper is present. You can touch what you are writing on. For me, computers are fictional in a way because the writing takes place in some kind of fictional digital world. If the computer collapses, then your screenplay doesn't exist anymore, but if you are writing on a typewriter, it is on paper, you can touch it. I feel like I lose a bit of the connection to the paper and that the paper is my work.

My process has changed with each film. *Together* was a film that changed in the editing room; it was really turned upside down afterwards. *Fucking Åmål* was edited as it was written. Another thing that is interesting is that I always believe that I am finished before I actually am. I don't want to write anymore, but I feel like I have to write again. So that is one of the problems. I am a bit lazy and I feel that I am finished when I am not finished at all. So I have to push myself to go back and do the writing. It is the same thing with the editing; with *Together* I felt like we were finished and we weren't finished at all, we had to do some more work. *Lilya 4-Ever* was very special in that it came very suddenly to me and very precisely, like a flash or something; it just fell into my head almost finished. I have never experienced that before. I was working on a different script about something else; it was actually an American movie. I was interested in some American things like health insurance. So then one day I was writing in my room and someone was whispering in my ear, "This is the film you have to do," and suddenly I changed. I called my producer and told him I'd changed my mind and he said, "OK." The whole process was very, very fast, which was good because otherwise I don't think we would have made that film, because it was such a difficult film to make in many ways, especially with the language and everything.

At one point you were writing a movie about health care in America. How did you feel that you could talk about Americans in such a convincing way? Had you ever lived there?

No. The world is open, and if you have open eyes you can see everything. I have never lived in Russia either, and I made *Lilya 4-Ever*. There is this book I read about a month ago called *Papalagi,* and it's from the 1920s, and it is written by some man who is from a primitive culture from some island somewhere. He comes to Europe in the twenties and he looks at the Western civilization with enormous skepticism and criticism, and he gives new words to things we take for granted, like money or clothes or cars or houses, or like the way we have jobs, for example, which he thinks is completely strange. For him it's, "But why is it that this person is only working with this thing and not that thing?" He sees things from the outside. I don't think that all of his analysis is correct but many are very strange and very interesting. When I am at my best I try to be close to that, someone who looks at something from a distance and misunderstands a lot but also understands a few things. I think that is the reason why *Fucking Åmål* is about girls, and why *Together* is about the seventies, and *Lilya 4-Ever* is about Russia, and why that script was about

America, and why my next film will also be about things that I don't really fit into completely.

What do you go through during your writing day when you are in your room alone and you are trying to create this universe?

I think you need some kind of energy and sometimes you need different kinds of energies, depending on what you are writing. For example, I am writing a script right now, and I felt like at one point I was listening to the wrong music. I usually listen to some very loud music in my headphones, but I realized I was listening to the wrong music because it made the script too aggressive. I was listening to lots of Marilyn Manson, over and over again, his latest record. But then I had to switch to something—it's a bit like an exorcism or something like that—that if I was a teenager today I would listen to. I realized that I was trying to write from the point of view of a teenager. It's not a movie about teenagers but this character happens to be a teenager and I wanted to get his perspective about things. So I tried to be a teenager today and find the music he would listen to today. So it's like I have to find some way that makes me focus completely in one direction. It feels a bit like dancing; you just try to feel like you are in the music with the writing and with the characters. It's like trying to be present somewhere. But actually that is the second part of the process. The first part is one long part; it is like having a child inside of you; you can't really push it out, you just have to wait until it is ready to come out. That is very important because you want the child to come out but it will not. If you try to push it out too early it is like an abortion, and you will kill the child. [*laughs*] It's a strange analogy, I know. But it's almost like you have to carry it for a long time, and if you try to write too early it gets destroyed.

Have you ever gotten pregnant by accident?

I think I am always pregnant by accident; actually. *Lilya 4-Ever* was very much an unexpected pregnancy because I didn't expect that at all. I never really know who the fathers are. [*laughs*] I am just a mother and I think they come to me when I sleep and I don't wake up. That's the first part. The second part is when I am just completely focused and then the third part is the rewriting, which is sometimes great and sometimes very frustrating, because you think you are finished and then you aren't finished.

My understanding of it is that during the writing process you are constantly making decisions which other decisions are reliant upon. You build this foundation and then if you discover you made a wrong decision, you then have to go back and reassess all the decisions you then made after that mistake.

That's true. It's one of the most frustrating things about writing. But it can also be wonderful because it can turn the script upside down in a wonderful way. For example, if you have a problem somewhere you can try and fix it by doing something completely different. In a script I am writing at the moment, there was a young woman and she had a friend, and at one time it just felt like there was something wrong, so I changed the friend to the mother of her friend. That changed everything because her mother said the strangest things. If you put the words of a friend into the mouth of a mother, that is very strange, and that created a very strange and interesting character.

When you are alone in a room and it's just you and the computer in front of you, how do you deal with feelings of self-doubt that crop up during the writing process, during those moments when you don't feel that great about what you are working on?

I go through that all the time. It is always difficult. I think there are two kinds of self-doubt. One is a kind of constructive self-doubt, that is a self-doubt when you are self-critical — "There is something wrong but I am going to fix it." That can be a very nice and interesting feeling because that is a feeling that gives birth to new ideas like "I am going to change this friend into a mother." But when you're feeling "This is bad and I don't know how to fix it," that is terrible. The problem is that it is like a virus that spreads into everything that you have written. Sometimes I can be sitting there, writing, and I can think, "This dialogue is so crappy." Then later I might go further — "Not only is this dialogue crappy, it is a symptom of *everything* I have ever written." So suddenly it is like "I am nothing and I have written nothing in my life." That's terrible. But on the other hand you have to go through a depression to get out and go through to the other side.

Do you write music into your screenplays or camera movements?

Only a few camera movements, when they are very special. My screenplays are very much just based on dialogue. I try to be very precise and simple when I write. Sometimes I write music but it usually changes when I make the film — it turns out to be something else.

Does listening to music when you are writing help you establish the tone of the script?

Listening to music is essential for me. When I listen very intensely to Marilyn Manson, I am not really sure I enjoy listening to it; it's more that I had to be there because it had some kind of tone that was close to what I was trying to write.

Ingmar Bergman paid you a famous compliment by calling you a "young master," which is quite something, given the long shadow he throws over world cinema, and in particular, Swedish cinema. But you seemed generally unaffected by the compliment; you were grateful but also took it in your stride. And you said you were part of a new generation of Swedish filmmakers who don't have to worry about where things stood in relation to Bergman. When did this shift take place?

I think Bergman's problem is that he never became popular. I think that is something he feels bad about. He is more like a phenomenon than someone who has ever been popular. Maybe sometimes it feels like foreign journalists see him as more influential in Sweden than he actually is. I wasn't working with films when he was, so I don't know how it felt at that time. Right now, I don't know. I think that a few generations ago you had to be either pro or con, you had to be friends with him or his enemy. There were people who tried to make films like him, and people who avoided making films like him. I have never experienced it, so I am not really sure. What is fascinating is that he is still looking at films. He sees one film every day at one o'clock. He lives on this small island outside of Sweden called Faro. He has his own movie theater, and at one o'clock every day he sees a film, and he sees all the new Swedish films. I think that is fascinating and maybe a little bit sad. Just the fact that he has seen my films is interesting. I know once or twice a year the Swedish Film Institute sends a truck down to his place with a bunch of prints, and he runs them at his little theater.

One day I was going to call him. I got his phone number and I was going to ask him if he wanted to sign something about protesting the fact that Abbas Kiarostami wasn't allowed into the United States. I called him once and he didn't answer, so I didn't call him again.

You say these ideas just come to you, but can you give me an understanding of where the idea for Together *originated?*

I think it had something to do with a feeling I had that had to do with being in a crowd. I have forever in my life been a person who felt like

I didn't like being in crowds or in crowded places. I think the film was my way of dealing with the fact that you cannot survive outside the crowd, you have to be with other people. Allegorically, that is what the film is about.

I think you are always drawn to these things by other, deeper reasons and you have to follow them. Sometimes, even when the idea for the film is superficial there still might be a deeper reason you are attracted to the idea, even if it seems arbitrary at first. You have to be aware of the fact that ideas don't come to you as wonderful flowers but more like small seeds. So I think the first seed of *Together* was born in two different places. One was when I was in an art museum with my wife and we were looking at some paintings, and I thought that doing a film on the seventies and everything that went on then would be a funny thing to do. I was looking at some Swedish art from the seventies, especially the political art from that era. And then we were discussing a book that my wife had read when she was a child, so that was one place of birth. I think another place of birth was just being in a crowd like that. It was a festival I was at, and there were so many people and there was smoke and people screaming, and I was so used to not liking being in places like that and I suddenly felt "This is great." I think that was the real birth of the story.

Did you do any character biographies for the script?

No. What I did was I wrote more scenes than there is in the finished film, but that was more like scenes I was interested in writing, but I didn't write biographies. That is something I am interested in for the future. I am interested in creating characters for the actors to jump into, and then for them to explore their characters more. I am not sure if I want to write biographies, or if I want to describe the characters and let the characters come up with ideas for scenes or improvising or in some way making it a looser script. That would be interesting in the future, but so far I have not done that.

Together *is told from different points of view. Was there ever a point where it was one person's story, or was it always an ensemble piece?*

I know it wasn't like that from the beginning; I know what was not there at the beginning: the perspective of the children. At the beginning I thought it was going to be such a chaotic film; and it would be such a strange set with all these grown-ups running around naked, I just felt like I didn't want to put children in that place. For a long time I just tried to avoid the children, but they just pushed themselves into the story, and they also pushed me to make their characters more and more important. So it wasn't there at the beginning, but at the end it was the most important perspective.

I was fantasizing about making this film when I was making *Fucking Åmål*. Sometimes we would talk about it, maybe we were just getting tired of making all of these scenes with teenagers and we were discussing the next time we would make a real film with grown-ups in it. I felt like "Now I am going to make a grown-up movie." But it didn't happen that way, at least not completely, but that was the intention.

Why do you think you are attracted to teenage characters?

I'm not sure I am—or if I am more attracted to their perspective. I think I am trying to find the childish perspective in myself the whole time as a writer. When people criticize me for being childish or naïve . . . to me that is just a compliment because I am just trying to find that perspective or that point of view, that way of looking at life, that reality. It goes back to what we said about building the Lego. This is my way of building my Lego and those strange starships and castles in the sky.

Is it also something about teenagers having less choices than adults who are in control of their destiny to a larger extent? They are living at home; they don't earn their own income, and they don't have the emotional maturity to make decisions for themselves, so a lot of decisions get made for them . . .

Yeah, but on the other hand they are not dead yet, but sometimes their parents are. They still have the chance to do great or bad things with their lives, and they haven't become stiff and boring. They are still changing, and they have a lot of imagination, and they are experiencing things for the first time instead of the hundredth time. I wouldn't want to be a teenager now; I think it is a very difficult time in life. I am very happy now; I feel much smarter today than when I was fifteen, but at the same time I envy some of the things I had as a teenager that I don't have today, like a childish, clear vision. My children say the strangest, most true things. Like my son yesterday, he's four years old, he said he wanted to go outside and sit by the table and look up at the sky and he wanted to make drawings of what he saw there. Then he wanted to hang up the drawings on a tree. That is so wonderful. I think that is what I want to do myself, I just want to go out and see—I don't know if I want to look at the sky—but I want to go out and look at the world and make these small drawings and then tape them up on a tree.

You have a really good feeling for what is happening in this world, the era, what was discussed during those times—I'm thinking of that funny scene where the kids celebrate that Franco has died—I was wondering if you did any research on the film?

I have met people both before making the film and after who have lived in communes. Some of them lived in communes when they were twenty or thirty years old, and some when they were five or ten years old. I am not really sure if the people who were twenty-five had a much clearer view of what was happening there than the child had. I think as a child you do understand quite a lot and you do see a lot of things. My four-year-old son knows there is war in Iraq, and they know about Saddam Hussein and Osama Bin Laden. It's a bit scary sometimes because you realize that they are probably listening to what you are saying more than you hope they are. [*laughs*] Sometimes you are discussing things that shouldn't be heard by those small ears. I think I had much more knowledge about what was going on around me than what my parents realized.

Some of the fundamentalist ideals that the people who live in the Together commune have are ripe for satire. How did you guard against being too ironic and making fun of people who are, in a sense, soft targets?

I think that if you really love someone, then you can criticize that person quite well. I felt so much love and sympathy for the people in the film that I felt I had to be very hard and critical against them, not because I hate them but because I really love them and I really sympathize with them. One journalist asked me two days ago through a short e-mail interview if this is some kind of major theme of what I do, people who try and fail or that they have ambitions and they don't succeed in achieving those ambitions. I don't think it is a major theme, but I do think I have a lot of sympathy for people who do try. I think there is too much focus in the world on people who succeed rather than people who try. I really like people who try, people who dream, people who want to change things. Some don't succeed in changing things, but at least they want to try and change things.

If someone with right-wing opinions just laughs at those people, then I don't really care because the movie is not made for them. Politically I think it is a film for the left-wing. It's a film saying, "Please, friends, let's not make the same mistakes again. Let's not be fundamentalists, let's not be sectarian, let's invite the neighbor who doesn't share our opinions, let's invite the people who listen to ABBA, and let's play some football." So I think that is the political message.

Their passionate arguments now seem slightly outdated and naïve. For example, one character talks about the coming workers' revolution and how the banks will collapse and how everything will change.

I don't think that's naïve; that's what I am dreaming about right now.

Fair enough. But you are also poking fun at him and embracing him at the same time. When you gave your acceptance speech at the Swedish film awards you said things like, "Don't eat meat," "Film doesn't belong in an opera filled with fat cats in tuxedos." Looking back on that incident, do you think someone can poke fun at your political beliefs thirty years down the road?

Yeah, but I still see myself as someone who is criticizing and making fun but always doing it from the inside, never from the outside. If someone criticizes me from the outside, someone with completely different political ideas than I have, then I don't really care. But if someone criticizes me or makes fun of me from the inside, with similar ideas to mine, then I will listen to that person. That's the difference. Also, I don't think it is outdated at all. I think we are living in a very, very political world, and I think more and more people are becoming aware of how the world is and what it looks like. I think they are becoming more and more aware of the enormous injustices there are in the world and the enormous problems that exist here. I can maybe regret a little bit about *Together* that I didn't make it radical enough, politically speaking. However, I think it works very well allegorically.

This is the problem with all alternative movements: they have to always be *against* things rather than be *for* things. I think it is so easy to criticize things. I know people who are living in a commune and say, "Why did you make fun of us? Why did you just point out the difficult side of things?"

Can you talk about the editing process? You said you planned the film one way; then you shot it, and then you edited it a completely different way. What happened?

I felt it was quite simple to write the script but then I thought it was very frustrating to edit the film. Some scenes were invented when we were shooting. There were some storylines that were interesting but got cut out because they didn't work. The structure of the film changed a lot in the editing. For example, if you look at the number of the scenes as it stands now, and you compare it to the edited script, it would not be 1, 2, 3, 4, 5, 6. It's more like 8, 3, 7, 1. It's a very different order. Some of those things I thought about during shooting, so I left some doors open. Consider the first scene when he comes downstairs and says, "Franco is dead, Franco is dead!" That was a scene we made in two different versions, because in one version Elisabeth, the sister who brings her children to the commune, was in the scene originally but then I started thinking that this Franco scene, which was somewhere in the middle of the film, maybe this is something we could use somewhere else. So we used another version where Elisabeth was not in the scene. I tried different alternatives. Then I had the idea of how each character could have their own film, and then I could put them one after the other. We tried that and it led to me wanting to make new scenes, because I wanted to include one of the children. It didn't work out because there were not enough surprises from one person to another, so it was more like a retelling of the same thing. But it was a good exercise.

I thought that having a unity of space gave the characters, at the least, a natural way of interconnecting.

That's one of the things I really enjoy as a director. I really enjoy creating these universes. I really enjoyed going into that house during production. That was the most fun aspect of making that film. You are walking down the street and it's the year 2000; then you open the door and it's 1975. I spent a lot of time there just looking and changing colors and changing chairs and moving things around. We found a lot of realistic books that could have been in this commune so I spent a lot of time reading those. It goes back to the way I try to be a bit childish about making films and having that childish sensibility. In that perspective I don't think there's a big difference between me and the Hollywood director, like someone who makes *Titanic* or *Star Wars*. It's like being this big child who is allowed to create this new universe. There is a connection there.

Together is a film that is shot mostly inside—there are a lot of interiors—away from the gaze of the outside world. There were precious few scenes where the characters interact with the outside world. Was that intentional?

I am interested in small bridges, not big famous long bridges. I am interested in bridges. There is a bridge in *Fucking Åmål*; there is a bridge in *Lilya 4-Ever*, I cannot really analyse why. The parallel to that might be that I am interested in these closed environments, like this house in *Together*. I am interested in writing a script one day that takes place in just one small apartment, and no one ever goes out from there. I think those rooms and those bridges are just symbols of things that go very deep inside of me, and I can't really analyse why. I am extremely interested in how people live and where people live. One of my biggest inspirations is just looking at different houses and looking at different areas and imaging how people live there, what kind of furniture they have, and what it is like to grow up there, and what it is like to be forty-five and alone in a place like that. So I am not interested in the architecture but the houses and the apartments; there is some kind of deeper symbolic level, but I don't really know what it is.

Rolf's problem with alcohol was handled in one short scene in having him emptying his liquor bottles in his kitchen sink and then later asking for a cup of coffee instead of a beer. Were you worried that this was not going to be convincing enough? It looked like it was a deep rooted problem for him.

Are you asking me to defend myself? I don't really know. What I could say is that I really don't feel that I can defend myself very much, because I don't really think I have achieved anything yet that is perfect in any way. I don't have problems with criticizing myself . . . I have really thought about this. There is not one single scene in any of my films that I am one hundred per cent happy about. There are things in every scene, in every detail that I would have liked to change. I have tried to find one single scene that I feel is perfect but I haven't found it.

Where did the idea for the Pinochet torture game come from? I thought it was brilliant.

I think that is something that is very realistic from my own childhood.

Really? You liked to play torture games as a child?

Yeah, we played Concentration Camp a lot. Children do play those things, then they grow up and forget about it or feel embarrassed about it. I think when you're a child you have to make some kind of attempt to understand the world you live in. I don't think I am unique in any way in this, but I think that most children do the same. I was very much aware of torture and kidnapping and poverty and injustices and starvation. I was very much afraid of being kidnapped.

Of a Stranger-Danger grabbing you when you were walking alone at night?

I don't think I was scared in real situations, but more when I was fantasizing about it. I remember when I was in kindergarten, I could have been four or five years old, children that age do know what is happening. I remember talking to this girl about a boy that had been kidnapped in Italy or something. The kidnappers had cut off his ear and sent it to his parents just to prove that he was in their hands. I remember afterwards laughing about it because those children were rich children and we weren't. Who would want to kidnap us? [*laughs*] Our parents couldn't pay that ransom.

I thought the casting was very good; each character has a very strong, individual identity. Did you take on any notes from actors on character changes?

If I wanted to make a new scene with them it would come from me. In the future I would like to expand that process into more of working with actors, having them suggesting scenes or changes. But so far that hasn't happened.

Knowing that you like to be in the crowd, do you think you'd like to get away from the writing process, since it is such a lonely experience?

I think I am actually going back to where I used to be; not enjoying being in crowds.

On numerous occasions I have seen your work compared to Jean Renoir. His films are renowned for being humanistic, treating each and every one of his characters with great sensitivity. Would you call yourself a humanist filmmaker?

For me humanist sounds like a word that doesn't really have a lot of meaning. I see myself as more of an aggressive and kind and religious and political filmmaker. We have been talking so much about *Together*, and it is strange for me because it is the film I think about the least. If your films are like children there is always something special about the first child and there is always something special about the smallest child and there is always something special about the misunderstood child. For me, *Together* is the misunderstood child. I am not sure if I have understood it myself and I am not really sure if I am happy with the reactions that it has received around the world.

Was it disappointing that your film did so well here in Sweden? I think it was number one at the box office.

I don't have a problem with many people seeing my films, but I never planned that. I think it was a little bit of a disappointment, because I saw it as more of a symbolical film, and it was seen as a comedy. On one level it was intended as a comedy but it was also very much a film that I felt had roots that went in different directions. Because of the success of the film, the whole root system of *Together* was a bit neglected. But it is also misunderstood by myself. I'm not really sure if I succeeded or failed with the film. I am not really sure if I can read what my own intentions were with it, and that is why it is special for me. But all of your children are special but in different ways. This is my misunderstood child that I don't really know what to do with. [*laughs*]

Lilya 4-Ever *is very different, tone-wise, than* Together. *Where* Together *is bittersweet,* Lilya 4-Ever *is something that you could call a social-realist drama. The tender humanism is still there, but also there is a much darker side of human nature on display. There is also a lack of hope there. Where did this dramatic shift in tone come from?*

Well, it's a small child, just a little baby still. I think it's the film that is closest to me right now. Yes, there is some kind of change between *Together* and *Lilya 4-Ever,* but for me it is more important to look at the previous films in the light of *Lilya 4-Ever* rather than the other way around. This is something that no one really believes, but for me it has been, on a very deep existential and religious level, the film with the most hope in it. I am always a bit ambivalent about if I should try to talk about what that hope is, or if I should just let other people interpret the film as they want to. But it is a film that I made to try to be able to live in this world. I survived it, so for me it is full of hope.

Was there anything that you wanted to add before we finish?

I read somewhere that someone wanted to be the first artist of the revolution. I want to be the first *director* of the revolution.

Which revolution is that?

The revolution.

Malmö, Sweden

Paul Laverty

14

PAUL LAVERTY

Sweet Sixteen

"Did you mean to set out to make a sixty million dollar
propaganda movie?"

Paul Laverty practiced law in Scotland before moving to Nicaragua to
work on human rights violations during the civil war in the mid-80s.
The director Ken Loach encouraged Laverty to write *Carla's Song*
(1996), based on his experiences in Nicaragua. They went on to col-
laborate on *My Name Is Joe* (1998), *Bread and Roses* (2000), *Sweet
Sixteen* (2002), and *Ae Fond Kiss* (2004), all original screenplays by
Laverty and garnering him the Best Screenplay Award at the 2002
Cannes Film Festival. Laverty lives in Madrid with his family.

Synopsis

*Greenock, Scotland, the present. Liam is a restless sixteen-year-old
struggling to realize his dream of providing a home for his mother,
Jean, when she comes out of prison, away from her abusive drug-dealing
boyfriend, Stan. She is completing a prison term for a crime that he
committed. Liam and his friend Pinball start dealing heroin and find
success despite the risks they are taking. Liam manages to find his
mother a home, but when she comes out of prison she has other things
on her mind.*

* * *

KEVIN CONROY SCOTT: *Paul, were you interested in writing when you
grew up?*

PAUL LAVERTY: Not at all, it was a total accident, though I used to get
a buzz out of writing surreal letters home to family and friends. I never
knew anybody remotely connected to writing or anything like that. If
someone had told me ten years ago I'd be writing screenplays . . . most
things in my life are accidents.

Were books a part of your household growing up?

Yes, but not in abundance. Although when I became a teenager I was reading all the time.

Were you encouraged at all to pursue the arts?

Not the arts, but both my parents were fantastically encouraging about anything I wanted to do. They didn't put pressure on me, they just said it's really important to try your best no matter the result. Very simple, very helpful. I'm the oldest of six kids. All of us have found satisfaction in our work. They gave us great confidence, and I'll always be grateful to them for that.

Am I right in assuming you're from Glasgow?

I consider myself from Glasgow. I was born in Calcutta in India, and sometimes feel I've been travelling since. My dad applied for the first job he could get after he qualified so we ended up in India by chance—he turned up with a Cromby and woolen coat in the middle of the summer. Then he got very ill with TB and he nearly died, so we came back . . . we were only there for nine months, time to take first steps, and off again.

Then we lived in West Scotland, a tiny wee village, two thousand people, so it was an absolutely fantastic childhood of freedom, coming back home only when we were hungry.

Then I left home at the age of twelve and never really came back except for holidays. I went off to seminary to study for the priesthood. Because of the Catholic and Irish connection with the city of Glasgow, some 80 per cent of the seminarians were Glaswegian. Within weeks I had a Glasgow accent and it's been a part of me ever since. I was with Glaswegians from the age of twelve to twenty, albeit not in the city. When I eventually went to study law in Glasgow, it just felt like home. It still does, though I don't live there; so many deep-rooted connections and memories, even apart from family and friends.

Going into the seminary is a pretty serious thing to decide at the age of twelve.

At the age of twelve it could have been a school for astronauts—two brilliant football strips and boots with screw-in studs was more important. I wasn't forced, dragged kicking and screaming, but my parents thought it would be an education for me.

In our village all the Catholic kids were put into one classroom, inside the larger Protestant school. Poor Mrs. Mills, our teacher, had to teach all the kids from four to twelve in a single classroom. Sectarian nonsense. We felt under siege sometimes. I failed my eleven plus (exam at end of primary school) which meant I would have been sent to a non-academic secondary school—seminary meant I had a so-called more academic education. So instead of studying joinery and metal work, I ended up declining Latin and Greek irregular verbs, which comes in very handy.

So basically between the ages of twelve and twenty you thought you were going to be a priest?

It was something distant, like a far off mist . . . Seminary was a complex experience. Many priests have been justly denounced for sexual abuse, and I found out later this happened in Blairs College, Aberdeen too. But my experience in the main was of decent men who imbued me with a rugged sense of equality. They weren't materialistic in the slightest. I think the experience made me independent and very self sufficient, maybe too much. I have many fond memories of many of the priests and fellow students. But at eighteen it was a big decision to go to Rome and study in the Gregorian University. Students came from all round the world. Dozens of popes have been educated there, and I was taught by Jesuits. I even served Pope Paul VI mass once in the Vatican! Terrible the details you notice . . . he had massive nostrils, at least from my angle, holding the good book as he read the Gospel. But it was a strangely claustrophobic experience, both socially and intellectually. I even remember our course on Marxism; designed to teach the main precepts, but more time was spent on demolishing them. I had great fun at the Scots college in Rome, but that too felt increasingly claustrophobic, and hardly surprising since we were all taught the same dogma since the age of four. I have a sense religious education at the end of the day is indoctrination and subtle mind control taught by the faithful (sometimes by crude repetition and sometimes by brilliant erudite Jesuit Professors), steeped in a powerful ideology, who are convinced they are doing God's will. Teacher and taught were caught in the same two thousand year rut. After all, "believing" was more important than thinking. Luckily, the Gregorian University is very close to the Trevi Fountain and I was saved from the Lord by my hormones . . . can you imagine what it was like after years in Aberdeen where it was so fucking cold, and then cumulative years saying prayers in Church, and then, aged eighteen, going down to see all those young, brown-skinned Italian girls messing around the fountain . . . like a miracle . . . Semtex of the mind and bloodstream. No amount of rosaries and confession can redeem that. To cut a long story short, trouble was on the horizon. When I finished my philosophy degree—I actually studied very hard—the Rector summoned me to his room and in all seriousness gave me an ultimatum: "We're giving you one week to change your personality." You couldn't write it. But I'll always be grateful for that experience in retrospect. When I got out of seminary I felt like a spaniel unleashed on a spring morning.

Do you still have pangs of Catholic guilt?

Quite the opposite. I think there are many types of religion. In Nicaragua I met a Christian-based community who were at the forefront of the war against Somoza. I met fantastic human rights activists and trade unionists who were all Catholics from the Christian bases in El Salvador, risking their lives for freedom and justice. They were amazing people. And then I saw right-wing people like the Cardinal in Nicaragua who was an ally of Reagan and the Contras, and who, as an apologist for these murderers showed his contempt for ordinary civilians. But for every bishop who has supported the rich and the powerful there are those grass-root activists at the forefront defending the marginalized

So after abandoning the priesthood you went on to study law?

After I got thrown out of seminary I had to decide what I was going to do, and I thought, first of all, that law would be interesting. It's a good career, it's a good training, and there was also the possibility of earning a living. I also thought it would be fun and mischief, and I would be dealing with people from all sorts of backgrounds. So I went to Glasgow to study law. And then after that I did a two-year apprenticeship at one of the top criminal law firms in Glasgow. That was a fantastic experience, really, because I prepared defense cases for some brilliant lawyers, everything from breach of peace to murder trials. I did a lot of welfare law, housing law, a whole span of things, and I realized how law could be used as an instrument. So, with a couple of colleagues, we ended up doing quite a lot of controversial cases. We were very young, in our early twenties, but we had great fun with the law and drove many of our older colleagues absolutely mad. It was a very exciting period of my life and it was also important to learn how to become practitioners.

Were you learning a lot about politics as well?

A bit about everything really, about life—because when you do law, you begin to see from the inside actually what people's lives were like. And I was amazed just how much poverty there was, how much desperation there was, and just the contradictions in people. And also just the incredible complexity of the human mind, the lies they would tell me as the defense of what happened, the crazy stories, how they got into a fight, how a murder happened. So it was a very rich experience of just meeting people, very exciting and exhausting because we were very pressurized. Most jobs don't have that diversity and I'm sure I'm still mining that now.

How did you then end up in Nicaragua?

Well, I saw a fantastic documentary by a Jesuit priest called Padre Gorostiaga, but I'd been reading a lot about Nicaragua anyway. It's hard to believe now, but in the early eighties the United States said that, after its relationship with the then-Soviet Union, Nicaragua was the most important foreign policy matter for them.

To cut a long story short, Somoza Senior was put in power by the United States like a dynasty, and then they eventually ended up with the final Somoza in 1979. Nicaragua was where the U.S. organized the Bay of Pigs invasion from. Somoza was absolutely America's man. As Roosevelt said, "He may be a son of a bitch, but he's our son of a bitch." In other words Somoza did what he was told; it was totally corrupt, his family controlled most of the businesses, terrible human rights abuses; they murdered trade unionists and human rights activists, until basically there was a revolution in 1979, a popular revolution made by a mix of socialists, Catholics, social democrats. They threw Somoza out on July 19, 1979. And the first thing that the "Sandinistas" did—they were inspired by an earlier nationalist figure called Sandino—was that they taught the population to read and write. That was just unbelievable—the second poorest country in the world taught themselves to read and write. Then they had mass inoculation campaigns, they wiped out polio, they redistributed land. There was a massive redistribution of power and the United States was scared that this was going to spread to the rest of Latin America. So they funded the Contras, who were ex-Somoza National Guard members, to go to the borders, and from there they organized terror attacks against Nicaragua. The idea was to bleed this revolution dry and to overthrow the Sandinistas, and that's exactly what they did. They started murdering anybody associated with the Sandinistas—health workers, the *brigadistas* who taught others to read and write, the cooperatives where the land would be redistributed. It was a systematic campaign of terror against the party, the army and also the civilian population who supported them. All despite democratic elections the Sandinistas won in 1984, which I witnessed.

I started reading lots about it. I was in my early twenties, and I wanted to go there. I didn't speak a word of Spanish, so I decided to save some money and learn Spanish. I went to the north of the country, which was a war zone, and I lived in a cooperative. Just by living there, you could hear the guns going off in the distance. The cooperative had armed guards at night, because not long before I arrived they'd blown it up. And I actually saw what the revolution was like, the nitty-gritty, the faces of ordinary people, their determination to change their world. They'd been taught by young students to read and write, which they never thought was going to happen. I saw how their lives changed when they were given land, how they were no longer treated as ignorant peasants expected to do their master's bidding.

It sounds very idealistic.

There were problems with the Sandinistas too; I'm not going to say that they were perfect, far from it. There was some corruption, but generally this revolution was an amazing human experience; it actually showed that this could happen in the rest of Latin America. And the United States crushed it, just like they've done with many other things. So I came back to work in Scotland for another six months, and the second time I went out to Nicaragua I could speak Spanish, so I worked for two and a half years for a human rights organization using the law. I went round the countryside talking to people whose families had been murdered or kidnapped, a lot of human rights activities. In a time of war, human rights becomes massively politicized just like it did in Iraq. The size of the population was less than Madrid, but Ronald Reagan persuaded the U.S. that Nicaragua was a "two-day march from Texas" and was a threat to U.S. security! Sound familiar? It was a tremendously strong experience, and out of that came *Carla's Song*.

How would you describe your daily activities there? Were you organizing people? How much danger were you in?

A lot of the time I was in Managua talking to delegations that came in from the States and Europe. Because human rights had been massively politicized, there were a lot of United States–backed human rights organizations there, and there were a great deal of lies being told. What I did was speak to delegations; I'd meet famous people, plumbers, ex-Vietnam vets, right-wing politicians and journalists. That was a very good introduction to the United States, and I began to realize how dangerous it was. I met ex-CIA guys like John Stockwell, and a guy who was involved in the My Lai Massacre in Vietnam who was guilt-ridden and was bringing peace activists into Nicaragua. And the same guys are probably there now in Iraq, because I just spoke to some human shields that have just come back form Iraq, and the parallels were amazing.

But the journalists were just absolutely determined to screw Nicaragua, which they did. The sustained misinformation was unbelievable. Sometimes I used to go and visit areas where helicopters had just been blown up, there were mines in the roads; something could have happened, so I was always lucky to stay alive. I remember once a documentary crew got blown up; you could see all the houses blowing up; I talked to people whose sons had been kidnapped or children had been mutilated, because they terrorized people, cut their breasts off, cut their bits off. These are people Reagan and Bush financed. It's not new and it hasn't changed but it's marked me for life.

What could you do for those people then?

Not very much. My job and the job of the organization was to get information and present that to the world, so we'd send our reports off to Amnesty International and others and just tried to have a truthful representation of what happened. Because President Reagan was saying, "The Contras are the moral equivalent of our founding fathers; they're struggling for truth and democracy and freedom, these people are freedom fighters."

At what point in working there did writing a screenplay set in Nicaragua become a tangible thought?

Probably towards the end of my experience, really. I was in a very privileged position because I was an eyewitness for two and a half years, and I found the investment made to screw Nicaragua absolutely fascinating. Sometimes you would see statements by the Pentagon, by the State Department totally corroborated with the supporters within Nicaragua, who were bought and paid for by the United States, coordinated with attacks by the Contras, all taking place within the same day; and what I began to realize about this propaganda campaign was how many bright and intelligent people were involved in trying to destroy this tiny little country, which then only had three million people. So I just found this a stunning phenomenon and I thought I really had to write something about this. I was sick of doing rights reports and articles. I said right, I'm going to write a screenplay about this, but of course I'd never written a piece of fiction in my life.

So you knew that there was a story to tell, and you had a lot of material from talking to all those people. But how did you find a way through it?

It was a very long process. I met a couple of documentary filmmakers out there, and I began to realize it's not a magical process. And if they can do it then at least I can have a try. I was absolutely determined to try and make it work. So I bought a couple of books about screen-writing, and I had to discover what a treatment was and all of that. I tried to put some order and give some shape to the story, and decided who the characters would be. So when I finished my time in Nicaragua, I had a detailed storyline, about twenty pages, and I just got a book out and I sent it to every producer under the sun. Because I'd no idea, I didn't have a clue.

Did people write back?

A lot didn't, and most people that did write back said, the subtext was clear! "Are you serious? You've never written a screenplay before and you want us to go to Nicaragua while there's a war on and make a political film?" So it wasn't a big seller, not at all. Then one day I was washing the dishes and Ken Loach phoned me up. I didn't really know a great deal about the film world, but Ken just invited me around and said, "We'll have a chat and a coffee in my office."

Had you had any familiarity with Ken Loach's work when you sent him the treatment?

I'd seen *Riff-Raff* and I thought there was a mischief there, but I hadn't seen his other films. Ken engaged with the material. There are very few people who are willing and open enough to take a chance with some-one who's never written before, and Ken does the same thing with act-ing. Martin Compston had never acted in his life before *Sweet Sixteen*. A lot of people would look at my CV and want to know if I'd seen *Mean Streets* or *Bicycle Thief* and what did I think of *The Birth of a Nation*? But Ken doesn't give a flying fuck about all of that. He was much more interested in what I'd witnessed myself. Some just talked. Right from the beginning he said, "It's a very, very long shot." But what he said to me was, "Why don't you just try and write some scenes?" Because I'd written as a lawyer, I knew how to put ideas on paper, but I'd never written fiction. Writing dialogue and narrative and story was such a quirky thing, and strange, I didn't know how to do it but I just wanted to try. I was keen as mustard.

So I went back home and really the first half of *Carla's Song* just popped out. It was great to be liberated from the political ideas behind it. I was picking all the details of the protagonists, all the choices, and I remember just this feeling of excitement. Ken was very encouraging about the scenes, and eventually it was presented to the Scottish Film Council and I got a commission to write the screenplay. I'd been on the dole for ages when I came back. I was doing a lot of solidarity work, at schools and universities, so it'd been a long time.

But I was absolutely, totally determined to make this somehow or other, and I actually believed from the very beginning—this may sound arrogant or crazy—but I just believed we'd get it made. I didn't realize it would take six fucking years . . . But I would still have done it if it had taken twenty years. I supposed really what I'd seen and what I'd witnessed had such an effect on me that I had to write something. But looking back I'd wished I'd made a better job of the screenplay!

So it wasn't about becoming a screenwriter, it was about conveying your experience?

Becoming a screenwriter was an accident. I love my job, I love my day and I love every single job I've been involved in. I would have done it for nothing because I get excited by it, especially things like *Carla's Song* and *Bread and Roses*. I mean, to do a film about cleaners and immigrants in LA, about trade unions, is not very sexy. I'm not daft, I know that, but it took us about six years to do that one too. So in a way you've got to engage with the material and be like a dog with a bone and not let go, and get absolutely determined to make it; otherwise it's not going to get done. You have to be the most determined person, and I've been very lucky with Ken—finding someone who engages with material in the same way. We had to shoot *Bread and Roses* in thirty days, that's really tight, so we had to cut things down. But you make choices and say we're not going to get a huge budget for that, but also keeping control of the material, which is really important.

I read somewhere that you and Ken Loach took a print of Carla's Song *to the village in Nicaragua where it was filmed?*

It was out in the countryside during the rainy season, and it was in a
wee square, and seeing those places again was magical. I didn't realize,
but it's happened again with other films: the cleaners in LA, teenagers
in Scotland, how seldom it is that so many people actually see people
like themselves up on the screen, and what a lift that gives them.
Because most people on screen are North American, rich, with chis-
elled good looks, and they usually solve the world's problems with
their cleverness and physical prowess. It always amazes me the reward
people have when they see something else than that; they see themselves on the screen, and it's almost like their experience is vindicated.
I never forget this old boy watching the film. I don't think he'd ever
seen a film; it must have been like going back to the first time in France
when the Lumière brothers showed that train and everyone thought it
was going to come through the wall. You realize what a wonderful
medium cinema is. That's why I was so glad to see *Lilya 4-Ever* by
Lukas Moodysson—you know, it's like a different experience, different voices, different accents, and I think that's what film does
absolutely beautifully.

*How do you decide what to write about? Does it come from you, or
do you and Ken sit down together?*

In general I think there is a fixation with "originality" as if it was
something pure, mixed in with attempts to claim ownership. I think
the best ideas come out of caffeine and talking. Ken and I are talking
about things the whole time, and we try to choose an idea that nour-
ishes us both. We talk, and then I've got to find something that I
really engage with, something that captures my imagination. What I
like to do is put something down on paper because by doing that
you're also delineating the parameters of the story, which is important. You're getting some sense of the world of the story and the
characters, and principally the premise, because if you don't get that
premise right you're screwed. I really think that is such an important
decision. If you get it wrong you're chasing your tail for years. If you
get it right, boom, it just feels good. I think we were very lucky with
My Name Is Joe and *Sweet Sixteen*. We got a little premise which
gave us the energy to get right to the end. Actually the first and last
drafts of the screenplay are very similar; they chop and change but
they're very similar. So what I do is just put something down on paper,
think laterally, scatter ideas all over the place and then I talk to Ken to
see if there's something there, providing we're both interested in the
material and he goes for it.

I couldn't believe we did *My Name Is Joe*. The very last day, as we were leaving *Carla's Song*, I'd already written the first draft of *Bread and Roses*, and he'd just done *Land and Freedom*. He'd done Nicaragua, which was difficult, and he said, "Do you fancy doing a little story in Glasgow." I went away to be by myself for a couple of days and I just thought I wanted to do something very personal. So I said there are two characters, Sarah and Joe, and I just described them. Pencil note, faxed it to London, Ken gets back to me and says that's quite nice, we should do that. I went off to Glasgow, walked the streets and tried to decide how I was going to put this story together, and that was *My Name Is Joe*.

I was interested in people who were a bit older, who'd made a lot of mistakes in their lives, who were in desperate need of love and attention but were scared by their previous experiences, who were very lonely and had this great need to communicate and to make up for lost time. Another notion grabbed me: one of the ten steps of Alcoholics Anonymous is the attempt to make a moral inventory of yourself. Now that's real meat.

You got a scholarship to write screenplays, I believe?

I won a Fulbright award. I'd written *Carla's Song* but it hadn't been made. John Cleese, I think, sponsored a Fulbright award so that one person from the UK could go to the United States every year, based on a competition. So I went down there and I was interviewed by John Cleese and Robert McKee, and also this guy who was a Colonel Blimp figure. He actually said to me, "If we give you this award, because you've been to Nicaragua you might not be allowed back into the country, and that'll be very embarrassing." And of course John Cleese and McKee were appalled at this guy, but I was laughing. So it was a surprise that I won. And I went to study at USC, the University of Southern California. I would have enjoyed New York a lot more but I wanted to do a Latino story, so when I went there I went to live in South Central and then I went to live in MacArthur Park, which isn't too far away from the campus at USC.

Out of all this came *Bread and Roses*. When I went to LA I went to live in South Central, near MacArthur Park. Just by the house I lived in and the characters in it, the life going on around it, the gangs in the nighttime, I could get a sense of a story. When I went to buy bread I would speak to all the gang members who were buying their bread; you could see all the scars, and because I could speak Spanish I could speak to them. And they're also stunned to see a white man there, and they're even more stunned to hear someone speak Spanish, so you talk to them and get them a cup of coffee. Most were from Central America where I had worked, so that broke down barriers. And then round the corner are all the Evangelical churches. The girl who lived in the flat above me, it was a short walk but she had a little knife in her handbag and she used to take her knife out and keep it in her hand from the bus stop to the flat where she lived. Details like that tell you a lot about how she lived. The guy downstairs was playing the same love song over and over again, and he was a white man. Just by being in the middle of it you can tell a hundred stories. You're not copying it, but it informs you.

I was trying to tell a story about the United States but also about the immigrants, and I can't club together the El Salvadorians and Guatemalans and somebody who comes from the mountains in Mexico; you've got to respect that their traditions are totally different, and because I hadn't lived in those conditions before, I had to do a hell of a lot more work on *Bread and Roses* and *Sweet Sixteen,* so I could understand everything. And then I went down to the border and went round the poor houses there; then I went to talk to trade unionists, people who'd been beaten up because they'd tried to form an independent trade union; you talk to mothers there who are just trying to survive. And by getting all that information, it just gives you a much better idea, and then you try to condense it. *Bread and Roses*—what was fascinating was that those people not only had two jobs but three jobs, two shifts a day, then working a job at the weekend, and then they start talking about their children who are left alone, and then you can understand why they join the gangs. Then you see a gang member who's got "Fuck L.A.P.D." written on his hat and you can use that. You build up a picture. And I like living in the middle of what I'm doing and that was a mad experience, living there and hearing guns go off and living near mad people, seeing all the people being thrown out of the mental health institutions. Some of the things I saw were totally surreal, like the blind woman with a blue stick in the traffic begging; you couldn't write that in a science-fucking-fiction piece, could you? Blind, four lanes of traffic going backwards and forwards and she was mad waving her stick about, and people would stop and pick her up and she'd do it again, and you think, "What kind of society is it that can allow that to happen?" Some of the things I've seen during my research are so wild and so surreal that if you put them in a screenplay it doesn't really make sense. People talk about a kitchen sink drama or social realism and it makes me burst out laughing because I've just seen so many mad and surreal things which are part of the scope of human experience.

How did you find your time studying at USC?

I wasn't a good student really. I didn't really go to a lot of classes. I was more interested in what was going on elsewhere really, but there was one brilliant thing which I would like to thank them for—there was a guy called Frank Daniels, who was Czech, he changed his name, and what he did every Thursday afternoon was watch one of his favorite films, *The Apartment*, say, and he would analyse it and break it down. That was great, I loved that.

What did you make of the film industry in Los Angeles?

I didn't have much to do with it. When I first went there I met a few agents. They were all very pleasant, but I could see that our interests were so different. I hadn't written a screenplay at that time; they thought I was a bit odd because I was living where I was living. I had a funny accent, so there wasn't that much shared interest really.

I have to tell you this one little story though, talking about the film industry. What happened at the school was that producers used to come in to talk to us. And the producers from *Clear and Present Danger* came in, the Tom Clancy novel, and of course the students at the film school are all fascinated. But the film did amaze me really, because right at the heart of it is Harrison Ford, the great hero of the CIA. So I asked the producer, he's really well known, "Did you mean *Clear and Present Danger* to be a true reflection of what happened with Latin American relations in the United States?" And he said, "Oh yes," but that he'd used Escobita instead of Escobar. I said, "That's interesting, because I think what a wonderful character Harrison Ford is, and peace and justice, searching for the truth. But if you actually look at what the CIA had done in Guatemala, overthrowing the regime resulting in over two hundred and fifty thousand civilians being murdered, then you look at what happened in Honduras, the death squads in El Salvador and more death squads in Nicaragua . . ." And I just went through the history of several countries and said, "Did you mean to set out to make a sixty million dollar propaganda movie?" And honestly I've never heard such a quiet room in my whole life. Then he just said, "You Europeans are trying to politicize everything." But what's fascinating about it is that they'd just adapted the Tom Clancy novel and gone through the process, picking Harrison Ford. And I think that people are so steeped in the framework and ideology that I don't think it actually occurred to them that they were doing a propaganda movie and totally telling lies about history. Ken and I are accused all the time about making political films, whereas that was a sixty million dollar entertainment film.

How did you get on with the other USC students?

They were pleasant. I thought it would be a fascinating course, full of young people from all over the States bursting with ideas. Maybe I was just unlucky with some of the tutorial groups, but right at the same time a young guy from Cambridge and his friend had sold a screenplay about a monkey and a policeman for a million dollars, and I remember it just seemed to be like poison, everybody wanted to sell their screenplay for a million dollars. I remember the hunger for it. I found the student population massively conservative. It's hard to generalize as I was there for such a short period with a small tutorial group, but the stories I came across, to my taste, were deadly boring and I couldn't be bothered with it anymore. So that was when I started just doing more research and joining the janitors.

That's just the problem with cinema though, it's motivated by money.

I can understand that, it's a process that costs a great deal of money and in a strange way our films are very commercial because everybody gets their money back. Nobody's going to finance if they're going to lose money, so we have a strong list of distributors in Europe that we use at the same time. It's only a modest return, but the point is we are making a film, the people who are financing us are making a profit, and we have control over the material. I don't suppose I'll get stinking rich by this. But you know we can't expect to be subsidized, we're not subsidized so Ken's films all make their money back, and that's important because otherwise people won't finance us for the next one, so I'm not idealistic about it.

I read that you wrote Sweet Sixteen *because there was a lot of unfinished business after you wrote* My Name Is Joe. *What did you mean by that?*

Walking the streets in Glasgow I met a lot of young people who'd never had a job in their lives, and I started talking to them and trying to see the world from their point of view. And I was fascinated by the choices that confronted them. For many of them, they would end up unemployed or working in McDonald's or a call center. They're hand to mouth, they never save anything. Then I met some young people who were selling drugs and they were making a fortune, and that choice is very interesting. Some people weren't using; I met a young girl who had bought her own car, bought her own flat, she wasn't educated, didn't use herself, but she'd done it as a career choice. And given the career choices that she had in her life, you could see why she did that. I met a lot of young people with wasted lives and had never worked in their lives, and there really wasn't the space in *My Name Is Joe* to deal with it, because I'd seen it almost uncompromisingly from Joe's point of view. And so then I decided to come back and look at young people, and also I think the choices facing young people now are much more violent than thirty years ago, when there was a much bigger chance of getting a job.

When you're walking the streets of Glasgow—do you take a tape recorder with you?

No. Would never think of it.

Is that a betrayal of confidence?

It's a way of separating people, really. A tape gets in the way of an ordinary conversation. I'm just trying to nose around and follow emotions. What I do is put something on paper, something that me and Ken want to do, then I just examine that notion and prepare to change it. And what I'd do is, on *Sweet Sixteen* for example, I'd go along to children's homes. You have to set that up because you're talking to very vulnerable children, so I set it up with the experts and they'd all seen *My Name Is Joe* and were incredibly open; it's amazing how many doors open because of that. I'm talking about experts and politicians who were very helpful. Then I went to junior prisons, I worked with people who worked with children, people who'd had that experience. A lot of people had become homeless, so I spoke to them. And what I do is walk the streets, see the area and I tried to get a feel for it. I'd bump into people and talk to them about their lives, and I'd find people incredibly open. I'd go up to kids on street corners and they might think you're a total wanker—"Who's this prick?" You know, then if you engage them in conversation and talk to them it's amazing how people, generally speaking, always want to talk. The same with people in LA, they want to talk about their lives; people are not asked about their lives, usually, and it's fascinating. I know it's sometimes exaggerated and sometimes they tell lies but in between the lines you begin to feel something. And it's not that you copy what's going on; I think the real challenge when you're writing a screenplay is to see the world from that person's point of view. Not to judge them but to actually get inside their skin and see the world from their point of view.

What is it about that personal point of view that really makes it effective?

I think we're contradictory creatures and the great thing about film I think is that it can bring us out into another world, and that essentially means trying to get into someone else's point of view. I wish we could do it a bit more really. I think that's the great problem with Iraq; I read yesterday that we dropped 1,800 bombs last Friday on to Iraq, on to 7,500 people, and this just flies over our heads. What's it like for the people living there, I'm just trying to imagine that, 1,800 bombs, you know? I think it's that ability to just try to be there and imagine them, and that's what I did. I saw a photo of a little girl in a lilac dress, pulled from the rubble, cut in half. The personal makes us human, flesh and blood, not "collateral" abstractions.

You and Ken Loach both claim that there are no film references in Sweet Sixteen, *that the material came from the people you talked to and what you saw. However, you could argue that the film follows a rise and fall pattern similar to many gangster films.*

When I was writing the story it didn't really enter my head. I was just trying to tell a story true to the premise and the characters. I was using traditional story techniques; a beginning, a middle, and an end, and we're following a critical period in someone's life; but I didn't sit there with film references in my head, I just tried to imagine Liam, imagine the premise; then you build up the relationships with the family, and then you follow your instincts and try to tell a story.

Once the first draft's done, what do you do after that?

I usually put something on paper, a very brief summary just to see if there's a notion in there that I get excited about. If we think it's interesting I'll do a lot of research and I'll just talk to everybody and anybody, organize things, things that I'd read, fill up notebooks which I never look at again; it's just a process of filling it up and writing new ideas, and then I reach a point where I feel I'm just absolutely bursting to get started. Call it pre-scriptural tension! You know, like you can't sleep, you're dreaming about it, and then I just have to try and write the first draft very, very quickly. That's the private bit, and the great thing is that Ken respects that space really.

How long does that usually take if you are trying to write it very quickly?

The actually writing doesn't take that long, most of writing is just thinking about it and imagining, then the actual writing process is about six weeks, two months, depending on interruptions. I can do that usually quite quickly but it's the time beforehand and having ideas and information, and just a feel for the world. So I get the first draft and I meet up with Ken and we just take it from the top and talk about it. We've also got a very close friend called Roger Smith who gets a credit as a script editor, and he's just like a troublesome, difficult bastard who always asks the really tough questions that you try not to ask yourself. He has great instincts.

Do you find that Roger identifies problems that you were already aware of but didn't have the courage to face?

Some things you know are wrong, you're just not happy with it and he's like an extra voice, someone we both trust, and he's got a real good grasp of structure, and we just talk about it. I've just got back from a session in Madrid, and sometimes we just talk about a scene for two bloody hours. But then we don't know why we're doing it but then we suddenly realized it's because there's a problem earlier in the script. So we just talk about it and then I go away and write another draft. But you can't write by committee, so you try and take the spirit of the conversation and look at it and then go back and do another one, trying to make it tighter and tighter. It's a continual process right until the very end. I find it's a totally organic process and I feel it's very fluid. And I'm totally involved in the casting process with Ken. We do it together. I do the castings and improvisations with them, and by the process of talking about the people we've met it helps us to find our own character in there, and sometimes we change things, not a great deal but the whole process is open. At that point I see collaboration as very important.

So it's a democratic process.

I wouldn't say it's democratic. We do different things. It's just me and Ken having good arguments. Hopefully we make progress trying to make the story tighter. For example in *My Name Is Joe* I had a subplot with some young people in it and I didn't want it taken out, but I could see why they had to take it out. Eventually the film is so tight and so economic and disciplined that there's just no space for anything that would take away from the story. The scenes themselves can work lovely, we actually had that in *My Name Is Joe*, some beautiful scenes and we lost them, and it was the right decision. I could see afterwards when it was up there on the screen, because we had some of the same arguments we had in the script as we had in editing, and then you can just see that the rhythm was wrong. Jonathan Morris is our editor, another man with great instincts, who is a gem to work with.

Were there some recurring arguments that didn't go away?

They're not so much arguments as questions in our mind, because I've come to realize that sometimes there's just no right or wrong, there's just different. And then sometimes I'd make a different call, Ken would make a different call, and then what you would do is just talk around and see what the strongest solution is. Again some of those things change after casting.

Are these conversations civilized?

We argue, but the thing is both of us don't think we're the fucking Pope, you know, there's no right or wrong answer. We just try to analyze it. Film is massively collaborative and there are no tantrums. I've got great confidence that we're trying to do the same thing. I'm not saying we would agree on absolutely everything.

Otherwise it wouldn't be interesting.

We just try and talk through the options and just try to be as clear about the consequences of making one decision rather than another.

Moving on to Sweet Sixteen . . . *can you tell me where Liam's dogged love for his mother comes from?*

I was going into these children's homes and I was just absolutely amazed at the chaotic lives that so many of these children had, absolutely abused by their parents, and they're still desperate to get in contact with them. Not all of them do this. I remember one guy who spat on his father's grave with delight because he'd been abused for years by his father, tortured and beaten up and that. You could see it was tearing them apart, and it came from that. It's very much rooted in the people. And also when you're a teenager you just think, "I'm going to sort things out now, I'm an adult, I'll get rid of that prick my mom's been with and I'm going to set up a nice wee house. I'm going to sort it out." And I think as a teenager you're much more determined to change reality in a way that when you're much older you realize you can't control people's emotions that way.

How did you handle the elements in the film that came from real life but are also similar to conventional staples of the gangster genre? I am thinking of the local crime boss being similar to characters you would see in both versions of Scarface.

Maybe this is the great advantage of not being steeped in genres! I'm unburdened with it, it doesn't bother me. I don't care. Obviously if there is some massive thing out there I'm going to try not to copy it, but at the end of the day I'm just going with the truth of the impulse when I'm writing. Hopefully I don't produce stereotypes. And I actually thought that boss was an interesting character because I found that a lot of the drug barons were investing in things; restaurants, houses, buildings, secondhand car lots, and also health farms, I thought that was absolutely brilliant; they're destroying kids in one sense and on the other hand they're creating this environment where people are tanning their bodies, toning their muscles, and to me that was a metaphor for this polarization of wealth.

Did you meet drug dealers up there?

Oh yeah, I'd go up and talk to them. Journalists do this all the time. Some of them were ex-users. I actually spoke to younger people on the streets who were selling drugs, I just went up to them and asked them. The younger dealers were all very jumpy to begin with, but you find that they're very open to people. You just tell them what you're doing, people are fascinated to talk.

Is it important for you doing the research process to be upfront with people?

Absolutely, I'm always upfront. Then the people trust you, they're very bright, they'd find out usually.

Humor is prevalent in your work. How do you handle tone in your films when you are dealing with such serious subject matter?

In many ways it's traditional storytelling, you just try to pace it. Some so-called working-class films, I'm not going to talk about names, but they make their working-class characters absolutely miserable and depressing, dour. And that's not my experience. My experience of working with people in Nicaragua, in LA, the days can be very exciting, they're taking the piss, they're bright, they're smart, they're irreverent, surreal things happen. I find among the tragedies are the most amazing stories, and I'm just being truthful with the three dimensions of the human personality I come across. Some of them are miserable bastards, but most of the time life is mixed. Generally speaking there are lots of shades and I just try and capture that.

I'm talking more about how you're mixing the shades together.

I think I'm being truthful to the personality of Liam. At the beginning of the film, before he's selling cigarettes, he spots a chance, he's selling, he's taking the piss with the people in there, enjoying it, but he's got his eye for the main chance.

In terms of reality versus research, I was thinking about how Liam and his mates go out and they start delivering drugs on their mopeds while delivering pizza for a local shop. In a way that's something that's probably truthful and comes from something that exists, but in other ways it's slapstick.

I'm aware of all this and you have to be careful, because at the end of the sequence there is slapstick. When that sequence finishes there's a woman coming down the stairs and she says, "You fucking scumbags, do you realize that person you are selling to is a mother with a two year old child? You're nothing but a fucking scumbag." So we play with slapstick then we kill it

Film is so tight and so disciplined that you have to be aware of what every single theme's doing, you have to feel your way through it, use your instinct and timing and sometimes you need time to come down, you can't have big high scenes, you need to change.

Are transitions something you spend time on?

Yeah, absolutely, every single time we change a scene we ask ourselves the same questions: "Does it work, does it feel right, does it test credibility, does it bring you on?" Because you want people to be right in there from the beginning and go right to the end without a break, without a false note in the film, and that's a really difficult thing to do.

Do you chart where you want to take the audience's emotion or is it just intuition?

I once went to a weekend course on screenwriting, which I still find very useful. There are things that work but there are things that are dangerous because they suggest that "professional screenwriters" work out every single scene beforehand and it just didn't work for me at all. If you plan it out like that, when you come to write it the characters surprise you and they take you in a way you never expected. So you might be trying to get over to one point, and actually the character takes you over to another one. So if you've got it all worked out beforehand I think maybe you'll end up with a tight structure but somehow it tends to lack energy and life. I tried it once that way and it didn't work for me at all. But at the same time you do need to have points. Graham Greene used to say, "You pick out a few points and you let your horse roam." I find that much more useful.

When you're working on your writing and things aren't going as well as you like, when your horse isn't roaming in the right direction, how do you push yourself through periods of self-doubt that crop up and threaten to ruin your day?

A great deal of writing for me is testing possibility, so in a strange way I don't mind testing a cul-de-sac that doesn't work, so I'll try it and I'll feel it and I'll work like hell on a scene and it might be only two or three days later I'll say it doesn't work, but for me it wasn't wasted. Because of that approach I haven't really had those moments of self-doubt. I don't want to seem very arrogant but I find that rather than having no avenues, the problem I've had is trying to put too many things in a screenplay, so what I've had to do from my first draft is not build up but cut down.

But I think what you're saying is a marvelous endorsement for research. It sounds like you've got so many different options that it is an embarrassment of riches rather than trying to grasp at straws.

I've found that every time I've come to do a story I feel I could do four or five different screenplays. I just always feel like the characters are all like, to use a little analogy, like birds in a nest. I find that I just feel like it comes to a point where I say I can't do anymore. I'm just determined to try to get this story out now. And what I usually find is that everyone's screaming for attention, all the different characters. Pinball could have been the main character, Chantelle could have been the main character, the mother or the grandfather could have been the main character, and the last screenplay I'd done I had great difficulty deciding whose story I was going to tell, and I actually went with a choice but I was so close to another one. I found all of those stories really, really interesting and all massively different. So the real choice was to make some really tough decisions.

How did you make those?

Well, you just try to work through which is the strongest, most complex, which is the one that will maybe try and communicate more of what you're trying to say. So they're all like wee birds in a nest going, "Me, me, me!" And you have to fucking kill them or they'll kill your screenplay! I really do feel that way about it. That's what happened with *My Name Is Joe*; there were a couple of kids there whose stories I wanted to tell so much, but I didn't realize I was going to come back and do *Sweet Sixteen*.

That's nice.

Because you've only got two hours, it's not like a novel where you can spread and grow out. I just feel it's so tight. That's the beauty of a novel. It's a different medium.

I think the dialogue in your films is wonderful; very local and true to the area you're trying to depict. How do you handle writing your dialogue? Many screenwriters consider that to be the hardest part.

I don't think so. I think it's the easiest part. It's the west of Scotland so I just know it. I've got a feel for it, so I don't have to think about it. I think the dialogue is by far the easiest thing in a screenplay. What I do is I make a decision to write neutral, neutral language, but I also did a lot of research into what these people said and their speech, so I tried to be truthful to it. But the west of Scotland, the first part of *Carla's Song*, I didn't even think about it, you hear it in your voice. Like I say, I think the premise and the narrative drive and the complexity of the characters are the most difficult aspects of writing, but not how they actually communicate, I didn't think about that.

It's nature.

I suppose the rhythm is in your blood.

Knowing that Ken Loach shoots in sequence, does that affect your writing at all?

No, but it affects the actors a great deal because they can live it in sequence. Like for Martin, he had to do the first scene first or he couldn't have done it, but he's lived that whole experience and you can see him growing and changing, the confidence in his face. And when he meets his mom in the suit at the end you can see that he's grown. He's got money, he's got people around him doing jobs and his confidence has grown, and he's sold people down the river and made some big decisions and you can see he's actually grown.

Can you talk me through improvisation in rehearsals and how you incorporate that into the screenplay?

There's lots of misconceptions about how Ken works. People put him together with Mike Leigh and he's the exact opposite; there couldn't be two more different ways of working. Mike Leigh, as I understand it, meets the actors, improvises the screenplay with them. Whereas I write the screenplay, then I meet Ken and we discuss it with Roger Smith. Then Ken never gives them the screenplay at all. But that's not a golden rule, it depends who the actors are. What we do is, to choose the actors, we meet them, we don't give them anything to read like other people do, which I find absolutely terrible. What we do is give them situations that are maybe close to something in the screenplay just to see what their natural instinct is, how it will be and how they operate. And also you see how quick and sharp they are, you see their face and their tone, all sorts of things; are they pleasant to look at, how fast are they, are they funny, are they convincing, truthful? You can figure all that out by doing those improvisations. But we don't incorporate what we learn from the improvisations into the screenplay; the screenplay's done way before we do that. But then when we come to actually shooting it in sequence, not every single word is tied down as if it's bloody Shakespeare. I mean, every scene in the film is in the screenplay; sometimes we cut some things down, and then when it gets back to editing, the dialogue goes back to about ninety per cent of the screenplay. I think a lot of people who are not working in film confuse dialogue with the screenplay.

What do you mean by that?

Imagine the exact words coincide, so the film is ninety per cent screenplay. But in fact the much bigger choices are actually the premise, the narrative, the characters and all the scenes; whether the actual words are exactly the same or not, I think that's a less important question. Like all these kids, we don't give them every single line of dialogue. They're chipping things in, throwing lines in. And Ken will let the scene run and run and run just to see what happens, and sometimes you get magic in it.

I thought the son of Liam's sister Chantelle had some great lines. For example, when they get back to the burning camper and he says to his uncle Liam, "Don't go in there!" It was just so tender.

That's building on the relationship with the kids and making sure Martin spends time with the boy, so you can't write stuff like that really.

So, you don't give the script to both professionals and nonprofessionals, am I right? When you're seeing people, is it both nonprofessionals and professionals?

We're open to anybody, but a lot of the time . . . we're not making *Maid in Manhattan.*

That film must be the antithesis of Bread and Roses.

You can tell by their faces and their bodies and their hands. I love that scene in *Bread and Roses* where one character is trying to get another to tell on other people who've been involved in the union. She's a real cleaner; she's never acted in her life, and she just looks up and her hand begins to shake and she's just not going to tell. And there's just everything about her that's just so truthful, you could never get an actor to do that, I don't think. Her hands, you can tell she's been a cleaner.

Were you on set during the filming of Sweet Sixteen?

I've been on set in every single feature since *Carla's Song.* We're close pals. It was very hard for me when we made *Carla's Song* because by the time we'd actually made the film it was ten years out-of-date. It was set in the war, the war had finished, so I'd been there, I'd seen things and knew Nicaragua; it was useful to be there.

And you'd canvassed Los Angeles and Glasgow.

So what we do is just like a continuation of the process really. After I've done the first draft of the screenplay I bring Ken to meet a lot of people I've met beforehand, so he familiarizes himself with the territory and then we talk and he gets to know them. He knows all the grassroots organizers, same as the grassroots people we met in *Bread and Roses.* And then we use them in the film, they become extras and all the marchers, and so the whole process begins to enrich itself. And then Ken will meet them and questions will arise out of that and we'll talk about it and change the screenplay. So the whole thing becomes organic, and then when we come to do the casting we pick people, and then we come to shoot the sequence; especially in *Bread and Roses.*

What does it do for these people when you talk to them about their life experience and then a year down the line you ask them to be in the film?

It's really beautiful sometimes, the people we've met, they've been wonderful people. That's why I like bringing the film to the people who helped to make it, who inspired it in the first place; it's a lovely thing to do. We did it with the cleaners in LA, we did it with the Nicaraguans—that's what I love about Ken, he came all the way up to this little spot in the middle of nowhere and we had to get a big generator in to power the projector and all that. In a strange sort of way it's a way of thanking and recognizing that they are the authors of the piece really. You can't copy a screenplay from life, that's ridiculous, but in many ways we've touched their experience and we've gained a great deal of insight from their lives through them. So I see it as a matter of respect.

I'd like to talk about a few scenes from the film, in particular. Can you take me through the opening scene, where, under a clear sky at night, Liam tells a group of children about the stars and then makes them pay money to look through his telescope?

I just really wanted the film to breathe a little bit. I think there are two things here really; it sets him up as a businessman, wheeling and dealing; he's taking the piss with the kids, he's very warm with them, he's taking money from them but then he's not taking money from others. But at the same time I think it represents a sense of wonder at this amazing world, beyond this little corner; it's just a sense of a child's imagination really.

It's also a sense of being an entertainer and also being very sweet-natured but tough at the same time as well.

It was really setting him up. At the same time as they're making money, they're taking the piss and enjoying it, a sense of *joie de vivre*. When you see the screenplay there's a lot more jokes in it. You know he's a wheeler and dealer, you know that they've got confidence, they've got cheek. But at the same time he's a kid who's got an eye to spot a business deal. So it establishes them quite well and, as you say, establishes the partnership and how close they are.

It also shows that Liam is pretty fearless, the way he sells cigarettes in a pub and takes the piss out of the pub landlord. He's not afraid of confrontation.

This was another thing that came out of research—I was absolutely amazed at how fearless these kids were, in a way it didn't make sense. I met a kid who'd had his nose broken three times and his arm broken, a really small kid, and he was fucking fearless, and that wasn't normal; normal children don't have that.

Where does that come from?

It's another thing that I found very strong and I think runs through the film; self-destructiveness. It's like the scene where Chantelle is doing Liam's wounds; it's a really important scene for me, and she says to him, "If you don't care about yourself, you don't care about us either." It's that sense of not caring and taking a chance and I think it comes out of desperation really.

The grandfather is an interesting character.

He's very important, though he has a smaller part. What struck me in those areas is that there are generations of unemployment. It's not just the parents but then the grandparents. Even for a lot of social workers, I spoke to them and they would tell me that in previous times the parents were drug addicts and sometimes the grandparents were addicts. Some of these grandparents are very young, they're in their forties. And also once you see that grandfather, you understand the mother. So it's a very small part but to me a very important part because it's a way of looking at the generations.

How did you come up with the idea of the grandfather siding with the boyfriend of his daughter rather than with his own flesh and blood?

Again, a lot of these guys are chancers really. But the grandfather and his daughter's boyfriend, Stan, they are like typical bullies really, they bully themselves and they're always looking for a boss figure in their community. So he's a complex figure, in one way he'll be loyal and then he's beating up his own grandson. He's actually making money and probably doing a deal with Stan; he's a dominant figure, in the mother's life as well. He's a typical bully really, he's bullied himself and bullies in turn.

This is when Liam and Pinball go out and sell the heroin they stole from Stan. I was thinking about how you structured this because you're covering a span of time where he's starting to get up on his feet as a drug dealer but you also have to take time to constrict it and expand it.

It's always one of the trickiest things to time a screenplay. The passage of time and pacing, and also because the mom's in prison, so I thought this is a way of him being intimate but also keeping contact; he's getting the camper for his mom so you have to keep that with the audience too, and you're building towards that. But you also get insight into his life. I think the secret of screenplay writing is, because it's so short, you have to try and get every scene to be doing about three or four things. It has to be tight. And also to do it in a way that the audience avoids feeling like it's just for information and it takes them out of the story.

Exposition.

If you can combine the information as part of the character development or part of the narrative so it all works together. Like the scene in the bar, for instance, where Liam is asked to stab someone for his new boss. It's a dramatic moment but it's also giving information. The boss really wants to know if he's capable of doing that. Again that was from research. I talked to a kid who'd stabbed somebody and I talked to him about it, so it's very much based on research. But at the same time it's a big, big step for Liam—"Is he prepared to do it?"

Chantelle's friend Suzanne—first of all she's very pretty, but you flirt with the idea of her being Liam's love interest but you don't really get into that. Can you take me through that?

I think for a start that all teenagers think about sex for about ninety per cent of the time! But there wasn't time for that. I was more interested in his relationship with his mom, his relationship with Pinball and his relationship with his sister. To have another love interest would have been distracting.

Did you find a lot with these people dealing drugs, that their dreams of living there are very much tied into the value of money? It's almost like a version of the America dream . . .

This is very important. If you look at their clothes and stuff, they have to get the best sneakers, certain jeans, the brand names, the sports car; so as part of their life they are presented with this dream which is totally out of sync with reality. That's what fascinated me about Greenock, the city in Scotland where *Sweet Sixteen* is based. Thirty years ago on that river, you know this is where they built that great ship the *Queen Mary 2*. In the previous century something like a third of all ships were built on that river; twenty years ago there were still lots of people working there, they had a routine to their day and got money in their hand at the end of the week; they weren't millionaires but they had the discipline of work, the fun of working with people, having to deal with people, and they also had a way of planning their life. Now those kids don't. The shipbuilding is all gone, and in its place they've got hamburger joints and call centers.

Those teenagers face much tougher choices than they did thirty years ago.

Because there's no infrastructure?

It's a bigger question. Are we going to take responsibility for communities, build local economies that work where people can plan their life and have some dignity? Are we going to depend always on distant boardrooms making decisions for us or have big battles with local politicians? My point is we've got to build communities that function and that was exactly the same thing that was underlining the janitors in *Bread and Roses*. Those communities don't work because people have to work at two or three jobs to make ends meet; those economies don't work, so we have to democratize economies.

So how's Greenock doing? You do see some signs of wealth and prosperity on the fringes of the film—the health club . . .

It's the polarization of wealth again, the rich and the talented, or the ruthless, will always find a way. The privileged or talented will always get out to university and escape. But there are lots of kids who'll not escape those areas; most young people can't leave and so you're left with lots of kids who'll never work in their lives. I met kids who'd never worked in their lives. I think that's taking away their dignity and taking away their ability to plan a future for themselves.

Was getting to know this area really important in helping you write the screenplay? Pinball's place serves as a lookout—did that help you in mapping the screenplay, mapping the geography?

The feel of the place bleeds into it. The river was very important. It's not so apparent to people who don't know it's history.

The River Clyde?

Yeah, the River Clyde. It's majestic, it's absolutely beautiful. Millionaires would pay fortunes to have the view that those kids have, but you have some miserable council estates overlooking these mountains with the wind coming up the estuary. So the Clyde works because of its history. It also works because in the past people know that there was tremendous work on the Clyde. And it also works because it's very stimulating and beautifully counterpoised against all this; some houses aren't too bad but some of them are terrible. So it works on all sorts of levels. A foreign audience might not catch all that, but I hope it's there for a local audience.

This is what I was talking about because you have the drug dealer working at this spa—it's ironic because he's in a health club . . .

It's another world, isn't it? This is the thing about doing research; when I walked around these areas, you felt like you were in another kingdom, separate rules, different expectations. I'll give you this example: I talked to a single mom who knew someone who just lived down the road to her and this guy, it's a drug thing again. This girlfriend lived with her boyfriend, there was some fight between families, so this guy kicked the door open, ran up to the guy, stabbed him, cut his spinal column; his girlfriend jumped on top of her boyfriend to save him and he slashed the girl. Now this girl is pushing her boyfriend around in a wheelchair. The police came round, didn't see anything. That's unimaginable to most people, that level of brutality and the idea that you just wouldn't tell the police. The world of the police, the world of getting jobs, the world of buying your own house, the world of where you're going to be in the future, your diet—it's actually like a separate kingdom with different expectations. They actually live ten years less.

In Cannes, a journalist from Rio de Janeiro said that Scottish accents are different but he recognized the kids, he recognized the choices they have in front of them.

Pinball is interesting. Liam is told to "take care of Pinball" by his boss and it's kind of an open-ended way of putting it.

It is, but given the context I didn't mean it was an order to go and kill him, but teach him a violent lesson. It's amazing how many kids in these areas have scars on their faces.

The confrontation between Pinball and Liam is very moving. Can you tell me something about it?

They're not caring about themselves and Pinball's so desperate for Liam's affection, isn't he? Pinball's taunting him because he needs him so much, it's like he loves him really. There are really lots of things going on in that scene; there are lots of things that say a lot about Liam. Pinball is not copied from any one person but from many I met in the children's home. Even the name, I just felt they were going backwards and forwards and all over the place. I was amazed at the chaos of their lives and they were very needy kids, very, very needy. In the same sort of way there was fearlessness and a sense of destruction; quite a lot of the kids were cutting themselves. I supposed all of that distilled into the character of Pinball. He's got nobody. Pinball says, "I would have done anything for you." That's shorthand for, "I fucking love you, I need you, you're the only person I've got in my life." And then, of course, it was inevitable that when Liam started climbing the greasy pole of opportunity that Pinball's a liability because he's unpredictable. But Liam made his choice, he went for his dream. He shows solidarity to some extent but at the end of the day he's going to be a bigger fish, and at least in my imagination I know what happens to Pinball. I think the chances are he'll start taking heroin, he'll be self-destructive, he'll lose contact with the only person he's close to. Liam has his sister and her little boy, and even his mom in a terrible sort of way.

That's interesting because Pinball always puts the relationship in jeopardy. I was thinking that he would be worried about losing Liam as a friend.

I sense that Pinball felt he'd lost Liam long before. We can see his confidence in the relationship dripping away, sometimes in very short scenes, but it's there and I felt for him as I wrote. Pinball wasn't based on any character I met, but distilled from the desperation I sensed from some of the kids I met before writing.

You said you weren't really a film buff—what kind of relationship did you have with cinema and film history at that point?

I guess I'm more interested in history than film history. I think it's a wonderful medium, I'm very excited by it, but I still don't consider myself a film buff. I'm much more interested in many other things than film.

Are you busy doing a lot of other things outside of film?

Yeah, I try to balance it, it's very hard actually. I've just had a wee boy, so before I was always travelling; now I suppose it's a big difference to my world. My partner is involved in filmmaking too, a right tough critic, she was actually the redheaded girl in *Land and Freedom*, so I blame Loach for that as well, the bastard . . .

London, England

Fernando León de Aranoa

15

FERNANDO LEÓN DE ARANOA
Los Lunes al Sol

"When things aren't working, it's like walking through a desert; you
don't like it but you keep walking."

Fernando León has written and directed three feature films: *Familia*
(1996), *Barrio* (1996) and *Los Lunes al Sol* (*Mondays in the Sun*),
which was co-written with Ignacio del Moral and stars Javier Bardem.
Fernando has won three Spanish Goya awards for his writing and
directing. He also works in documentaries and writes screenplays for
other directors in Spain. He lives in Madrid.

Synopsis

Northern Spain, the present. Santa is the leader of a group of unem-
ployed friends who were shipbuilders before the industry closed
down. They spend their days in a bar opened by their friend Rico.
Among the regulars: Amador, who has become an elderly drunk;
Reina, who works as a security guard, which for some of his comrades
is dismayingly close to being a policeman; José, whose wife Ana has
taken a job at the cannery; Lino, a middle-aged man with a teenage
son, who puts on a coat and tie each morning and goes off to inter-
view for jobs that go to younger men with skills he lacks. The men
amble through their Mondays in the sun, battling with the many
debilitating facets of unemployment.

* * *

KEVIN CONROY SCOTT: *Fernando, you were born and raised in Madrid.*
Can you tell me about what you were interested in as a teenager?

FERNANDO LEÓN DE ARANOA: I always liked drawing and spent a lot
of time doing that, and I always thought I was going to earn my living
as an illustrator. In fact, that was my first job. I worked for four years

at an advertising company, drawing storyboards—it was the only thing I knew how to do.

I was going to study drawing at university, but there was a problem with the date of the exam, and I was too late for it. So I went to my second option instead, and started a degree that lasted five years and was called something like Science of Image and Sound. But I never thought I would work in film—I always wanted to draw. I never even liked movies very much.

You didn't?

No, I hadn't seen a lot of movies. Later when I started studying film-making I saw more, but I never thought about it before then.

If you'd made your test on time and were drawing now, what kind of work would you do?

Well, it's hard to make a living as an illustrator. Probably I would have liked to have done comics. But I did some illustrations for newspapers and magazines in Spain for four years, and that's probably what I'd be doing now . . .

The degree I did was more about the history of communication and filmmaking. Most of my classes were about ethics, economics, history, literature, it was very theoretical. We got a camera for three weeks in the third year and we made some short films, but it was very hard because it was a very small camera and we couldn't use it outside the university. It wasn't a very good course. For me it was OK, it wasn't a problem, because I was trying to write, and every-thing we did was concepts—ethics, sociology—and I was able to use that later. But people who were trying to go into filmmaking were very unhappy because they were always asking why they couldn't use the camera . . .

Did your parents encourage you to be creative from a young age? What kind of environment did you grow up in at home?

It was a very regular middle-class family, and I think they were progres-sive and very liberal about what I wanted to do with the rest of my life. I was a good student, and then they left me alone: "If the boy wants to draw then let him draw, if he wants to make movies then let him make movies." I have to say that they never went against my decisions.

And were politics something that was discussed at the dinner table?

Sometimes, and I think that it was close to left-wing. When I was thirteen or fourteen, we went to live in Guatemala for a couple of years because my father was working there. In Spain he was an official in the Department of Employment, and he helped at the Institute of Professional Information, which is a kind of university for people who can't go to university. They show people how to learn a trade, and this is what they were trying to do in Guatemala at that time. It was after the earthquake in 1976; my father went as part of a collaboration mission to review the country and help people get some kind of work. And the whole family went with him. I think that was very important to me, because I realized something about another country. The people I saw in Guatemala made me realize that it was a very poor country compared to Spain. I saw another kind of culture and a very hard way of life. Every day was a struggle. Even the relationship of the army with the population was very difficult. I remember the people who worked for my father took some electronic microscopes to Guatemala, to show the locals how to work with them. Then a couple of days later the army went into the place they had set up for education, and they broke the whole thing. The army didn't agree with what the Spanish people were doing there, with their kind of mission. There was a lot of Spanish involvement in some of the Latin America countries at the time. I was very young, but I was aware of things from TV and conversations, and I think that a lot of that has stayed with me in some way.

We might return to this when we talk about Mondays in the Sun *and how it deals with unemployment—how it may relate to your dad.*

In fact, I researched *Mondays in the Sun* in very different places, and one of them came up after my father called an old friend of his, a man who was working in the welfare and unemployment office in Spain. Then I interviewed some people who worked with my father when I was very young.

What about literature? I read that you'd written some short stories, so I was wondering when your interest in literature started and if you had any literary heroes growing up . . .

I used to read more often than go to the movies. I remember reading Robert Louis Stevenson. I don't know when I started reading people like Raymond Carver or Tobias Woolf. But I love short stories, I always read them.

When did you actually start writing your own short stories?

Well, once I started to study filmmaking I wasn't very involved, I was always thinking of leaving. I was nineteen years old and it was very boring to me, everything was like mathematics; the axis of the camera, the size—I wasn't interested in it. Then a friend of mine took me to a screenwriting course, a three-week course which was *very* interesting. Each week we would have a different teacher, and Laura Salvador was the first. I remember the first day was the only day that all three teachers were together, and one of them said, "What is a script?" In Spanish it means "a guide"; a guide for shooting. In English it's a different thing, writing for the screen, but in Spanish it's a guide because they say this is only useful for the shooting, after you've finished it doesn't mean anything. It's a work in progress, not a novel. Laura—who loves to write—she heard this and was very angry and said, "Excuse me, a script is everything!" And the other guy, who was younger, said, "Sometimes the script is nothing, sometimes it's everything!" But I feel very close to Laura and I think, as she said, that the script is everything.

That course was the first time I had the feeling that I'd discovered something. Before that, I'd never written a lot, this was the first time. And the way Laura and the others talked about their job was so passionate and wonderful to me that I listened and thought, "If these guys talk this way about their job, I want to do it." And on this course we started talking about characters, about relationships—it was very different to the mathematics. This was more like literature, it was about passion and love and hate and revenge.

Then I got the feeling this was what I wanted to do with my life, and so I almost forgot drawing. And at that time, when I started writing, I had no thought of directing movies, I was only interested in screenwriting. Six or seven years later I changed my mind and directed *Familia*, my first movie. But until then I worked only as a screenwriter and I was very happy.

You asked about the short stories . . . when I discovered writing on this course, I started writing short stories too. And then I sent a story into a contest, the first story I ever wrote, and it was a very prestigious organization with about two thousand short stories competing. And I won the second prize. I was nineteen, and the first prize went to an established novelist in Spain who writes wonderfully, so it was crazy. I think I was very lucky. But then I thought, "This works, I can do it."

Have you ever thought about publishing a collection of your own short stories?

I don't have very many. I haven't published my short stories because most of them are already in books with other short stories. Over the course of fifteen years this has only happened six or seven times.

Are you interested in writing a novel at all?

I always say that I would love to do it. I am very interested in it, but I'm not too sure. I'm so involved in making films that it's very difficult to actually think about writing something as long as a novel. I think that you need to be very focused and relaxed. In fact, the thing is that I enjoy filmmaking a lot until I have the last draft of the script, then, in my opinion, the trouble starts. When I was young I was very quiet, and so because of my character I think it was easier for me to work as a writer than to direct, because when you direct you have to talk to so many people. When you write, you write alone or maybe with one other screenwriter, but with filmmaking you have to deal with so many other people. I hate it, really, I hate directing. I think that when you write, you write what you want to write, and when you shoot, you shoot what you are able to shoot—because the actor is not exactly the one you want, or you're not having a good time with the weather or the production company. But when you write, there is no problem, everything is perfect. When I shoot I try to keep the movie as perfect as it was in my mind. And my opinion goes down during the shooting. At the end of *Familia* my first assistant used to ask me, "What do you think of this movie?" I think he meant in relation to the script. And on *Familia* I said I thought we got about seventy per cent of what I thought was in my mind.

What was Mondays in the Sun?

I think about the same, seventy—no, seventy-five per cent. Don't get me wrong, there is frustration when you write, too. Sometimes you don't find what you're looking for but the only difficulty is you. And I don't feel frustration when I write, but when I shoot I can't bear it. I can't reach what I want.

How did your screenwriting course influence the way you set about screenwriting yourself?

I think that people like Laura Salvador and I, when we write, we write more than just actions. She is more expressive in her screenwriting, and I think I learned a lot from her. My way of writing is similar to hers, which is more expressive.

I think at the beginning, even though I read all these manuals about how to write a screenplay, I was very nervous and obsessive about plot and how to make the movie work. As were many of my friends who became writers—we were going back to mathematics again! When I worked as a screenwriter I used to work to rules a lot, and each time I was writing new scripts I was trying to lose them. They were useful, but each time I was trying to pull them apart and think more about the characters.

In the beginning when I started to write a script I promised myself I wasn't trying to construct anything; I was trying to destroy it, and just think about character. I remember I gave a script to my friend who was a screenwriter and he told me I was crazy because the plot didn't start for thirty-five minutes. I think that if you understand the characters and you are involved with them you are going to be there, listening to what's going on and you're going to be involved in the movie even if there are no plot points.

So how do you know that you're keeping the audience's attention with a story that doesn't have these huge turning moments?

Sometimes through humor. But I think that the main way is through the characters and when I write I try to connect with them, I try to understand them and have an effective relationship with them, even with the smaller characters. For example, in *Mondays*, the guy who is in the shipyard, he only appears in a couple of sequences in the movie, but when I write that character I try to be very close to him and understand him. I think I know who he is even though he is only in two sequences.

Do you construct biographies of the characters?

I don't write three pages about a character because I think that's very boring. Sometimes you think of things and write them down because later it's useful for the actors, but I don't usually work that way. I used to write a lot and then there are a lot of sequences which finally are not in the script but they gave a lot of information about the character. My first scripts were about two hundred pages, but then I knew a lot about the characters. Then you take out sequences. In each movie it has been different. For example in *Barrio* there were three main characters, three fifteen-year-old boys, and I started worrying about them and then one day I remembered something that I'd learned in philosophy classes that Aristotle said about the three souls of the man; one is the head, one is the chest, one is the . . . I don't know how you say it . . .

The cojones?

Yes! Because there is the rational soul, the will, and the passion. I thought that those boys were the three souls, because the three of them are part of the one character. But I didn't have to force the characters to be this, it just happened in a lot of other ways, each one was one of them; Rai was the guts, or the balls, Manu was the will, Javi was the more rational. That's why I think that Javi is the one who'll survive because he's more rational and he thinks before he acts. Rai never thinks. That's why somebody kills him at the end of the movie, because he's more instinctual. That was useful for me to organize that movie.

When did you become interested in making documentaries?

In the beginning I was writing for television shows, and then sitcoms, and then drama, each time it was longer. Finally I started to write feature movies for directors. At the same time I had some friends, one of whom was very close friends with Paul Laverty—Javier Corcuera from Peru. We worked together at university and then became friends and one of them had a camera, a Betacam, and we used to go to places to shoot things just because we loved to do it. We went to Bosnia during the war in 1994. Some friends knew people who were living there and then we went there to shoot.

Wasn't that dangerous?

Yes, I think it was. When I told my mother I was going away I never told her that I was going to Bosnia. But it wasn't a long shoot, just fifteen days. We worked fifteen or twenty hours a day because there were a lot of things to do there, a lot of interviews and reports to put together. The most interesting thing was that in that final week we went to Serbia, which was interesting because the Serbs didn't used to allow European cameras inside because they were angry with the Europeans.

Were you nervous about your safety at all?

Yes. To go to Serbia we had to cross the frontier, and this was a very difficult thing because there is a movie, *No Man's Land* . . . it's a great film with a very interesting script. It's very symbolic, just two characters. I think it's very interesting and very similar. The no man's land is the land between the two sites; it is six kilometers of land and we had to cross it. We had United Nations protection and we were in a car and we had a tank in front of us and another one behind, and we crossed six kilometers. There were mines there and they picked the mine up, passed by, and then put the mine back on the road. I was very nervous. It was like a slalom to avoid the mines. We were very afraid because these mines were from the First World War and they explode just looking at them, or so they told us. We were very scared.

How do you go about writing a documentary?

This has changed a lot too, because in the beginning there was just a commentary, which was the first one, we didn't write anything. We researched, we talked to people in Spain who were from Bosnia, and we talked about the war. We wrote the questions and that was it. Every day we were there we had to make decisions. After that we had to shoot several commentaries. As a filmmaker I've only shot one of them, in Mexico about the Zapatistas, the National Liberation Army in Mexico run by Subcomandante Marcos. I worked with Javier Corcuera on another one which was called *The Back of the World, La Espalda del Mundo*, and in this I was the screenwriter and he was the director. This was very different because we did a lot of research and then we wrote a script, which changed a lot. It was interesting to do.

You wrote a script so you had an idea to structure the documentary, and then it changed once you started actually getting the interviews?

That's it. The producer wanted to do a commentary, and I wanted to do it too but not with the tour, a march of protest all the way to Mexico City, as I thought CNN and Spanish television was going to be there and we couldn't do it better than them. So I didn't want to do it until we could think of an idea which was that if this was the march, instead of shooting it like news material, we would find a different way of doing it. We went to a little village and we shot how this little village was waiting for them. The idea was that we spent fifteen days on this commentary shooting how they were waiting; so the whole structure is like a countdown, and just at the end of the commentary they arrived.

It must have been quite stressful to shoot when they marched into town and you want to follow all these people that you have been filming.

Yeah, it was because when they were on the stage talking to the people, we were shooting at our characters, which were the people of the community. The teacher, the musician, we were shooting interviews, and then at the end we were shooting our people. But that day I had a third camera, a camera from Mexico. For me that day my focus was on the people of the community, their hopes and their expectations were the main thing.

How did you get access to Subcomandante Marcos?

It was very difficult.

His identity is very well protected.

Yeah, and those were very bad days because there was a lot of pressure on him because of the government, and the whole march was very tiring because it was crazy. They didn't have a lot of time. A couple of weeks before they left we sent him some letters through people we know who are close to him. We tried to reach him through a lot of different ways and finally when I talked to him he told me, "My God, you came to me from everywhere!" I said, "I'm sorry Marcos, I had to do it." He was saying, "Who are you? Why are so many people telling me about you?" We knew some interesting people near him, a lawyer, a woman who was the mother of somebody who died in jail in Mexico and she's important in this movement. Through her and other people we sent letters. When we were in Mexico we went to a village that is close to them and is a place where from time to time they go and hold a press conference. We were there for three days and we tried to interview him but it wasn't possible, we had to leave because there was a lot of pressure. In those days the International Red Cross was going to protect them but four days before, the Red Cross said no because the Mexican government wanted them to say no. Then it was a problem because the whole thing was very dangerous. Because of this we couldn't reach Marcos and we had to leave because we had to start work. Then at the end of the tour, three days after they arrived in Mexico, we were leaving Mexico so we sent him one last letter saying it was important that we see him but that we had to leave. We told him the flight we were taking and when and asked him to call us and then we'd stay; otherwise we had to come back to Spain to do the casting for *Mondays in the Sun*. Then we were in the airport, the cameraman and me, the rest of the crew had put their luggage on the plane but we waited. Then they called us, the cell phone sounded and the producer picked up the phone and they said, "Wait one more day because he wants to do the interview." So the cameraman and me, we stayed, and the rest of the crew were on the plane. That night they called us back at the hotel and it was Marcos, he called us at the hotel! Then the following day we did the interview; he said we had to be there at four p.m. "and I will be there at five because I know you are very slow as you have to do the lights and everything." Finally, he came at four too, which was great because we were talking for an hour before shooting the interview, which meant I was more relaxed.

I'm sure the Mexican government would have a few queries for you about that interview . . . Moving on, can you tell me something about your first paid screenwriting job?

I remember it very clearly, it was an important step! I had the feeling I was professional and it was great. I think I was twenty-one years old, I think it was the fourth or the fifth script that I'd written. For a couple of them I'd had some grants from the Spanish government but I never sold them to any production company. But selling one was good for me because I thought this works, and somebody thinks this can be a movie. Then after a few years I sold one to a production company but it was never made. The first three or four scripts that I wrote were never shot, I got paid but they never got shot.

That's not too bad . . .

This happened about three times and the fourth one I sold to a production company and then it got made. All of these were assignments; they gave the idea to me. Usually in Spain at that time they wanted us to write comedies, they thought that it was more commercial because in Spain at that time the only Spanish movies that worked were comedies. I wrote for TV for a few years and then they'd call me and say they wanted a comedy like this one, which was a very good one, and I'd say, "I can write a different one, but not that one!" But they wanted ones like that, so I did it, of course.

So writing comedy has come to you easily?

Yes.

How did you find writing for these TV comedy shows, was that easy work to do?

The thing is, I was so happy writing, I discovered writing so late that I spent a lot of hours doing it because I had to write the things I hadn't written before. The time I lost practicing my drawing I had to make up for by practicing my writing. I was writing a lot and then I started writing for sitcoms and it was very interesting because I love dialogue, and then that was that kind of setup because the dialogue and the characters are very important. And I think this was very good for me, like a school, because I wrote a lot of sitcoms and then I had the feeling that I was learning how to create characters and write dialogue. It's funny, because the first movie they shot from a script that I had written was from a sitcom but the main actor liked it very much and wanted to do a feature with it. But in the beginning it was the first episode of a sitcom, then the producer called me and said they had more money now, that they could use exteriors, and I said, "I don't want exteriors!" Sometimes the thing is, if you have a lot of money you can shoot in the country or on the streets but I love writing for characters up close. I must be more like Polanski because I like situations in close-up.

Your second feature, Barrio, *was made in 1998 and takes place in a suburb of Madrid. My understanding is that the poster had a jet-ski locked to a lamppost, is that right?*

Yes, that's right.

Can you tell me about Barrio *in comparison to* Familia, *about what you learned from both of them, screenwriting-wise?*

I think I wrote the script of *Familia* very quickly, but I never sold it to a production company because I liked it a lot and I put it in a drawer because it was a very small story. The whole movie is in a house, it's a very low-budget movie because you don't need anything, it's only a house and a family. But it's not a real family; it's the story of a man about fifty-five years old who is alone for his birthday so he pays actors to play the roles of the family. The movie is about how the family works, because my idea was that the family is a theater, so the actors will play roles. The movie was exactly that, it was funny because there were a lot of strange situations inside the family; the brothers have sex but they were not brothers because they were actors, but at the same time it's funny because it's like incest. So it has humor but at the same time I think it was a very bitter comedy, sometimes it was sad.

A dark comedy?

Yeah, I think so. I thought I should shoot that movie because my experience with scripts was that sometimes when I saw the finished movie I wasn't very happy, mainly because of the tone of the movie, which I found to be very obvious.

You were more subtle.

I would like to think so. But in *Familia*, it was the kind of movie that depends on the director because the tone is so fragile that one director can make a thriller; another one can make a very obvious comedy, so I thought I should shoot it myself. It was a very low budget movie so finally I found a producer to do this movie. *Familia* and *Barrio* are very different. I think in *Familia* the plot is more important, and in *Barrio* I was thinking more of characters.

So that was a big shift for you?

Yes.

And Mondays *is an extension of thinking in characters.*

Yes. When I wrote *Familia* I tried to create characters that were more interesting but the idea was so strong, so that was the most important thing in the movie, not the characters, even when I tried that. In my opinion *Familia* is more effective. As a young writer you're trying to show yourself in the script and the script for *Familia* is a bit exhibition-ist, like a brilliant exercise of a good student. I think it's more of that kind of movie and *Barrio* is more personal. In my opinion, *Barrio* was more difficult to write than *Familia*, because *Familia* had this brilliant idea and the plot. And the comedy situations were easier to write at that time than *Barrio*, because *Barrio* paid more attention to the characters and the feelings of the characters so it had to be more respectful to the characters, so to me it was more difficult. That's why when I started to write *Barrio* I thought about not constructing anything. I had to destroy it, had to be very pure, and not to use screenwriter tricks.

Such as?

Things like condensing time or ellipses, other things that are useful and very necessary when you're writing a script. It happens with the actors too; when an actor has played twenty movies he has a lot of tricks, and he can do something in front of the camera that works but is not good. It works, but it's maybe what people are expecting.

Like a certain facial expression?

Yes, like a kind of smile, because there are a lot of famous actors who use this because they have to. And sometimes writing is very similar because you'll write something you know is going to work but it doesn't mean that it is good. Sometimes you have to think this is not so pure; I tried to do it with *Barrio* because with other scripts that I had written I found that sometimes you finally use the things you have learned from writing a lot of scripts or sometimes you realize that you use similar structural tricks. So I tried to avoid all of this when I wrote *Barrio*; I don't know if I managed it but I tried.

You're thirty-five years old but you've already written and directed three features, numerous feature films for other directors and also worked on three TV series. You must write quickly, so could you tell me how you go through the writing process, from idea to first draft?

It's very different, it depends on the movie. I have an idea, like in *Familia* it was family as a theater, and then I used to write a synopsis and then a treatment. I used to write all this stuff, but in these last two scripts I have been spending more time on research. At the beginning I didn't use a lot of research. I thought that you could imagine everything, I was very inexperienced. I thought you could imagine everything and you could write a movie about the war without going there, but I don't think that way now. One of the first movies that I wrote, a script for Fox Searchlight, it hasn't been filmed, but we did a lot of research and it was great because in doing a lot of research I learned about the characters and then when I started writing I was wanting to write the best movie ever because I loved the characters. I thought that they deserved a good movie. This was three years ago and since then I have researched a lot. *Mondays in the Sun*, the research was great for the movie. I had a lot of feelings, situations, and characters, but not only things for the scripts, a lot of things for me.

So you can understand the characters.

Yes, and later I can tell the actors the things that I learned from the research. Research is great because it allows you to go into a different life and it's a good way to learn things.

What do you do with the research when you've got it? What's the next step of the writing process?

I used to do the research when I had a story, at least when I had a synopsis or even a treatment. I have the treatment for the movie I am writing now, and I've started to do the research now; maybe it's a little bit late because I have the structure and the characters, but it's still useful because you can still find characters in situations and you learn how they speak, how they talk. I think after this I will write the first draft. Usually the first draft of the script is pretty useful; maybe eighty per cent of the first draft is the movie. Sometimes, sometimes not, but at least the ones I have directed have been that way. The first draft of *Barrio* was very close to the final movie. Then I used to write five or six drafts. I changed a lot of the dialogue to make it sound as real as possible; sometimes I'd take out a character of a secondary plot. But usually the first draft is very close to the finished film. That used to be a good sign, sometimes when you have to change a lot of things in a script and you do fourteen drafts and you have a problem with the script because it is full of . . .

Different colored paper?

Yes, that's a bad sign because it means you have a lot of problems and you have to repair them, it's like a tire with a lot of patches. I think that a script like that is never going to work. Scripts that are written in less time usually for me are the best.

You write pretty quickly, for example how long did it take you to write Mondays?

Sometimes I write very quickly, maybe because of my time writing sitcoms when I had to be very quick. When I was twenty-four I was very quick. I would write a script in a couple of months, approximately a couple of months for *Barrio* and *Familia*. *Mondays* took me more time. I wrote it with Ignacio del Moral and the thing is after *Barrio* I was very tired and I vowed never to shoot anymore, just to be a screenwriter. After *Barrio* I wrote a couple of scripts for other directors, and then I started to think about *Mondays in the Sun* and I started talking to Ignacio. This took a lot of time because he works as a television screenwriter and he was very busy, so we didn't have much time. We wrote a treatment and then we stopped; when we had the first draft I went to shoot *Caminantes* in Mexico, and then I went back to the script. I think this is great because if you let the time pass by on a script then you can see things you didn't see in the beginning, it's useful. Overall it took a year to write *Mondays in the Sun.*

When you're working, how much do you write per day, when it's going well?

When it's going well . . . I don't know, maybe seven or eight pages.

How do you handle those moments when you feel like it isn't working, how do you handle the self-doubt?

I think, when it happens, and it happens a lot, I think it's right to go on, not to stop. Sometimes it happens because it doesn't work and you are very slow, and of course you want to call somebody or go out, so you do. And then after a few days of writing a lot you are very slow because you're not happy with what you're writing. I just try to go on. If I'm writing a sequence and I don't like it, I don't like the way they're talking, what's going on, then I try to keep writing even when I don't like it. To go forward and then maybe four sequences later it will become nice again. This is the good thing about computers because you can go back and do revisions, not drafts but revisions before the draft.

So you just leave it?

Yes, because I think that sometimes it's a problem for that day and when you come back to that sequence . . .

Ah, you're in a different mood, you feel different about the day.

Yes, that's it. Sometimes you go back and you have the same problem and sometimes you have to fix things and change things, but when things aren't working it is like walking through a desert, you don't like it but you keep walking. Like in the desert you don't stop, you just keep walking, and maybe you die! I tend to keep walking and then maybe the second time it's right.

Sometimes you write alone and sometimes with a partner. Which do you prefer and why?

Usually when I've written scripts for other directors, when the production company has given me a contract, most times I've written with another writer. It's funny. I used to write with people that I like as writers and as people. Then when I have written my own scripts: *Familia* and *Barrio* I was the only writer and *Mondays in the Sun* was with Ignacio, who is a close friend of mine and I love how he writes. It's very different. I love to write alone more than writing with somebody, but when you're in the desert it's great to write with somebody because then you're not so alone and sometimes you can see different things.

And how did you and Ignacio work together?

I worked with Ignacio before in television. He writes theater plays, I think he's very good with dialogue. I think we worked well together because ten years ago we were writing for television and he's very quick too; we have a lot of fun writing together. Then when we are working on the structure and characters in the treatment I love to write with someone like Ignacio because you can say things that may be silly but it's OK, he doesn't mind. That's nice because you are with somebody and you can talk and give each other ideas. I think it works. But I think I prefer to be alone to write dialogue because sometimes it's very difficult to write dialogue with somebody because of the music of the dialogue. I think all of us have a different ear for music and some-times it's difficult to write dialogue with somebody because you hear things in a different way, the music of the words. But I think on *Mondays in the Sun* we worked together a lot on the structure, we changed it a lot of times, put in new characters, took away some, and then when we had a treatment we liked we started writing the dia-logue, but I think I worked more on the dialogues than he did because I was going to shoot the movie.

I understand the idea for Mondays *was based on a true story—I was wondering where that came from?*

There were a couple of newspaper stories. I remember the first one was at the beginning of the 90s and I read a story in the newspaper about something taking place in France.

They love their strikes in France!

Yes, they're good at it! There was a movement of unemployed people, they weren't violent, they were funny. They were unemployed and they used to go to a big restaurant in Paris in a big group and have a big dinner, then when the bill came they would say they couldn't pay because they had no job. Then sometimes they called the police and it was in the paper. They did this too in the supermarkets, transporta-tion. In Spain we read a lot about this in the news, and one of the names of the movements was *Mondays in the Sun* because when they were going to do something on a Friday, they would say this Friday is a Monday in the sun for us, which was a way to say it's a day of unemployment, but it's fun, more hope and more positive.

So it's actually an expression in Spanish?

It's not a very popular expression.

If you're unemployed, you'd know it, right?

Yes. They use this expression and think everyone knows what it means but it's not a popular expression. In the beginning the movie was similar to this idea, it was more aggressive and the characters were more like the people who went to the restaurants.

How did you get away from that idea?

I think it always happens that you always want to write that kind of movie, more aggressive, but the writing process takes so long that you change a lot of things. This always happens to me; you take so much time to do all the work that you put everything you have in, you rationalize too much and sometimes you finish with a movie different to what you wanted to do, which was more impulsive. I think I wrote a movie about how things are, not about how they should be.

Can you tell me about your specific research, did you videotape people or interview them?

For the research I'm doing now, I use a camera for part of it but for the other I'm not because when you have a camera it changes things. I shot something last week about two girls working in prostitution and they were trying to speak in a different way, unnatural. But on the opposite side I've spent time with them and it was great.

Do you take a tape recorder?

No, I just remember.

It's better for developing trust, isn't it?

Yes, it is, and you always remember the interesting things. In *Mondays in the Sun* the research was very interesting, because I was writing the script and I saw images the same as the ones at the beginning of the movie on the TV, the fights between the workers and the policemen, and these were real. This was three years ago, I was writing the script and I saw the same images on the TV and what was happening was that there was fighting and three or four hundred workers of the shipyard said no as they didn't want their colleagues to be hurt fighting. And then I got in touch with them to ask if I could go there with a camera and they said yes, they were inside the dockyard for a month; they stopped working and the policemen were trying to get them out of the dockyard but they couldn't. I went there to the dockyard and we spent a week there with them, and there was some discussion of the situations and what they should do; it was very interesting. I shot some interviews but the most interesting thing was to hear them talk about their work. They call themselves working class and the way they talk about work is interesting because they were very respectful to the work.

Almost like a Marxist.

Yes, because their work is their only possession, they said they were working class and work is the only thing they had and they couldn't allow the other people to destroy their profession, because they were closing a lot of shipyards and buying ships in Korea. The way they talked about their jobs, in my opinion, was very emotional. There are dialogues in the movie which are exactly the same, for instance when Javier Bardem says something like, "This is not about our work, it's about the work of our sons, thinking about the next generations and fighting to defend them." That's very close to what they said, it was great, and it was very emotional. I think that I learned a lot there for the movie and most of it was related to dignity. We did this for a week and then I wrote a sequence in the movie in the bar, near the end, and it's a translation of one of those discussions, almost literal. In those meetings with the workers it was terrible because they would bring their wives, and sometimes the wives were the ones who would stand up and talk in the name of their husband. The wives were explaining to the other workers why her husband had to say yes to the conditions because they had to pay for things, and it was terrible because you can see the husband beside her, and it was embarrassing.

You said that this film consists of local, everyday stories and I was wondering what you meant by that?

I think that I was trying to say something like when I write it's interesting for us as writers to look at things that are close to us, and sometimes you have to just write films as if you were in the American industry about cops and this is not our life or our culture. I was thinking that we should look to the things that we have close by and not things far away. It was a joke because I am myopic, I only see things when they are very close to me, and I think that's a myopic way to write. I am interested in seeing things that are very close to me, and I never focus on things far away. I think that the best stories are in the smaller situations.

Small story, large reflection.

Yes, and I think that we have to look for stories in the useful things; there are stories in the common people.

At what point did Javier Bardem get involved? I was wondering if you wrote the part of Santa for him and if that affected your writing?

Not really, because I never think about the cast as I write the script, because then you write a role for an actor and then they don't end up doing the movie, so it's stupid. Sometimes you can't avoid thinking about somebody but I try not to do it. I try to create the characters and not to think of actors. It was that way for this script. When I wrote the first draft I never thought about who was going to be Santa, who in some ways is the main character in the movie. He's very important because he's the leader, the pillar of the film. He reminds everyone who they are. He is important but I never thought about Javier. Then I went to see *Before Night Falls* in San Sebastián and after five minutes I knew Javier could be Santa.

You could see it in Before Night Falls *and it's such a different role?*

Just because of that. I thought he is so good he can do whatever he wants. And Reinaldo Arenas is so different to Javier Bardem; he is very strong and Reinaldo is very fragile. I always thought that Santa was older than Javier is. Javier was thirty-three years old at that time and I wanted Santa to be forty years old. But when I saw the movie and went for coffee the following day with my first draft and read it with Javier Bardem as Santa, it worked because the character could be a bit younger, and I knew that Javier could play thirty-eight years old. So I told him and he liked it a lot; he called me the next day and was very excited with the story and with Santa; it was a very unconventional role. This was one year before shooting the movie and he waited.

So he really helped get the film made?

I think so.

How do you feel about the comparison between Mondays *and Ken Loach's work?*

I always think, "What will Ken Loach think about this?" I like him a lot and I like his work a lot.

So you're happy with those comparisons?

I'm happy, of course, to be compared with somebody who I think is one of the best filmmakers in the world. I think Ken Loach would think this too, that sometimes journalists like to use this trick; it's a very easy way to talk about the film. I think that there are probably some similarities in the subject and the way of dealing with it but not everything is the same. But I liked the comparison, I'm happy. There were some comparisons made with the Italian neo-realists and with Ettore Scola. In some terms I think *Mondays* is similar to the neo-realists because of the way they treat the characters but I love the way that British social films, like Ken Loach's, use humor, sometimes it's a different humor—very dry—and the Italians sometimes are more poetic. Sometimes I like this comparison because of the approach to the characters. Sometimes I think it's more like Italians than the British.

Do you think unemployment is an affliction like alcoholism; that it's hard to get out of its grasp once it takes hold?

I chose a special age for these characters, a difficult one, being forty.

Why is that difficult?

It's like a gap between two things, it's not well-defined. In Spain they say that there's a kind of unemployment which is the people who are in their fifties who haven't worked for the last ten years and it's the worst time for them. There is a phrase for them in Spanish which, translated, means "long time unemployed." It's difficult because it's hard for them to get back into work. In some sense I think Amador is close to this situation, which is why he is a hard character, more involved with the workers and the end of his story is more dramatic. But from the beginning I thought that this was a good age for the characters because things aren't very clear for them. Like José, he spends a year unemployed, but he still doesn't realize his situation, but his wife has figured out what is going on. Maybe he's thinking every day that it's going to change, he doesn't realize that it might not. I think it's more subtle because the relation of each character is more subtle, it's more fragile because everything can go great or everything can go really bad.

Is there something about that age where you also start looking back rather than looking forward?

If they were twenty-five years old then this working class mentality doesn't exist and people want to work in anything because they don't have a family to support. When you are like these characters then it's different because they are professionals, and they want to work and be well-paid.

Once you do that job that's beneath you then you kind of get stuck down there, don't you?

You only want to go up, but maybe you can't. I feel that José is very confused. When I wrote his character I always thought that he was very confused about his situation, and his wife knows what's going on. It's like he's lying to himself; that's why when I wrote and I talk about unemployment as being the main part of his life, he doesn't think that it is. He thinks that unemployment is something that happens to other people, and then he starts to have a bad time in his situation. For me the age was important; still you have to work a lot, but you have worked a lot already, then you have a notion of what work should be, you have a lot in front of you.

Why did Santa want to emigrate to Australia? To me it seemed like a very escapist fantasy considering how well he knows the harsh realities of his life.

I think there are a couple of things there. First, he is the strongest fighter but at the same time he has no roots anywhere. People came to the towns to work and then when the industry broke down most of them were out of work and without roots, and I think Santa had no roots and that was a problem for him. That's why he lives in this small hotel and he always has different girls.

He's searching.

He's searching and he knows he's probably going to leave this town. The real thing that's important to me was that I wanted him to talk about emigrating, and when he talked about Australia I wanted him to talk about Utopia. I think that Santa is more idealistic and he always brings humor to the movie. I think he's the hope inside the movie. I liked him to be the one who talks about how things should be, when he talks about politics he says how he thinks it should be. But when he's talking about other things, like Australia, he's talking about how things should be when really his situation is the opposite.

José's wife, Ana, works in a fish cannery and is obsessed with the thought of smelling of fish when she gets off work. Was that something to suggest that some jobs are only just better than unemployment?

I think that's the work she has to do, which she doesn't want to do. Like Lino—he wants to do any kind of work, and Santa always tells him not to go to more interviews. I think I was trying to talk about temporary jobs as well as unemployment. They are only six month jobs which are precarious. I was trying to talk about how some jobs are trash jobs because the work that Ana does is very hard and they're contracted for six months at a time. When you're contracted for three years you have to change contracts so before you've done three years they stop you and you have to start from the beginning again. It's terrible. I wanted to talk about this kind of precarious work too. José was trying to talk about what happens to a couple. José is feeling bad that it is important to have his wife working.

Where did the idea for Sergei's character come from? It seems unlikely that a former space cadet would end up in Spain, but it felt completely real.

The fact is in Spain there are a lot of workers who came from Eastern Europe, a lot of Russian and Polish workers who are in construction and manual labor—very cheap and temporary work. Most of the time they are people who had very good careers. This happens a lot; people have skills but they cannot use them. I wanted to put an immigrant in the movie but it couldn't be a very big character because I didn't have the room. I wanted someone to represent the immigrant workers; I like the Slavic culture and the people so I made him Russian and then I had the idea of him being a trainee cosmonaut, which was a little bit crazy, but I found a kind of poetry in it because in some ways he is like a cosmonaut because of the way he thinks. When we wrote the script, Ignacio and I tried to put in a different problem related to unemployment of each character; with Lino it's the problem of age, with José it's his relationship with his wife. Santa is more combative, Sergei is the immigrant. Each one of them represented from a sociological point of view one of the impacts of unemployment, each one of them represents a different way to live through this situation.

Can you tell me something about the baby-sitting scene where Santa and his friends cover a baby-sitting assignment for a teenage girl who ditches the job so she can go out with her friends? Santa and his mates sit in the back garden, sipping expensive drinks while the toddler watches TV. The tone is very funny, but it's also very realistic.

It's funny because some people wanted to take this out of the movie; the producer and even Ignacio thought that, so I fought very hard because I like it too. I loved to write those sequences, which are a little bit out of reality, fantasy goes into reality a little bit and then there is poetry, just a little bit, not too much. I love writing that kind of sequence and it's difficult to shoot it because I want to make it real but sometimes it's difficult. For me it is important to hold on to this scene because it was one of the last fun moments in the movie. After that sequence things get worse for them, after this there is the whole thing in the bank so I wanted to have this to lighten it.

When Santa sweetly reads the bedtime story for the boy he is baby-sitting he starts to read a story about a grasshopper. It is a fable that Santa interprets as political and he passionately informs the child that the story is a lie, that the grasshopper is politically motivated. Where did that come from?

I think it came from Santa's mind because when I was writing at that point I was very close to the mind of the character, and this is the first moment in which I wrote what the character is saying for themselves. Then later you read it and sometimes you think, "I have written this?"

Is it your subconscious that's written it?

Yeah, I think so. When I wrote it I was thinking like Santa, which is that everything is political. I could talk about everything as Santa does. Another thing, with José, is that he always asks Amador about his wife, like in the bar, he always asks about his wife and I didn't realize this. When we were shooting the last sequence he says it again, and I realized that José says it because he always has problems with his own wife, so that's why he's always asking.

It's a very somber theme and also the pace of the film is not very rushed — how aware are you about the pacing of the film when you are writing?

I knew that the rhythm of the movie had to be quiet because we are talking about unemployment. In many sequences they have nothing to do, they are under the sun and this is the title of the movie, this is what it's about. We were worried about the scene where Javier Bardem talks about Australia; this has to be a long sequence and it's fifteen minutes into the movie, so we were worried that people were going to leave the theater. And I always asked the actors to talk slow, it was important because of the subject of the movie. It was the same with *Barrio*, we used to say it was a terrible story but softly told; you can tell a horror story but with nice words. I tried to give each character good moments and realistic moments. If you see them laughing and having a good time you are going to feel close to them and then in the bad moments you are going to be more concerned. I also can't avoid it. I always use humor to tell things, in real life too, using humor to make things softer but sometimes harder.

What kind of future do you think Santa and some of his friends have?

My idea was always to have an open end for the movie, because I think their lives were open; so the most organic thing I could do with the script is have an open ending in which they are moving and they don't know what's going to happen. One of the most important things is that, no matter what happens, they are under the sun and they have laughs; it's difficult but for their own dignity they know it's not their fault. It's like finding hope inside the situation. I don't know what's going on with them. I think that maybe they've learned something and I hope that Santa has reminded them who they are and that they should stay together; they have to keep close and I hope this worked for them. The sequence at the end of the movie where Ana was going to leave but she stayed: I always thought that six months later she would leave. This is because she had to stay to help her husband, she didn't choose to stay because she wanted to.

Then we went back to the place where we met the workers and did a screening for them; we were very afraid of what they might think. But it was nice. The thing is that talking with them about Ana, about the wife, they told me they liked her because they felt like it was a homage to their own wives, because some of them had to leave because they drank; conditions were difficult, there were a lot of broken marriages, but they thought that Ana represented the wife that supported them and stayed even when everything was very difficult. They said the wives were important and it was great to see them. Then

I said, of course, "Ana was always going to stay!" I think it showed me that you can be more dramatic than reality is. I thought she would leave but they taught me that reality wasn't going to be so hard, they loved each other so she would stay.

Los Angeles, California

16

DAVID O. RUSSELL

Three Kings

"Just take whatever is inside of you and speak from that."

David O. Russell wrote and directed the independent hit *Spanking the Monkey* (1994), a comedy about incest. He also wrote and directed a comedy about adoption, *Flirting with Disaster* (1996), which starred Ben Stiller, Patricia Arquette and Alan Alda. He adapted and directed *Three Kings* (1999), the only American movie ever to be made about the Gulf War, from a script that was in turnaround at Warner Brothers. The film stars George Clooney and Mark Wahlberg. His latest film, an existential detective comedy, *I ♥ Huckabees* (2004), stars Dustin Hoffman, Lily Tomlin and Jude Law.

Synopsis

Iraq, March 1991. The Gulf War has just ended and U.S. soldiers Troy Barlow and Conrad Vig find a map locating the bunkers where Saddam Hussein has hidden gold bullion looted from Kuwait. Major Archie Gates convinces them, along with their staff sergeant Chief Elgin, to help him steal the gold. The four soldiers locate the bullion and Saddam's soldiers make no attempt to stop them because they are busy suppressing local rebels. Reluctant to abandon them to their fate, the Americans decide to take the villagers with them, even though it's against official U.S. policy.

* * *

KEVIN CONROY SCOTT: *Books were revered in your house when you were growing up. Were there any particular authors you read at that time whose lives or careers you wanted to emulate?*

DAVID O. RUSSELL: Yeah—probably J. D. Salinger or F. Scott Fitzgerald. Those were the two big guys. I wouldn't have had Fitzgerald's "rich" thing going on, but I liked what he wrote about social classes. I read some more interesting people too. I feel as though I should be saying some more obscure French authors . . .

Don't worry, it's not that kind of interview.

Okay, so those two guys, and probably Mark Twain too; *Huckleberry Finn* had a big influence on me, and I also thought Twain was very cool as a gadfly, as a social critic, a satirist and a humorist.

I believe your first short film was a documentary called Boston to Panama?

I did it as an activist, mostly. I always thought I would be a writer because I had worked in Central America during the early years of the Nicaraguan revolution, teaching literacy there. Then I did some of that in Boston's South End, and I used the writing as a political empowerment tool. In other words you get people who don't know how to read or write and in the process of learning to read and write they write their own stories, and they realize it's not a mystifying language that's owned by the rich classes, but it's something in which they can express themselves as well. They wrote stories in English and I published them in a little magazine, and everybody took it to the media. Then the magazines would go out to little adult education centers, and the immigrants would see the work they'd done in the magazine and in my documentary, which was a video of one guy's life in particular. It's the story of how this guy from Central America was struggling to live in Boston, where people were slashing his tires and stealing his mail. The film was a struggle for me because it was a creaky process where I used the facilities at the local community college to make it. I was cutting from one deck to the other, there was no editing system, so you'd have to stop the deck exactly where you wanted to cut to, and then cut the other deck in. So it was stone-age editing . . .

Apparently in college you were interested in writing fiction and doing critical work. When did you start focusing on filmmaking and, in particular, screenwriting?

You know, for some reason I think I never took it seriously as a vocation—maybe because I grew up in a house with books, and I thought fiction writing was the only way to go, really. I was too laden with middle-class expectations—though I bucked all of those by growing up to be a leftist and a screenwriter, neither of which fit those expectations. I always loved movies, I loved them from my soul. I'd go to the same movie five or six times and I would relive them in my head for weeks and months, probably to a neurotic extent. And I've always said that all those great movies of the seventies were my film education. Then I just started making films, badly. When I came to Boston, I didn't understand the very thing I'd been teaching my students, which was that you should just take whatever is inside of you and speak from that. I think I thought of film as some artifice that had to be fabricated to be deserving, and so my first short films are sort of weird in that respect. I don't like to show them too much anymore because I don't think I knew what the hell I was doing. I didn't know anything about putting a movie together.

When you became serious about what you were doing, you moved to New York City and took a series of jobs, including work as a journalist and script reader for MGM. I've done reading work too, so I know it's one thing to be an analytical reader who can give good notes, but quite another to actually go out and write a screenplay . . .

Well, the first script I wrote was a horror thing, because that was considered to be a hot genre where you could quickly get very good and get started.

Was this during the Nightmare on Elm Street *phase of the eighties?*

Yeah, but I made my horror film political. I'd worked on toxic waste issues in a mill town in Maine so I said, "OK, you have these mill workers in Maine who are toxic mutants and they go down to New York City and start attacking and contaminating the Wall Street people who have bought and sold their factories." So it was like a yuppie-destruction horror picture. It didn't get me anywhere. Actually, that's not true, I met my wife through it. She was at New Line, but she "didn't respond to the material."

What was the problem?

I don't know, I should pull it out and look at it again . . . but I do know that in general what I thought I was learning was how to express what's inside of me and what I care about, and to turn it into some kind of cinema. There was a lot of groping around in that regard. For example, I had an idea of a guy in a Chinese restaurant who eavesdrops on every table and writes very pointed, personal fortunes to everyone, and that got me some grant money to make a short film. In the end I decided it was too cute so I tried to write it as a feature and spent two years on it. It would have been a nice comedy in some respects, but I needed to do something deeper, I think. It's a *little* bit similar to what I'm doing now, if only in the sense that I think there was something there about wanting to have an interface between people's lives.

I understand that you outline anything you're going to write. Can you take me through your process in going about that?

Well, first there's whatever it is that excites me about the idea, and then sometimes you have fragments or pieces of a story, and then you have scenes that you love and think are really great, and then character ideas — all these things aren't necessarily meshed together, but I list them all in columns, like characters. I've actually distilled it down so that I will take each character and write an arc from left to right, and then I try to find links between those arcs, between the stories of each character, and then I curtail them and condense them into one story. It can be a long process of trying to figure out what *the* story is — if it's interesting enough, whether it's going too much in the direction of one character, how do you pull it back? That's always a fight: "Whose movie *is* it?"

You said that you like to write at a friend's house because you found the writing process to be lonely. Is it really that hard for you to sit down and work on your own?

Well, you're still working by yourself when you're at a friend's house. But somehow it's easier just having somebody around to go get a coffee with when you want to take a break . . .

Do you find it's easier to break through certain kinds of problems if you're able to vocalize them?

Absolutely. It's nice to have someone to talk to about it. I've actually started collaborating for the first time on a recent project, and that's made it a lot less hard. So far it's been entirely my idea that I've developed, but I want help in figuring it out, and realizing it.

So you come up with so many ideas, you just need help expressing them?

I have billions of ideas. The problem is making them as good as they can be. Sometimes that's a long, hard process, so it's nice to know you don't have to do it by yourself. It's also good to just have someone there as a critic. And I also like to bounce ideas off certain people who work in my office sometimes, but we keep it in a hermetically sealed environment — because it would be too damaging if you let in too many people too soon. It gets confused, so you just keep it sealed, and then you start letting people figure out what makes sense.

Why do you think screenwriting is, and this is your own description, "excruciating and painful?"

Excruciating? Screenwriting? Well, I was probably referring to the lonely arduousness of it all. It's not easy to write a good movie; some movies just come popping out, but not all of them do, especially if it's an ambitious idea. Those are the ones where so often I'm halfway through the writing and I'm saying, "Why don't I just write something simpler?" I mean, I recently finished a rewrite of a new project that reminded me of the Chinese restaurant one, because it's about two existential detectives, one of whom will be played by Dustin Hoffman. People bring their cases of existential crisis to these detectives, and they investigate. So there is some eavesdropping, like in the Chinese restaurant, but it's only a little bit. I ran into Dustin Hoffman the other day and told him I had a new draft, we were chatting, and he kept saying, "Congratulations." And I said, "Why do you keep saying 'Congratulations'?" and he said, "Because I know how hard it is." And I appreciated that—someone knowing how hard it is to rewrite something, to shorten it or improve it. I think endurance is a big part of being able to be a good writer—to persist in trying to find the best answers, even when they're not presenting themselves to you yet.

Apparently Warren Beatty told you that it's just as hard to read a screenplay as it is to write one. Can you tell me why you agreed with that?

I have a very hard time reading a screenplay. People give them to me and I don't like to read them because I'm working all day on screenplays, so it then takes a lot of energy and concentration, because I like to put myself entirely into the script. But also I think you can totally misread a screenplay—many of my scripts have been completely misread by people, including the present one and *Three Kings*. The executives pass on it, and then they come up to me afterwards when the film is out and they say, "Oh my god, I didn't understand what you were trying to do and now I see! And it's so terrific, please come back to me." And you come back with the next project, and they say the same fucking thing—"I don't understand what you're doing here . . ." So you say, "Remember you said that about *Three Kings*, and then you said you really loved it . . . ?" And it goes on and on.

So yeah, I think it is hard to read a screenplay. You know, Dustin Hoffman asked me to read my new script to him aloud. It took three days to sit with him and read it, but he wanted to really hear it, how I feel and hear the script myself.

Is that because he wants to get your tone? Because your tone is very unique—you shift gears, you're always on a kind of high wire . . .

Exactly.

After Spanking the Monkey *and* Flirting with Disaster, *two films that the critic Graham Fuller called "neurotic family comedies," you made*

the $50 million Three Kings, *which you called a "political war film."
Can you tell me why as a writer you wanted to switch gears that way,
or increase the size of the canvas?*

That's a damn good question, and I look back and go, "Why the hell
did I do that?" But again, I think it's another one of those cases where
you're writing and you don't understand why you are going through
that process. You just feel you need to do it; something is drawing you
to tell that story. Obviously, making that film got me to where I am
today, where I feel very clear about what I want to do: smaller films
that are sort of more about strange, spiritual matters, which is most
dear to me. But for some reason that was not crystal clear to me at the
time. Part of it was a curiosity about the movie business that I just
hadn't got out of my system; and then you make a studio movie, with
a stunt department—for some reason I was drawn to that—and, having done it, I could not be *less* interested in repeating it. Let alone the
genre aspect of the heist, which just bores me to tears.

In your video journal that accompanies the DVD of Three Kings, *we
see you during pre-production, cycling to a casting session. You're not
in the back of a studio car, you're whizzing down Central Park West,
and then you bump into Spike Jonze . . . and your world seems quite
small and hermetically sealed. Then later, during production, you're in
a hotel conference room round a table with sixty other people, all
looking to you for an answer. I thought that, juxtaposed, those two
images said a lot.*

Yeah, that's just sick, isn't it? I was like God Almighty with how many
people were working on that film. It's really good to work with a
skeleton crew—I want to work with the smallest crew possible from
now on. Having a gigantic crew can be problematic because half of
them treat it very impersonally because they've just come off a string
of five movies. It's not a good energy to have on the set, when you've
slaved away at something for years.

   I have a lot of things that are in me, and movies take so long to
make that I suddenly woke up and thought, "Jesus Christ, let's bust
out some more jams! Let's get some more of me out there." And I still
have that, there are whole parts of me that I think by the time I tell all
my stories I'll be ninety years old. I want to get some of my politics out
there, because I was in Central America during a very unstable period—well it's always unstable—and I was always drawn to that.
Another reason I was drawn to *Three Kings* was because I wanted to
make a male movie, I didn't want my next movie to revolve around
women, like my first two movies.

You alluded to your distaste for the heist aspect of the plot in Three Kings. *Did it ever occur to you to take that element out of the plot?*

Good idea . . . No it didn't, and it would have made my life a hell of a lot easier. For some reason, I was like an autistic who gets hung up on one idea, even if it doesn't make sense anymore. I probably could have made a much more interesting movie if it had just been about the characters—a *M*A*S*H**—like comedy.

It seemed as if throughout Three Kings *there was a tension between what you need to do with the story and what you wanted to show about the American soldiers fighting in Iraq. I thought the cultural elements were very well-observed—such as the soldiers sneaking booze into their camps, the journalists angling for a story . . .*

I'm gonna say two things about that. First is that I'd like to think we did the action in an original way; secondly I felt as though we offered a very good political metaphor for the naïveté of the soldiers. This was through their green feelings, that they didn't have a satisfying experience in the war because they didn't get to fight and wanted to take something with them as a souvenir of their time in "the war." That goal of wanting to take something with you—either experience or a material possession like gold—is sort of like the oil: we get it and then we leave everyone behind. Which is what we do with these societies, we suck their resources out and leave behind these really fucked-up situations with repressive dictators, which is exactly what we did at the end of the Gulf War. I thought that was a huge hypocrisy. At the time I couldn't believe no other filmmaker was interested in exploring those themes and that war.

Three Kings *has become a very important film, especially in the current political climate. How do you feel about America's strategy in Iraq today?*

The whole thing just smells bad to me, it just feels as though it's based on really stupid oil policies and stupid ways of living our lives here that we could have changed a long time ago, to a better way of living in the world where we aren't so resource-dependent and wasteful. They obviously want to build an empire and have bases all over the world, and I don't think that's such a great idea. I also know how brutal Saddam Hussein is, since many of the people who worked in our movie had been torture victims of his. He's such a good dictator—if there was like a Top Ten Dictators list, he'd be right up in the top three because he is so brutal, that's how he can hold power. He killed his own sons-in-law . . .

You researched and wrote Three Kings *over a period of eighteen months. Can you take me through the process?*

It's nice to have somebody helping you, an assistant that the studio pays for who helps organize all the book research. You also search out certain veterans who were there, you develop relationships with them, like I had a relationship with a Navy SEAL named John Rottger who was in Iraq, and he became one of my technical advisors. It was the same with Jim Parker. He was another one of our advisors, and he actually had the experience of witnessing Saddam crushing the demo-cratic movement after the Gulf War. Jim saw his soldiers cry. American soldiers were crying, not understanding why they weren't supposed to do anything when they saw people who were their enemy a week before killing innocent civilians.

We also found some awesome books on the war. One of my favorites was a book that featured photos from the *Los Angeles Times.* It had a pictorial history of the war comprised of the day-by-day front-page color photos from the *Times* throughout the war. What I liked about it was the color; it was the first daily newspaper to run color photos. And I liked the look of it so much that we tried in the cine-matography of the film to make the colors super-saturated, the way they look in a color Xerox copy and on the cover of the *LA Times,* where the color really explodes. A lot of CNN footage gave us that vibe as well.

There was also a book by Gilles Peress that was hugely helpful. He's a famous photo-journalist who did a book called *Telex Iran,* photographs from the Iranian revolution in 1979. It really informed how I wanted *Three Kings* to feel and look. That book has a very strange, ominous feeling of chaos amongst normal lives, brought on by political turmoil. There is amazing foreground-background deep focus in those photos. It's really an amazing book, and I carried it around with me relentlessly. I also met a guy who I should also give credit to—John R. MacArthur, who is an editor at *Harper's* who had written a book about the media in the Gulf War. It's called *Second Front: Censorship and Propaganda in the 1991 Gulf War*; it sort of corroborated for me the experience that I tried to distil into the film.

And pieces such as the detail of the soldiers sneaking booze in, how did that come up?

Soldiers would tell me that they snuck liquor in with mouthwash bottles, and you'd see snapshots that soldiers had where they'd be drinking out of something that looked like a Listerine bottle but it would be Jack Daniel's or something. We'd get a lot of pictures from guys who'd been in the barracks. They had a lot of free time, so they were giving each other really badass haircuts, taking pictures of each other and all that shit.

There's something homoerotic about it—like being in prison, a lot of guys hanging out with each other.

All of them lifting weights . . . Yeah, there was, for sure.

Three Kings is a mixture of genres. First of all it's a war film, then it's a heist film with different parts. If the first third is a comedy, and the middle third is an action film, what would you say the last third is?

"Political melodrama?" I've never heard it broken up in thirds like that, but I think that'll work. I like to think they're a little bit more interwoven than that, but that sounds fair enough.

Music is an integral part of the storytelling. Do you listen to music to help you establish tone?

I tried that with *Three Kings.* When you're writing and listening to music you tend to intoxicate yourself. I think music is dangerously seductive. You can play music and kind of do some aural masturbation about what the movie would feel like, and that almost can preclude the work from actually penetrating directly into what you are trying to get across. I don't like films that rely too much on music.

It's interesting that you have inserts of the home lives of your three main characters. One was a baggage carrier, another was obsessed with guns, the other had a newborn baby at home. Do you like doing character biographies when you write?

Yeah, I give all the actors multiple-page histories.

You wrote Spike Jonze's part with him in mind. And yet I don't think he had acted before. So how does that work?

Spike's a friend of mine, and he was at the time I was writing this. He has this energy, he's also a prankster—so that I just started to consider him as this character. And once I started picturing him as that guy, physically, it started to make sense. I think Spike has a certain inner sense of himself; he took to that character very well, and he started to fuck around with the idea in a very jokey way by manipulating the voice and playing around.

Brentwood, California

François Ozon

17

FRANÇOIS OZON

Under the Sand

"You don't have to tell the audience everything."
Translated by Landa Acevedo

François Ozon studied directing at the famous Paris film school, La Fémis. He has written and directed numerous short films and several feature films including an adaptation of a play by the famous German director, Rainer Werner Fassbinder, *Water Drops on Burning Rocks* (*Gouttes d'eau sur Pierres Brûlantes*) (2000). Ozon is also responsible for revitalizing the career of Charlotte Rampling in films like *Under the Sand* (*Sous le Sable*) (2000) and *Swimming Pool* (2003). In his musical comedy, *8 Women* (2002), Ozon directed France's most famous leading ladies: Fanny Ardant, Catherine Deneuve and Isabelle Huppert, to name but a few, as well as making a star out of Ludivine Sagnier.

Synopsis

Paris, the present. Marie has been happily married to Jean for twenty-five years. During their summer holiday in the southwest of France, he leaves Marie sunbathing on the beach and goes to swim in the sea. But Jean never returns. Has he left her? Did he commit suicide or drown? In complete denial and without a body to mourn, Marie conducts her life in Paris as if Jean was still there.

* * *

KEVIN CONROY SCOTT: *You made dozens of 8mm short films when you were a teenager, can you tell me something about them? I'm curious to know how you approached them as a writer.*

FRANÇOIS OZON: It was very interesting for me to begin with Super-8 because I didn't have anything to record sound with, so I had to write my stories without dialogue, and explain everything just by using the images, the actors and the situation. So I had to work in a particular way, like the first directors of silent films, and very quickly I picked up a sense of the image and of making the story very visual. That's also why I now try to make my films without dialogue as much as possible, or to just use dialogue that isn't so direct, because I don't like it when things are conveyed by the dialogue. Then again, it depends—8 *Women*, for instance, is all about the dialogue and its different flavors. But having said that, at certain moments in that film you can close your ears and just look at the actresses, and that's enough . . .

But Under the Sand *is very sparse in terms of dialogue.*

Yes, well, the beginning of *Under the Sand* could be shot on Super-8; it's like the films I made when I was younger. It's a man and woman who are just going through their routine, "Do you want some wine? Do you like the wine?" And when I first showed the film to an audience, they said, "It's a nightmare, they don't speak to each other." And I said, "They do speak, they just don't say anything important." And that's what happens in life too. Screenwriters will very often put too much information into their dialogue because it's easier to tell the story that way. But if you put everything into the dialogue, you don't need to cut the film together and try to make the subtext work.

What kind of relationship did you have with literature when you were growing up? Did you have a lot of books in the house?

Yes, because my mother is a French teacher so she had a lot of French literature. From an early age my parents told me that I could read anything I wanted. They had very open minds to the idea that when you're an artist, anything is possible. They said, "When you make art, there's no problem, you can do anything—you can kill everybody in a book or a film or a painting, just because it's art." So when I was young it was possible for me to read the Marquis de Sade or other writers who weren't writing for young people . . . When I was very young, ten or eleven, I loved Zola's books because they are very realistic, very much like documentaries. And the stories were always full of sex, which, to a young boy, can be very exciting. His novels weren't directly about sex; it was more subtle and alluded to, but you could always, even as a child, imagine different levels in reading the book.

What about cinematic heroes? I've heard you speak of Fassbinder and, by proxy, Douglas Sirk.

Yes, but I discovered those kinds of directors very late.

Was this when you attended the esteemed national film school in Paris, La Fémis?

Yes, it was during my time there. When I was younger, I was like every other child; I saw stupid films by Walt Disney. But I do remember having the chance to see films by Rossellini and Alain Resnais, and then suddenly I realized that movies were not only there to entertain. They could be thoughtful and deep, and touch your own life. It was a shock for me to see *Germany: Year Zero*. It's a film about an eight-year-old boy just after the Second World War finishes. He lives in Berlin, the city is totally destroyed, and he tries to survive with his family, but finally he commits suicide. A very dark film. But as a child it was very important for me to see it, because I was the same age as the young boy. The director I loved when I was sixteen, seventeen, when I started to become a *cinephile*, was Eric Rohmer—which is ironic, because he made entire films out of dialogue. I understood very quickly that people in his films would discuss life and other matters, and then Rohmer would show that there was a contradiction between their words and their actions. It was very important for me to understand that. Also I like that there is always a documentary approach to the way Rohmer makes his films. It's very natural, very realistic.

Before you went to La Fémis, did you ever try your hand at writing short stories or prose?

No, I don't really like to write. I write because I want to film. First I have the image in my head and *then* I have to write, because I need to communicate and share my work with the team that will make the film with me. When I made my Super-8 movies, I didn't need to share, I was alone. I had the camera, no sound, and I lit everything myself, it was just me. And I'd tell the actors, "Do this, do that, and that's it . . ."

At what point in your teens did becoming a writer-director become a very serious ambition for you?

I realized that when I began to make my Super-8 movies that it was exactly what I wanted to do. Before then I wasn't sure what I wanted to do exactly, maybe I could do theater . . . but once I took the Super-8 camera from my father—it was the camera he made the family home movies with—I realized directing was for me, because I could be hidden by the camera, and yet I could also express myself and make very passionate things without revealing that it was me who made them. I liked the idea of being behind a camera saying very personal things, using other people. It was like wearing a mask, and I liked that because I was very shy at that age. I eventually lost that shyness by making movies—because as a director you have to explain what you want, you have to express yourself and communicate with people.

What kind of training did you receive at La Fémis in terms of screen-writing?

I learned more about screenwriting by making my movies alone on Super-8 than I did at La Fémis. We saw a lot of films, which is a good thing, because every day we were seeing classics by Bresson, Renoir, John Ford. But I can't say I learned much about writing there. Once you make your own films and work job after job, you learn many things. That was the good thing about La Fémis, there was no com-mercial risk. You had the money to make your film, and you don't care if it is good because there is no financial risk. You have the money to try, and if you fail it's not important because you'll do better the next time. At La Fémis we had to do some screenwriting exercises and write scenarios, but it wasn't where I learned how to write screenplays. I would say I really learned from the little films I made with my friends.

Were there people you met at La Fémis who influenced you?

I met three important people there. Joseph Moter is a director of Super-8 movies and *only* Super-8 movies. He made us do an exercise with a Super-8 camera because the Super-8 reel gives you three min-utes to shoot something—it's not like digital videotape now where you can shoot for two hours. The fact that you have only three minutes means that you have to plan ahead about what you want—because it was expensive for us to get the film developed, we had no money. So we had to think in a precise way about what we wanted. One of his exercises was to ask us to edit in the camera while shooting, so we didn't waste film or cut anything together at a later stage.

The good thing about short films in general is that it's easier when you have a long time to express exactly what you want to say, but when you only have ten minutes, you have to go directly to your sub-ject without the idea being a cliché. That is the difficulty of making a short film, to avoid caricature. That's why short films are very often so bad, because there's only one idea at play in the story.

Do you think that your apprenticeship in Super-8 is the reason your films are so lean now? There's no fat to them.

Yes, I agree with that. I remember Eric Rohmer came in to the film school to talk to us, and he taught us a lot about economy in our films. It's funny, when you meet Eric Rohmer you're waiting for him to tell you some very profound things. But he just talked about money . . . He was talking about his film *Full Moon in Paris*, and he explained to us where he bought the cheapest possible carpet for the film. He said, "It's a very good shop, you have to go there if you need carpet." [*laughs*]

Just going back, Jean Douchet was the second of the important people I met at La Fémis. He was one of the editors in chief of *Cahiers Du Cinema* along with Eric Rohmer, and he showed us many films and he was really interesting. The third important person was Claudine Bouché who was Truffaut's editor on *Jules et Jim* and other films. She taught me many things about editing. Have you seen any of my short films?

I read about one that dealt with two boys on a beach who are in love. One of them puts on a dress, and initially you showed him putting it on, but—

Yes, and instead Claudine told me to cut to him wearing the dress already, and that was much more effective. I had loved seeing this boy put on this dress, I thought it was funny and sexy. But when you cut to it after he put the dress on, it was much funnier.

Claudine Bouché has since helped you edit some of your feature films. Is there anything that you have learned from her that has helped your writing?

She used to come in at the end and help me with the final touches. She told me the same thing that Joseph Moter told me—you always have to think about the editing, when you write the script and when you shoot the film.

What about her notion of cutting into a scene after it has started, as late as possible? Does that help you with economy in your screen-plays?

You still have to shoot the entire scene, but sometimes you know you'll cut out the first half in the editing. There is a scene in *Under the Sand* where Charlotte Rampling is back in Paris a few months after her husband disappears. She's gone out to dinner, and I shot the beginning of the dinner but I didn't use it, because it was stronger to begin in the middle or the end—then you don't know where you are, and the audience is very excited because they don't know what's going on. You don't have to tell the audience everything, they're very clever, they're thinking all the time. If they know everything, they just sleep through the film. But in the screenplay you have to explain everything on paper because you have to find the money from the financiers. [*laughs*] That's the problem with scripts. Very often I know I overwrite some scripts to explain my film, knowing that I will cut certain scenes or won't shoot them. But I need those scenes of explanation to show the financiers so they can understand the story in their terms.

You've never worked in Hollywood but I know you have had a lot of experience in Hollywood promoting your films and seeing American films. What do you think is the major difference between European screenwriters and their counterparts in Hollywood?

The difference is—especially in France because I am speaking for myself—we don't have many screenwriters on a film. For me, I am alone and I don't have the weight of the production on me, I do what I want. But I love that in American movies they can be so very direct; they're not afraid to say things. Sometimes in France we fear that because we think it's vulgar. But Americans have this freedom because they think only of the audience. Sometimes in France we don't think enough of the audience.

Do you think Hollywood will ever get around to letting their audiences, and I am using your words here, "be adults in front of the images"?

Well, it's because there is a tradition of entertaining in America. For me, it's important to allow some slack into the film and ask the audience to take up that slack. When I'm a spectator I like to be involved in the film, to have a place, not only to look passively at the film. I want to be a participant in the film.

In setting out to make Under the Sand, *you said, "I wanted to give my audience the opportunity to identify with the characters in one of my films." What did you mean?*

I think very often in my films I put a distance between the audience and the characters. In American cinema, right from the beginning, the idea of the identification is with the characters. Distance can be good for a film like *8 Women*. But for *Under the Sand* it was important to identify with the character. I wanted to put the audience in the head of this woman because it's not easy to understand why she thinks her husband is still alive. I wanted to present all the feelings of this woman, and the difficulties of mourning.

In terms of a French audience and its expectations, what do you think is the difference between a French blockbuster and an American blockbuster?

I think the American blockbusters are better. [*laughs*] We try to make it like the Americans, but I think it is best to leave the Americans to do what they do best.

Can you take me through your writing process, starting with where the idea for the story originates?

I never have a problem with inspiration or imagination. I have many ideas and many possible projects. When there's an idea that has been in my mind for a while I will pursue it. In fact, *Swimming Pool* is about this process of creation.

So where did the idea for Under the Sand *come from?*

From a memory of being on holiday with my parents. We always went to the same beach in the south of France. Each day we would always see the same people, including a Dutch couple, who were about sixty years old. One day the man went into the sea and he never came back. I saw this woman waiting for her man, and the helicopters searching for the body. I remembered seeing her with her husband's belongings. As a child it was a shock for my brother, my sisters and me. We asked, "What happened to this woman, did she find the body, did she stay in France?" For me it was like an enigma. I made the film so I could try to find the answer to this mystery.

So you have the idea. What next?

Then I need to leave Paris, go somewhere and to be alone for one or two weeks so I can work. I begin to write it and by the end of that period I have the whole project. Then I have to think about it and work on it for another two or three months. Then I go off and I am alone again to concentrate on the idea. Then, after the second time, I give it to friends to read and we work together.

What is it at this point, an outline?

No, it's a total script, but it can change. Or sometimes it's only forty pages so I have to enrich it somehow.

You had numerous collaborators on Under the Sand—

Yes, many women! [*laughs*] Emmanuèle Bernheim, Marina de Van and Marcia Romano. I needed a feminine point of view—three of them, in fact.

Can you tell me something about how you worked with them?

They didn't write anything, but I spoke with them a lot. For instance, Marina is a director too and also an actress. She was in my films *See the Sea* and *Sitcom*. She helped me for the second part; I wrote the first part of the film about the south of France on my own because it was a memory of my childhood there. We went out and shot that beginning and after that we stopped shooting. It was only then that I started to write the second part of the film. At this moment I began to think of things from another point of view, because I'm not a fifty-year-old woman. So each woman co-writer helped me with different aspects of that perspective.

Emmanuèle Bernheim, she is a very famous writer here in France, helped me with the relationship between Charlotte Rampling's character and her lover. There was a simple thing she helped me with, a scene where they are in bed making love and suddenly she laughs. I wanted her laughing, but I didn't know exactly why. Emmanuèle asked me, "Why?" And I said, "Because she is used to being in bed with her husband, who's very heavy, and this guy is very light." The difference in weight is funny to her. But when the man asks her, "Why are you laughing?," we didn't know what to answer. Emmanuèle suggested that maybe she could just say, "Because you are light." Sometimes to find a very simple solution you have to talk for a long time . . .

My work with my co-writers is always a conversation about the film; it helps me find exactly what I want to say. You know, it's very rare to find exactly what you want to say at the beginning. You have to work on the script many times. You need time to think; you need another point of view to consider things from. Even sometimes when you are shooting it can change, because you wrote the script in December and you shot the film in July and during those six months you have changed, you are different, so maybe you need to adapt. If you have a new idea or a problem in your life, everything can change.

What do you think your script would be like if you had to work on your own?

I would need more time to make a film. If I wrote on my own I would be like Kubrick, you know, needing five years to write a script . . . I like to work quickly, so I like to work with people who can help me work faster. For me the script doesn't have to be perfect. You must have the idea in the script, but during the shooting I want to have freedom so the script doesn't paralyze me. Once I start shooting I don't even read the script anymore.

Did you do any particular research for Under the Sand?

Yes, I did some research for the drowning at the beginning of the film. I read many things about what is done when bodies are discovered at sea in the south of France. I met some lifeguards to explain to me how it works. I also went down to the morgue.

What about talking to women who are going through grieving problems like Charlotte Rampling in the film?

I met a psychiatrist who specializes in the difficulties with mourning. I went to see him in his office and I explained the scenario: "The film is about a woman who never found the body of her husband who drowned at sea, so she starts to imagine that he is there with her in her flat even though he's probably dead." After I told him that he thought that I was the one who was crazy. And I said, "No, no, it's not for me, it's for the film!" And he said, "It's the same thing." [*laughs*] I asked him if he thought a woman could go on acting like her husband was alive and in her life even if he disappeared in a drowning accident, and he said that it could happen. Most importantly he told me, "She's not crazy, it's the only way for her to be alive, to imagine that he's present." So the specialist was good for my mise-en-scène because I didn't want to show her as a crazy woman.

Do you listen to music during your writing day?

I don't like to, but sometimes it can happen. When I was making that short film about the boys on the beach, I was writing a caricatured scene about lovers arguing. It was a cinematic cliché. Suddenly I heard a song I knew when I was young called "Bang, Bang" by a French singer, Sheila. It is a very sad song about nostalgia. "When we were young we were in love and now we are finished, when we were children we were innocent." So I had the idea to put the song in the film, and one of the boys sings it. It's a way for him to say things to his lover even though the lover doesn't want to hear the song anymore. Through the music you understand exactly what's going on between the two characters.

You do something very similar in Under the Sand *when Charlotte Rampling is shopping for groceries in the supermarket. There is that melancholic song that says something about the end of the summer.*

Yes, it is a beautiful song. At that moment you don't know if it is a song at the supermarket or if it is a song in her head. Because it is a song about separation and the end of the summer, and it's very sad, but she seems very happy at this moment because in her life she has her husband at home and her lover. It is the scene just before she gets the information about her husband's body being found. So it's a poetic moment.

Here's a personal question—

Oh no, something sexual . . .

No, no. It's just a question about writing. When you are at home alone and you are writing and it's not going well, how do you handle the feelings of self-doubt that crop up?

I stop writing. I can write only if I have an idea for the film. I'm not in front of my computer every morning asking myself, "What can I write today?" It's happened before where I don't write for three months because I'm not completely inspired. When that happens I just leave it alone. If I'm writing a scenario and I can't figure something out or I am unhappy with it I will leave it alone and let my subconscious work it out. I'll go to bed unhappy with a scene, but when I wake up sometimes I will find a solution to it. Sometimes I'll watch a silly program on TV and the problem will solve itself. You have to be very sensitive and open to everything that is around you all the time, because you will pick things up.

Paris, France

Neal Purvis and Robert Wade

18

ROBERT WADE AND NEAL PURVIS

Die Another Day

"What's the worst situation that Bond can get into?"

Robert Wade and Neal Purvis have enjoyed great success in Hollywood. Responsible for the two latest films in the globally successful James Bond franchise, *The World is Not Enough* (1999) and *Die Another Day* (2002), their other produced screenplays include the drama *Let Him Have It* (1991), *Plunkett & Macleane* (1999) and the 007 spoof, *Johnny English* (2003). In 2004 they co-produced *Return to Sender* and the *Wild & Wycked World of Brian Jones* from their own original screenplays, while preparing the next James Bond film. Both Wade and Purvis live in London.

Synopsis

North Korea, the present. Agent 007, James Bond, escapes detention by the North Koreans by driving a high-speed hovercraft through a minefield in the Demilitarized Zone. From Hong Kong to Cuba to London, Bond circles the world in his quest to unmask a traitor, Gustav Graves, and his ruthless right-hand man Zao, to prevent a war of catastrophic proportions. On his way, he crosses paths with the beautiful Jinx and Miranda Frost, who could be accomplices or spies. In a palace built entirely of ice he experiences the power of a high-tech weapon. This leads to an explosive confrontation back in Korea, where the mission began.

* * *

KEVIN CONROY SCOTT: *I'd like to start by asking each of you if you could tell me something about your upbringings, and what part books played in your household then . . .*

ROBERT WADE: My mom was an artist, a sculptress, and there were lots of books at home but there wasn't any "bookishness." I used to like reading, and at school English was the subject I was into. I couldn't do anything else, really. So I always thought it would be cool to be a writer in Paris—that sort of thing. Then when I was about fifteen, I got more into movies.

NEAL PURVIS: My dad was a photographer, so I was brought up with the smell of fixer all over the place. I read a lot in my teenage years, but for me I think it was really about going to see a lot of films. Going to the cinema on your own is the defining thing about liking films—it's that thing of coming out of the cinema in daylight . . . I joined a couple of cinema clubs when I was sixteen, ones that only dealt in 1940s movies and got a very strange crowd—older people eating sandwiches with the crusts cut off.

RW: I made videos as a teenager. You know the old video equipment where you had the camera and a massive suitcase thing that was the recorder? Black and white.

Neal, what sort of books were you reading when you weren't seeing films?

NP: Oh, I was going through a very pretentious phase. All your Sartres and your Camus. A little bit of Kafka on the side.

Was it your shared interest in film that brought you together?

RW: We met at university, Kent, which at the time was the only place you could do film theory as a major. I'd seen a lot on BBC2 late at night, the sorts of films where there was always a good chance you could see a naked woman. I got into French movies that way, Bertrand Blier.

NP: For me, Bertolucci, the earlier stuff. That, again, is a bit pretentious . . .

RW: Scorsese. But that's the normal thing.

NP: Humphrey Bogart movies.

RW: And Laurel and Hardy, actually . . . But at Kent it just happened that we were put into shared bunk beds in a college where there were only four rooms with bunk beds. We had both stipulated that, a., we wanted to live outside of college if possible, and, b., we didn't want to share. But instead we were flung together.

So you were both eighteen and in bunk beds?

NP: Yeah. And that helps you talk long into the night . . .

RW: And then you left after a term.

NP: Yeah, I didn't like it. The music had started by then, hadn't it?

RW: Yeah. We were in a band together.

NP: After I left, we still kept in touch. I went to polytechnic to do a Film and Photo Arts BA, which was half theory and half practical. We still have the band—we've been playing pretty much the same songs for twenty years now, so we're very tight.

This would have been the late seventies, early eighties. Were you into that post-punk scene?

NP: I suppose so. I rather liked the New York stuff. In those days, Television, and the usual Velvet Underground, Stooges sort of thing.
RW: We were quite good musically but the lyrics weren't any good.
NP: Yeah, we were mainly an instrumental band.

So how did screenwriting come into play for you?

RW: Neal was doing his practical film degree, and by now I had graduated in pure theory. My original plan was to go to the National Film School, but at Kent they were very academic: they were trying to create a generation of teachers, and so they really looked down on anyone who actually made movies—they were actively discouraging about that. I got a First and could have got a scholarship and gone to UCLA if I'd been thinking. But I thought there was all the time in the world, so I was mucking about with the band. Then I moved up to London and we got a place, and while Neal was doing his graduation I was writing a script, about two blokes in London. And we met someone who had some money who was prepared for me to direct it, Neal to edit it, and he would help me to rewrite it and put up money to get it going. We got an office on the Strand, and he bought this car that featured in the story: a convertible, fifties sort of car.
NP: Pink.
RW: And we sort of edged towards this thing and we rewrote it together during the summer of the LA Olympics, 1984, when Frankie Goes to Hollywood were number one.

Did you know anything about screenplay format or technique?

RW: Not at all. We didn't even know what a script looked like.
NP: At my college, even though you'd make your graduation film, there were no real scriptwriting lessons or lectures.
RW: That Syd Field book may have been out, but you couldn't get hold of it. So it was really hard to get on, but eventually we did get hold of a script called *Agatha* directed by Michael Apted at that time. And from that we could see how you laid it out.

So you came by a script from a director who you were to work with about fifteen years later in The World is Not Enough?

RW: Yeah, oddly enough.

NP: We also wrote a Bond theme in the band. We haven't played that to the producers yet. We're biding our time . . . So we wrote our script, but we didn't really have a clue as to how to get it made. And neither did the financial wizard who was going to produce it. So we would just get *Spotlight,* the actors' listing guide, and go through and get a cast. I think we actually sent it out to people.

RW: By this stage I realized that I couldn't direct it so we got the name of a film director who was going to be doing a big movie and sent it to him—Robert Bierman, who did *Vampire's Kiss* . . .

NP: He later did *Keep the Aspidistra Flying,* also known as *A Merry War.*

RW: And he read it and really liked it, and was extremely nice to us and said, "Whatever you do, don't be told there's a lot wrong with this because there isn't."

NP: But we were there in leather jackets and hair sticking straight up. Rob had these big mutton chops.

RW: We were sort of rockabillies. Robert Bierman introduced us to people, including his agent, and she managed to determine very quickly that it wasn't going to get made.

NP: She handled that script, but she wouldn't take us on because we were so unknown and would have been too much work for her. And yet we've ended up with her. We moved there about seven years ago.

What happened with the script?

NP: Well, we got a big six-page article about us in *The Face* magazine. And so we thought that we'd arrived. But the option on the script went to a couple of different people over a couple of years, and nothing came of it.

RW: What happened then was that we took a year off and played golf. That's the other good thing about having a partnership.

NP: There was an assumption that you write one script, get it made, and then write another one. So when this one wasn't really happening, we played golf.

Would you say you were any good as screenwriters then?

RW: We got better . . . But we also realized that that wasn't quite how you got on. We're going to be talking here about one of our more big-budget movies, but actually our taste was kind of quirky, quite dark stuff.

Bertrand Blier's movies, you couldn't get away with them in Britain. They're edgy material and somehow because it's Gallic and subtitled, it's not so controversial. We then tried to write a script about an elevator boy at The Savoy called *Fin du Siècle,* about a guy who realizes that his great grandfather had murdered Byron, and he becomes a sort of serial killer, killing in literary ways. It was good stuff. That was when we hit on the thing of doing a structured document, a scene-by-scene breakdown, a beat sheet really. We wrote it out and stuck all these bits of paper together.

NP: It went right across the room. I suppose the things we were trying to do were all commercial ideas.

RW: With humor. We wrote a script called *A.K.A. Lucifer* and that was three stories about the devil over one story. The last line of that was, "You're all going to die. Women and children first."

How long did it take from when you were first writing screenplays till you got your first screenplay produced?

RW: Six years.

NP: That was *Let Him Have It,* which was a departure for us, because it was more serious than what we had done before. We set out to make it light throughout, and then it got serious. We really thought that if that didn't get made, we might give up on screenwriting.

RW: We started at a terrible time trying to make movies. But we didn't want to write for television; we wanted to write a proper movie, and yet no films were being made in this country. There was *Chariots of Fire* and then everything went wrong after that. That's when we were just getting going. It was really difficult to get a movie made, and we thought that if you can't get a depressing period melodrama made, we might as well pack it in. Luckily it did get made. And that was because it was serious. People can latch on to something if it's serious. It's much more difficult to sell something quirky.

What sort of work did you do to make ends meet?

RW: We'd get option money for different things and sign on a lot, social security. And we also would ghostwrite pop videos.

NP: Once again, you would do a lot of those and get no money. But if it got made, you got a hundred quid.

RW: And that was a lot of money in those days. Then we did a number of treatments for things—not off our own backs, but if someone wanted a series or something. This was 1985. Before that, we did get paid to write scripts, not just for options. We adapted a novel for what was our second script, a novel by Tony Parsons for Tim Bevan and

Eric Fellner at Working Title before they broke through with *My Beautiful Laundrette.*

NP: We did some pop promos for Tim Bevan's video company, which gave us access to their photocopying machine that we were able to come in and knock scripts up on.

RW: That was a big deal in those days.

Do you remember any tough lessons you learned about screenwriting and the film business in general during this time?

RW: I think that when you start out you tend to write lovingly and to overwrite enormously. When we look back on our early scripts, they've been worked and worked on to a point that is completely irrelevant in terms of getting a film made. My brother's been writing recently, and his scripts have some great stuff in them but there's also tons and tons of description—which is what we were suffering from.

But another thing about that period, I think, is that the fact that there were two of us made it much more bearable.

NP: That thing about just keeping on going while other people gave up. There were a couple of other partnerships, and they dropped by the wayside.

Why did you decide to keep going?

RW: I don't know. We weren't making a lot of money, and we were sweating while we worked. I remember there was a book we wanted to adapt, and our agent phoned up and said the producers weren't interested in us. They knew who we were and what we had done. A few years later, they came to us with that book and we just thought, "Right, we don't want anything to do with *you,* because nothing's changed except that maybe we're more bankable." I don't know about dogged determination, but we knew what we were doing was good. It was just the pictures that got small . . .

You broke through with Let Him Have It. *How did you get on that project originally?*

RW: We were around at that time when everyone was floating around wanting to make movies, but there weren't many writers around. A guy called Rob Warr was in the music business but wanted to move into the movie business—he was married to a woman who worked at Working Title, Tim Bevan's video company. He had originally been the one who brought Tim and Eric in to the Tony Parsons novel about the music business which was supposed to be a version of *Sweet Smell of Success*. It was a misguided enterprise that everyone has chosen to forget. But Rob Warr had been at the same school as Derek Bentley, the guy who got hanged in *Let Him Have It*. And he said, "This would make a big movie, why don't you look into this story?" We were resistant, but then we started looking into it, and got a researcher.

NP: The researcher was Will Self, now a very successful novelist.

RW: So Will did this research, and we started to get interested and said to Rob, "We'll write it if you find some money." He then teamed up with a guy called Luc Roeg, a very successful promo producer.

NP: Music videos were doing well even when the film industry wasn't.

RW: So we wrote the script, on spec. And it was a very depressing thing to do, because the story is so harrowing. But we felt that we had a lively vehicle. It was about these two boys who can't relate to the outside world. One of them is retarded and the other's dyslexic and a kind of livewire. It was about two morons having fun, finding their mode of expression and then suddenly being in trouble with the law. So it was supposed to be a fun journey that went horribly wrong. What was bizarre was that the first director attached to it was Tony Richardson, and he said that this was the first thing he had wanted to do in ten years or so.

NP: We were in LA for a while working with him on the script, which was good but weird, because there we were in sunny LA, in a Hollywood house, and this whole thing was written about rainy Croydon in the fifties.

RW: So we worked with Tony and then he excused himself because he needed some money, I think, and he went off to direct *The Phantom of the Opera*. And then Alex Cox came on board, who had done *Sid and Nancy*.

NP: We've worked with a lot of directors, but Tony and Alex were two of the best by a long way.

How did the writing process evolve through working with a director? Did you get notes; were you sent away for another draft?

RW: We had a solid script and it didn't change very much. When Tony Richardson came in, he gave us very broad strokes.

NP: If the film was really about this Derek Bentley then Tony wanted to see him in every single scene, whereas we had split it up a bit more.

RW: He emphasized it was about the generation gap, the distance between the father and the son, and the father ends up not being able to save his son's life. It's very moving in that way, and Tony focused on that.

NP: I also remember that he said, "You should take the films you really like, and put that into a film you really like." In other words, if you like something in a particular film and you understand it, then don't be afraid to put that sort of thing into your own film. That was a learning thing.

So you had a film made in 1991 and then the next one in 1998. But in-between you were also working in Los Angeles for Disney, right?

RW: What we're credited for and what we actually *did* out there, there's a lot more . . . Chronologically, *Let Him Have It* came out and we went to America for the opening, and got ourselves an agent in Hollywood, a guy called Tom Strickler who we've stuck with as he's progressed through different agencies. We were brought in as "the director's writers" on a Disney picture that wasn't a great movie, but we were glad to do what we could.

NP: The great thing about that is to just do eight weeks or something and then you're off.

RW: We then wrote a spec script, *Return to Sender*, and that was optioned and nearly got made, and it got us work in America. It's totally an American movie. Actually, it's just been made by Billie August, with Connie Nielsen, Aidan Quinn and Kelly Preston.

Did you have any problems writing an American film?

NP: Not then, no.

RW: We had meetings with studio people, and they were really surprised that we were English. *Return to Sender* is like a Sidney Lumet picture from the seventies, a genre picture. We're all brought up with American movies here, so in a sense "genre dialogue" is less of a foreign tongue than it might be.

RW: We started work on it in 1989, and got the script right in 1992, and then we worked with Vincent Ward on it.

NP: He then did a Robin Williams movie called *What Dreams May Come*.

So how do you guys work together as a writing partnership? What goes on when you're writing? Do you pace the room trying to work things out?

RW: Well, we walk from the bar to the table. When we're hatching a plot, we spend quite a lot of time together. And the process is that in the morning we drink coffee, and then you've drunk so much coffee that you need alcohol, and during that there's a little window where we have some good ideas.

NP: During the hatching period, the mornings would be each of us on our own, and then we meet up early afternoon to discuss things, and that may go on into the early evening.

Where would you say your ideas come from?

RW: Well, with the *Bond* films, that's very extensively discussed with the two producers, and it's very hard to say whose ideas are whose.
NP: That's sitting in an office for hours and hours, very concentrated.

Is a lot of that already laid out by the history of the franchise?

RW: No, it's not set in stone, it's really up for grabs. For instance, in *Die Another Day*, there's very little of Moneypenny—in fact, at one point, she wasn't even in it and we thought we had to get her in somehow so we came up with the idea of her as a virtual character. That came actually two days before shooting. We did know we needed to have a Q scene, and introduce the new Q.

You go through the process of the nuts and bolts of the plot. Once you've agreed on that, do you go and write an outline?

NP: Well, depends on the job at hand. The way we prefer to do it is to go straight into a scene-by-scene breakdown, then split up and take a couple of scenes each. On a daily basis, you do five pages each of consecutive scenes, or maybe one scene. Then I'll e-mail my stuff to him and then he'll join them together, and we carry on.
RW: I guess what we like to do is to get the pages out rather than kill ourselves on the actual finer points of the scene, because sometimes it's much better to get pages up than let it be ahead of you. Because you can do as many treatments as you like, and even after it's changed for the first time, when you find a way to do it—it will change again and again. And also because there are two of us, we're going to get fed up with it and change it whether someone else wants to change it or not.
NP: And what's good is that when there are two of you, you owe it to the other person to get your pages done, because if you don't you're letting the side down.
RW: Whereas if you're on your own . . .
NP: You don't need to. You can let it go to the next day.

How do you guys handle any conflict between you about what you've both written?

NP: We don't have that problem. Generally, we're fairly specific about what we're going to achieve. You know where it's going. We're not the sort of people who write and work it out as they are going. We know pretty much what's going to happen. When we were younger there might have been some conflicts, but life's too short for that sort of thing. We're very clear what we're going to do and we just do it.

You obviously have a very clear understanding of your strengths and weaknesses. Do you have certain roles?

NP: Rob's quite good at doing all the verbiage at the beginning of the script.

RW: But that's only because I take an interest in it! I thought at one point we were quite good at dialogue, but I think we need to work harder on it than we used to.

NP: The problem is that things get changed so much and then it can slip.

RW: I picked up some drafts of *Die Another Day,* and it's depressing because there are some good lines that were in there for ages and ages and then they get cut.

NP: I read in William Goldman's book that he thinks the first draft is his; then after that it's everybody else's. I agree. The first draft is the one we like the most.

RW: Things do get better as well but . . .

NP: It's when perhaps you have a little more time to do what you want. And when you get into production, there's such a rush on all the time that everything's different.

RW: Getting back to that question about strengths and weaknesses — those *Bond* films, they're really hard to do; but perhaps one thing we're quite good at is coming up with unusual ideas, things that you wouldn't expect. The Bond script, they're beaten down and down until they're left just as an element.

The hovercraft idea, for example.

RW: Things like — actually the director Lee Tamahori thinks he came up with that — the diamond shrapnel. It was our idea and then it got cut out and he thought of it as well.

NP: We had different hovercrafts in our original conception, ones we found on the Internet that fly eight feet off the ground and that can glide across the minefield.

RW: And that went over water too. But that wasn't what I meant about original ideas. What I mean is slightly weird elements is what we're good at. But one of our weaknesses is to try to put in too many ideas. I know this in theory but can't put into practice, that films are really simple and should be. They're not meant to hold lots of ideas, and they don't work when they try out too many different ideas. When we write something, we fall in love with an idea and put in more ideas because we like them. And we shouldn't; you should just lose those ideas, but it's really difficult not to. You get entertained by putting those ideas in.

NP: Entertained by yourself, more like it.

Have you found your writing has become more simplified as your career has progressed?

NP: Not really. I've found it hard all the way along. In fact, the first script is in some ways the easiest because you don't know as much. It's like the perfect golf swing.

Obviously music is a big part of your friendship. Do you listen to it while you're writing?

NP: I think you can listen to stuff you know. But if it's something new, it's difficult to work because part of you is listening to it. You use it more as a blocking-out thing to concentrate.

RW: I listen to music partly because if I'm in a café and I don't like the music they're playing, I'll put my headphones on. Or if there's a particularly annoying conversation going on I'll block it out. So it's partly to tune out and also to get in the right mood. We rewrote a script a few years ago, which has now been made but not based on our script whatsoever. It's called *Highwaymen,* and we took it and went off in a different direction and the people who have made it have not even seen our draft. It was all about a guy using a car as a murder weapon, and it's a very unpleasant film. And I listened to Nine Inch Nails and Prodigy and that kind of stuff. Nowadays, if I ever listen to that, it gets me back into that horrible world of that film and it really depresses me, so I can't listen to it anymore. But writing a *Bond* movie is great because you've got soundtracks to every *Bond* movie if you want as a theme in the background.

How do you let each other know when one of you suggests an idea and it does or doesn't work? Is it diplomacy or instinct?

NP: Desperation, isn't it?

RW: We generally agree.

NP: In the beginning of *Plunkett & Macleane,* two people meeting over a body that they intend to get the jewel from and then having to swallow it, that clearly seemed . . . you latch upon something and we have similar tastes.

RW: But that goes back to that problem of trying to get too many ideas in because you know that in the end, you're going to have to get rid of them. We've been doing a rewrite of a Michael Douglas picture, and it's difficult because what the studio want it to be is a thriller, but no one gets murdered and there's no threat. So it's more like a David Mamet thing, in a way. But because the theme is modern art, there are so many things that are interesting to us that they really are a problem. We've got a script of 130 pages. We're going to have to get rid of some of the ideas we really like. Maybe that's our problem: we don't have a mechanism of editing it before we do it. But if you aren't allowed to put that in, it's not interesting to do that as a writer. You've got to try. Who said you have to kill your babies?

Going back to your process of writing, do you do character biographies or treatments?

NP: We don't like doing treatments because you're virtually writing the whole thing there and then.

RW: In a dry way, whereas if you get in and try to work on the scene it's different.

NP: We don't like doing it but it is useful to do character biographies. Half a page each.

Who makes the decisions about the characters?

RW: Another weakness that we have is over reliance on back-story and the trouble is when you do a character description, the tendency is to get into that back-story and there's a danger to that. You make the character more interesting to yourself by giving them a back-story but if you then dwell on it, it causes problems. The story should move forward into the future.

NP: We don't do it in a particular, easy way. We muddle through all the time in lots of different ways. It just helps that there's two of you to help bring you back on course.

How do you handle the moments of self-doubt and try to get around that as a writer?

RW: When we wrote that boxing script, we had some periods in that where there were some true, unsolvable problems, and I just remember I went to Belgium because my wife happened to be there. And I went there to try to get a new way of thinking about that, and it's not a place I'd recommend going even though the *croque monsieurs* are good. And I just went through agony, and I can't even think what the problem was now. You just have to keep going and having two of you means that you do.

Do you find one of you playing cheerleader to the other, with one picking up the other when they're down?

NP: Well, we're usually complaining about the same things. You're either happy about something or not happy about something.

RW: I might be more bothered about something . . .

NP: And I have to calm him down about something. Things have changed a bit over the last few years by doing *Bond* because you're caught in a different world both creatively and time-wise. You just sort out problems, whereas if we went back into trying to do stuff like *Radio Riviera* recently we'd have problems.

RW: We'll get over those.

NP: I know, I know, but we're in a sort of unreal writing place.

RW: It's probably more like writing a hit TV show in that there's a kind of sense of moving forward.

NP: We don't really suffer from blocks for too long.

RW: One way of solving the problem is putting it off and doing something else in the script. It's a different situation at the moment. It's kind of like childbirth. Women forget once they've had the baby the excruciating pain.

NP: On *Return to Sender* we even bought a couple of books on scriptwriting because we thought structurally it wasn't right, and we couldn't work out where we had gone wrong. But they were no help.

And how did famous Bond *producer, Barbara Broccoli, come to read your work?*

RW: The drafts of Plunkett and Macleane that we were particularly pleased with, our agent passed around Hollywood, and she read it and liked it and then invited us in and we made them laugh.

NP: I think *Tomorrow Never Dies* was just coming out and they wanted to inject a bit more drama back into Bond because that had gone a bit action-y. What with *Let Him Have It* and *Plunkett & Macleane*, which was probably the best thing we have done as a script—

RW: Not the movie, but the script we did before we got fired from it.

NP: It was character-based and had imaginative action but it was serious as well. And that fulfilled what they really required on Bond. We went in with a lot of ideas the second time, including the Thames chase and the female villain.

RW: The good thing was that we didn't go in with any hopes. Normally you go into a production company and you don't get to meet the boss, you get to meet the development person. And we just got shown straight in to Barbara and Michael Wilson in a massive office which was totally intimidating. But because we weren't really prepared for it or expecting anything, we didn't put any ideas on the table. The worst thing is when you put an idea down and they throw it out. Then you might be out of it.

How does writing for Hollywood and for the British film industry compare?

NP: In Hollywood, they want to know absolutely everything you're going to do before you do it. And if you change it from what you said you were going to do, they'll go along with that but they want you to edge it back to what you originally talked about. They work really hard and expect you to work sort of harder than you feel is fair. They just want to keep on going and going when you know it's not necessary, and you know that you'll do a good job by it and you don't need to tell them everything.

RW: You get to a point with a script when you know that it's pretty good and then it's all diminishing returns after that. You know that you could make it twenty per cent better, but in the Hollywood process of going at it, going at it, going at it before you've even got a director maybe, you've lost what it had.

NP: So when things go from a draft, the rule is that you don't get them back again so when you lose something good, that's the last time you see it.

So how does it feel to be rewritten?

RW: Well, there's two types of being rewritten. There's one which is against your wishes, and there's the other which you're perfectly happy about.

NP: Will Davies did a good job on keeping a fair amount of things in *Johnny English* when it all had to be changed.

RW: In that instance, it was just that we couldn't go back and work on it, so that makes you more philosophical about whoever is going to take over.

NP: What was bad about *Highwaymen,* was that they went back to a draft before our draft.

RW: Because it was a change of producer.

NP: We didn't get rewritten, but that script is dead now and no one is going to see the film. And I'd rather it had been rewritten and had been made rather than never be rewritten at all.

RW: In the case of *Plunkett & Macleane*, you don't blame the writer that comes on, you just have to look at the whole situation, but there was a big mistake that got made.

NP: We were rewriting it in the first place, but from scratch, so it felt like our own.

RW: It was moribund and we gave it life, which was good.

NP: But that was the worst experience of all.

RW: That was terrible because we were very proud of that script.

What about rewriting other people?

RW: Well, for instance, we're rewriting a script by David Henry Hwang, who did *M. Butterfly*, and he's done a good job on the script. We haven't spoken to him. I think what he got to was a point where he didn't want to carry on. You could see the gulf between what the producers wanted to do and what he wanted to do. And, equally, we took over and they want something different from what we thought that they wanted originally. I admire what he's done, whereas there are other times when you take over a script and you don't like what they have done. You can't complain about being rewritten, but it's just circumstances whether you've been made to jump or are pushed. That makes the difference.

So how did you come up with the fire and ice premise of Die Another Day?

RW: We were thinking at that time about dictators and that when they get pushed, they want to get going. Our original idea of the character was Colonel Moon, because that is literally what they do; they take diamonds because they're the most concentrated form of wealth and the easiest to get rid of. So we started off with that idea, which then became an arms deal, and we'd been thinking about North Korea as a very scary place and a parallel with the Iron Curtain because we'd had the idea of Bond being exchanged. Those things fell into place.

NP: We had a lot of ideas and it slowly balanced out into the film. Thematically it was about mucking about with nature and what's real and what's not.

RW: Also there were all sorts of things, he's literally the son of this guy. We had had this idea of the mirror in space, which the Russians really had and put one in space but it broke. It's natural and harmless in nature.

So the sun and the light and the heat came from that. And the cold, actually in a fairly arbitrary way. Barbara Broccoli had suggested using an ice hotel as a setting. So Iceland came out of that. And the idea was using a very cool blonde, the Miranda character in contrast to the hot Jinx.

Can you tell me more about the conversations between you and the Bond producers?

NP: The conversations are long, from ten in the morning till four in the afternoon. All you're doing is talking about interesting things you've read or seen.

How long did that process last?

RW: A long time.
NP: Because unlike *The World is Not Enough* where we had a release date even before we started talking about the story, we went in once every week or two and took three or four months to get a storyline.
RW: But they're very intense discussions. I happened to see a thing about the Eden project and that gradually put two ideas together.

So what's it like coming up with these ideas and then going on set and seeing seventy people setting it up?

RW: Five hundred probably. It doesn't feel real.
NP: Every page of the script costs a million dollars. Actually slightly more. So when you finish a page in a café, you can go, "That's a million."
RW: What was bizarre was that we went to Cádiz where they filmed the Cuba stuff. And we had no intimation as to how much work had been going on down there for three months.
NP: You walk out into this beach bar, have a drink and then you hear they built the whole thing.
RW: There's a scene on the rooftop there, and there's rigging, stairs and an elevator just built to get up there to do that shot.

So you kind of feel like God for the day, having created this universe while drinking tea in your local café?

RW: It's really a fantastic feeling. All the work that goes into it, really clever people working flat out—and you dreamed it up in the first place.

There must have been a lot of people weighing in with their opinions. How do you deal with feedback from the producers and the studio?

NP: Well, you're sort of protected by the producers. You're kept away from the massiveness of it all so it's a surprise when you see how much is going on.

RW: The director comes to you but he talks to the producers as well. Once shooting starts you just have to accept it's not your baby anymore.

NP: They're shooting for six months on the whole thing and on pre-production for five months, so there is time to see, everyone's nice about it all.

RW: We had a very nice director, so that makes a huge difference. We could equally have had a horrible experience, I'm sure. It's like Pierce Brosnan was concerned about carrying the expository dialogue in a couple of places, and he let us know that and we took that on and tried to address it. Now some directors would have a problem with the actor talking to the writer, but Lee saw it as one less worry for him to deal with.

How much writing did you actually do during the filming?

RW: We wrote every day.

NP: For a lot of time we were playing catch-up on what we should have done before. The whole third act, the location changed from being on a beach to being on a plane.

RW: Originally we did have a plane, but that was how they got to this giant indoor beach. And then a month before production, there was a decision to change that to this huge plane.

NP: And we were involved in that right over Christmas, so when they started shooting we were trying to polish things a few days before they occurred. So we had a list on the wall of things we had to do and have done before they reached that page.

Where did that come from?

NP: It was stuff we knew needed work. Notes the director might have had.

RW: For instance, the end of the movie is always a concern. And because it's not an immediate worry, it's going to be shot at the end, you get on with this, get on with that.

NP: We get a lot of freedom because we can polish what we want.

RW: Apart from the general shopping list, we weren't in any hurry to go off and do anything else, whereas maybe we should have been off, and maybe we would have worked harder.

NP: We felt in a privileged position because we were working on it all the way through and could guide it where we could.

Were there any moments when you had to write things that you weren't too fond of?

RW: Really just details. Sometimes you think, wait a minute, that's doubling up on something that has happened before, it's redundant.
NP: There are a lot of practicalities that go on. But dramatically, there's only really one thing that we were annoyed with in the way we thought it would be done, and it had to be re-shot down to about three lines because the film would be too long. That was annoying to do that because it was unnecessary.
RW: If you don't agree with something visually, that's not really your business. You might argue something gets in the way of the drama, if there's something crap distracting from the story, but the director's in charge so you've got to bite the bullet. I'm talking about the electric armor which we weren't keen on. You just have to weigh all these things up, on the whole.

And this is the 40th anniversary and the 20th Bond film with a lot of in-jokes and references. How did you go about that?

NP: I think that the Q workshop was the big one. That's fun because it was meant to be that if you didn't notice it, it didn't matter. It's not meant to stand out.
RW: It was a bit of a mind-boggler because here was Pierce Brosnan sniffing the shoe of Rosa Kreb who tried to kill Sean Connery. What does this all mean?

Was it difficult to write dialogue in an action film for a woman who had just won an Academy Award?

RW: We were well into shooting when Halle Berry won the Oscar. Before she went off, she was in a red leather catsuit, strapped into a robotic arm being tortured by lasers. And then she went off and came back and got re-tied. We did pay slightly more attention to the dialogue after that. It's funny, Judi Dench was up for the same Oscar.
We had a scene which Judi and Halle were both in and they hardly speak at all because she speaks mainly to Michael Madsen, so we did try to get more dialogue in. Our approach with Jinx was that we always felt she should act like she's a character who's got her own movie. She's wandered out of her own film into James Bond's movie. If Bond walked into your movie, he would have been a strange presence, and that was the original idea. Ironically, we've just been working on the Jinx movie and hoping that that's going to come off.

How did you deal with the product placement on such big movies as Bond?

NP: They generally work off the script, and if they find Bond shaving they'll find a partner for that.

RW: We would have liked him to have a wet shave but it's a *Bond* movie so . . .

NP: And if he's flying they look to an airline. Apart from the Aston Martin, which we knew was going to be in the film—which was great, we weren't going to complain about that—everything else came from the script. We're not restricted in any way.

RW: You know it's associated with so much of that corporate sponsorship. My own feeling is that it's not really intrusive. It's the marketing of the movie that makes you think it's there, but when you watch the movie you don't really notice it.

Is it hard to find a replacement for Russia in plot terms, or do you look to the modern world today?

RW: We saw the 38th Parallel as a fantastic image and the fact that it's full of mines. Bill Clinton, who was president at the time we started writing, said it was the scariest place on earth, and we did think it was a flashpoint. And we were also trying to think, "What's the worst situation that Bond can get into?" And it's to be held prisoner in North Korea. You couldn't get much worse than that.

NP: It also seemed in keeping with Fleming. Oddjob was Korean. North Korea seemed to represent the last hard-line Communist country.

RW: And Kim Jong-il does wear Dr. No suits. He likes Swedish models as well. He also liked *Bond* films. Or he did. Part of the process of working with the producers is reading what is happening in the world and what might happen. It's a really difficult one. The film has to be escapism in a way and entertainment, but we did lose a lot of our audience in North Korea.

NP: They were going through an anti-American phase and thought it was an American movie.

How concerned are you with keeping reality in an action movie?

RW: There is a big debate about the surfing on the wave thing. It was a great idea, but whether it was an implausible level of action, that is another question. There are times when you just want to go for it. When you think about justifying it in terms of entertainment then it can be difficult.

NP: All the things come from what we've read about.

RW: The invisible car is based on something real.

NP: The gene therapy, even though it's an old movie conceit, now that's also credible.

So your method is taking a truthful premise and extrapolating it a bit?

RW: Yeah, but you don't want to make a movie with something totally implausible.

When you're writing do you have an internal barometer to gauge where the audience will go with you?

RW: I think you just have to think in terms of being an audience member yourself.

NP: Michael Wilson is very strict as to how close things are to reality.

RW: He's pretty good on logic. But it's like the virtual reality thing in the movie. Would it really be like that? We're not there yet but it's such a fun idea, let's do it. And if the audience laughs, then it forgives us and you still believe in the storyline. There are times when this particular film doesn't quite get the balance.

NP: I think you should not have too much action because you lose people who forget the characters.

RW: They get bored. They lose their connection with the character, and that's the danger with Bond movies.

What's the hardest part of writing Bond movies?

NP: I think it's finding a story that contains all the things you want it to.

Do you find you have to write around thrilling set pieces of action?

RW: It's odd, because we can see the action, then it becomes the province of the director and the team. Then it becomes a self-contained thing.

NP: It would be great if there were some action things that already existed, that you can pick and choose what you want but it's not like that. There's one stunt that exists that wasn't in the Bond movie that they tried to get into the last reel and was difficult to put in. There's an example of something that existed but it's not going into the film.

There's a lot of technological weaponry featured in the film. How extensive did your research have to be?

NP: We probably have a couple of sessions on the Internet and science magazines.

RW: In that film there's gene therapy, the space theme, the hovercraft which was changed; there's the virtual reality thing, the invisible car, the eagle project, the ice hotel, the airplane . . .

Was it difficult to keep a balanced tone throughout the film because you're doing so many different things and covering so much ground?

RW: The thing with *Bond* films is that they do have sweep, and that's fun. I think the tone of this movie is a little bit unequal. It starts off quite gritty, and I think that's the best stuff. Then it gets more fun and it's "James Bond" again and a full-on ride. So it's really difficult and I think it manages quite well. I do think it's an unusual mixture and the consistency of tone—Bond is the only constant in it.

NP: I think you're left in the hands of the director in terms of tone. We could say that the second part of the ice-palace stuff could have been done in a grittier way itself.

Where did the idea for the opening set piece and the curtain raiser come from with the night surfing? Bond lands on the ocean, off a parachute, and stylishly surfs his way to shore.

RW: We had this idea of night surfing and originally it was that the psychotic Colonel Moon is making his guys surf at night.

Straight out of Apocalypse Now.

RW: Exactly.

NP: For surfers, some of the best waves are at night so there is a thing of night surfing. And we thought, "If they're wearing infra-red goggles, what's the problem?"

RW: So the idea is that he's doing this to his guys, one of them breaks his leg and shoots him and stuff, and then Bond infiltrates them. But then it was decided that was too much story to tell on the surf, as it were, so it became just a clever way to get into a heavily fortified country.

NP: They thought the opening sequence was timing out too long, and there were limitations even on this, so we cut it down completely. The introduction happens with the punch bag scene instead. He was fiddling with the hat we see at the end of the film on the plane originally.

RW: So, it is a quite complicated bit of story with Bond distracting and hijacking a diving dinghy. On that level of plausibility you could say, why didn't he get the guy at the other end, why did he have to go into Korea to do this? But at that point, you don't understand what's going on anyway, so you don't question it.

Was the film shot in sequence?

RW: To quite a large extent.

How do you pace your action sequences? And how much is your idea followed when it comes to the budget and logistics of the film?

RW: We had less shooting in the compound. They made much more of that. They built this bloody great compound so then you've got to blow it up. It's irresponsible.
NP: We do suggest what we think it should be, but then the second unit director and the director and the producers just go off and do it and try and push it as much as they can.

How many drafts did you get through?

RW: So many. If you include the thinking process, we started in July 2000.
NP: It's nearly two years seeing as we were working all the way through the shoot.

What software do you use?

RW: We use a thing called Screenwriter 2000.
NP: We don't like Final Draft. It doesn't seem to be as sophisticated.

And what about that scene where Jinx comes out of the ocean, like Honey Ryder in Dr. No. *It was written at one point totally naked, wasn't it?*

NP: Tastefully done, of course. She's naked in this draft which is in keeping with the original *Dr. No*, the novel.

The scene where she meets James Bond reminds me of a speech in The Big Sleep *where they're talking about a racetrack and it becomes so charged with sexual innuendo. Are those sorts of films a model for you?*

RW: Yeah, absolutely. Humphrey Bogart's so controlled and self-contained. And the women as well.
NP: Talking about the stress of trying to change something on the day of something so gigantic—we were on our way to the airport to

Cádiz, because they weren't going to shoot because the weather was so bad. And then the weather cleared up and we got a call that they were going to shoot—that water was freezing—and they're going to shoot it right now. And the whole scene was written as dusk—the predators come out as the sun goes down—the language of the scene was built around sunset imagery, and suddenly they were having to shoot it in the blazing midday sun. So could we change the dialogue to reflect this? It stayed like that for a year and suddenly it's being changed. You can't think of anything; you're getting out of the car, you're walking down and you go through all the crowds to get through the set to a crew of a hundred down there. And they're rehearsing it with the director. And moments before as we're walking across the sand, we thought of just putting in the word "usually" instead of "always."

What about the sword fighting scene that features Madonna. It seems so anachronistic . . .

NP: There was a certain amount of resistance to the sword fight because it seems so old-fashioned and in the days of *The Matrix* will this go down with people and how can we do it differently?

The old-school clubby environment seems to make it OK.

NP: It's known as Blades, which is the name of the gambling club that was in Fleming's books.

And you get to write lines for Madonna.

RW: We did have a really good line—"Cock fights aren't my style," but she wouldn't say it. She said it the other way round, "I don't really like cock fights."

This is a Bond *film with quite a dark tone. Was it your way of trying to humanize James Bond?*

RW: I think it's interesting that he is an assassin. That is the internal baggage he carries around, and it's quite nice to see him in that mode. What makes him an interesting character to us is how he is that, but he also lives life to enjoy it. We didn't encounter any resistance to the idea of his being incarcerated. Getting caught makes him human, not a superhero. The aim is to give him a chance to shine, because we're all here to watch James Bond. So the harder you make it for him, the better the picture, the greater the enjoyment.

You're dealing with forty years of history and nineteen previous films. In some ways limitations are very liberating and in other ways very frustrating.

RW: That's what made it a hard job. Of course, there are a million things that haven't been done . . . but what's great here is that we've got a young villain. Which is sort of to do with Pierce's age as well. So that's sort of new.

NP: Pierce is a man whereas Graves is almost a wild kid, a boy. I thought this whole scene was really well filmed as well.

RW: And yet the funny thing was that the director was a bit wary about it, and it was put off and off and off and then turned out to be one of the best things in there.

NP: The way they do the betting was influenced by an old Terry Thomas movie called *School for Scoundrels*. What's great as well is that these two men hate each other. And it's that simple.

Exploiting Bond's ability to be a loose cannon as a flaw as well as a plus.

RW: For us it's come from the producers being so knowledgeable — and also that's what Pierce is really like. And that's why we have Miranda Frost to talk about Bond in that way. It's trailer stuff because they can cut it together. It's entertainment.

NP: Pierce is bleeding as well, which you don't see very often.

So where did the idea of the abandoned Tube station come from? Vauxhall Cross?

NP: We didn't have any choice over the location. And we wouldn't have called it that.

RW: There are a lot of these unused Tube stations and there's one really near the Bond office in Downing Street, Down Street — it's where Churchill held secret meetings during the war.

NP: This is quite subtle because he's going past an old shooting range here. All of it is a nod to the beginning of *Moonraker,* the novel.

How did you feel about reintroducing the Q character?

NP: We were quite conscious about trying to take it back to the former Q. Even Desmond Llewelyn changed over the years. We tried to get it back to the original bad relationship they had in the early sixties movies.

RW: We were also very aware of Desmond's passing. So John Cleese refers to "my predecessor" and Bond initially refers to Cleese as

"Quartermaster"—a nod to the origins of the name—and only uses the endearment of "Q" at the end of the scene once he's realized that this man is really quite clever and good at his job.

Have you had any feedback from the true Bond devotees?

RW: Yeah, I think it was appreciated.

NP: What was interesting with this film is that it polarized people quite a lot. People either loved it or hated it. Normally it's just a *Bond* film.

Were you nervous about the invisible car?

RW: We were very pleased that the director liked it because we suggested it originally, but we weren't sure anyone would go for it. The idea is that in Iceland or in the desert when there's not much contrast in the background it's invisible, but in an urban environment you'd be able to see it.

NP: So it came down to that first shot, which worked because it's a gag. But really it shouldn't have been quite so . . .

RW: It should have been darker. And if it had been really dark, you would've forgiven it.

NP: Q says it's "as good as invisible." It's a camouflage, not a cloaking device.

Do you find that you try to structure your scenes on a high note?

NP: Well that was the Q scene and you have to end it like that.

How aware are you guys of the whole Austin Powers thing when you write dialogue?

NP: Those films are only really spoofing the sixties Bonds, anyway—which weren't really that crude, but more exotic. And we tried to stay on that side of things. But you would have liked to have the choice . . .

RW: We actually—believe it or not—tried not to do many puns, but we ended up with a movie full of them.

NP: The director was encouraging.

RW: Because it creates a sense of fun. And that's a good instinct to have. It meant that the first hour of the film is great fun, even though it's quite gritty . . . But somewhere along the way, with all this fighting going on—the balance gets a little lost. And this happens because these things are very difficult. As Stephen Frears told us "Art is easy. It's entertainment that's hard."

London, England

Guillermo Arriaga

19

GUILLERMO ARRIAGA

Amores Perros

"You do not choose what you write, it chooses you."

Guillermo Arriaga is the author of three novels and a collection of short stories. They include *Night of the Buffalo (El Búfalo de la Noche)* and *A Sweet Scent of Death (Un Dolce Olor de la Muerte)*. His first original screenplay, *Amores Perros* (2000), was directed by Alejandro González Iñárritu, starred Gael García Bernal and was nominated for Best Foreign Picture at the 2001 Academy Awards. His first English language script, *21 Grams* (2003), was also directed by Iñárritu and starred Sean Penn, Naomi Watts and Benicio Del Toro. He lives in Mexico City with his wife and two children.

Synopsis

Mexico City, the present. Octavio is the teenage owner of a dog named Cofi. He enters Cofi into an illegal dog-fighting contest, hoping to win enough money to enable him to elope with Susana, the wife of his aggressive brother, Ramiro. A near-fatal injury to Cofi prompts a reckless car chase that ends violently. Middle-aged businessman Daniel abandons his wife and children to set up house with a beautiful young model, Valeria, who is tragically injured when Octavio's car crashes into hers. Meanwhile, El Chivo, a revolutionary turned assassin, witnesses the accident and looks after Cofi, only to find that caring for the dog leads to a life-changing epiphany.

* * *

KEVIN CONROY SCOTT: *Guillermo, can you tell me something about your parents and the way they brought you up?*

GUILLERMO ARRIAGA: One of the most important things in my life has been my family. My father and my mother have always believed that education and culture are very important: they travelled a lot, read a lot, they like good films—so my brothers and sisters and I, we were always discussing these kinds of things. We had politics and culture; those kinds of things were interesting to my family.

I believe you've said that your father thought that having a Ph.D. was the most important goal you could achieve in life?

He never taught us to be aware of money or having a good professional position. He doesn't care about that. He only wanted us to have the tools to do what we wanted in life in the best way possible. That's why he believes in education; and he thinks that education is not only having a Ph.D. but it's also a way of *understanding*; a Ph.D. gives you more tools to understand life in a better way.

You've been a father yourself for more than a decade. Has that helped your writing?

A lot, because it made me understand that love and hope really have a meaning. For me, being a father is the most important thing that could happen in my life, it's beyond anything I have ever lived through. It makes me much more humble, much more down-to-earth, and it allows me to understand human beings in a more profound way.

Is that because your perspective has changed—because you are now responsible for a life you have created?

Yes, it makes you understand that you can no longer be doing whatever you want in life; someone else can be greatly affected by your actions. If something happens to your kids, it makes you very scared. And it shows you that there is a *link* to life, that life goes on, that you have an influence in the world through your children. Also, kids always say things that allow you to understand life in a more playful way. When we were filming *Amores Perros* I took my son, Santiago, and my daughter, Mariana, to the set during the post-accident scene. It's a terrible thing to witness: a guy is spitting up blood, a woman is trapped in a mangled car. In the middle of this scene, Mariana asked me to take a walk—she was seven years old at the time. And as we walked away from the set, she asked me, "Why do they make such horrible films?" And I said to her, "I *wrote* this film. What do you mean, it's horrible?" She said, "Why did you write this film?" and I said, "Because it's what's in my heart." And she said, "What a horrible heart you must have!" [*laughs*] So these things make me humble . . .

Can you compare the neighborhood where you grew up in Mexico City to the one Octavio, Ramiro and Susana live in, in Amores Perros?

My neighborhood was divided by one street. One side was very dangerous, and the other was kinder, more middle-class. So some parts of it were tough.

You got into a fight every day when you were growing up. Why was that part of your behavior? Was it down to self-defense, or something else?

It was a place where, in order to be respected, you had to fight for yourself. You had to prove yourself all the time. I had someone cut me when I was fourteen; I lost my sense of smell when I was thirteen because someone punched me in my face too many times. When I was eleven, my older brother stepped into a puddle and splashed water on a girl, and her brother—who was a twenty-five-year-old Vietnam vet—got angry, but instead of taking it out on my brother he hit *me* with a baseball bat. He almost killed me—the last blow was to my neck, and I couldn't move from my neck down for three hours. Another time when I was ten, I went outside to take some sun and some old guys took cigarettes and burned my stomach. So yeah, my neighborhood was kind of violent . . . but it had some good things about it too.

You first got involved with theater at school, didn't you?

My father first sent me to what was considered "the best" school, but they were like fascists there. I had a big problem with that, and as a result I was expelled. Then I went to another school, a very cool place, very liberal. And theater was obligatory there, so we began to read a lot of plays, starting with the Greeks and then the Spanish and then Shakespeare. We had to direct, produce and act in these plays.

What age were you then?

Twelve.

You put on your own plays at the age of twelve?

Yeah. By the time I was fifteen, I had already acted, directed and produced twenty or thirty plays.

Around this time you also developed, independent of your parents, a passion for hunting. Can you explain how that came about, and why you still like it so much?

The Latin word for "passion" is to suffer something. It's something that's out of your hands. Hunting is something like that for me; it's very difficult to explain. I think hunting is at the roots of all humanity—we are a hunting species. It's very sad to see that some communities who no longer have a sense of nature are now against hunting. I like hunting because it allows me to understand contradiction. For me, contradiction is the truth for everything. And in hunting, there's beauty, there's death and there's cruelty. You feel guilty, you feel happy—there are a lot of different feelings. You pursue something to kill it, and then you feel bad because you have killed it.

You've been quoted as saying that you're not fond of a new political correctness that is surfacing in Mexico. Obviously, hunting is not the most politically correct hobby, so what would you say to those people who ask, "Why are you hunting when you don't need to? When you can go to the supermarket to buy your venison?"

You don't need to go see films, you don't need to play soccer. You don't need to read poetry; you don't *need* to do a lot of things. It's not about economic needs; it's about spiritual needs, emotional needs. Hunting allows me to be closer to beauty. It's my way of understanding nature. What these politically correct people forget is that ecologists must defend human nature before anything else. We as humans have a pact with nature that means death and cruelty, and a lot of other things. Now that we're becoming so bland and nice and so terribly repressed, we're losing our sense of contradiction. It's like the people who take their dogs and put ribbons and bows in their hair. They're taking away the essence of being a dog; I call it "dogness" or "dognity." [*laughs*] Joseph Campbell, the anthropologist, in one of his books he says, "In hunting societies there was no need for human sacrifice. Human sacrifice began with cropping and agricultural societies." So I think if we repress our involvement with nature, we will become crueler and meaner.

You like dogs, but you hate cats, right? I don't understand how you can hate cats.

I have a clear reason to hate them. When I was a kid, I loved animals, and I had a lot of them. Among them were small chickens and rabbits. And guess who killed them . . . ?

But you should appreciate why the cat did what it did . . .

It's a hunter! Absolutely, I know, hating cats for this reason is one of my contradictions. [*laughs*]

You suffered a boxing injury in 1984 that turned out to be very significant. Can you tell me something about it?

I had a friend who was really training to box for the Los Angeles Olympics, and I thought I wanted to go too. Because I'd been getting into fights almost daily since I was a kid, I thought I could be a boxer. I thought I could be a *heavyweight* because there are no heavyweights in Mexico; there aren't any people of my height and size in my country. So I thought I'd go to LA and lose my first fight, but at least I could say I was in the Olympics. [*laughs*] While I was training I got a pain in my chest and numbness in my left arm. I went to the doctor and I found out I had an infection in my heart; it was nothing serious if you took care of it right away. But I continued training, and the muscle of the heart got irritated, and suddenly I was on the verge of having a heart attack. It was very swollen and full of liquid. The pain was unbelievable, an incredible burning sensation. My left arm felt like a cat was inside it, scratching around. There was nothing I could do because it was a virus, and the doctor told me, "I have good news and bad news. The good news is that you are not a hypochondriac. The bad news is that your heart is in very bad shape. We don't know what's going to happen, you must go to bed. You can't do anything else." So that night I was worried and I looked at my hands and I thought, "Maybe these will become the hands of a corpse. I must do something with them. I must leave the world different from how I received it." I always wanted to be a writer, but at that time I thought I had no talent. But lying on that bed, I changed my mind: "I'm going to write: I don't care if it is published or not, I am going to write." So when I overcame that infection in my heart, I began writing. A year and a half later I had a second infection that was much stronger. It was then that I decided to be a writer, no matter what.

How were your first efforts at writing? Pretty bad?

No, no. One of the first books I wrote was when I was twenty-five-years old, a collection of short stories that was recently published, *Retorno 201*, the address of my house when I was growing up. In Mexico the first edition sold out in one month.

But even before that, you were a professor in Mexico and chairman of your department at the age of twenty-three. How did this happen at such a young age?

Everyone in my family has been a teacher at some point, except for my mother. When I was a student, the director of my department told me he was going to expel me because of my bad grade-point average. I told him he was mistaken and he looked up my name and saw I had the best average in my class. He had mistaken me for someone else, so we started talking and he was impressed and he asked me if I wanted to teach there. After asking around to other professors and my colleagues he found out I was respected, so I became the chairman of the department after I graduated.

Did you enjoy teaching at that age?

Of course, but I was very young and it was difficult because I had no experience as a professor. So being a chairman and having some influence on my own professors and having students that were older than me was tough—I had to gain the respect of everyone by working very hard.

Then, after your heart condition, when you were twenty-nine, you won a place to be a writer in residence at the National Institute of Fine Arts (INBA) in Spain. And I understand your work was not well received at first . . .

There is a brilliant writer called Hugo Hiriart and he oversaw the eight of us in this program. I wrote a novel and he took it and said, "Who the hell told you that you are a writer? This is shit!" He threw the manuscript into the air and the pages went flying everywhere. "This is the worst thing I have ever read in my life," he said. In order not to kill him, I made myself count to ten, and then I had to count again. Then someone else in my group said, "Yeah, it's a very lousy novel." I said, "Shut up or I'll beat you." So I picked up my novel and said to Hugo, "You don't have a fucking idea of what literature is about!" [*laughs*] Years later I asked him, "Why did you do that?" And he said, "Because I wanted to see if you had the guts to be a writer. If you can stand rejection then it means that you are a writer. If you can't stand rejection it means that you don't have the personality to be a writer."

That novel turned out be A Tale of the Splendors and Miseries of the Guillotine Squadron and How It Contributed to the Legend of Francisco Villa. *How soon after this incident was it published?*

It was published four years later.

So by the age of thirty-three you had been a university professor, writer in residence and a published novelist. It looks like you had some luck early in your career. What do you tell writing students of yours who complain that they haven't had so many lucky breaks?

First of all, you create your own opportunities. I am tired of these people who say, "I have all this talent but I have no opportunities." We must remember a writer that comes from a very little town in the middle of the jungle; his name is García Márquez. He comes from a place that is not even on the *map*. When there is talent, there is talent, and when you have talent you have to create your own opportunities. You must trust your work. I always say, if your work has legs it will walk and run. If your work has no legs, it won't happen. It doesn't mean you have to go to editors at publishing houses and invite them to lunch. But I am happy that until now I've had no need to go and knock on doors—my work has spoken for itself, it has its own legs.

You've got Attention Deficit Disorder (ADD). How does your short attention span affect your writing?

In a bad way and in a good way . . . It affects it in a bad way because I spend a lot of time in the process of writing, because I do a lot of things when I am writing other than writing. For example, I'll take a shower or go take a walk with the dog, or call my friends; I do so many of these things in between the actual writing that I actually now consider it a part of the writing process. As a result, it takes me a long time to write because I have a lot of problems concentrating. But I think that having ADD allows me to understand the world through intuition instead of reason. Outside of me there is chaos but inside of me there is order. I can walk into the desert for hours without any reference, and I can know exactly where the camp is. I know exactly which route I have taken. It is the same with my novels, because I can have these maps in my mind, making these kinds of structures. I understand it perfectly; I do not get lost with the structure.

Why do you think that internal coherence comes from having ADD?

When you have ADD you are not able to go from A to B to C to D—you have no linear reasoning. You hop from one place to the other, where your attention takes you.

So you have no control over where your mind wanders?

I do now. But when I was in primary school I didn't.

That must have been why you got expelled from the fascist primary school.

Yeah, my teachers thought I was mentally impaired . . .

To make some extra pocket money when you were a professor you started producing, directing and writing radio and TV projects?

As a university professor I like teaching but I don't like the academic world. I don't like the researching and the pompous meetings with the professors. Academic writing is a lot of masturbating. I think the academic world is different in the United States because it has influence on the political and social life of their country. But here in Mexico it's very difficult; the academic world is completely out of touch with reality. I think I would be betraying my students if I didn't have professional experience outside of the university. Since I was eighteen I've done lots of things, writing for newspapers and other things. One of those things is directing. I have directed a lot of documentaries for TV. I love directing documentaries.

Why?

Because it allows you to go into the understanding of someone else's life. For example, the documentary I am most proud of is about Down's Syndrome persons, I refuse to call them kids. I discovered their sexuality, their need of independence, of self-esteem, of love; they are very creative; they are wonderful painters. I spent a lot of time with these people. Then I directed a short film for television with Down's Syndrome actors. It wasn't very spectacular but I was happy because I made something about people I respect in a way that hadn't been done before. So when I was working in television I was not trying to make commercial stuff—they were always educational and cultural things. I have made a series on Mexican cinema called *Out of the Frame*. I made some science programs for teenagers and even something on magicians.

So you tried to pick up every experience you could?

I think a degree in communications is the last renaissance career, because you are studying philosophy, psychology, sociology . . . everything. I am interested in *everything*.

How does working in Mexico differ from working in Los Angeles?

Mexico hasn't been "professionalized" the way Hollywood has. The industry here is very loose, there are no rules. You have to go to the producer and fight with him, he gets angry, you get angry. Sometimes there is money, sometimes there is no money. It is more romantic, but it's not very professional compared to Hollywood.

This is a big thematic question that you must get a lot . . . but do you consider your work to be male-oriented or macho? Amores Perros alone has dogfighting, a hit man, revenge fantasies . . .

I don't think it's a male thing, or at least that's not my intention. I don't even know if I can talk about it—because you do not choose what you write, it chooses you. I'm not trying to make a statement about macho things. For example, with the hit man I tried to portray him in the most tender way possible.

Is El Chivo living his lifestyle because of his own choice? It seems like from the money he makes by killing people, he could afford a better quality of life for himself and his dogs.

No, he feels betrayed by his politics and what happened with that. He had a goal for society, then everything crumbled for him. He feels that he's in a black hole and there's no way out. So he is now the most despicable, meanest human being you can imagine.

Can you take me through your creative process, how you work when you're writing?

Almost everything I write, I dream about first. I have some unclear ideas in my head when I go to bed, and then the next day something from my dreams just sticks in my mind. I never write anything in the middle of the night or take out a recorder. If the dream is interesting and valuable enough, it will stick to me. If not, I don't have to worry about it because it wasn't that good. In the middle of the night you'll think you have some brilliant ideas, and you'll wake up and write them down and read them later and you discover that they're shit. It's embarrassing to read some of that stuff . . . So it's not like the stories come to me whole cloth, but I do get little pieces through my dreams.

So you have this idea from a dream and then it conjoins with something else, then once you have that you have a pretty good idea of the story. What do you do then?

I never outline the story, never. I once went to a seminar by one of these gurus of the screen, and this person said, "You must know everything about your character." I thought, "Fuck, there's no way!" I want to have dark parts of my characters' history so they can surprise me. Also, I can't have an ending already, because when I don't know the characters they can show me the ending as I get to know them. That's why I don't like to do research of any kind. I like for the characters to grow up inside of me. There are two kinds of writer: there are those who don't have any kind of internal way to order things inside themselves, so they need structure, page thirty, page sixty, and so on — and I don't blame or criticize the professors or the students of that discipline. But I think there is another kind of writer who has a different kind of approach to structure. *21 Grams* goes back and forth all the time, and I had a perfect understanding of where it was going. I never got lost or thought that I needed a plot point here, or for something to happen in the second act. I never think that way. That's not to say the other way is bad — it's just that myself and other writers have a different internal process. It's intuition.

How did you learn all of the things that first-time screenwriters make their mistakes with? I'm thinking of explaining too much, having scenes that run too long, improbable exposition . . .

I made a lot of mistakes. If you read the first drafts of my screenplays you would never hire me again. They're awful. One of my biggest mistakes is to allow anyone to read my first draft. I think the only person who can read it is my wife; she's the only person who knows it will get better . . .

Why can't you take the first draft any further than just an unpolished draft?

For me, the first draft is when you vomit up the idea. Then you have to order it. What happens with most writers is they think the first, second or third draft has to be perfect. That's not true; you have to reorder things constantly.

Didn't Amores Perros *go through thirty-three drafts?*

Yes, but it was much closer to the finished film in the first draft than *21 Grams* was. I am ashamed of the first draft of *21 Grams* and I made the mistake of showing it to Alejandro González Iñárritu. I'll never do that again . . . So now the first draft I deliver to someone is actually my tenth draft. Sometimes you get lucky with the first draft, but not often. I think that this is the thing you are going to give to the world, so you have to struggle with it. As Kafka said, "Writing is a fight against death." Because writing gives sense to your life, your work transcends you; it goes beyond you. And if it goes beyond you then you must make it in the best way possible.

Does that mean you are anal or meticulous about your writing?

I am meticulous, but not anal. Someone with ADD cannot be anal about their writing . . . It's just that you want it to be as perfect as possible. Although the imperfections make the work beautiful, I would hate to have a perfect work; I would prefer to have a contradictory and imperfect work that will continue to move me and the people who watch or read it.

You work during the evenings so you can spend time with your children during the day. Can you take me through your writing day?

I can't write if I'm not fully concentrated. That means I have to begin to relax. In the evening I like to spend some time with my wife, talking to her and being with her. Then I put my kids to bed. I can't go from a meeting to writing; I have to put the engine down. I know I'm relaxed when I sit down at the computer and my hands start to type and the words start to flow. Music for me is very important when I write, it helps me get the tone. That can be the tone of a character, the tone of a scene; it can also be the counterpoint. Sometimes when I was writing 21 *Grams*, during the saddest moments of the story, I wrote with very happy music. So the music doesn't have to illustrate the tone directly.

How did you come up with the notion of putting dogfighting at the center of Amores Perros? *It works well both in terms of plotting the narrative and giving us a unique metaphor for life in Mexico City.*

I had the ideas for two novels I was writing, one was called *Good Fellas* and the other one was about hit men. But I realized that they weren't working so I tried to connect them. I had a dog when I was young, who is the original Cofi. He escaped from my house and killed many dogs in my neighborhood, because he was ferocious. So I had this personal background with dogfighting, even though I never fought my own dog. I was aware of it, but it wasn't professional—more like two guys who knew each other saying, "My Doberman against your Rottweiler, to the death." So I had an idea to write this novel based on part of my past. But the first draft of *Amores Perros* was completely different; it was about middle-class kids fighting their dogs. That wasn't working so that's when I decided to go to Shakespeare. I could start to see how dogs were relating different elements of the script with each other and that dogs can express a lot of who you are. For example, I can't see myself being the owner of a petite, red ribbon poodle . . .

What kind of dog do you have?

A Labrador.

You studied Shakespeare when you were younger. Did that influence your writing of Amores Perros? *I think you once said something about pushing your characters to extremes . . . ?*

Shakespeare puts a filter on every one of his characters. For example, this guy loves that woman, but this guy belongs to the family that hates the family of the woman he loves. Or this other guy wants the power, but in order to get the power he has to kill the king who is his best friend, while the person who is pushing him to do it is the king's wife. This is what I mean by a filter. Shakespeare's stories have very clear objectives: I want the power, I want her love, I want revenge. They are very basic and very strong. So when I had these problems with *Amores Perros*, I thought I would work Shakespeare into the story and have a character with a very strong objective, the love of a woman. He's gonna fight for that woman and he'll do everything he can to have her—but that woman is going to be married and then pregnant, and she is also the wife of his brother. These Shakespearean filters can change everything.

But if you overdo the filters, aren't you in danger of making a melo-drama?

I don't care . . . [*laughs*]

Then there's the influence of William Faulkner in your work. I read The Sound and the Fury, *and I have to admit I was completely lost after reading the first seventy pages. Can you take me through how you discovered Faulkner, what he means to you?*

When I first read *The Sound and the Fury* I thought it was one of the most hateful experiences of my reading life. I just couldn't understand what this guy was trying to do. But suddenly I began dreaming of Faulkner's characters, and I began to realize that in that book there were very important things. It can be very, as you say, "melodramatic" to have a guy who's retarded and who has raped his sister. But Faulkner also has filters; he was a great Shakespeare follower and a great follower of the Bible, not as a religious man but as a literary man. So after reading the book, I realized that there was not only one way to tell stories. Every novel of his has its own way to be told. Faulkner went on to write *As I Lay Dying* and *Absalom! Absalom!* and *A Light in August*, and every one of them is told in a different way.

Is this why the character dictates the structure of the story, rather than the structure of the story dictating the character?

It's why I'm not too much into the three-act structure. When you want to tell a story of how you had a car accident, you don't begin, "I walked out of my house at 7:30 a.m. At 7:35 a.m. I stopped at the gas station. At 7:45 a.m. I had my first turning point . . ." You don't tell stories that way. You say, "I was driving and suddenly this car came from nowhere and I was blind-sided!" Then you might add, "In the morning, I had a beautiful breakfast, and there was a beautiful woman, she served me fried eggs, and I vomited them . . ." That's how we choose to tell stories. So that was the biggest lesson of Faulkner. The great writers always have the filters.

I think Faulkner also said that writing a novel is as difficult as building a chicken coop in the middle of a hurricane with one arm tied behind your back.

I think he falls short with that description . . . [*laughs*] I think that writing is both tough and easy. It's tough because you are by yourself. For example, when you direct and you don't know what to do, you just ask someone, "What do you think about this shot?" and someone will respond, "I think that one's better." So the director says, "OK, let's try that." I remember when I was writing *A Sweet Scent of Death* I woke my wife up all the time and would say, "What do you think about this . . . ?"

Could you work with a writing partner?

I always work on my own with the novels. But with the screenplays you always have the input of the director, the producer or even the DP.

So it's like you have co-writers. Still, in the end you are alone, that's what is tough about it.

What's easy about writing?

It's not as tough as being a prostitute.

But some writers are prostitutes . . .

Yeah, you're right . . . *[laughs]*

Amores Perros received a lot of critical acclaim but it was also criticized by some for its second act. Not because the story of Valeria and Daniel isn't interesting but because there's a switch in tone from a kinetic, roving story to an almost static chamber piece of paranoia. Was this something that you were aware of during the writing process?

I like to take risks and gamble in my work. I don't know of a film that can have two very different tones in it. So I was obsessed with trying it. I have a Marxist education: Marx is very Hegelian, he has a dialectic theory of thesis, antithesis and synthesis. I said to myself, "OK, let's have a point, counterpoint, and a result." That's what I was doing with Valeria's story, I wanted a counterpoint. The first story that took place was on the outside and was full of characters thrashing around, and suddenly you have two people in a closed apartment, almost in an absurd fantasy. So you go from a very realistic point of view to an almost surrealistic point of view. Of course we've had that criticism from a lot of people so we tried an exercise of presenting the film without the second part. It didn't work; *Amores Perros* is awful without the second part.

Why is that?

The first story is about two kids fighting for the throne of an absent father; the second story is about a father who has decided to become absent, and the third one is about a father who is absent who wants to return. In the second one he leaves everything for a very dumb model, for a cost. So they were interconnected and I thought that the second piece helped to complete the structure of *Amores Perros*. Let me get this straight: Goya Toledo who plays Valeria and Alvaro Guerrero who plays Daniel are very good actors. But I was thinking of the model as being nineteen years old and the man as being forty-five. So it was more of a father–daughter relationship. It's not the same seeing a woman of thirty having her leg cut off as it is seeing that happen to a nineteen-year-old. I think Goya and Alvaro did a terrific job, but it would have been much different to have more of a father–daughter relationship. But most importantly, I'm still happy about this shift in tone because it has that contradiction I love. I don't regret it in any sense and I'm happy that *Amores Perros* is imperfect. It's also a wider portrait of Mexico City; you have the lower class, the middle class and the upper class.

You mentioned that the chain of events in the narrative of Amores Perros *couldn't have happened if Cofi the dog were not accidentally let out of the house. Am I right in assuming that this idea of chance is a prevalent theme in your work? It ties in with the idea of people's lives intersecting through car crashes, something you called "Nature's Revenge" on man pushing technological limits.*

There is a Spanish philosopher who says that man is himself and his circumstances. In the case of *Amores Perros* you have characters who are much more themselves than the circumstances. For example, Octavio has a terrible accident but he returns to Susana and he still says, "Come with me." [*laughs*]

He's still going for it.

And I think that these kinds of accidents provide the places you are going.

You've written a car-crash trilogy. Can you tell me something about the first in the trilogy, the screenplay that hasn't been made?

It starts with a car accident. It's a story where the father of two teenagers died. One of them was with him in the car and the other wasn't. Two years later he is very angry and decides to look for the driver of the other car.

You mentioned that the battle between Octavio and Ramiro is not Cain against Abel; it's Cain against Cain. This also happens again with Luis and Gustavo, the brothers who want to kill each other through El Chivo. But why is it "Cain against Cain"?

I think that human characters are not just good or bad. We're driven by very strange forces that make us much more similar to Cain than Abel. It doesn't mean that Abel was the bad one, he was just jealous. I think that Cain portrays much more accurately what human beings are, all the contradictions we have. We can think of Octavio as a very nice kid, but actually he's the most monstrous of them all. That's what I want to do—to create monstrous characters who can be loved. I think that El Chivo is terribly monstrous too.

Don't you think monsters are capable of being reformed in certain ways? El Chivo has an epiphany . . .

I think that there are moments in life when you understand life much better. Both El Chivo and Octavio have those moments.

When Octavio and his brother are shown earning money in different ways for Susana—I understand you thought it was the weakest moment in the film?

Not the weakest, I just don't like it as a writer—because I don't like montages; I think they are weak by themselves. It's like cheating. But they work, and I think it worked very well in *Amores Perros* and I don't regret it.

Why is it cheating? It's just condensing time and showing narrative progress.

I don't think Orson Welles cheated in *Citizen Kane* when Kane is having breakfast with his wife. That's elegant, that's the way a montage can work. But I think most montages are not elegant. You just put music in, and it's too easy. What is amazing about cinema is that it's a very conservative medium. In the 1920s you had literature by Virginia Woolf, James Joyce, William Faulkner and Juan Rulfo, making these back-and-forth stories, and the world of literature accepted them. Then we had Picasso making paintings with one eye here, the mouth in a chest, the ear on the wrong side of the head and it was accepted. They said, "OK, that's a woman!" But cinema can't do this; it's stuck where it started.

But don't you think that has to do with the cost of the medium? If you're writing a book or painting a picture, you only need one person in a room, alone. Motion pictures require an army of people and a lot of money. Don't you think that's why audiences have to understand the movie—because the financial investment is so much larger?

Exactly, that's why it's so conservative. But I think audiences are becoming much more sophisticated and educated. We also have to consider that cinema is still a very young medium. It's only a hundred years old. It's still learning.

In your introduction to the published screenplay of Amores Perros *you mentioned that love can represent both pain and hope: the crossroads between life and death. Can you explain what you meant by that?*

We have this corny view of love as something mellow and happy. That's not true. Think about how painful it can be—fall in love with your best friend's wife, then you'll find out . . . Love by itself is painful, because it means that you have to cancel part of you to have that relationship; you have to make some compromises. You have to spend time with that person; that can be painful in certain ways. Love also takes you to the meaning of death. When you lose someone you love, you are also experiencing death in some way, you are dying. Death represents itself not only in the definitive way. It also marks you in more subtle ways—like when your hair starts falling out and leaves you bald.

So where does hope come into this?

Love, with all the pain it brings, is still the only hope we have as human beings. Because love means to give yourself to another one, and that person then gives themselves to you. This pain reshapes you. And sometimes it's in the darkest places that you can find hope.

Mexico City, Mexico

Acknowledgments

Thanks to Peter Hobbs, who put me in touch with Debbie Holmes. She arranged my interview with Michael Haneke and traveled from Vienna to Paris to translate. A special thanks to Carlos Cuarón, who introduced me to Guillermo Arriaga, a great novelist who has become a mentor and, I am pleased to say, friend. Thanks to Richard T. Kelly, who got me started by suggesting a place to study, and thanks to Rachel Alexander for giving me the idea to do this book. Thanks to Natalie Pearce who helped me enormously when I started putting this book together. Thanks to my agents, Clare Conville and Patrick Walsh, for looking after me, an even bigger thanks to my editor at Faber and Faber, Walter Donohue, who gave me this opportunity and took a chance on a novice. And how can I forget Lee Brackstone? Who, "Without him, none of this would have been possible." Those are his words and for once, he's actually right. Thanks to my beloved family, in particular The Original who gave me sound advice, as per usual. And, finally, thanks to Landa Acevedo, who translated the interview with François Ozon and put me up in Paris during my stays there. Shami says there are many good times ahead.

Kevin Conroy Scott
London, April 2004

Kevin Conroy Scott began his film career in the mailroom at New Line Cinema before becoming a script editor at their London office. He earned his M.A. in Film History at Birkbeck College, University of London. He has written and directed two short films and now works in London as a literary agent and freelance journalist writing about film.